DATE DUE	
JUL 0 7 2004		
OCT 3 2006		
NOV 2 1 2006		

WITH
REAGAN

Edwin Meese III

WITH REAGAN

THE INSIDE STORY

EDWIN MEESE III

REGNERY GATEWAY
Washington, D.C.

25282790

Grateful acknowledgment to The Bettmann Archives for use of their photographs "Girl kisses runway" and "Meese testifies" and to Roger Sandler for use of his photograph "Preparation for 1979 announcement." All remaining photographs are from the Ronald Reagan Library/White House collection.

Library of Congress Cataloging-In-Publication Data

Meese, Edwin.
    With Reagan : the inside story / Edwin Meese III.
      p. cm.
    Includes bibliographical references and index.
    ISBN 0-89526-522-2 (alk. paper)
    1. Reagan, Ronald—Friends and associates.   2. Presidents—United States—Staff.   3. United States—Politics and government—1981–1989.
4. Meese, Edwin.   I. Title.
E877.2.M44   1992
973.927'092—dc20
                                      92-4222
                                        CIP

Published in the United States by
Regnery Gateway
1130 17th Street, NW
Washington, DC 20036

Distributed to the trade by
National Book Network
4720-A Boston Way
Lanham, MD 20706

Printed on acid free paper
Manufactured in the United States of America

96 95 94 93 92   10 9 8 7 6 5 4 3 2

To my wife, Ursula,
and to our children,
Mike and Ramona, Scott, and Dana

ACKNOWLEDGEMENTS

THIS BOOK DISCUSSES RONALD REAGAN and his presidency, and examines one of the most significant periods in the history of our country. As a participant in the Reagan administration, a fortunate place from which to observe that era, I am grateful to the many people with whom I had the privilege of serving, and especially to those who assisted me directly, both during that period and in the writing of this book.

First and foremost, the entire nation owes a debt of gratitude to the late William J. Casey. Without his timely entrance into the leadership of the Reagan campaign, the Reagan presidency might never have become a reality. Later, as director of central intelligence, he was a principal supporter and promulgator of the Reagan Doctrine, which resulted in the liberation of millions of people throughout the world. Bill's post in the Reagan cabinet capped a lifetime of public service as lawyer, businessman, philanthropist, and leader. He was a good friend and a true patriot.

I wish also to acknowledge my gratitude to the other cabinet members, the sub-cabinet and agency leaders, and the many other appointees with whom I served and whom I am proud to call my friends. Our common bond—our service to President Reagan—is reflected in the Reagan Alumni Association, which continues to flourish.

Both in the White House and at the Department of Justice, I was blessed with very dedicated and highly effective members on my personal staff, men and women who gave me invaluable assistance and whom I consider part of my extended family. To all of them I express my heartfelt appreciation.

I also want to acknowledge my deep gratitude to the members of my FBI protective security detail and transportation team, who looked after me so diligently during my tour of duty as attorney general.

A special note of appreciation goes to the three ladies who served successively as my administrative assistants at the White House and at Justice: Florence (Randolph) Procunier, Marilee Melvin, and Cathie (Appleyard) Hurlburt. Their loyal and devoted service, and their ability to handle with skill a myriad of complex details and varying requirements, made an impossible job possible.

Throughout my government service and during the writing of this book, an essential source of strength for me has been the love, encouragement, and support of my wife, Ursula, and our children: our son Mike and his wife Ramona; our late son Scott; and our daughter Dana. It is to them that this book is dedicated.

The Heritage Foundation deserves great credit for its unique contribution to the success of the Reagan administration, and I extend my thanks for the cooperation and encouragement I have received in the development of this book. It has been a genuine pleasure to work with the fine people at Heritage, and I am particularly grateful for the friendship of its president, Ed Feulner, and its executive vice president, Phil Truluck.

My own staff at Heritage has been a tremendous help to me in many endeavors, including this book. I want to thank Cathie (Appleyard) Hurlburt, who made the transition with us from Justice to Heritage, serving as my administrative assistant until last July. I am also grateful to those who served as my research assistants: Julia (Warriner) Boles, Linda Matisans, Rob Schmults, and Jeanine Chase. Special thanks go to Karen (Keywood) Kohl, my research assistant and new administrative assistant, who spent long hours typing the manuscript and working on all the many details essential to the completion of this book. Without her invaluable assistance, this could never have been accomplished.

The National Archives and Records Administration has been of great help in facilitating my research and locating documents and photographs. This organization, which became an independent agency of the federal government during the Reagan presidency, is truly unique in preserving vital historical documents and information. I am particularly grateful to National Archivist Don Wilson, Assistant Archivist John Fawcett, Edith Prise, Douglas Thurman, and Mary Finch. Their professional skill, courtesy, and understanding were exceptional.

I greatly appreciate the encouragement and assistance in preparing this book of Ken Cribb and Brad Reynolds, my counsellors at Justice, and John Richardson and Mark Levin, who served as my chiefs of staff there. Ken and John were also with me at the White House. All of them have contributed valuable ideas and suggestions and have helped in many other ways.

My thanks also to Alfred Regnery and his publishing organization. Al's innovative approach to publishing and marketing as well as his constant support and gentle prodding, have been very important to me. I am also very grateful to Jennifer Reist, who has coordinated the many facets of publication with remarkable calm and understanding along the way. I am also grateful to Peter Hannaford, Lou Cordia, and Megan Brockey for their assistance.

Finally, I want to thank two people who made this book possible. While I take full responsibility for its contents, and for whatever blame may arise, they have been invaluable partners in producing this volume. Patricia ("Trish") Bozell has demonstrated remarkable skill and patience as my editor at Regnery Gateway. She has labored at all hours of the day and night in this endeavor and has been a most friendly and kind person to work with. My editorial teammate, Stan Evans, has combined a great memory for details with true journalistic skill as we worked together in the research and writing of this book. To both Trish and Stan I extend my deepest gratitude.

EDWIN MEESE III

Washington, D.C.
1 May 1992

CONTENTS

INTRODUCTION

A FEW MONTHS BACK a former government colleague said to me: "You know, if someone had gone into a Rip van Winkle trance in 1980 and awakened ten years later, he would have had a hard time knowing Ronald Reagan had ever been president, or at least that he had done anything to speak of in the White House."

The comment had some merit. Media treatment of events that unfolded in 1990 and 1991, at home and abroad, often ignored the policy achievements of President Reagan, or else disparaged the eight-year record compiled by his administration. In some journalistic wrap-ups of the 1980s, Reagan's name was barely mentioned.

My response to my colleague's comment was to turn the analogy around: A person who had gone into a coma in 1980 and awakened in 1990 would certainly have been aware that *something* had happened in the interim, and that it must have been tremendous. Such a modern day Rip van Winkle would have gone to sleep in a nation that was undergoing a political-economic crisis on the home front while reeling before the challenge of Soviet communism abroad.

By the end of the 1980s, however, everything had been transformed. The U.S. economy was completing the longest peacetime expansion in American history, raising the average income of everyone. And overseas, the change was even more dramatic: the communist menace was undergoing its terminal spasms of collapse.

These generalizations, in fact, understate the enormous changes that swept over America and the world in the past decade. If we recall the grim facts of our national situation when Jimmy Carter was in the White House, and compare them with corresponding facts ten years later, the transformation is even more apparent.

In domestic affairs under Carter, we endured crippling shortages of petroleum, double-digit inflation and interest rates, a large and growing burden of federal taxes, and high and rising levels of unemployment. And the domestic economy was suffering from "stagflation"— an almost unheard of combination of inflation and low economic growth.

In foreign affairs the situation, if anything, was even worse. Not only were fifty-two Americans being held hostage at our embassy in Tehran, but the forces of communism were making inroads in virtually every quarter of the globe. America's citizens, allies, and security interests seemed everywhere in danger.

In the latter 1970s, the roster of countries taken over by Marxist revolution was long and ominous: Vietnam, Laos, Cambodia, Angola, Mozambique, Ethiopia, and more. In the final years of the Carter presidency, the Soviets invaded Afghanistan; Marxist-Leninist regimes took power in Nicaragua and Grenada, and El Salvador was being threatened with a similar fate. And a Marxist leader was installed in Zimbabwe-Rhodesia—with the backing of the Carter government.

Strategically, there was widespread consensus that the defenses of the United States were inadequate to protect our people and our interests. Military experts pointed to a "window of vulnerability," which would allow the Soviets to inflict colossal damage on the United States, thus crippling our capacity to respond—our only deterrent against attack. Given this American vulnerability, members of the Western alliance were openly doubting the value of our strategic guarantees to Europe.

As this summary suggests, the prospects facing the United States in 1980 could scarcely have been worse. Nor did the authorities in the nation's capital have any strategy to improve our situation. We were told, in essence, that we would have to learn to accept these conditions on a permanent basis. Learn to do with less gasoline; submit to the ever-rising burden of taxation and the slowdown of the economy; sit by idly while Marxist forces took over one country after another; and hope that through agreements with the Soviets, we could persuade them, by appealing to their charitable instincts, not to exploit our growing weakness.

Ronald Reagan, needless to remark, saw all these matters differently. Above all else, he repudiated the notion that the problems we suffered had somehow fallen on us from the sky, and that we could do nothing about them. The troubles we faced, he said, resulted from mistaken government policies, not from any decree of fate or some "malaise" among the American people. The country and its basic values, he believed, were as sound as ever. If our nation adopted proper policies, he concluded, we could reverse the record of decline in both domestic and foreign affairs.

To an extent that not even his staunchest admirers could have predicted, Reagan accomplished these objectives. He pushed through an economic program that spurred phenomenal economic growth and advanced a national security policy that turned the Cold War tables on the Soviets—inducing the collapse of the communist regimes of Europe and the idea of Marxism itself.

In combination, Reagan's domestic and foreign policies sparked a worldwide revival of the cause of freedom. Other nations sought to emulate what was happening in the United States, to adapt it to their own use. Reagan's program of lower taxes, reduced inflation, and less government intervention became a worldwide recipe for growth.

In sum, our Rip van Winkle of the 1980s would have awakened to a world that had been radically changed in ten short years. From a situation in which freedom was embattled, often losing, amidst uncertainty of its principles and prospects, he had come to in a world in which the idea and practice of human liberty were triumphant. Our sleeper would have had trouble believing he had returned to the same country—or even the same planet.

That, in briefest summary, was the "Reagan Revolution"—in America, and in the world. I firmly believe that, when the history of the twentieth century is written, the chroniclers will conclude that, as President, Ronald Reagan led the cause of liberty to an unprecedented victory over the forces of oppression and slavery. The Reagan era will be seen, I am convinced, as the hinge of history in the modern era—comparable in its way to the allied victories of World War II.

But somehow, looking back from the vantage point of the 1990s, the realities of the previous decade and the perceptions of it have become disconnected. Eight years of remarkable progress are being either ignored or disparaged by journalists, academics, and "instant historians" who write articles and books on this era. Likewise, there has been a blatant attempt to distort the impact of Ronald Reagan's leadership during this period and to derogate or deny his accomplishments.

Having been an active participant in the policy-making process of the White House and having led a major department in the executive branch, I know from firsthand experience that Ronald Reagan had a primary role in the decisions and the philosophy that governed his administration. I was there when he translated the principles of liberty, limited government, and free-market economics—which he had been studying and advocating over the quarter century I was with him—into the successful policies and programs that characterized his presidency. I therefore feel an obligation to share my personal experience and direct knowledge of what really went on during the eight years that turned around this nation and transformed the world.

This book is an attempt to tell part of that amazing story in a way not told before. As mentioned, many accounts of the Reagan era have appeared, some by journalists and policy analysts, others by people who in one capacity or another served in the Reagan government. Some of these works provide important insights into various aspects of Reagan's tenure. But too many paint an erroneous picture of the President, his policies, and the results.

Especially misleading are those journalistic treatments that suggest Reagan was not in charge of the government, that he was "disengaged," ignorant, a mere puppet of his staff. As a witness to the events that took place, and as a direct observer of how decisions were made, I have set forth in these pages an accurate account of many major events and critical issues.

Equally false accounts accuse the President of negligible or harmful policy outcomes—"irresponsible" tax cuts, a "wasteful" defense buildup, intransigent global dealings, illegal activities (Iran-Contra), and similar complaints. These pages address these allegations in detail.

Some memoirs of participants in the Reagan government do indeed give an accurate picture of what took place. Among the more valuable of these are Martin Anderson's *Revolution*, Caspar Weinberger's *Fighting for Peace*, Constantine Menges' *Inside the National Security Council*, John Lehman's *Command of the Seas*, Paul Craig Roberts' *The Supply Side Revolution*, and—though I disagree with some of the personal comments that it offers—Don Regan's *For the Record*.

In no way do I mean to slight the contributions made by these and other authors. Indeed, I have drawn on their researches and recollections at several points, where, for example, their detailed knowledge of defense or fiscal policy complements my own. Most of these memoirs focus on a particular period of the Reagan presidency or a particular aspect of public policy.* I strongly recommend these books to those who seek additional information on the Reagan government.

Other books on the Reagan era, sad to say, come under the heading of backstairs gossip or score-settling. These have provided sometimes sensational fare and momentary scandal for the news media, but little by way of substantive understanding of the President's policies and actions.

In the pages that follow, I have sought to present an overview of the "Reagan Revolution" in all of its dimensions, as I witnessed it, and as revealed in the documentary record. These include the question of Reagan as a political personality; his methods of operation; his qualities as a leader; his philosophy and domestic program; his goals and accomplishments in the realm of foreign affairs; and the net impact of all these matters in terms of national policy and global power.

In addition, I have tried to supply an understanding of crucial

---

* The book that provides the most complete overview of the Reagan years is the President's own memoir, *An American Life* (New York, Simon and Schuster, 1990). This is the best source, of course, on Reagan's plans, reflections, and motivations. Even this memoir is limited, however, in one essential aspect: the President likes neither to claim credit for himself nor to apportion blame to others. He is thus reluctant to stake a claim for himself in history.

episodes in Reagan's public career—turning points that led to particular outcomes, and why events unfolded as they did. In many cases, both in terms of political occurrences and of substantive policy decisions, my views will vary from those that prevail in many of the conventional histories.

My observations of the Reagan era differ from most in two respects: I served with Reagan, on a more or less continuous basis, from the earliest days in Sacramento in 1967 until the final months of his presidency in 1988. As legal affairs secretary to the governor, then as his chief of staff, as a campaign official in 1980, as counsellor to the president, and finally as attorney general, I was privileged to work with him closely over a long span of time, and in several different capacities.

Second, my various roles with Reagan involved, preeminently, policy matters. While these initially focused on the field of law enforcement (and would again at a later date), they touched on virtually every facet of domestic and foreign affairs, covering the entire spectrum of issues before the nation. I was thus well situated to observe his level of interest in, and knowledge of, a multiplicity of topics.

This policy emphasis is the major feature of the narrative that follows. My objective is to document what Reagan was able to achieve in substantive terms across a broad range of governmental concerns, not only to set the record straight, but to show how policy outcomes have affected the American people, and, in the case of foreign affairs, other people throughout the world.

Whether we live in an economy that is functioning, or not; whether we can make a living, buy the things we want, and keep the fruits of our labors, or not; whether the world is peaceful and secure, or not—these are the things that really count in government and politics, in the eyes of the average citizen.

And this Reagan always kept in mind. The concerns and aspirations of the average citizen were the touchstones of his career in government and accounted for much of his success.

Understanding what Reagan was able to achieve, and how he was able to achieve it, is essential in order to appreciate the historic changes that occurred in America and the world in the 1980s. Equally to the point, learning the proper lessons of that decade can guide us toward successful policies in the future, just as the failure to learn those lessons will cause us to repeat the mistakes of the pre-Reagan era.

Given this focus, the present book is in no sense a personal memoir of Ed Meese. While some autobiographical details are briefly supplied, they are offered merely as background, to establish the nature of my relationship with Ronald Reagan.

By the same token, when I touch on episodes where I was personally involved, my object is to cast light on Reagan's policies and decision-making process, based on my knowledge of the situation. I have accordingly not dwelt much on personal battles in which I was engaged, in Senate confirmation hearings and elsewhere, except to the extent that these were part of a broader pattern that affected the workings of the Reagan government.

I am well aware that conventional histories of the period contain many references to such controversies, including a number of statements and comments that are inaccurate. I leave these matters to be addressed in more detail at a future time—perhaps in a separate book. This volume, however, is confined to portraying the Reagan presidency, not my own endeavors.

Discussion of the Reagan administration necessarily involves some particular individuals and the roles they played. In this regard, my instincts are much like those of the President. I don't like to speak ill of others, and I have tried to avoid anything that has the appearance of score-settling or personal rancor.

But some things that occurred in the Reagan era in terms of political and/or policy results cannot be understood without discussing the people involved, and the differing methods that were employed in trying to influence decisions. I have limited personal references to what was absolutely necessary to provide an accurate account.

It is my hope that the events and issues depicted in this volume will provide the reader with an understanding of how a dedicated president came to office with a well-defined program, how he unceasingly worked to implement that program, how he remained true to his principles throughout his tenure, and how the outcome touched not only a nation, but the entire world.

WITH
REAGAN

1

TAKING COMMAND

O F THE MANY CRITICAL DATES during Ronald Reagan's quarter century in political life, none was more important than Tuesday, February 26, 1980. This was the day of the New Hampshire primary election, climaxing a month of dogged campaigning in bleak and bitter wintry weather. This was doubly a day of decision for Ronald Reagan, for it involved not only his chances of victory in this vital contest, but the very survival of his campaign for president.

Just a month before in the Iowa caucuses, Ronald Reagan's high-flying campaign—in which he had been positioned as the "inevitable" nominee in late 1979—had crashed to earth. He had lost the caucuses to George Bush by 2 percentage points. While numerically small, this margin suddenly shifted the momentum from Reagan to Bush and was quickly played up by those who had opposed Reagan from the beginning. The establishment news media and politicians were only too ready to proclaim the end of the Westerner's challenge and to see the campaign come back into the hands of more "appropriate" contenders. Unless he won New Hampshire, there was every likelihood that Reagan's candidacy would be finished.

3

Although as yet unpublicized, behind the crucial battle for victory in New Hampshire, equally serious troubles were disrupting the campaign organization itself; for several months a tense struggle had been building among the campaign leadership. Arrayed on one side were campaign manager John Sears, who had run the Reagan delegate hunting operation in 1976 against Gerald Ford and who was back for the 1980 effort, plus a group of campaign operatives who had come on board as his assistants.

Those whom Sears viewed as being "on the other side" were veteran Reagan staff members who had been with the governor since the early days in California. These included Lyn Nofziger, former communications chief in Sacramento; Mike Deaver, longtime aide to the governor; Martin Anderson, director of policy and issues in 1976 and again in 1980; and myself, who had served as Reagan's chief of staff from 1969 to 1975 and as a close advisor ever since. The problem we faced was like an Agatha Christie mystery novel: the original Reaganites kept disappearing.

First to go was Lyn Nofziger, forced out of the campaign in August 1979 on the grounds that he was not doing an adequate job of fundraising. As a specialist in press and communications, Lyn had never claimed to be a fund-raiser; yet that was the job Sears had assigned him. Alleged problems in this area then became the pretext for eliminating the most politically knowledgeable of the Reagan veterans.

Next to leave, in November, was Mike Deaver. He had been appointed as a coequal with Sears in the campaign structure; Mike was to oversee the administration and operation of the campaign while John concentrated on strategy and planning. Yet, for several weeks John and his associates had excluded Mike from important campaign decisions, had added staff without consultation, and were rapidly dissipating limited campaign funds. To resolve this untenable situation, a meeting was scheduled for the Sunday after Thanksgiving at the Reagan's home in the Pacific Palisades area of Los Angeles.

When Mike arrived at the appointed hour, he found that Sears and two allies had come to the house early and were sitting with the governor and Nancy, who were obviously very worried. He quickly learned that John and the others had mounted an offensive against *him*, delivering a litany of complaints and an ultimatum: either Mike Deaver went or they would go. The Reagans were completely taken aback by this emotional confrontation. While they had sensed some unrest among the campaign leadership, there had been no warning of an imminent blowup. Losing such well-known political operatives as Sears and his colleagues could be devastating to the election effort— particularly since the news media viewed Sears as giving credibility to the campaign. But Mike was particularly close to both the Reagans, and they were grateful for his long and devoted service. Mike showed his loyalty by breaking the impasse himself. To save Governor Reagan from having to make such an agonizing decision, Mike announced that he was leaving the campaign and abruptly walked out of the house.

Next came—or went—Martin Anderson. Martin, another old Reagan supporter and key member of the 1976 campaign, had been recruited early in the 1980 campaign as director of the policy staff, operating out of the Los Angeles headquarters. Having worked on the Nixon campaign in 1968 and subsequently in the White House, Martin was a brilliant expert on all phases of domestic and economic policy. But when he learned that Sears had secretly installed a rival policy group in a new office in Washington, D.C., Anderson returned to the Hoover Institution at Stanford University, where he was a senior fellow, rather than engage in a fruitless series of internal battles.

By February 1980, it had become my turn. For several weeks Sears and his colleagues had conducted a whispering campaign against me, apparently hoping to undermine my position as the last Californian to have direct access to Governor Reagan. Then, in February, the struggle came to a climax. My attempt to bring in some new help for a faltering campaign was viewed by Sears as obstructing the total control that he apparently required.

At a tempestuous meeting with the governor and Nancy Reagan, Sears demanded that I also be removed. At this, the governor, I am glad to say, balked. For some time he had suspected that the problem was not with all the people whom Sears kept accusing, but with Sears himself. In addition, there was a serious communication problem within the campaign, even between the campaign manager and the candidate. During the New Hampshire campaign, Sears had increasingly withdrawn from the general activity, remaining in his room at the headquarters hotel or huddling with his close confidants, away from the rest of the campaign staff. There were also fundamental differences in campaign philosophy between the "grassroots" approach that Reagan favored and the high-level, strategic machinations that were Sears' hallmark.

Accordingly, by New Hampshire primary day, Reagan had decided that Sears would have to be replaced. We were lucky that an excellent new leader was available—former Nixon official, lawyer, and business leader, William J. Casey. Among his other attributes, Casey had first-rate connections in the financial community, which was important, since in addition to its other troubles the campaign was almost out of money. Casey proved to be a top-flight campaign manager and would figure prominently in the history of the Reagan era.

Having determined to drop Sears, Reagan decided not to make the changeover until the afternoon of the primary election day. He did not want the new arrangements to disrupt the New Hampshire effort, nor to be seen as merely a reaction to that election, whatever the outcome. That afternoon, at the campaign headquarters hotel, he called in Sears and his lieutenants and told them of his decision. The governor said he was sorry, but that he felt it was the only thing to do. He also told them that Bill Casey would assume the position of campaign director. They, in turn, wished Reagan well and quietly left the hotel. Key supporters around the nation, along with our campaign staff, were quickly notified and the news was then released to the press. They were totally surprised and somewhat dismayed since Sears had been close to many of them. The big question was: Could Reagan survive the loss of his campaign manager and principal strategist as well as other key staffers?

In results well known to history, Reagan won the New Hampshire primary, plus most of those that followed, and went on to become the nation's fortieth president.

The confrontation with Sears showed a Reagan not usually talked about in the conventional histories: a man capable of taking tough-minded actions and making hard decisions when these were needed to get the job done. This was not an easy thing for him to do, as I knew from going through similar experiences with the governor in California. Firing anyone was a painful ordeal for Reagan, for it evoked the traumatic memory from his boyhood when he had seen his own father lose his job—on Christmas Eve. But when he was convinced that such a step was necessary, he went ahead and did it.

Well before the firing, Reagan had moved to take personal control of the campaign. Sears' "above-the-battle" strategy in the Iowa caucuses had resulted in the loss to Bush, and grassroots complaints about the Sears approach, already numerous, had intensified. The Iowa defeat was more than a wake-up call; it was a four-alarm fire bell for the Reagan candidacy.

In many respects, these problems were a replay of what had happened four years earlier when Sears, managing the campaign against Ford, ran Reagan as if he were already president. It was, as Lyn Nofziger said, a "Rose Garden strategy without a Rose Garden"; it lost key primaries in New Hampshire and Florida before Reagan took the gloves off in North Carolina and started hitting on the issues. In 1980, Sears again attempted to run Reagan as though he were above the hurly-burly of debate. And again it failed.

With the rude results of the Iowa caucuses still rankling, Reagan at last abandoned Sears' approach. Rather than being aloof and above the battle, the governor went into high gear in New Hampshire, going from town to town, meeting with the voters, answering their questions. This was Reagan at his very best, forcefully expounding his view of America, of the Republican party, and of the issues that faced the republic.

Thus, in the New Hampshire primary, we had a campaign with a management pointed in one direction and a candidate in another. Something, obviously, had to give, and it was also obvious what that something would have to be. In late January 1980, shortly after the Iowa defeat, some members of the candidate's "kitchen cabinet," a group of Reagan's longtime California supporters augmented by others from around the country, convened in Los Angeles. Bill Casey, who had been active in staging the Reagan kick-off dinner in New York in November 1979, was in attendance.

At this meeting, almost all of those present expressed their concerns about the way the campaign was going. They knew from their own experience how effective a campaigner Reagan could be, but felt that the governor was not getting his message across, particularly to voters in the East and South. Bill Casey listened quietly and then spoke up, saying that Reagan needed to sharpen his focus on the issues. He volunteered to help out in that regard, having played a similar role in the Nixon campaign in 1968. Bill impressed us with his knowledge, experience, and dedication to the cause, and with the fact that he viewed the issues, and the kind of campaign needed, the same way that Ronald Reagan viewed them.

After the meeting, Mike Deaver and I had dinner with Bill, and it was even more apparent to me that he would be an ideal person to help manage the campaign. I discussed this matter with Reagan, and he asked Casey to come up to Massachusetts and talk with him. Bill Casey's arrival at the campaign hotel and his meeting with Reagan precipitated the blow-up by Sears. Apparently Sears viewed the introduction of Casey as an attempt on my part to seize control behind the scenes.

Just for the record, nothing could have been further from the truth. For one thing, Bill Casey was a powerful personality, just as strong and distinctive as Sears himself, and someone of much greater independent stature in the world of politics, government, and finance. Had I wanted to exert Svengali-like political control of Reagan—something of which neither I nor anyone else was capable—Bill Casey would have been an unlikely cat's-paw.

In reality, the campaign was in deep and serious trouble, and something had to be done about it. I had been functioning as a part-time consultant to the campaign while continuing to teach as a professor of law at the University of San Diego Law School and directing the Center for Criminal Justice Policy and Management there. For several months I had watched the campaign situation deteriorate and staff morale plummet.

When Mike Deaver departed at Thanksgiving 1979, I almost left too because of my unease over the way the campaign was being led. But, instead, the governor and Mrs. Reagan invited me over to their house and asked if I would come on board full-time. I had always found it difficult to turn down a request for help from the Reagans, and especially now, considering the stakes involved in running for the presidency.

I therefore made arrangements to cut back my teaching to almost nothing and to turn the management of the Criminal Justice Center over to my associate director. From then on, I spent about 80 percent of my time on the campaign and, after that fateful day in New Hampshire, about 110 percent. I was in the campaign for one reason only: because Ronald Reagan wanted me there.

After the departure of Sears and his lieutenants, Bill Casey took over the campaign while I became his principal deputy with the title of "chief of staff." Lyn Nofziger, Mike Deaver, and Martin Anderson came back on board, as did others who had been disaffected by the Sears approach. It was like a breath of fresh air. Bill and I immediately met with the campaign staffers in Los Angeles and with the regional political directors, many of whom had been demoralized by the Iowa loss and the general atmosphere of confusion.

Elements of the campaign that had been in conflict began to work together and new volunteers arrived to join the enthusiastic team operation. Particularly important, the financial situation began to brighten. Treasurer Angela "Bay" Buchanan, who had valiantly tried to improve the fiscal system under the Sears regime, now received full support. Management was strengthened by the recruitment of Verne Orr, Reagan's finance director in Sacramento, as the campaign director of administration. And Finance Chairman Dan Terra, ably assisted by Helene von Damm (Governor Reagan's secretary in the state capitol), rejuvenated the campaign fund-raising effort throughout the nation.

The changes made that February 26, I am convinced, were essential to Ronald Reagan's success in 1980. Not because Bill Casey and I were organizational geniuses, but because we had the common sense to allow Ronald Reagan to be himself—something the previous management had not done.

That showdown in New Hampshire also highlighted many aspects of Ronald Reagan's character as a candidate and a leader, qualities that made him unique in the recent history of our politics. And it revealed, in the starkest terms, the difference between Reagan's brand of politics and the conventional view of Republican electioneering.

Reagan's strength in politics, from his first appeal on behalf of Barry Goldwater to his own campaigns for president, was his ability to communicate directly with the American people. He enjoyed campaigning, enjoyed the crowds, and enjoyed delivering his message to them, not simply on television, where he excelled, but in person.

Reagan drew emotional sustenance from his audience and their responses. And it was from those responses that he learned how most effectively to get his points across. It was in his campaign appearances—in the literally hundreds of speeches that he made in his lifetime—that he set forth his views of America, its problems, and its opportunities. Campaigning was a forum, not simply for stating his ideas, but for informing and energizing those who shared them.

For all these reasons, Reagan worked hard on the communication that seemed so effortless for him—reading, researching, developing new information, shaping his presentation, making points with good-natured humor and personal anecdotes. Until he was in the White House, when time demands obviously would not allow it, Reagan wrote virtually all his own speeches, set down in a distinctive shorthand, on the now-famous four-by-six inch cards. He also read a great deal, gaining information and carefully formulating his views. In countless trips in airplanes and automobiles, I remember him constantly at work, either preparing his next speech or searching for new ideas.

All of this was done to present a vision of America—what it had been, what it could be, what it would someday be again. It was a powerful and remarkably consistent vision, as these pages will show. And it resonated with the voters, for one simple reason: It was their vision too, a vision based on the traditions of our country and on the application of some fairly basic rules of common sense. That outlook, and the issues that comprised it, were the very essence of Ronald Reagan as a political leader.

It was this unique quality—so different from those of most political figures—that brought about the New Hampshire changes in campaign style and leadership. The relationship between John Sears' approach and Ronald Reagan's was complex and, in some ways, contradictory.

Martin Anderson put it well when he stated in *Revolution*, "[W]ithout John Sears it is doubtful if Reagan would ever have become President. . . . But it is also true that if Reagan had not fired Sears in February 1980 . . . it is doubtful that he would have been elected President of the United States."[1] Sears unquestionably gave Reagan's candidacy credibility with the Eastern press. Also, John and those he brought into the campaign had much greater knowledge of and experience in national politics. But for all their obvious talents, Sears and his assistants seemed ignorant of the reason for Ronald Reagan's political success. Their own view of politics—so different from Reagan's—focused almost entirely on strategy and technique. To them, everything depended on deft maneuvers, back room alliances, projecting the proper "image," packaging the candidate for the media, and so on.

In this perspective, substantive issues were not that important. From my observation, Sears had little interest in issues as such. In political terms, at least, he viewed "issues" as necessary ingredients in campaign politics, since the candidate had to talk about something, rather than the substance of policies by which the country could be aroused to action.

A related aspect of the Sears campaign style was his distrust of Reagan's judgment and ability—which Sears was often at few pains to conceal. From his attitude, he believed that Reagan needed to be packaged, programmed, and kept away from the voters as much as possible. His aversion to Reagan's interest in issues translated into an uneasiness about Reagan himself. Sears preferred what might be called a "Wizard of Oz" technique, in which the candidate was a phantom projected on a screen, while political "experts" stood behind the curtains, turning the cranks and pumping out the smoke.

These two attitudes converged into a third, which was really the overarching motive of the whole approach: that Reagan should be an establishment candidate. Sears was closely attuned to the Eastern press corps (and well treated by them) and he took his cues accordingly. He tried to present the Reagan campaign—with himself as mastermind—as something of which the establishment media would approve. This meant, among other things, steering Reagan away from his strong espousal of conservative policies.

Seen in this way, Reagan's problem in New Hampshire was merely part of a much larger and continuing problem, a problem that had existed from the beginning of his political career and would last throughout his years of service in the White House: the gulf that existed between Reagan's conservative, issue-oriented approach, and what passed for the conventional wisdom in our politics.

In the usual view of things, elections are not won by talking seriously about the issues, at least not of the sort addressed by Ronald Reagan. By the conventional standards of the establishment pundits, Reagan's political views were absurd, irrelevant, and unpopular with the public. And if these views were not fit to get elected on, still less were they appropriate to govern with.

This view of Reagan surfaced early on, in his first race for governor, and continued over the span of a generation. No one professing his strong opinions, it was said, could get elected to major office. When he won the governorship over Democrat Pat Brown by almost a million votes and went on to a triumphant reelection in 1970, the prevailing wisdom seemed to have been thoroughly repudiated, but its advocates were able to come up with an explanation—one that was dragged out again and again when Reagan won two landslide elections to the presidency.

Reagan, you see, won elections, not because of his posture on the issues, but in spite of it. He won, that is, because he had ingenious managers, or because he was the "great communicator," or because he had an affable personality, or because he was "the Teflon President." Whatever the variations on the theme, one thing was clear: Reagan never won any election because of the positions he had staked out on the issues.

This view of Reagan had obviously been accepted by Sears, who constructed his campaigns for president accordingly; since Reagan's conservative stands were unpopular, while Reagan himself was well liked, it was necessary to distance the candidate from his conservative ideology.

This analysis of Ronald Reagan and the issues is important not only as a retrospective on the 1980 campaign, but because it touches on themes that surfaced repeatedly throughout the Reagan presidency.

Time and again, some in the Reagan entourage sought to maneuver the President away from his most deeply held beliefs, to package him in noncontroversial terms, and to make his program acceptable to the Washington establishment.

Once Reagan was in the White House, this approach became known as "saving Reagan from himself." According to countless stories in the Washington media (and numerous books that have chronicled the administration), Reagan left to his own devices was a hopeless ideologue, out of touch with "reality," someone who had to be carefully coached and guided by his more sagacious staff members and advisors. The purpose, invariably, was to get Reagan away from his "ideological" views so he could do the "pragmatic" things required to govern.

In both political and policy terms, I believe this was a complete misreading of Ronald Reagan and of his tremendous impact on the politics of our country. Given Reagan's historic successes, not only as a candidate but as governor and then as president, it was roughly equivalent to saying that Babe Ruth should have learned how to bunt or that Samson would have looked better with a haircut. It was not only wrong, it missed the point about the man entirely.

As was amply highlighted in the contrast between Iowa and New Hampshire in 1980, and in many other instances, a Reagan severed from the issues *lost* in popular appeal and effectiveness, while a Reagan who spoke out directly and forcefully on the issues won. He was indeed the Great Communicator, but *what* he was communicating was the basis of his appeal. To cut him off from his convictions was to disconnect him from the source of his political power.

2

REAGAN AS LEADER

ONE OF THE MOST ASTONISHING THINGS to me is to read the numerous accounts of the Reagan era that portray the President as an essentially passive figure, somehow disengaged, ignorant of the facts, or incapable of leading. This is a totally false depiction of the Ronald Reagan I knew and worked with closely for a quarter of a century.

Reagan was, in fact, a tough and decisive leader, one of the best I have ever known or seen in action. He had a friendly and nonconfrontational manner, but it was coupled with resolve and strength. Far from being ignorant, he was widely knowledgeable on a host of issues—often much more so than his detractors. And rather than being passive, he was capable of standing his ground against all comers, including self-important staffers who occasionally believed they could or should persuade him to substitute their own ideas for his most deeply held beliefs.

On the face of it, the Reagan-as-empty-vessel theory is somewhat ludicrous. From the treatments of Lou Cannon of the *Washington Post*,

Bob Schieffer of CBS, or Laurence Barrett of *Time* magazine, you would be at a loss to explain how such a vacuous individual could have been twice elected governor of our nation's largest state, much less win consecutive landslides for the presidency. Or how such a person could have successfully reversed the course of national policy and produced so many historic changes.

Clearly, such achievements are at odds with the conventional media picture of Reagan as a pliable front man, or as a rigid ideologue out of touch with the American mainstream. The truth is, Reagan was a very strong leader; more, the strength of his leadership was the vital factor that brought about historic change in Washington and in the world, the ramifications of which continue into the 1990s. A man of lesser conviction and tenacity would have made little headway against the seemingly intractable problems that confronted the nation in 1980, the power of the special interests, and the inertia of the huge establishment entrenched in Washington.

Having been at the President's side through numerous crises and fateful hours of decision, I can testify that he was capable of handling enormous challenges with a calmness and perseverance that were remarkable. The public got a glimpse of this inner toughness during the assassination attempt of March 1981, when Reagan faced his personal travail with courage, stoicism, and humor. His behavior at that moment of peril was entirely in keeping with his true personality and the history of his life, both before and after the shooting incident. This is shown by a brief look at several instances which demonstrated his firm and often courageous leadership:

Reducing Taxes. On the domestic front, the most obvious illustration was the President's tenacity in seeking, and obtaining, an across-the-board, historic reduction in federal income and corporate tax rates. This greatly improved the well-being of the American people and the economy, while also changing the dynamics of the American political system.

While the merits of the tax reduction program are discussed in a subsequent chapter, suffice it to say here that no such changes would have occurred without the dedicated personal leadership of Ronald Reagan. Had he not projected the program in the 1980 campaign, and then insisted on following through, no such reduction would have been possible.

The reason Reagan's leadership was vital is well known, of course, to anyone acquainted with the workings of our national political system. The engine of Washington is fueled with tax money; Congress, the bureaucracy, and the special interest groups all want more of it, and the reigning ideology says they should have it. An administration trying to cut back the flow of tax money challenges the establishment's most vital interests.

At the time, misgivings about cutting back taxes extended into the Republican party and the administration itself. Repeated efforts from within the GOP and the administration were made to undercut the Reagan program and to force the President to back off from his pledges.

But by sheer will power and his own considerable powers of persuasion, and aided by some staunch allies in Congress, the President persevered to the end. At no point in the tax debates of 1981 did he ever lose faith in the rightness of his cause, and he constantly exhorted his cabinet, staff, and members of Congress to move forward with the programs. And in the end, he prevailed against the establishment, the Democrats, and the GOP doubters. Hardly an example of a passive, empty-headed president.

Fighting Inflation. Second only to the Reagan tax program in restoring the health of the economy was the dramatic reduction in inflation rates that occurred from 1981 on. Much of this reduction, of course, was the responsibility of the Federal Reserve System, which controls the rate of increase of the nation's money supply (though some of it should also be credited to increases in production, which provided more goods for dollars to chase).

While the President's role in affecting money supply growth is limited by the independent status of the Federal Reserve, there is a crucial psychological-political link between the White House and the Fed. In times of recession, it is tempting for presidents to engage in Fed bashing, demanding that the money supply be gunned to produce a flurry of economic activity. This diverts attention from White House and legislative policy, while frequently causing the Fed to revert to easy (and inflationary) money.

During the grim recession days of 1981-82, before the Reagan economic program had had a chance to take effect, the President was under obvious pressure to "bash" the Fed and seek easy money. But he steadfastly refused. On the contrary, he often conveyed to Fed Chairman Paul Volcker (through myself and others) that the administration stood by the Fed in following a path of prudent money growth, even though the President himself was under great criticism because of the recession. Again, a case of decisive leadership and political courage—though one seldom publicized.

National Defense. If Reagan's tax reduction plan was the centerpiece of his domestic program, rebuilding our defenses, in all their aspects, was the foremost achievement of his national security policy. He not only devoted more money to defense, but deployed new weapons systems and—when necessary—used U.S. military and economic resources to protect our security interests.

While the Reagan defense buildup was not nearly so massive as his critics have suggested, there is no doubt that his policies reversed the long-term decline in the support of our military forces. And he persisted in this effort despite the outcry of many in government—including some members of his own cabinet—that projected defense spending would have to be curtailed in order to reduce the budget deficit.

Reagan's determined policy sent an important message to the Kremlin in the early 1980s. It also had tremendous consequences a decade later when America went to war in the Persian Gulf; without the weapons developed through Reagan's insistence the United States would have been sorely pressed to deal with Saddam Hussein. Tomahawk cruise missiles, Patriot defenses, "smart bombs," and the like were all deployed on Reagan's watch.

The PATCO Strike. Another crucial episode of 1981—the August strike of the air traffic controllers—reverberated both domestically *and* internationally. Through the years, the American people had become accustomed to public sector union walkouts, which though illegal had prompted little or no response from government leaders.

Action against the Professional Air Traffic Controllers Organization (PATCO) must have seemed even less likely considering that air traffic control is a highly specialized occupation and crucial to the functioning of the nation's aviation system—and that the union was one of a few to endorse the President's bid for election in 1980. Given all that, the union leaders must have calculated that forceful action by the President was a remote possibility.

But when then-Secretary of Transportation Drew Lewis brought this issue to the President, he never hesitated to make sure that the law was enforced. During our several meetings on this subject Reagan was absolutely firm. He gave PATCO the opportunity to obey the law and set a deadline. When they refused, he ordered the striking controllers fired and legal action was taken against the union and its leaders. When Drew and I met with his staff on the crucial day before sanctions began, no one doubted the commitment and support of the President. The message to the nation was clear, and the public response was highly favorable. We are informed, moreover, that this action had a sobering effect on the Soviet leaders, who also had become accustomed to seeing American Presidents back down before a serious challenge. The PATCO action convinced them that Reagan was someone who had to be taken seriously.*

INF Deployment. A similar message was transmitted to the Kremlin in the dispute over deploying Pershing II and Cruise missiles in Western Europe, which was debated in 1981 and 1982 and finally accomplished in 1983. These deployments were undertaken over the heated opposition of the Soviets, the "peace" movement in the West, and the many experts who felt we should postpone or cancel deployment as a concession to the cause of arms control.

The President's performance was especially notable when compared to that of the Carter administration, which had backed off on deployment of the enhanced radiation weapon (the so-called neutron warhead) in response to organized public pressure. Reagan's willingness

---

* As Prof. Richard Pipes put it, "The way the PATCO strike was handled impressed the Russians . . . and gave them respect for Reagan. It showed them a man who, when aroused, will go to the limit to back up his principles." (Quoted by Laurence Barrett, *Gambling with History*; New York, Doubleday; 1983.)

to forge ahead, despite the media uproar and the threats from Moscow, went far to convince the Soviets that he meant business, as witness the INF accord that was signed in 1987.

Grenada. No single event did more to dispel the Vietnam syndrome of the 1970s than the liberation of Grenada from Marxist despotism in October 1983. This was the first such deployment of American forces since the Vietnam War, and the first time in Cold War history that the communist takeover of any state had been reversed by military action. As we know from their secret communications, the message on both of these counts came through to other communist leaders loud and clear.

The liberation of Grenada stirred fierce resistance from the U.S. Congress, from the media, and, as sometimes occurred in such situations, from a number of people in the Republican ranks as well. On top of all this, it came in the immediate aftermath of the tragic death in Lebanon of 241 U.S. Marines, victims of a bomb attack by suicidal terrorists.

Yet the President never wavered once he had determined that U.S. lives and Free World security interests, as well as our integrity in carrying out treaty obligations, were at stake. As described in a later chapter, this historic turning point in the battle for the Caribbean, and in the Cold War generally, was brought about by the resolve of Ronald Reagan, as well as by the skill and valor of our fighting men. Again, it shows a character very different from the media portrayal of a lethargic, passive president, manipulated by others.

Reykjavik. The President's greatest single departure by far from the conventional wisdom was his proposal for a Strategic Defense Initiative (SDI). In pursuing this objective, Reagan took on a whole array of formidable opponents: the arms control establishment and its doctrine of "Mutual Assured Destruction" (MAD), some elements of the military, liberal Democrats in Congress, pragmatists within the Republican party, and so on. Most of all, however, he took on the Soviets and Mikhail Gorbachev, who used all his wiles to get the President to drop the program.

The climax of the campaign against SDI occurred at the October 1986 summit meeting at Reykjavik, Iceland, when Gorbachev proposed the abolition of the program as the price of large reductions in offensive weapons. Many in the United States wanted the President to accept this last-minute deal, which would have won him worldwide plaudits. But the President stood like a rock, steadfastly refusing to surrender SDI.

In all these episodes, the pattern is clear. Far from being manipulated, programmed, swayed, or meekly argued out of his position, the President persevered for what he believed, battled for his policy positions, and made the hard decisions that only he could make. That was the Ronald Reagan that I knew, not the addled figure depicted by his critics.

This quality of toughness in Reagan, of going against the popular tide if he thought he was right, was also evident in some of the less popular episodes of his presidency. In 1985, for instance, just about everyone thought he should cancel his controversial trip to Bitburg, Germany, when it was discovered that former SS troops were buried in the cemetery there. But Reagan insisted on going through with the trip because he had promised German Chancellor Kohl that he would. Equally unpopular, needless to say, was the administration's initiative toward Iran, which was strongly opposed by senior members of the cabinet. Again, for good or ill, the President personally made the hard decision to proceed.

The President's critics are aware, of course, of these many instances of Reagan's toughness; most were major episodes, not only for the Reagan government, but for the history of our country. But rather than give him credit, they simply shift into another mode of criticism. These cases, they instruct us, are examples of Reagan's "stubbornness," or his commitment to a "rigid ideology." Thus, by a kind of rhetorical Catch 22, the President was damned if he did and damned if he didn't: if he was flexible, it meant he was weak and manipulated; if tough, he was a stubborn ideologue.

In fact, like most successful executives, President Reagan combined both toughness and flexibility, more or less in opposite fashion from that suggested by his detractors. He kept his eye on the main objective at all times—astonishingly so, considering the number and complexity of the issues involved—and seldom could be deflected from his course. But in determining how to reach his goal, he was willing to listen to different points of view, and to try different methods if the original approach didn't work.

This combination of attributes was most obvious in his skill as a negotiator, a talent for which he has not received adequate credit. He had a definite theory about this, and he prided himself on his abilities—an attitude that was borne out by events. From dealing with the Democrats in Sacramento to playing high-stakes global poker at Geneva, Reagan proved that he knew how to bargain.

The foremost element of his bargaining strategy was to stake out a position that, so far as he could determine, was *right*—whether in economic policy, foreign affairs, or reform of the courts—defined as in the best interests of the American people. Then, by various approaches, inducements, or collateral measures, he would move persistently toward his objective.

This method, which fit with the other facets of Reagan's management technique, meant that he was always firm in his goals. If he felt his bottom-line position was in danger of being compromised, he was willing to walk away from negotiations, or let the other party do so—which somewhat surprised the Soviets, who weren't used to this type of behavior by an American president. Reagan was confident that firmness would actually increase the likelihood of a sound agreement in the end.

At the same time, Reagan was willing to compromise on details, so long as the overall agreement was moving toward the desired objective. His flexibility in this regard was also a surprise, often to his more conservative supporters. But once again the final outcome, as shown by the Cold War struggle, indicates that Reagan knew what he was doing. He was willing to take 80 percent, or 50 percent, today, in order to return for the rest tomorrow. His unalterable purpose was to keep the process moving in the right direction.

Reagan's penchant for delegating to, and consequently relying on, his staff is frequently cited by critics as a weakness, suggesting that he was merely a creature of the people around him. This is nonsense. Every president brings to the White House his own unique management style, the product of his personality, background, and experience. And each style has its strengths as well as its points of vulnerability. The test of a management style is the results.

The idea that a president or any other chief executive can enmesh himself in all the minutiae of a complicated organization is self-defeating, even if possible. Hundreds of problems and thousands of details are involved in managing something as vast as the federal government, details that no single human being could ever master.

The problems with attempted micromanagement were apparent in the case of Jimmy Carter. It wasn't simply that knowing all about energy policy, the Middle East, or any other major issue was beyond the capacity of any single human being, though that is certainly true. It was also that the attempt to absorb so much detail distracted the President from looking at the overall picture and establishing workable priorities.

Reagan, in contrast to Carter, was a big picture man. Carter could tick off a list of inconsequential details about some aspect or other of federal policy, but seemed to have little idea where he wanted to lead the country. Reagan did not immerse himself in details, but he had a true vision of what he wanted to accomplish, and how the various components of his policy fit together. It enabled him to govern with certainty and consistency.

Reagan's approach was to establish his goals, state them clearly to his staff, and rely on them to handle the details. He wanted, for instance, to reduce the federal burden of taxation and control the growth of federal spending; slow the rate of inflation that was debasing the value of our currency; rebuild the nation's defenses after a decade of depletion; and reduce the threat of nuclear war by developing a system of strategic defenses.

In order to accomplish these objectives, he would listen to policy experts, consider various legislative packages, call in the military or the scientists to discover what was feasible, and so on. Once he established the goal, he expected others to develop the detailed options to achieve it. He would decide on the plan and leave its implementation to those responsible for carrying it out. Reagan's approach was to hire the best people he could find, give them responsibility, and then turn them loose to act. He didn't look over their shoulders, demand constant updates, or otherwise try to monitor their every movement.

This method worked well in Sacramento, where the people around him understood his style and operated according to his ground rules. While the staff had its share of strong personalities and human frailties, there was also a high level of *esprit de corps*, a willingness to work together as a team.

There are, however, potential problems in such an approach, as well. Success depends on the assumption that the people on whom the chief executive relies share his vision, accept his decisions, and abide by the rules, such as insuring that he receives full and accurate information—things we took for granted in Sacramento.

But in Washington, we discovered that some observed different ground rules, which could lead to different outcomes. When staffers had their own agenda, and sought to use the decision-making process to press for a policy different from Reagan's, his reliance on the staff made him vulnerable—either to being deprived of needed information or to having his decisions diluted after the fact.*

Reagan's background in motion pictures and television was obviously relevant to the way he practiced politics, but not in the simplistic fashion suggested by his critics—that he was merely an actor, playing a part or reading lines that had been scripted by others. The facts belie that image. His "role" in politics and government, and the "lines" he spoke, were scripted by only one person—Ronald Reagan.

Nor was it merely that, as a professional actor, Reagan knew how to speak in public or was comfortable before a microphone or a camera. Thousands of actors and actresses, after all, are adept in this regard, but few have been successful in politics, and none has come close to achieving what Ronald Reagan did.

---

* One other aspect of Reagan's personality made this approach a source of vulnerability—his essentially trusting nature. His rule of thumb was that people meant well and were doing what they said until proved otherwise. Once people were on the team, he accepted them essentially at face value. He was reluctant to believe ill of them, or impute bad motives, and was especially reluctant to fire someone if there was any other alternative. Although the instances fortunately were few, there were some who took advantage of Reagan's trust, as will be discussed later.

Reagan's background as an actor accounted, among other things, for his penchant for delegating responsibility. Having acted in movies, and later in television, he had learned to depend on others to bring him options or proposals for decision, and then to allow those persons to carry out what he had decided. In that profession he was accustomed to having people present scripts, or ideas for television programs, and he would choose among them.

As governor, and then president, he followed much the same practice. He depended on his cabinet and top staff members to bring matters to him for decision. Having set forward his vision and main objectives, he expected people to bring him specific plans to which he would say yes or no; or he would mould different options into a program with which he was comfortable.

As an actor, and because of his natural disposition, Reagan knew how to relate to people. It wasn't just a matter of appearing on a screen, or talking into a microphone. Reagan was likeable and wanted to be liked—both by the general public and by individuals. He disapproved of the politics of personal attack, by himself or others, and preferred to conduct compaigns on the level of policies and ideas.

This helps explain his "Eleventh Commandment" approach to California Republican politics ("Thou shalt not speak ill of any other Republican") and his frequently expressed desire to wear the "white hat" in the political drama. He didn't want to be the heavy, a role that suited neither his friendly nature nor the positive message he was trying to convey.

In keeping with these qualities, Reagan was an excellent person to work for—or with, as he would put it. He was almost always upbeat, optimistic, enjoyable to be around. Courteous to everyone, he was seldom overly demanding or given to bouts of anger. Nevertheless, Reagan was human, and could on occasion display flashes of anger, usually when he was frustrated—such as by an obdurate Congress or an overcrowded schedule. His impatience with the schedule usually occurred when he was torn between his desire to continue a conversation with a guest in his office and his reluctance to keep the next visitor waiting. His sense of courtesy to others and his disciplined adherence to his schedule were both offended whenever he was running late.

Even the explosive news of the Iran-Contra connection could not keep him from an appointment with an important African political leader (about which more later).

One essential aspect of Reagan's personality was his sense of humor. He would enliven a meeting with jokes, which he told flawlessly, and had an endless store of tales, often about Hollywood. His less friendly biographers like to point to this as suggesting that he wasn't a serious person. This completely misses the point. Reagan's humor was part of his personality and contributed to his management style by reducing tension and keeping up morale. He knew that laughter was a tonic for people who were working long and hard on contentious matters. Besides, he was a first-rate joke teller—another attribute from his show business past.

Some have intimated that Ronald Reagan was less than warm to members of his staff and did not have a close personal relationship with them. They utterly fail to understand the private Reagan. While he never tried to be "buddies" with those who worked for him, he was always friendly and genial, and if anything, too easy a taskmaster. He rarely criticized and usually left any disciplinary action to those who headed his staff. At the same time, he rarely praised those with whom he worked closely. As Martin Anderson has said, "He seemed to have the attitude that we all should do our best: he should do his and we should do ours. And one does not get special thanks for doing what one should do." [1]

Nevertheless, Ronald Reagan had real feelings for his close associates during their times of crisis. I will never forget when I returned to Washington, D.C., after learning that my son had been killed in an automobile accident. I went directly from the airport to my office and had been there only seconds before the President and Nancy Reagan rushed into the room and threw their arms around me. They literally wept with me and consoled me at the worst time in my life. They both attended the funeral and then invited my family and me to use Camp David for several days to get our lives back together. There was no question in my mind about the depth of the Reagans' feelings and their support for us during this terrible time. I can recount similar instances, such as their presence on my fiftieth birthday, when a surprise party was held for me after work in the Roosevelt Room of the White House. Again, in 1987, when the press was attacking me daily, President Reagan made a particular point of putting his arm around me—in full view of all the news media—after the press conference in which he announced the nomination of Anthony Kennedy to the Supreme Court. He wanted to make sure that the reporters knew of his support. And it did wonders for my morale.

Reagan himself was a highly organized and disciplined person underneath his relaxed and genial manner. This also reflected his actor's training—intensive preparation followed by natural delivery. He would prepare hard for events such as public appearances, speeches, debates, and press conferences, spending hours doing homework on the major topics of political dispute. With his strong sense of priorities, he would concentrate keenly on things he knew were important.

That concentration, too, related to his training. He was a "quick study," able to focus intently on things and to absorb information rapidly. In fact, he had a remarkably retentive memory, recalling things that he had read years before to make a current point. (This greatly annoyed his detractors who, unaware of the matters he would cite, would automatically—and erroneously—assume they were incorrect.)

Even Reagan's skill at negotiation related to his motion picture experience—not as an actor, but as head of his union, the Screen Actors Guild. The techniques he employed in dealing with the Democrats in Sacramento and Washington, or with Gorbachev at Geneva, were those he had honed during extensive negotiating sessions with heads of the motion picture studios.

Perhaps the most significant skill that Reagan carried from Hollywood over to Washington was his understanding of the public. He knew the American people, and he knew how to talk to them. This had nothing to do with "reading lines," and everything to do with knowing what those lines should be: what to say and how to phrase it, what would be understood, and what would impress his audience. He knew how to deliver a message, to be sure, but his greatest ability was in knowing how to formulate the message in the first place.

3

SACRAMENTO

WHEN REAGAN RAN for president, one of his most obvious and impressive credentials was that he had been chief executive of the largest state in the Union. It would be hard to imagine a better training ground for the managerial job at 1600 Pennsylvania Avenue. With over 20 million people, California was larger than 90 percent of the countries on earth; had it been a separate nation, its gross national product would have been the seventh largest in the world.

In addition, California is a prototype for many key developments, both good and bad, in modern living. It has many blessings—a great climate, a varied agricultural and industrial economy, many high-tech industries, and a multifaceted and hard-working population. But it also has, and had, many problems—high taxes, urban sprawl and traffic congestion, environmental disputes, crime, a large welfare class, and so on. At the time Reagan became governor, the state was facing disruptions on its college campuses and a major fiscal crisis. And the legislature with which he had to work was controlled by the political opposition.

The challenge to Ronald Reagan, citizen-politician and newcomer to the halls of government, could hardly have been greater. But during his eight years in Sacramento, he met it in superlative fashion. What he did, and how he did it, rewrote the textbook on American politics. I was proud to have played a part in helping him with that task.

Given my long association with Reagan, some background and explanation of our work together may be in order. I am by training and profession a lawyer. I considered the governor—later the President— in a sense as I would a client: someone who deserved my best counsel and effort. I tried to do a professional job for him in all respects, as I would have for any client. And while always valuing Reagan's friendship, I did not consider myself, nor did I wish to be considered, a faithful family retainer. In other words, I did not want to be in a position where I could not give him my honest and objective views.

Nor was I, when Reagan ran for and was elected governor in 1966, a participant in his campaign or a job-seeker in his administration. At the time, I was a deputy district attorney in Alameda County (which includes Oakland and Berkeley) and I taught an evening seminar at Boalt Hall, the University of California School of Law. Then as now, my foremost interest was in the field of law, legal-constitutional issues, and law enforcement.

As a county official in a state where such offices were nonpartisan, I had little to do with politics, although I was active in civic and community organizations. My work increasingly involved law-and-order issues, including those pertaining to disturbances on the campus and elsewhere, which were blossoming at the time. At the DA's office, we worked closely with the local police departments, including the University of California and Berkeley police, to maintain order and prevent the disruption of educational pursuits. Reagan's forthright comments on this issue during his 1966 election campaign appealed to me.

My family had lived in the San Francisco Bay area for over a century and had long been engaged in governmental activity, but always at a local, nonpartisan level. My great-grandfather had come over from Germany in 1850, journeyed to San Francisco by covered wagon, and in 1878 moved across the bay to Oakland, where he became active in civic affairs.

His son, my grandfather, was a city councilman in Oakland in the early 1900s as well as treasurer of the city of Oakland. My father served for fifty years in local government, as a court clerk and as the treasurer and tax collector for the county. He served in the latter capacity from 1946, when he was first elected, until 1970, when he retired; his nonpartisan elected office was a factor in my avoiding partisan politics.

At the District Attorney's office, I had been in the thick of dealing with the Berkeley disturbances; I was on the scene, having been assigned there by the DA to advise the police, during the mass arrest of protesters who had taken over Sproul Hall. And I later participated in the prosecution of the 773 people arrested. In addition to that background, I had general prosecutorial experience and had been active in training police officers in many subjects, including the control of riots and disturbances.

I had, however, taken no role in partisan politics. Thus I was more than surprised when I was invited to join Reagan's staff.

In truth, I wasn't anxious to leave my position in the DA's office since I enjoyed trial work, had advanced rapidly in assignments, and believed that I might someday become one of the senior executives in the office, perhaps even district attorney. Considering that I was then in my middle thirties, I felt I had made a good beginning in a career in law enforcement, a profession I considered highly important to the well-being of society.

I mention this to underscore that my connection to Reagan, from the outset, was not political, that I had not looked for a job in his administration. I was recommended to him because of my law-enforcement experience—important in view of the problems at Berkeley and because the previous governor had left some sixty people on death row awaiting execution. The new governor needed someone to deal with these and whatever other legal issues were sure to arrive at his doorstep. (I later learned that Sen. Donald Grunsky, one of Reagan's staunch supporters in the state legislature, had recommended me to Reagan. I had met the senator during the two years I served as legislative advocate for the California District Attorneys and Peace Officers Association.)

After preliminary interviews with Tom Reed and Phil Battaglia, two of Reagan's key advisors, I drove up to Sacramento one day in the middle of December 1966 to meet the governor-elect, still uncertain whether I wanted to work in a state administration. In the half hour we spent talking about the concept and practice of criminal justice, we focused on how the governor's powers of clemency should be used in death penalty cases. I was so impressed with Reagan's grasp of these subjects, and the near identity of our views, that I accepted the job on the spot. The title of the post was initially extradition and clemency secretary, which translated to legal advisor to the governor. Later the title was changed to legal affairs secretary.

In this position, I was responsible for capital punishment issues, prison matters, pardons, commutations, and extraditions, as well as liaison with the legal, judicial, and law enforcement communities. In addition, the governor asked me to help organize responses to campus and other disorders, including working with state and local police agencies and providing liaison at scenes of disturbance. (Over the next three years I saw a lot of flower children, and some vicious attacks on police officers.) Also, at the governor's request, I developed a system for evaluating judicial candidates—another issue on which he had campaigned in 1966.

Among other matters, Reagan wanted to remove cronyism from the courts and to insure that California had highly qualified judges who understood and believed in the law. (In California, although judges faced voter approval or disapproval on a periodic basis, most of the appointments were initially made by the governor.) To this end, we established in each county a judicial evaluation panel consisting of a representative of the local bar, a judge of the superior court, and one to three other people who knew the candidates. It proved to be an excellent method for upgrading the quality of judicial nominees.

This experience with the California judiciary had obvious relevance to the program President Reagan would institute in Washington fifteen years later. At the state and national level alike, Reagan's commitment to appointing judges who would apply the law in a manner faithful to its intent was carried out with diligence, and, in my view, was one of the most important and constructive legacies of the Reagan era.

Many developments in Sacramento presaged what was to occur later in Washington. One of the earliest decisions the governor had to make was a capital punishment case involving a convicted murderer, Aaron Mitchell, who had killed two police officers. Reagan's predecessor, Pat Brown, had opposed capital punishment, and strong efforts were being made to abolish it before both the California and the U.S. Supreme Courts. On my recommendation, and despite loud public outcry by opponents, the governor allowed Mitchell's execution to proceed. That sent a message, early on, that Reagan was prepared to make some tough, and controversial, decisions.

A similar message, at another level, went out at Reagan's first meeting as a member of the University of California's Board of Regents. A great deal of criticism—and not just from Reagan—had swirled around the performance of UC President Clark Kerr. It was generally believed that Kerr had not been firm enough in dealing with student disorder, and the belief was accompanied by speculation as to how long he would last in the Reagan era. It turned out not to be very long—due primarily, it seems, to Kerr's own miscalculation about the novice chief executive.

Almost immediately after Reagan's inauguration in January 1967, a meeting of the Board of Regents was scheduled. Although the governor was by statute a member of the board, Reagan's predecessors had only rarely attended regent meetings. But because of the unruly conditions on several campuses and widespread misgivings about the quality of the university's leadership, Reagan felt he should participate actively. At Reagan's first meeting, Clark Kerr abruptly submitted his resignation, which many interpreted as a *pro forma* gesture to test the will of the fledgling governor. According to the ruling wisdom, Reagan, a political neophyte, couldn't afford such an upheaval so early in his term and was thus expected to ask the regents not to accept the resignation. Kerr's tenure would therefore be secure. If this was Kerr's thinking, he was about to receive a shock.

Reagan never wavered; he handled his first major test with both firmness and finesse. Meeting privately with the other regents, he told them they should not be influenced by the fact that this was his first meeting or that the press might try to embarrass him if Kerr were removed so quickly after his arrival on the scene. If the regents were inclined to accept Kerr's resignation in the best interests of the university, the governor continued, by all means they should proceed to do so. He was prepared to take any adverse comment from the news media or Kerr's supporters. The regents promptly returned to the public meeting room and accepted Kerr's resignation. Clark Kerr was on his way out.

Reagan's action set the stage for his dealings with the university. Particularly concerned about campus disorders and the disruption of academic functions, he urged college administrators to take strong action and vowed to give them his full support. He offered state law enforcement officers and even, on occasion, the National Guard to back up campus and local police. I was given the responsibility of planning and coordinating this response. The governor was determined that professors and students who wanted to pursue education would not be hampered by bullying dissidents.

Nor would Reagan allow protesters to intimidate him. In one memorable episode, a large and unruly crowd assembled in front of a campus building in which the Board of Regents was meeting. The governor's security detail wanted him to skirt the demonstrators by entering through the rear door. But Reagan, refusing to submit to the scruffy gang and sneak in, walked right by the protesters—thereby making a forceful demonstration of his own.

At the same time, Reagan was more than willing to engage the students in reasonable dialogue, and did so on numerous occasions. He met with the presidents of the various student bodies, hearing them out and offering his views. In fact, he frequently talked with people of divergent viewpoints who had something to say, provided they were willing to say it in a civilized fashion. He sought a wide range of opinion and was determined not to be a "sheltered" chief executive.

As always with Reagan, matters of taxation and government spending were a high priority and commanded much of his time. Having campaigned in 1966 against high taxes, he was deeply disturbed to find, on taking office, that the previous Brown administration had used accounting tricks to spend nearly a million dollars a day more than the state was receiving in revenues. This fiscal sleight-of-hand was discovered when a transition team, led by Caspar Weinberger, looked into the state's financial situation.

Pat Brown and his colleagues had conveniently changed the method of accounting; in the revised system, fifteen months' revenue was used to pay twelve months' worth of bills, thus avoiding a tax hike just before the election. That left what was then regarded as a whopping deficit, at least $167 million, for the new governor. In California, like other states (but unlike the federal government), a balanced budget must be submitted each January for the next fiscal year.

Even with the fiscal savings immediately instituted by the new administration, Brown's carry-over deficit forced Reagan to take the politically embarrassing step of asking for a tax increase during his first year in office. But characteristically, the new governor faced up to the problem and dealt candidly with the people of California. In his inaugural address and in subsequent televised messages, he told them about the mess he had inherited and how he planned to restore the state's financial integrity. Along with higher taxes and controlled spending, he pledged that if and when there was a surplus in the state treasury, the money would be returned to the taxpayers. He kept this pledge in 1968 and on three other occasions; over $5 billion in taxes was returned to the people during Reagan's eight years as governor.

On the spending side of the ledger, Reagan announced that he would "cut, squeeze, and trim" to reduce the cost of state government. In doing so, he adopted several methods that would reappear in Washington. One innovation was the Business Task Force, consisting of two hundred top leaders of the business community who looked into every department and agency of state government. They brought back a report with hundreds of recommendations for cost-savings and greater efficiency, which Reagan proceeded to implement, saving hundreds of millions of taxpayers' dollars—an obvious precursor of the Grace Commission which he appointed while in the White House.

Early in 1969, I became executive assistant to the governor and chief of staff, succeeding Bill Clark, who had been appointed a superior court judge. In this new position, I directed the governor's executive office, served on the cabinet, and had management responsibility for the National Guard, the Office of Emergency Services, and the Office of Criminal Justice Planning. At that time California had over forty departments and major agencies of state government— obviously too many components for the directors to meet regularly with the governor. Accordingly, they were divided into four "super-agencies," each headed by an agency secretary. These four agency secretaries, along with the director of finance and the governor's executive assistant, formed the governor's working cabinet. For formal cabinet meetings, they were joined by the lieutenant governor and the other elected statewide officers of the governor's party.

Ronald Reagan believed strongly in cabinet government, using this forum as his primary means of obtaining policy advice and information. The cabinet would meet with the governor several times a week. On some occasions—such as when the conclusion of the legislative session left him with hundreds of bills to sign or veto, or when the legislature sent him the annual budget—the cabinet would often meet with the governor from early in the morning until late at night, day after day.

This system had many advantages which Reagan prized. First of all, it allowed all of his top policy advisors to present their side of any given issue. Second, when he had made his decision on a matter, the cabinet heard it directly from him, not through some staffer. Third, since all of his top executives could participate directly in the decision-making process, they were committed to abide by the result. The governor was scrupulous in following this system. When department heads or others would try to buttonhole him in the hallways, or anywhere else, he would just smile and say, "Well, we'll have to roundtable that"—that is, discuss it through the regular cabinet process.

Another major problem for California during Reagan's tenure as governor was the growing social welfare budget. At a cabinet meeting in 1970, our finance director reported that welfare and educational outlays were squeezing the budget to the point where demands for another tax hike would inevitably follow.

After the session, I met with the governor and suggested we set up a task force on welfare reform to isolate the causes of the spending and design a new system from the ground up. As a result, he assembled a team of experienced public officials who shared one qualification: they had never served in a public welfare agency and therefore could take a fresh look at the welfare problem. After several months of fact-finding and analysis, they produced a report on welfare reform which came to be known as the "Blue Book," the color of its cover. It identified abuses of the system, and proposed many solutions designed to keep ineligible people off the rolls and increase benefits to the deserving. One new feature of the program was to allow the counties to keep the money they saved by weeding out ineligible recipients and finding delinquent fathers to pay for child support. Previously such savings would have been returned to the state treasury, leaving the counties with the work but none of the savings.

This set of proposals became a major point of contention between the governor and the Democratic legislature—and a major test of both Reagan's communicating and bargaining skills. Reagan proposed to deliver an address to a joint session of the legislature to present the welfare reform package, but the Democratic Speaker of the Assembly, the late Bob Moretti, refused to approve it. Reagan thereupon took to the hustings and the air waves with the speech "they wouldn't let me deliver to the legislature."

In it Reagan told his listeners, "If you want welfare reform and to control the cost of welfare outlays, then keep those cards and letters coming"—to Bob Moretti. In due course, as Reagan described it, "Moretti came by my office with his hands raised and said, 'Okay, I give in.' "* The negotiations, personally led by Reagan, ensued.

The package we came up with was highly successful, not only in curbing runaway welfare costs in California (at least while Reagan was in office) but in its immediate impact on the national scene. At the time, the Nixon administration was pushing a program called the Family Assistance Plan (FAP), which would have federalized most

---

* I participated in these sessions as a member of the governor's team opposite Moretti and then State Assemblyman John Burton for the legislature. The negotiations were strenuous, starting at eight or nine in the morning and often lasting until ten or eleven at night and continuing for almost a week. After the basic principles were agreed upon, I took over the negotiations for the governor, Burton led them for Moretti, and we negotiated for another week or so on the details.

aspects of welfare, established the principle of guaranteed annual income, and increased the costs of the system enormously.

But the success of the Reagan program in California derailed the FAP express train: the Reagan experiment proved that welfare problems could be handled effectively at the state level. It also indicated that the principles and incentives utilized in California could be employed at the federal level.

Or so thought Sen. Russell Long (D-La.), then chairman of the Senate Finance Committee, who asked Reagan to testify about the California plan before a hearing in Washington. The governor complied, emphasizing the importance of maintaining state responsibility in this area. He did this even though some governors had asked that welfare be federalized, hoping to transfer the growing expense to Uncle Sam rather than provide savings for all taxpayers. Reagan's testimony, and the success of the California experience, were significant factors in the demise of FAP.*

Another major initiative of the second Reagan term in California, with obvious national implications, was tax limitation. We established a task force under Lewis Uhler that came up with a proposal for holding state taxes and expenditure increases to corresponding increases in the economy. This was put to the test in 1973 in a special state initiative election. The numerous special interests that benefited from expanded state spending conducted a massive, often deceptive campaign, and the proposal was narrowly defeated. But it paved the way for California's famous 1978 ballot initiative, Proposition 13, which reduced property taxes throughout the state. It also set the stage for the national mood of tax revolt which was a key ingredient in Reagan's presidential victory two years later.

---

* Interestingly, the principal author of FAP was Daniel P. Moynihan, then an aide in the Nixon White House, now a liberal Democratic senator from New York. The details of the program, and the Reagan approach in California, are well described in Martin Anderson's book, *Welfare* (Hoover Institution). Among other positive impacts of the Reagan program, Bob Carleson, who had been appointed state director of welfare in California to implement the reforms, was invited to Washington to fill a similar role in the federal government. Others who worked on the welfare package, including Ron Zumbrun, Chuck Hobbs, and Jack Svahn, also went on to distinguish themselves in other, related positions.

In still another initiative of the early 1970s, Governor Reagan appointed a task force to look into the criminal justice system. One of its principal findings was that serious felons, when caught and convicted, seldom went to prison. In their zeal to rehabilitate, rather than incarcerate, convicted criminals, courts and other authorities had been sending them just about everywhere but to jail. Fewer than one in ten of the felons were actually serving prison time. The task force, unsurprisingly, recommended much tougher sentencing, along with technological and procedural improvements for their apprehension and a general upgrading of the adjudication process.

These and many other episodes in Sacramento showed Reagan as an effective politician, chief executive, and advocate for the public. But most remarkable was the variety of Reagan's initiatives and creative approaches. From courts and crime, to welfare, tax limitation, and control of spending, he was constantly seeking ways to make the government more efficient, more responsive, and less expensive.

As governor, in other words, Reagan was not content just to manage the situation that was handed him, to conduct business as usual, and to rest with the status quo. He wanted to change things for the better, and he never relented in his efforts to get the job done. All of this he would later duplicate in Washington.

One aspect of the Sacramento experience relevant to Washington— mostly by way of contrast—was Reagan's approach to the press. Almost every week he would hold a press conference in which members of the news media would ask him about administration plans and proposals, pending legislation, or controversial issues—all unscripted. The give and take was vigorous, and by common consent the governor managed it in superlative fashion. There was no hint that Reagan needed to be "handled" by his staff, or shielded from meetings with the press and public.

That scenario, of course, was very different from what too often occurred when Reagan was in the White House. The distinction points to important differences in organizational arrangements and the approaches of Reagan personnel. In Sacramento, the staff system and the people around the governor complemented his style of management.

Central to his operation was the idea of a cabinet government. Reagan has an important attribute, which was demonstrated both in Sacramento and in Washington; he is a good listener. In cabinet meetings, sessions with his staff, or conferences with visitors he would ask questions, raise issues, and offer observations. But his special talent was to hear what everyone had to say—to keep still until others had spoken and think carefully about what he had heard before making his decision. He viewed those meetings as a valuable means of gathering information, where completeness and accuracy of the presentations were highly important.

Understanding this, Bill Clark and I tried to stimulate the flow of information to the governor and ensure that people with important interests in or knowledge about a subject had the opportunity to talk directly with Reagan.

Other ground rules applied as well: Once Reagan had made a decision, we considered the debate closed; the option chosen was the policy of the administration. We didn't try to change the options Reagan had selected, reopen questions he had already answered, or otherwise manipulate the process—either before or after a decision. All of us realized he was the one who had been elected governor and that our job was to provide full information, respect his decisions, and carry out his policies. There were few turf battles and even fewer news leaks. Efforts to manipulate the media and thereby influence executive decisions were not tolerated, either by the governor or by his top officials. As a result, the Reagan administration in Sacramento was noted for its harmonious working relationships—and corresponding benefits for the people of California.

4

CARTER'S FAVORITE OPPONENT

I N THE AFTERMATH of the 1980 New Hampshire primaries, Jimmy Carter's press aide Jody Powell and pollster Pat Caddell were toasting their candidate's victory against Democratic challenger Ted Kennedy.

According to journalists on the scene, Powell and Caddell were immensely pleased, not only with Carter's showing against Kennedy, but also with what was happening among the Republican hopefuls. "They were very happy," the *Washington Post* reported. "Carter had just demolished Kennedy and *Reagan, the man they wanted Carter to face in the fall election*, had taken care of Bush. Furthermore, Sears—the most respected of the Republican strategists—was out" (emphasis added). [1]

There is other evidence to similar effect: Jimmy Carter and his staff were champing at the bit to run against Ronald Reagan, figuring he would be the easiest Republican to beat. In view of what happened the following November, the rationale for this peculiar notion needs explaining: the reason Carter's people thought Reagan would be such a pushover is that this was what they were being told by the conventional wisdom.

James Reston of the *New York Times*, for instance, suggested the GOP nomination process was "being run by the Democratic National Committee." Carter and his people had cause to be concerned about Gerald Ford, John Connally, Howard Baker, George Bush, or John Anderson—all of whom would be tough challengers in November. "A Ford-Anderson ticket," Reston opined, "would have given him fits":

> But now Carter is left with Reagan alone, and if Jimmy and the Georgians and the Democratic National Committee could have planned the whole thing, this is precisely how they would have worked it out. . . . Republicans are compassionate people. . . . They are giving Carter . . . their favorite candidate, and Carter's favorite opponent—Ronald Reagan. Seldom in the history of American politics has a party out of power shown so much generosity to a President in so much difficulty.[2]

The ironic wit of this analysis was surpassed only by its depth of insight. That Reston and other supposedly knowledgeable people actually believed such things is testimony to the delusion that passes for knowledge in our elections. The error involved not only under-estimating Ronald Reagan (a mistake habitually made by his opponents), but also a complete misreading of the forces at work beneath the surface of our politics.

The date of Reston's column is significant. This piece appeared on March 21, 1980, less than a month after New Hampshire; its premise was that the Republican struggle was over, that Reagan already had the nomination in his grasp. While technically not the case, this was true in substance. If Reston and other like-minded pundits had understood how Reagan had accomplished this, they might have revised their jovial estimates of his weakness.

The fact of the matter was that, after breaking out of the stranglehold applied by Sears, Reagan exhibited amazing vote-getting power. In a span of three weeks, he contested nine primary elections and won seven. After winning New Hampshire, he achieved a three-way standoff with Bush and Anderson in liberal Massachusetts and

Vermont (March 4), rolled over Connally in South Carolina (March 8), and swamped all his opponents in Florida, Georgia, and Alabama (March 11).

Faced with these rapid-fire successes, Reagan's opponents began falling by the wayside. Connally had staked everything on South Carolina, and lost. Howard Baker, having lagged the field in most of these elections, withdrew. Bob Dole, John Anderson, and Rep. Phil Crane were still in the race, but few believed that any of them had a chance of beating Reagan.

The only viable opponent left was Bush, and for him it all came down to Illinois, on March 18. Having lost to Reagan in New Hampshire, settled for a tie elsewhere in New England, and been swamped throughout the South, Bush had to make a showing in Illinois. If he couldn't beat Reagan in this large Midwestern state, his chance of winning the nomination as the campaign moved West to Reagan country was nonexistent.

The primary was complicated by the fact that two Illinois candidates, Anderson and Crane, were competing on the ballot, and that Reagan himself was an Illinois native. More decisive than these items, however, was a four-candidate televised debate held in Chicago on March 13, in which Crane attacked Anderson, Anderson attacked Bush, and Reagan came over as humorous, poised, and fully in command of the situation. (Noting that price controls hadn't worked under the Roman emperor Diocletian, Reagan added, "And I'm one of the few persons old enough to remember that.")

When the votes were cast, Reagan far outpolled favorite-son Anderson (48.4 to 36.7 percent) and beat Bush by almost five-to-one (11 percent). That outcome prompted analysts to believe the Republican nomination struggle was effectively over, and that Jimmy Carter was going to face his "favorite opponent" in the fall. A more sensible view might have concluded that a candidate who in three weeks had disposed of Baker, Connally, Dole, Bush, Anderson, and Crane knew a thing or two about campaigning.

In the Reagan camp, however, none of us was taking anything for granted. While Reagan had bolted to the front of the pack, two dozen primaries were yet to go, and the candidate had to keep campaigning.

The free-spending days of late 1979 and early 1980 meant that money was still a problem, and Bill Casey had to continue paring payrolls and pinching pennies—though Reagan's near certain victory was naturally helpful in fund-raising. (Our main problem at this point became the spending limits imposed by federal statute.)

As it happened, Bush staged a late comeback of sorts in Connecticut (one of his home states) and Pennsylvania, and came close to Reagan in Texas (another Bush home state). But these hopeful signs for Bush were too little and too late; by May, Reagan was routinely winning primaries by margins of two- and three-to-one (74 percent in Indiana and Tennessee, 68 percent in North Carolina, 76 percent in Nebraska).

By May 20, when Bush salvaged a final victory in Michigan, Reagan was winning the Oregon primary and wrapping up enough delegate votes to assure his nomination. All told, Reagan had won twenty-nine of thirty-five primaries, and had triumphed in every section of the country—from New Hampshire to California, from Florida to Idaho, in Alabama and Montana, Illinois and Nebraska. Jimmy Carter was going to get his wish, and then some.

With Reagan nailing down the nomination at such an early date, he and his campaign team were able to lay careful plans for the convention in Detroit. Our goals for the convention were essentially four: (1) to adopt a solid platform that would reflect the traditional values of the nation, the GOP, and Ronald Reagan; (2) to bring the various Republican elements together so that the party could go forth united in the fall; (3) to choose the strongest possible running mate who would help with this objective and with the general public; and (4) to use the convention as a showcase for the candidates and the themes that would be projected in the fall election.

All of these objectives were accomplished. In terms of platform, superb work was done by the committee headed by Sen. John Tower. Martin Anderson and Richard Allen, faithful sentinels of the Reagan program, worked with the committee to produce an excellent document that not only reflected the conservative values of Reagan and the party, but projected a sense of optimism about the future of the country—an essential part of Reagan's outlook.

Working with Tower on the platform committee were a group of younger Republicans from the House of Representatives, including Trent Lott of Mississippi and Jack Kemp of New York. Both would be heard from later, Lott moving up to the Senate, Kemp becoming a leading exponent of the Reagan tax program in Congress and then, in the Bush administration, secretary of housing and urban development. Also scheduled to play a prominent role in later developments was the chairman of the platform subcommittee on energy—a youthful congressman from Michigan named David Stockman.

In terms of party unity, candidate Reagan took special pains to heal divisions in the GOP, both prior to and during the Detroit convention, and did so quite successfully. One notable step was a fund-raising dinner held with his former Republican opponents to help pay off their campaign debts. Another was to have various of them speak at the convention itself, and/or become involved in the campaign to follow. Considerations of this sort weighed heavily as well in his selection of a running mate.

In the course of binding together the differing elements of the party, Reagan had several conversations with former President Gerald Ford. Despite their sometimes heated differences in the 1976 campaign, the two had become friendly in 1980; when some who opposed Reagan had tried to get Ford to run against him, particularly after Bush began to falter, Ford refused to be drawn in. Relations between the two by the time we reached Detroit were cordial.

Out of this renewed relationship emerged the idea of a "dream ticket," with Reagan as presidential nominee and Ford in the number two position. Reagan had made a *pro forma* suggestion of such a ticket in talking with the former president, at the urging of mutual friends, and was surprised when Ford in essence said he would think about it. The idea was then seriously considered by our campaign advisory team and—as soon became apparent—by Ford's people as well.

In terms of uniting the party, the "dream ticket" had appeal, as it also had for the fall election: though defeated by Carter in 1976, Ford was a familiar figure on the Washington scene, having served as president, vice president, and for many years as a member of Congress. His presence would reassure many who viewed Reagan as a wild man from the West; and having a former president on the ticket would help close any perceived "stature gap" between Reagan as an outsider and Carter as the sitting chief executive.

Accordingly, the possibilities of such a ticket were hashed out in a series of meetings, lasting many hours, between representatives of the two sides. Speaking for Ford were Henry Kissinger, economist Alan Greenspan, and Rep. Dick Cheney of Wyoming, Ford's White House chief of staff. Representing the Reagan camp were Bill Casey, Dick Wirthlin, and myself. However, in the course of these discussions— and in an interview that Ford himself gave Walter Cronkite— insuperable problems with the "dream ticket" concept began to surface.

Above all, should a Reagan-Ford ticket be elected, it appeared a kind of "co-presidency" might be sought—Ford having certain areas of responsibility, and power, beyond those customary for a vice president. I had no doubt that, from Kissinger's standpoint, this meant control over important facets of foreign policy and arms control, in which Kissinger himself, it's safe to say, would have played a prominent role.

From my perspective as a negotiator, this was a complete nonstarter (from Ford's side of things, we were getting signals that the former president had some problems with the idea himself). I didn't think that Ronald Reagan had campaigned for president in 1976 and again in 1980 to wind up with others calling the shots on foreign policy—or to barter away any other aspects of the executive authority conferred on the president by the Constitution.

Casey, Wirthlin, and I ultimately advised the governor against such an arrangement, which was exactly the way he was tending anyway. Ford had reached the same conclusion, which he communicated to Reagan on Wednesday evening. The "dream ticket," and any prospective co-presidency, went by the boards. The governor decided, almost immediately, that George Bush should be his running mate, bringing most of the positives associated with Ford but without the prospect of a "co-presidency." This was the course that I personally favored and had urged the candidate to follow. Bush provided geographical and intraparty balance, experience in the federal government, and—as evident over the course of the preceding campaign—a gentlemanly manner and basic agreement with Reagan on the issues.*

Though Reagan had now decided on Bush, speculation was still rampant, in the media and the convention hall, about the "dream ticket." The governor knew that if the delegates went home that night thinking Ford was to be the vice presidential candidate, only to learn the following day that this was not so, disappointment and recriminations in some quarters could sour the proceedings. He therefore decided to go to the hall before he himself had been formally nominated and clear the air—announcing that, should he receive the nomination, Bush would be his running mate.

In doing this, Reagan not only went against the counsels of those who wanted the "dream ticket," but also against the tradition that says the presidential candidate doesn't make a personal appearance in the convention hall before he actually has the nomination. But he felt it was important to gain control of the situation and eliminate potential discord over a false issue. His instincts were correct, and the dramatic visit to the convention enhanced respect for his personal leadership.

Coming out of Detroit, a logical, and necessary, change occurred in Reagan's strategy. Prior to winning the nomination, the campaign had been a matter of proceeding state by state, primary by primary, to secure the necessary delegate votes. Campaigning at this stage is very much a retail business. Now it became necessary to go wholesale, to project the governor as a national candidate: not simply a parochial contender from the West, but someone who could appeal strongly to every sector of the country.

Equally important, we needed to reach out to a broad range of Americans. A major feature of both the platform and the speeches at

---

* Bush's most famous policy disagreement, of course, had been when he described the Reagan program of supply-side tax rate reductions as "voodoo economics." Once on the ticket, however, Bush became a supporter of the Reagan economic program and continued as a low-tax advocate himself in the 1988 campaign with his "read my lips" pledge of no new taxes (broken in 1990). To those who asked about Bush and "voodoo economics," my standard reply was that he had experienced an exorcism in Detroit.

the convention was the appeal to constituencies in our population—ethnic minorities, urban Catholics, blue-collar workers—that hadn't traditionally voted Republican. These were also the leading themes of the campaign analysis prepared for us by Richard Wirthlin. Our message was that a Republican party of traditional values, economic growth, and jobs offered them a better prospect of effective government than did a crumbling New Deal coalition.

Reagan strongly believed in this message, having made the transition from Democrat to Republican himself, and he tirelessly preached it in his campaign appearances. Settings were chosen to highlight this message—an urban streetscape in the Bronx or a steel mill in Ohio. The campaign was to be one of optimism and inclusion, conducted on a national scale.

In keeping with these goals, we moved the major elements of the campaign from Los Angeles to the Washington, D.C., area, in order to be nearer to the major population centers—most of which, other than California itself, are east of the Mississippi. We would also be nearer to the Republican National Committee, and to the national media, which are overwhelmingly based in Washington and New York. In running a national campaign we had to consider all these factors, and the commuting times from California to the East were just too great.

The governor and Mrs. Reagan therefore temporarily took up residence in the Washington region. We arranged for them to use the former home of Bill Clements, the past deputy secretary of defense who had become governor of Texas. Near Middleburg, Virginia, not far from the home of Sen. John Warner, the house was beautifully located in the Virginia hunt country, about an hour from Washington, and thus a good rest stop for the candidate and Mrs. Reagan between campaign appearances. It also had a large converted barn that was useful for meetings and debate rehearsals.

At our campaign headquarters off Columbia Pike in Arlington, Virginia, directly across the Potomac River from the capital, we set up shop with Bill Casey as campaign director and myself as chief of staff and principal deputy. Verne Orr was in charge of administration, Drew Lewis handled our relations with the RNC, Bill Timmons was our political director, coordinating all field operations, and Cliff White—

who had orchestrated the Goldwater delegate hunt of 1964—was a consultant to Bill Casey. Others who worked on the executive staff as deputy campaign directors included Bob Gray, Mike Deaver, Dick Wirthlin, and Lyn Nofziger, along with Martin Anderson and Richard Allen as senior policy advisors. As we assimilated people from other campaigns, Jim Baker of Bush's team also joined the staff.

The traveling party that moved around the country with Reagan in a chartered aircraft usually included Deaver, Nofziger, Anderson, and on occasion Dick Allen. Jim Brady, who had come from the Connally campaign, handled policy communications. Stuart Spencer, a California political consultant, also helped out on the plane. This provided Reagan with the logistics, press, and issues people he needed with him as he traveled. All of them were experienced, sharp, and knowledgeable about Reagan, which meant he had an excellent backup team available at all times.*

Those of us who were at campaign headquarters on any given day would meet at 7:00 or 8:00 A.M. to go over plans for the day, coordinate strategies, and deal with any problems. Bill Casey and I both had temporary residence at the Skyline Towers apartments in Arlington, and we would meet many mornings at 6:30 so that we could review developments and lay out projects for the day before the first formal meetings began at the office. Bill's wife, Sophia, kindly provided breakfast, even at that early hour.

While Dick Wirthlin's polls suggested Reagan's issues were scoring well with an electorate tired of "malaise" after four years under Carter, there were some underlying problems. Beginning in August, and continuing into the fall, a lot of commentary suggested that Reagan's candidacy was stumbling. In particular, there was intensive coverage of what the media said were "gaffes" by Reagan—supposed misstatements that showed he didn't know very much about the issues.

A quest for gaffes had been a prominent feature of the 1976 Reagan primary campaign, during which various media critics alleged that Reagan had misspoken about Social Security, "welfare queens," and

---

* In addition, we set up a twenty-four-hours a day operation unit, headed by Bob Garrick, so that someone would always be on hand to alert us to developments in the news and to keep contact with the traveling party in whatever the time zone.

other topics. That drill would be repeated when Reagan was in the White House. These were prime examples of what I call "gotcha" journalism, and were usually based on media unfamiliarity or disagreement with what Reagan was saying rather than inaccuracy on his part.

Reagan's alleged 1980 gaffes consisted of saying he had some doubts about the scientific basis of Darwinian evolution (doubts shared by scholars such as Jacques Barzun and Gertrude Himmelfarb), that he felt the government of Free China on Taiwan should be extended official U.S. recognition, that the Vietnam War was a "noble cause," and that the economy under Carter was in a "depression" (when the official experts said it was only a "recession").

The greatest of Reagan's supposed misstatements occurred in Steubenville, Ohio, in early October, when he said that emissions from trees and other vegetation were heavy contributors to ozone pollution, so that simply controlling man-made emissions wouldn't solve the problem. This was considered hilarious ignorance on Reagan's part, with reporters making jokes about it in print and hecklers decorating trees with signs that said, "Chop me down before I kill again."

Though treated at the time and in subsequent histories as an example of Reagan's foot-in-mouth disease, this episode actually proved the opposite. As often occurred, Reagan had done his homework and knew what he was talking about; the people making fun of him did not. Several scientific studies have shown that trees *are* substantial contributors to ozone pollution and that controls on man-made emissions accordingly won't cure the problem—exactly as Reagan had contended.[*3]

The media "gaffe patrol" meant little as far as individual episodes

* For example, the September 1988 issue of *Science* magazine, in a report based on the findings of researchers at Georgia Tech, said: "Hydrocarbons emitted by trees appear to play a much larger role than originally believed in producing the high ozone levels that plague many U.S. cities." Using satellite data, Dr. William Chameides and his colleagues at Tech's School of Geophysical Sciences determined that wooded areas of Atlanta emitted approximately as much hydrocarbons as did man-made sources. "The strategy of reducing man-made hydrocarbons has not been effective," Chameides said, "because after you remove the man-made hydrocarbons, the hydrocarbons from trees remain. . . . It is when natural hydrocarbons from trees are mixed with man-made nitrogen oxide that ozone is produced and our air quality is threatened." So much for Reagan's ignorance.

were concerned, though we felt the cumulative impact might be troubling. What Reagan said about trees and pollution was of small import to the average voter, who was typically worried about the economy, taxes, inflation, keeping a job, buying a home, and so on. These were the issues on which Reagan continued plugging away, in his usual effective style.

In fact, it is hard to think of a presidential campaign in recent memory that has been so oriented to specific issues as that conducted by Reagan in 1980. In domestic matters, he hammered repeatedly on the themes of reducing taxes, getting government spending under control, cutting back over-regulation, and the need for a stable monetary policy. All these things were required, he said, to get the economy moving again—and all were completely different from the standard practice of the federal government.

In matters of defense and foreign policy, Reagan talked of the need to rebuild our military, to stand up for American and free world interests overseas, and to counter Soviet expansionism with a policy of "peace through strength." These topics were touched on over and over in major speeches, campaign appearances, and debates. Nearly all of these issue stands, too, were unpopular with the establishment—but popular with the voters.

Transcending and embodying these two groups of issues was a larger theme that was the hallmark of Reagan's campaign, and of his presidency: his faith in America, his optimism about the future, and his conviction that proper policies would restore the nation to its former greatness. The "malaise" idea that had arisen in the Carter era was anathema to Reagan; the problems we faced, in his analysis, were not the fault of the American people, but of mistaken measures adopted by the government. Reagan's message of hope, and opportunity, so different from the standard litany about the "limits of growth," resonated with the voters.

The domestic centerpiece of Reagan's campaign was his proposal for an across-the-board, 30 percent cut in personal income tax rates over three years. This was the essence of the so-called "supply-side" program being promoted in Congress by Kemp and Sen. William Roth of Delaware, and was part of the platform adopted in Detroit. The idea had appeal politically because most people like lower taxes and because it addressed the question of economic growth which greatly concerned the electorate.

The tax program, however, was being treated as another Reagan "gaffe," a pipedream that could never be adopted, or would have disastrous consequences if it were. The merits of the program in budgetary and economic terms are examined in chapter 11. In the early fall of 1980, it was a political question and needed to be addressed in terms of the election. Fortunately, in this respect, the campaign had the services of Martin Anderson, an excellent economist experienced in the arts of political communication.

Martin had been instrumental in drafting the original Reagan tax position and was intimately familiar with all the arguments about the wisdom of cutting taxes. He accordingly assumed the task of putting together the relevant economic numbers including assumptions about inflation, GNP growth, and revenues, to show how a cut like that proposed by Reagan would play out in budgetary terms, and also what impacts it would most likely have on the economy.

In his book, *Revolution*, Martin has recounted his efforts in this regard, the briefing data he supplied to the campaign, and the speech of September 9, 1980, in which candidate Reagan forcefully laid out the economic case for his proposal. It was a first-rate performance in all respects and supplied an effective answer to those who dismissed the Reagan economic program as a gimmick. This presentation was tremendously important, since it directly addressed the voters' concerns about taxes, inflation, and jobs.[4]

As the campaign unfolded, these and other underlying issues began to cut strongly in Reagan's favor, as Wirthlin's poll results revealed. But media concentration on Reagan's alleged gaffes suggested a possible vulnerability—uncertainty about the candidate as an individual, since he was in various respects an unknown quantity to many of the American people.

The Carter campaign and Reagan's critics in the media sought to exploit this uncertainty by spreading alarm about Reagan as a loose cannon and extremist who could not be trusted with the presidency. Given the enormous power of the office, and in particular the authority over life and death decisions and the awesome power of nuclear weapons, fears about such matters can be deadly—as the job done on Barry Goldwater in 1964 clearly demonstrated.

As Dick Wirthlin's campaign analysis had foreseen, the Carter effort to discredit Reagan *as a person* was a conscious and deliberate strategy. An August story by James Perry and Al Hunt in the *Wall Street Journal*, for instance, put it that "Carter Plans to Win by Depicting Reagan as Shallow, Dangerous." The main themes of this attack were to suggest that Reagan was a racist and warmonger, as well as being ignorant and irresponsible.[5]

In direct reference to Reagan, for example, Carter said such things as "hatred has no place in this country. Racism has no place in this country"; that the election would determine, among other questions, "whether we will have war or peace"; and whether "America will be unified, or, if I lose the election, whether Americans might be separated, black from white, Jew from Christian, North from South, rural from urban."[6]

These charges angered Reagan, understandably, since anyone who knows him at all knows he is not a racist, and since (as discussed later) he was the opposite of a warmonger. In fact, the Carter charges went so far they even caused a backlash in the press about Carter's "meanness." The Carter people thereafter tried to make him seem less mean; Carter himself even went on television with Barbara Walters to say, in effect, that he wouldn't do it anymore.

The basic thrust of the Carter attack continued, however, not simply because Carter *was* mean, but because this was the only campaign strategy available to him. Given the state of the economy and the disarray of our situation overseas, Reagan's goal was to make the election a referendum about policy and about the state of the country under Carter's stewardship. Carter's goal was to make the election a referendum *about Reagan*.

It was in this context that the question of a Reagan-Carter debate had to be decided. By mid-October, there was a difference of opinion among our campaign leadership as to whether Reagan should debate. Any such confrontation carried great risks, and also great potential benefits. The perceived risk was that Carter, sitting president and

experienced technocrat, would come over as much more knowledgeable about all the minutiae of government, making Reagan seem an
ignorant outsider by comparison and reinforcing the opposition message of his unfitness.

The potential benefit was that a strong Reagan showing, according
to our poll readings, would in all probability win the election. An
added benefit, perhaps the major one, was that anyone watching
Reagan on TV would have a hard time believing he was the ogre Carter
was portraying. The imponderable was whether we were ahead or
behind—the accepted wisdom being that, if you're ahead you don't
want to debate, and if you're behind you do.*

The question was hashed out at a meeting of most of the key
campaign operatives at the Waldorf Astoria in New York in mid-
October. Present were Lyn Nofziger, Dick Wirthlin, Bill Timmons,
Jim Baker, Mike Deaver, Bill Casey, and myself. The group was
divided on whether the candidate should debate.

As usual, however, one vote constituted a majority—the vote of
Ronald Reagan himself. The candidate was not only confident of how
he would fare in a debate with Carter, but felt, in a sense, a moral
obligation to engage in it. As he put it, "If I'm going to walk in another
man's shoes, then I should face him one-on-one, so the American
people can hear our differing views of the presidency and judge
between us." On that basis, the Reagan-Carter debate issue was decided.

Debate negotiations with the Carter camp and the sponsoring
League of Women Voters were conducted by Jim Baker—part of our
effort to integrate Bush campaign members into our operation. Preparation for the debate occurred at the candidate's temporary residence in
Middleburg, where he went over the issues with his staff and took part
in rehearsals during which he was peppered with tough questions.

---

* I personally had no doubts about Reagan's abilities as a debater. He had debated Bobby Kennedy,
Ralph Nader, and Bill Buckley—three of the most formidable figures in our recent political history—
and had more than held his own. He had virtually assured his win in New Hampshire by seizing
control of a debate with Bush (the famous "I paid for this microphone" episode), and nailed down the
nomination by emerging as the winner of the four-candidate debate in Illinois. Just about the only
debate Reagan had lost to that point was the one in Des Moines the preceding January—when he
didn't show up.

Two years later, these preparations led to a tangential issue when the Reagan campaign was accused of absconding with a handbook that the Carter people had compiled for his preparation. A congressional committee even conducted an investigation in 1983, and much time, energy, and resources, paid for by the taxpayer, were spent without result. The entire dispute—something the Democrats and media like to call "debategate"—was just another variation on their usual theme: Reagan couldn't possibly have won the debate—or, for that matter, the election—on the merits; some gimmick or skullduggery must have given him the advantage.*

The debate occurred on October 28 in Cleveland—a week before the election. For Carter and Reagan alike it was a final roll of the dice, with the election riding on the outcome. In terms of formal debating technique, Carter undoubtedly scored some points, exhibiting his familiarity with government and mastery of detail, and making methodical appeals to every key constituency of the Democratic coalition. But in terms of presence, personality, and magnetism, Reagan came through in his usual impressive fashion. Right from the start, when he walked across the stage to shake hands with Carter, a gracious gesture, he seized a kind of physical initiative.

Throughout, Reagan's genial and likeable personality dominated the affair. The most notable sally was his response to Carter's attempted onslaught on the subject of Medicare legislation. With a shrug and a smile, Reagan said, "There you go again . . ." The humor and decency of Reagan were manifest—as they usually were when he made a speech or appeared on television. On these grounds, he won the debate hands down—reversing the outcome two decades earlier when Jack Kennedy had won on style points over Richard Nixon.

Reagan, however, didn't win *merely* on style. He continued with his

* Actually, the Carter debate materials, later found in the files of the debate preparation team, were virtually useless—routine information readily available from public sources without any hint of strategy or confidential inside information. No such materials were used by Governor Reagan in the debate preparation, nor were they needed. Even the existence of that information was not known to those of us involved in the debate rehearsals. Reagan, furthermore, knew full well what the issues would be in his debate with Carter: exactly the issues discussed throughout the long weeks of the campaign. Reagan also knew what he thought about these matters and what he wanted to say about them.

powerful issue appeal, best summed up in the next most-memorable line from the debate, "Are you better off now than you were four years ago?"—a very effective way of reminding people of the troubles the country had suffered under Carter, with double-digit inflation and interest rates, rising taxes, energy shortages, and repeated setbacks overseas.

In the end, it was the *combination* of personality and issues that won the debate, and the election. By being his likeable self, poised and humorous, Reagan effectively disposed of the fears that Carter and the media had been trying to engender, thus letting Reagan's advantage on the issues come to the forefront. All too obviously, the Ronald Reagan that people saw with their own eyes was neither a warmonger nor an out-of-control extremist. And once that insinuation was laid to rest, Carter's campaign was virtually over.

An "X" factor, however, still hovered over the election. This was the question of the American hostages being held at the U.S. embassy in Iran. The problem had been a key negative for Carter, not only because of the distress of the hostages and their families, but also because it underscored the weakness of America in its dealings overseas. Though Reagan had done nothing to exploit the issue (he had not even mentioned it in his kick-off address), it obviously could have been a major element in the campaign.

This negative, we realized, could be turned to a positive, if Carter could somehow secure the release of the hostages before the voting. All of us in the campaign leadership were concerned that Carter might manipulate the situation to bring the hostages home on election eve, thus eclipsing the real issues before the country.

This was hardly paranoia on our part. Carter had shown a penchant for using the hostage issue when he could. During the Democratic primaries against Kennedy, he employed a "Rose Garden strategy" to avoid debate, on the grounds that he was too preoccupied with the hostage problem. All the while, he and his aides were taking plenty of time calling Democratic movers and shakers in primary and caucus states to make sure they stayed in line against the Kennedy challenge.

Among the most notable examples of Carter's use of the issue occurred in the Wisconsin primary. Kennedy had recently won in New

York and Connecticut, and Carter badly needed a win in Wisconsin, where Democratic voters are quite liberal. On primary day, Carter called a press conference to announce "progress" in the hostage negotiations—at 7 A.M., in time to make the morning news shows. As a Democrat quoted by Martin Schram of the *Washington Post* observed, "the 7 A.M. thing crossed the line. Carter no longer seemed decent and honorable, but manipulative."[7]

While we monitored the situation as best we could, the question of negotiations between Carter and the Iranian regime was something over which we had no control, subsequent charges to the contrary notwithstanding. Our best tactic was simply to warn against the possibility of an "October surprise," to inoculate the public against an emotional response if Carter were able to arrange for the hostages' return immediately prior to the voting.

In the event, the deal that Carter was apparently trying to make did not come off, and the hostages weren't released before the election. This fact became the basis for subsequent false charges that the *Reagan* camp was planning an "October surprise," by somehow interfering with Carter efforts to secure the hostages' release. As it happens, this theory has been refuted by exhaustive inquiries in *Newsweek*, *The New Republic* and other sources not usually friendly to the Reagan administration.[8]

As with "debategate," such charges in my view sought to obscure the underlying significance of the election. To those in political/media circles who thought Ronald Reagan was a laughable pushover, the November returns must have been a terrible shock. It was inconceivable to them that such a person could win the presidency on his merits. Therefore, they concluded the whole thing must have resulted from some plot.

Reagan's long march through the election season of 1980 ended much as it had begun nine months before in the wintry precincts of New Hampshire. By campaigning forcefully on the issues, he had connected powerfully with the views and values of the American voter. That was something a lot of people didn't understand—or didn't want to.

5

PREPARING
TO GOVERN

I N THE EARLY DAYS of the republic, a newly chosen president was
not inaugurated until March—four months after he had been elected.
That interval reflected the longer traveling times, the actual counting
of the electoral votes, and the more leisurely ways of a former era. In
1933, it was shortened a full two months, by constitutional amendment,
to cut down the lame-duck period of the outgoing chief executive.

While that change was helpful in many respects, after November 4,
1980, many of us in the Reagan transition team at times wished we had
those extra weeks. The transition from one administration to the next
is a complex affair. The federal government is a huge enterprise: it
spends hundreds of billions of dollars every year, employs 6 million
people, and administers hundreds of bureaus, commissions, departments, and agencies. For a newly elected president and his team, who
up until election day have focused all their energies on winning votes,
the sudden shift, preparing to control this vast machinery, is daunting.

In our particular case, we had all told seventy-seven days between the election and the President's inauguration. This short time seemed even shorter because Reagan had promised major changes in the federal government's way of doing things. The size and inertia of the bureaucratic machinery of our national government make changing its course something like turning around a battleship, only more so. In this case also, the captain and crew had just come over the side of an unfamiliar vessel.

Given this challenge, we knew we would have to move decisively if we were to redeem Reagan's pledge of instituting important changes. Yet we could not begin any real planning until after the election was over—and won. We had learned from the experience of other candidates how "dividing up the White House offices" had detracted from the election campaign. Besides, planning to govern before being elected would smack of smugness and have a negative effect on the electorate. People don't like someone who thinks he has the election "in the bag." Reagan, particularly, had always campaigned down to the wire; he constantly worried about being a latter-day Thomas Dewey. Nevertheless, I knew that we had to prepare at least in part for the transition before election day. Martin Anderson had described the chaos that Richard Nixon and his team encountered when they tried to cope with the appointment of personnel after the election of 1968. Some advance thinking had to be done about how to fill the hundreds of executive positions at the top of the federal bureaucracy and how to handle the flood of applications that was sure to inundate us should Reagan win the presidential contest.

Late in 1979 an old friend, Pendleton James, had asked me what he could do to help Reagan in the coming presidential election. I told him that he could best use his talents by preparing a plan for the presidential personnel operation—just in case we won. Pen, a leading professional in the executive search business, had served as a presidential personnel staff member in the Nixon White House and was well qualified to oversee the personnel-picking process that would face a new administration.

When I first mentioned this to Pen, he thought I was joking; the following spring, when the subject came up again, he asked if I were serious. I assured him that I was, and he began quietly to plan for a personnel operation from his Los Angeles office. In September of 1980, he moved to a small office in Alexandria, Virginia—away from the campaign headquarters—where he assembled a small staff who were not involved in the campaign itself. Most of them had had previous experience in other administrations. In two months this group, many of them working part time in the evenings, had compiled the necessary data on some three thousand appointments that would have to be made. They also developed a system for recruiting qualified candidates and handling the thousands of expected recommendations and applications.

All of this was done in such a quiet way that no one in the campaign—or the news media—learned of it. Even my own contacts with the personnel planning group did not interfere with my campaign responsibilities. I would sometimes meet with Pen James at 6:30 in the morning at a restaurant near campaign headquarters and then attend evening briefings, from 9:00 to midnight, at his Alexandria office. When the President-elect appointed me director of the transition on election day, we were ready to go with Pen's operation.

Setting up and staffing the transition was a major undertaking in itself. Overall, we had more than one thousand people working on it, 311 paid for by federal transition funds, another 331 who served for $1 token salaries, and the remainder serving as volunteers. We were allotted $2 million in public funds, the same amount the Carter transition team had received in 1976. Unfortunately, due to 50 percent or so inflation in the interim, this hardly covered our expenses. Thus, under a ruling from the Federal Election Commission, we raised private money—$1 million—for a Presidential Transition Trust Fund. As it turned out, we spent less of the taxpayers' money than the Carter team had in 1976–1977 ($1.75 million v. $1.78 million).

The transition operation was divided into several components, organized to accomplish the vast array of projects that had to be completed within two-and-a-half months. Transition staff members included both those who had served in the campaign and others who were recruited because of their prior experience in the federal government. Many joined only for the short term, contributing their expertise without any thought of appointment in the administration.

By far the largest element was the Executive Branch Management division, led by Bill Timmons, who had served ably as campaign political director and who had had extensive experience on the White House staff and as a leading Washington business executive. Bill sent teams into seventy-three departments and agencies to survey their activities and prepare a detailed briefing for the new appointees who would soon take them over. The briefing books included organization and staffing, major functions and responsibilities, pending policy issues, and a preview of the problems that existed or were soon likely to arise.

Reagan's 1980 campaign had been served by policy task forces that comprised "the largest and most distinguished group of intellectuals ever assembled for an American political campaign."[1] Nearly fifty groups, with over 450 advisors, studied numerous areas of foreign, defense, domestic, and economic policy and provided hundreds of recommendations. During the transition, the Policy Research and Development division, led by Ed Gray, produced position papers on subjects from welfare reform to crime, energy, the economy, and many others. Ed had served as Reagan's press secretary during the gubernatorial days and knew his mind very well. He was later to become director of the office of policy development in the White House.

With all the policy planning and research going on, someone had to keep track of the whole process, so I created the Office of Policy Coordination and placed Darrell Trent in charge. Darrell had served as Martin Anderson's deputy during the campaign, overseeing domestic policy research at the headquarters while Anderson was with the candidate. He had had experience in the Nixon administration in several capacities and was a senior fellow at the Hoover Institution at Stanford University.

The transition effort was aided greatly by a project of the Heritage Foundation, a public policy research and education institution based in Washington, D.C. Although a relative newcomer on the Washington scene, at least in comparison with its more liberal counterpart, the Brookings Institution, Heritage was rapidly becoming known for its outstanding work. Established in 1973, this nonpartisan organization described itself as dedicated to the principles of free competitive enterprise, limited government, individual liberty, and a strong national defense.

In the fall of 1979, Heritage determined to help in the transition in the event a conservative president were elected. It set out to answer the question, "What is the conservative agenda, particularly for the 'first 100 days'?" The foundation assembled several hundred people in teams that examined virtually every major agency of the federal government and then recommended changes. These studies and proposals were brought together in *Mandate for Leadership*, published early in 1981. Even before its publication, *Mandate for Leadership* began to take effect because a draft manuscript was sent to our transition team and to the press in November 1980. In fact, President Reagan gave a copy of the book to each member of his cabinet and directed them to read it.

This major accomplishment put Heritage "on the map" as far as Washington decision-makers were concerned. Indeed, many leaders in the federal government were appointed by President Reagan from among the Heritage staff and the contributors to *Mandate for Leadership*. The president of Heritage, Edwin J. Feulner, Jr., a talented executive with experience both in the federal government and academia, provided expert advice to the new administration in varying capacities.*

An important part of the transition was to establish relationships between the incoming White House team and Congress, particularly its Republican members who would be the President's indispensable allies on Capitol Hill. One of the happy surprises of the election had been the turnover of leadership in the Senate, to which a majority of Republicans was elected for the first time in over a quarter of a century. Sen. Paul Laxalt, an old friend of Reagan, who had served as chairman of the campaign, became the President's principal representative with his colleagues in the Senate.

In the House of Representatives, Rep. Tom Evans of Delaware brought together a group of key Republican leaders and served as their chairman. During the campaign, Reagan had built up considerable

---

* On two occasions he took leave from Heritage to serve as a special consultant in the White House on specific strategic planning projects, and throughout the two terms he was an informal advisor to President Reagan and members of the cabinet. At the same time, Heritage was fiercely independent and did not hesitate to offer constructive criticism when it felt that the administration was going astray.

good will with his congressional colleagues by assisting them in their campaigns. Many of the newcomers to Congress knew that Reagan's strong showing had helped win their own victories. To cement this appreciation and to ensure a good relationship over the next several years, we recruited Tom Korologos, a Washington, D.C., public affairs expert, as our principal legislative liaison leader. Tom's business was to understand and deal with senators and congressmen, at which he was excellent. He also was invaluable in guiding new executive nominees through the arduous Senate confirmation process.

The administrative, financial, and logistics arrangements for managing the transition effort were a major task in themselves. Fortunately, Verne Orr, who had done an outstanding job of overseeing this type of work in the campaign, took over as director of administration. He was assisted on the financial side by Angela "Bay" Buchanan, who had been the campaign treasurer. Together they made sure that the limited resources of the transition were used to maximum benefit. And since much of our financial support came from the federal government, a whole new maze of rules and regulations had to be followed.*

An important part of the whole process was the strategic planning directed by Richard Wirthlin. He brought together all of the policy and personnel activities of the transition, and in addition gave thought to how the President would deal with the public, the media, and Congress. During the campaign, Dick had headed up the public opinion survey work and had been heavily involved in planning and strategy. His close assistant, the late Richard Beal, later headed the White House Office of Planning and Evaluation. To house the transition apparatus, GSA provided several floors in an office building at 1726 M Street in Washington, D.C.

One of the roadblocks in recruiting people to serve in the administration was the maze of laws that governed federal personnel—the Ethics in Government Act, the Privacy Act, the Freedom of Information Act, and so on. Highly detailed forms, running to hundreds of pages, had to be filled out, while the FBI and the Internal Revenue

---

* Particularly helpful here was M. Peter McPherson, a Washington, D.C., attorney, who had been primarily responsible for our initial negotiations with the General Services Administration and other elements of the federal government in establishing our transition operations.

Service undertook intensive investigations. Dismayed by these bureaucratic demands, some well-qualified individuals declined to serve; those who persisted were subjected to long delays in getting clearances. All of this made filling government slots difficult.

Ronald and Nancy Reagan had returned to the West Coast for a brief rest before plunging into the work of taking over the highest office in the land. The President-elect planned to work out of his home, in the Pacific Palisades area of Los Angeles, during the period between the election and inauguration, with trips to Washington whenever necessary. Accordingly, across the street from his home, we set up the West Coast branch of the transition organization and Reagan began to appoint the members of his cabinet and other top officials.

Naturally, all of the transition activity received great media attention. Much of the speculation centered around the appointments, but the transition process itself drew attention since it was the largest in history. To deal with the news representatives, we had a public affairs office for general information and two press operations, one at transition headquarters in Washington and one at the President's office in Los Angeles. Jim Brady, who was later seriously injured by an assassin's bullet, took over in the nation's capital. His good humor and skillful handling of reporters established a reservoir of good will for us all. In California, Joe Holmes held regular briefings outside the President's home and provided as much information as possible. To save possible embarrassment, we had a cardinal rule that nothing would be said about anyone who did *not* get appointed.

Reagan decided to have eighteen members in his cabinet: the traditional thirteen heads of executive departments;* the counsellor to the president; the director of the office of management and budget; the director of central intelligence; the permanent U.S. representative to the United Nations; and the U.S. trade representative. While some of these posts were immediately filled by the President, others required an intensive search.

As always in such matters, there was much speculation about who

---

* The secretaries of state, treasury, and defense, the attorney general, and the secretaries of the interior, agriculture, commerce, labor, health and human services, transportation, housing and urban development, energy, and education.

was going to get what post, and even more rumor-mongering. To which I responded, "Those who know aren't talking, and those who are talking don't know." That also fit a lot of other rumors that appeared in the press throughout the Reagan era.

Despite the usual delays, the cabinet selection was basically completed by Christmas 1980. We then presented the cabinet to the public in groups, emphasizing the team concept the President wanted in his administration.

The President had five criteria for selecting the cabinet and other positions. First, commitment to the Reagan philosophy and program; second, the highest integrity and personal qualifications; third, experience and skills that fit the task; fourth, no personal agenda that would conflict with being a member of the Reagan team; and, fifth, the toughness needed to withstand the pressures and inducements of the Washington establishment, and to accomplish the changes sought by the President.

Again, the California background and Reagan's personal history are important here. When Reagan was elected governor in 1966, as a novice citizen-politician, he didn't have the usual long list of commitments and political associations picked up through years of wheeling and dealing in the party system. He therefore felt free to go out and hire the best available talent to help him staff the government.

Reagan's basic approach was to come up with people who did not want, or need, a job in government, but who would serve if called upon. In seeking such people, he relied on his "kitchen cabinet" of supporters in California, who were not interested in such jobs themselves, to help him with the talent search. By and large, the process worked very well in Sacramento, and we incorporated elements of it in what we were doing in the nation's capital.

Prospects for cabinet, subcabinet, and other positions were submitted from every possible source: people volunteering themselves or their friends; recommendations from campaign supporters and workers; recommendations from Congress; and people from our campaign task forces. The personnel division, under Pen James, sorted through all of these and listed those people who fit the five criteria.

The Executive Personnel Advisory Committee, the new name for the "kitchen cabinet," was a valuable source of candidates. The committee included some of Reagan's original supporters from California as well as those from around the nation who had backed him during the 1980 campaign, including Jim Baker, Mike Deaver, Pen James, Helene von Damm, and myself, all of whom would assume leadership positions. The group was chaired by William French Smith, a close friend of and personal lawyer for Reagan. The group's meetings were held in Bill's downtown law office, where Reagan met with us to go over the lists of prospective appointees, a lengthy and time-consuming process, but necessary.

After the recommendations for each cabinet position had been winnowed to a short list, the President would discuss his final decision with a small group of us at his house. At the very outset, he told us of his initial decisions: Bill Smith as attorney general, Cap Weinberger at Defense, Bill Casey at CIA, and Dick Schweiker at Health and Human Services. He had previously asked me to become counsellor to the president, with cabinet rank. David Stockman had waged an effective campaign to become the head of OMB. As for the other posts, a search was still in progress.

Of critical importance, given the international situation, was the post of secretary of state. Both Cap Weinberger and Bill Casey had been suggested for the position. But the President believed that he needed them at Defense and CIA, and their fine performances in those posts bore out his judgment. George Shultz was also considered for State, but the fact that he and Cap were both then working for the Bechtel Corporation weighed against his selection at that time.

This led us eventually to Al Haig, who had been recommended to Reagan by former President Nixon. Haig had been an aide to Nixon in the White House, serving initially with Henry Kissinger and then as chief of Nixon's staff. He had gone on to become commanding general of NATO and was known as a hard-line anticommunist. All in all, he was thought to have the credentials and experience needed for the job.

Rumor had it, however, that Haig wanted to run for president—which he eventually did in 1988. Since Reagan did not feel it would be appropriate to select a cabinet member who might use the office as a stepping-stone to a presidential campaign, he asked a few of us—Bill

Casey, Pen James, Jim Baker, and myself—to meet with Haig and discuss the question. After he reassured us on this point, we reported as much to the President who then offered the post to Haig.

Of the original Reagan cabinet, Haig was probably the best known. Al had formidable abilities, and a temperament to match. My impression was that he saw himself as the only professional among a group of amateurs. Whatever grain of truth lay there (most of his peers were people of great achievements in public and/or private life), it made working in a collegial atmosphere difficult for him, and for others.

Al had very definite and often very good ideas about the need to counter communist aggression in the Caribbean, about putting a halt to terrorism, and about other elements of our foreign policy. On matters of arms control and defense, he had a somewhat "Eurocentric" view, apparently dating from his time with NATO. This, too, was a point of difference with those of us who felt that we should not let our friendship with Europe override other policy considerations.*

George Shultz, who replaced Al Haig as secretary of state, brought a much less combative public style and much lower-octane rhetoric to the State Department. In cabinet meetings, he was low-keyed and invariably supported the President's policy goals, though he and Cap Weinberger had frequent policy exchanges that reflected the differing viewpoints of the Defense and State departments.

Another early appointment in the foreign affairs field was Jeane Kirkpatrick, who was named United States permanent representative to the United Nations and a member of the cabinet. Known to the President through her writings, Jeane was an invaluable addition to the Reagan government. As ambassador to the United Nations, she spoke eloquently and forcefully in behalf of the rule of law, reasserted our

---

* In the long run, it was Al's insistence that he alone, as the "vicar of foreign policy," should advise the President that led to his leaving the administration. The President not only had pretty definite ideas of his own concerning foreign affairs, but he also preferred to "roundtable" issues with several advisors, whether or not they had a specific portfolio in that field. Thus he welcomed input on international matters from Cap Weinberger, Bill Casey, Jeane Kirkpatrick, and others of us on the National Security Council, as well as from Richard Allen and Bill Clark, assistants to the president for national security affairs.

national strength and values, and became the nemesis of those who liked to "blame America first" for the ills of the world.

Jeane saw eye to eye with Bill Casey and Cap Weinberger on most issues, especially those pertaining to our defenses and to the Soviet-Cuban challenge to freedom in this hemisphere. While Jeane's UN duties kept her from the day-to-day activities of the National Security Council, she was a powerful supporter of the "Reagan Doctrine" and other elements of the President's program.

Cap Weinberger, the choice for secretary of defense, was part of our team from California. Cap had impressed Reagan with his extensive grasp of fiscal data when he served as director of finance in Sacramento during 1969–70 and had gone from there to serve in the Nixon administration as chairman of the federal trade commission, as both deputy director and director of the office of management and budget, and as secretary of health, education, and welfare. He brought to our fledgling administration valuable knowledge of the ways of Washington.

Because of his previous budget-cutting experience, Weinberger had been nicknamed "Cap the Knife," and many expected that he would continue this same proclivity as secretary of defense. But when he saw how badly our military forces had been depleted by the neglect of the 1970s, he determined to rebuild them. This put him in conflict with some other cabinet members, especially David Stockman, and with many in Congress, but history will surely confirm that Cap was right.

Some may have thought it strange for Reagan to appoint his campaign manager, William Casey, as director of central intelligence with a place at the cabinet table. But the President had developed a friendship and respect for this brilliant and accomplished man, whose appearance and manner of expression sometimes obscured his intellect. Bill had had a multiplicity of careers—businessman, author, government official, and, in World War II, European director of secret intelligence for the Office of Strategic Services (forerunner to the CIA). In addition, he had an excellent grasp of politics, as he showed in the 1980 campaign.

In cabinet councils, Bill was a stalwart supporter of the Reagan program, with a concentration on the Soviet threat, the communist insurgency in Central America, terrorism in the Middle East and elsewhere, and many other intelligence-related issues. Bill, a voracious reader, had a wealth of knowledge on many subjects. As head of the CIA, he drove its operatives to develop more complete and accurate data on the many intelligence challenges that we faced.

In the field of foreign policy and national security affairs, Richard Allen was selected National Security advisor. A lifelong student of defense and foreign policy issues, Dick had an encyclopedic knowledge of the Soviet Union, communism in general, and the forces operative in the Third World, as well as matters pertaining to strategic defenses, technology transfer, and related issues.

On the domestic side of the cabinet, a key appointment was that of secretary of the treasury. Don Regan had been one of the three cochairmen of Reagan's campaign kick-off dinner in New York, held in November of 1979. He was the chairman and chief executive officer of Merrill Lynch, the leading investment firm, and was well known for his management skills, forcefulness, and accomplishments. Similar to the President in his Irish heritage and humor, Don was committed to the Reagan goals from the start. He also oversaw the development of a tax reform program, which he presented to the President in 1984 during his final days as treasury secretary.

For his secretary of the interior, the President-elect naturally looked toward the West, where much of that department's work is done. He focused on a brilliant lawyer, James Watt, who was then leading the Mountain States Legal Foundation, a public interest law organization with an active involvement in environmental matters. Jim came to Washington with tremendous energy and outstanding ability as an advocate for Reagan principles. As a result, he earned the enmity of liberal pundits and environmental elitists. Jim set an outstanding example of common sense and balance in dealing with environmental issues.

One campaign official who had made a great impression on Reagan, and who could have served in any one of a number of cabinet positions, was Drew Lewis. A businessman from Pennsylvania, he had run for governor in the 1970s and had been a leader of the Ford delegation from that state in the 1976 campaign. Reagan was impressed with

Drew's management ability, loyalty, and integrity, as shown—ironically—by his refusal to abrogate his 1976 commitment to President Ford. Because of his business background, including the successful turnaround of a defunct railroad, Drew was appointed secretary of transportation. This proved an excellent choice, as was revealed later during the illegal strike of the air traffic controllers.

In appointing cabinet members whom he knew well, Reagan would often make the offer over the telephone, sometimes surprising the recipient. When considering people he knew less well, he would invite them to a series of private interviews, usually at his home. I remember meeting Sam Pierce, a lawyer from New York, at the Holiday Inn Hotel and escorting him to the Reagan home one rainy day in December. Reagan liked Pierce and shortly thereafter asked him to serve as secretary of housing and urban development. In the same manner, he selected John Block, who had been director of agriculture in Illinois, for secretary of agriculture.

In previous administrations, the positions of secretary of commerce and of labor were usually given to political supporters of the President. This was true with Reagan also, but we were fortunate in finding two individuals who were peculiarly qualified to hold those posts. Malcolm Baldrige, the chief executive officer of a successful manufacturing firm in Connecticut, had championed the Reagan cause from the start. His hobby was riding in Western rodeos, which immediately struck a responsive chord with Reagan. Baldrige championed American competitiveness in the world market and raised the Department of Commerce from a position of relative obscurity.*

For secretary of labor, Reagan went to another supporter known for his Irish wit. Raymond Donovan, executive of a construction company in the New York–New Jersey area, had been a major factor in obtaining support for Reagan in his home state delegation. In addition, having been very successful in labor-management relations in the heavy construction business, he was an ideal person to initiate a new era in Republican labor relations. He embarked on major changes which

---

* Killed in a tragic rodeo accident in 1987, Baldrige was so widely respected that Congress authorized an award for manufacturing quality that bears his name.

reflected the administration's concern for the well-being of the individual worker rather than that of the labor bosses and their monolithic unions. Ray accomplished a great deal, despite being plagued by false allegations of misconduct, all disproved.*

The last cabinet member selected was Terrel H. Bell, secretary of education. A former commissioner of education in the Department of Health, Education, and Welfare during the Nixon administration, he came aboard committed to Reagan's goal to abolish the current Department of Education. An enthusiastic, almost sycophantic, booster for the President at cabinet meetings, Bell left the administration after four years and wrote a book with some surprisingly barbed references to his former colleagues.

The culmination of the transition process occurred on January 7, 1981, when Reagan convened a series of meetings in Washington to review the work of the transition teams, as well as Wirthlin's plans, and to prepare for the incoming administration. These meetings were held in Blair House, the impressive series of buildings across Pennsylvania Avenue from the White House, which normally house visiting heads of state, but in January 1981 served as temporary quarters for Ronald and Nancy Reagan before their entry into the White House proper.

At 9:15 in the morning on January 7, accompanied by the others designated to hold top staff positions in the White House office, I briefed the President-elect and Vice President-elect on the schedule for the day. After taking time out to visit with an influential member of the Senate whom Paul Laxalt had brought in, Reagan sat down with his foreign policy and national security team. Besides George Bush and myself, the group included Al Haig, Caspar Weinberger, Bill Casey, Richard Allen, and Jim Baker.

We spent the morning discussing National Security Council procedures, major foreign policy issues, and plans for rebuilding our national defense establishment. Reagan again committed to spending whatever it would take to achieve military strength "second to none"

---

* When his ordeal was finally over, and he was exonerated, Ray made a poignant statement that reflects the plight of many falsely accused members of the Reagan administration: "What office do I go to to get my reputation back?"

in the world. In addition, we were briefed about the situation in Iran, and the President again stressed that no one in the incoming administration should say anything that would undercut the authority of the Carter government in handling these negotiations.

That afternoon the planning shifted to economic policy; Haig and Casey were replaced by Regan, Stockman, and Martin Anderson. Alan Greenspan, an important economic advisor during the campaign, also joined us, as did a new group of White House staffers. Another new participant was Edwin Harper, a very talented businessman whom the President-elect had persuaded to accept the dual roles of assistant to the president and deputy director of OMB.

Now the talk turned to tax cuts, monetary policy, the budget process which was so clearly spiraling out of control, and the need to slow the growth of federal spending. Reagan insisted that major changes were needed to stem inflation, reduce unemployment, and stimulate real economic growth. He also directed that the two subjects of that day— economic revitalization and rebuilding our defenses—were to be the top priorities of his first six months in office.

In a subsequent meeting of transition officials with the President-elect and Vice President-elect on January 15, Reagan reviewed plans for advancing these priorities through executive initiatives, projecting his legislative program, and developing a communications strategy. He particularly wanted to plan how best to use the power of the presidency to sustain his base of popular support and mobilize it in behalf of the changes that he sought. He was aware of the need to establish a working relationship with Congress and the bureaucracy, as well as with the media.

As I watched Reagan at these preparatory meetings, it was evident that he was ready—even eager—to take over the presidency. The months of campaigning had given him a clear vision of what the nation required to regain its economic strength and sense of purpose in the world, and he was confident that he had the policies needed to attain these goals.

6

IN THE WHITE
HOUSE

THE ADMINISTRATION of Ronald Reagan, fortieth President of the
United States, began at noon on January 20, 1981, when he took the
oath of office and was sworn in by Chief Justice Warren Burger.
Reagan then delivered an eloquent inaugural address to a crowd assembled at the West Front of the Capitol, with the Washington Monu-
ment and the Lincoln Memorial as a backdrop.

President Reagan spoke of a new beginning for America, the greatness of our traditions, and the challenges that faced the country. It was
a stirring speech, repeating many of the themes he had sounded in the
campaign and setting the stage for the policies he would pursue in the
Oval Office. Indeed, with its references to the burden of taxation and
the need to curb the power of the federal government, it was probably
one of the few such addresses to embody, at least in general terms, an
actual legislative program.*

---

* "In the present crisis," the President said, "government is not the solution to our problems;
government is the problem . . . It is my intention to curb the size and influence of the federal

71

As the President assumed office, the portents were extremely favorable. When the day began, the weather had been cloudy. But as Reagan spoke, the overcast skies cleared, and the scene was bathed in bright sunshine. Then, shortly after he had concluded, we received the news that the U.S. hostages in Iran had been released and were on their way to freedom. In all respects, an auspicious beginning.

Although the day of inauguration is usually given over to ceremony, the President took time to perform one item of official business. He went to the President's Room in the Capitol—an ornamental chamber reserved for the chief executive—and signed an order instituting a hiring freeze throughout the federal government. This fulfilled a pledge he had specifically made in his acceptance speech in Detroit six months before. If not many other people remembered that promise, Reagan did.

Afterward, the President attended a luncheon in the Capitol Rotunda with members of the cabinet, White House staff, leaders of Congress, and other dignitaries. It was here that we learned about the release of the hostages, which the President announced to the assembled guests and media. From there, he proceeded with Mrs. Reagan to lead the Inaugural Parade, take his place in the reviewing stand, and enjoy the festivities of the afternoon.

Once the parade was over, several members of the senior staff joined the President in the Oval Office, all of us still in formal inauguration morning coats and striped trousers, before returning to our hotels to prepare for the inaugural balls. Again, though this was a day of ceremony, some people had their minds on business— particularly Secretary of State-designate Al Haig. Before leaving the White House I went to my new office in the West Wing and found Al there, along with Richard Allen. Al wanted to give me a document, one that would later loom large in administration annals.

It was a draft National Security Decision Directive (NSDD), ready

---

establishment and to demand recognition of the distinction between the powers granted to the federal government and those reserved to the states or to the people . . . In the days ahead I will propose removing the roadblocks that have slowed our economy and reduced production . . . It is time to reawaken this industrial giant, to get government back within its means, and to lighten our punitive tax burden."

for the President's signature, which would establish an extensive net-work of committees and interagency groups with authority to coordinate various aspects of U.S. national security policy. I told Al that we would examine the draft, and turned it over to Dick Allen for his review.

The rest of the evening was devoted to celebrating the brand-new presidency of Ronald Reagan at the inaugural balls. The real work of the administration would begin the following morning.

It is a cliché of American politics (an accurate one, unfortunately) that many people run for office just for the sake of getting elected. Winning a position, and the fame and power that go with it, seems to be the point; the uses to which this authority will be put are less important. The problem is captured in the movie, *The Candidate*, in which the hero spends all his energies getting elected, and when he succeeds turns to an associate and asks, "What do we do now?"

That question didn't have to be asked on the first day of the Reagan administration. Not only had the President spelled out repeatedly what he wanted to accomplish in general terms, he had a very definite program for doing it, and a set of priorities for how it was to be done. No one needed to sit around and scratch his or her head and wonder if this or that might be a good idea; instead, there was a need to implement the program the President had already developed.

The transition period and Reagan's pre-inaugural meetings with his incoming staff and cabinet had stressed this outlook, and it would be reemphasized throughout the opening days of the administration. Our chief priority on the domestic front, he emphasized, was to revive the economy, a program in which his tax cut proposals were the central element. On the foreign scene, the foremost objective was to restore America's defensive strength, as a precondition for reestablishing our leverage on a host of other issues. These were goals to be accomplished, not debated.

To do this, the President knew we would need a specific game plan. During the transition period, Dick Wirthlin had developed a strategic outline of initial actions to be taken during the administration's first 180 days, from the inauguration until early August, when Congress traditionally recessed for the summer. This was the time span, in our calculations, in which we had to make a determined effort to accomplish our objectives.

The Wirthlin plan envisioned, first and foremost, a strong initiative on tax and budget issues. This would coordinate our legislative thrust with the communications efforts to be led by the President and supported by others in the administration. The idea was to exploit the force of public opinion—to remind the legislators of who had elected them—and thereby counter the special interest pressures we knew would be mounted in opposition to the Reagan program.

This was the prevailing attitude on January 21, when the Reagan administration began its operations. At about 9 A.M., in the Blue Room of the White House, members of the cabinet and White House staff took the oath of office, and then got down to business. At 10:20 A.M., approximately, the President held his first cabinet meeting. Of key importance in this discussion, to no one's surprise, were the issues of spending and taxation. In this connection, each member of the cabinet was given an OMB monograph on spending control.

The President also made it clear that he believed in cabinet government—that the cabinet would be the forum in which policy issues were to be discussed—thus establishing the foundation for decision-making. At noon, the President had lunch with Jim Baker, Mike Deaver, and myself. Speaking about the decision-making process, he again stressed the importance of the cabinet. As in Sacramento, he explained, the place for hashing out the issues was in the cabinet sessions, not through buttonholing exercises in the hallway.

Further cabinet meetings were held that week, on January 23 and January 24, again stressing the economy. Also on the 23rd, the President had his first meeting with the Republican congressional leadership in the White House to brief them on his economic program, followed by discussion in the cabinet of prospects for congressional support.

Symptomatic of Reagan's mindset were some of the moves he made in the earliest days of the administration. While most of the initiatives he wanted to take required cooperation from Congress, there were some things he could do on his own, and he proceeded rapidly to do them—as with the hiring freeze he authorized at the inauguration.

On January 27, for instance, the President signed a memorandum to the various departments of the government, ordering reductions in spending for consulting contracts, office redecoration, and other non-essentials. On the same day, he signed an order setting up a Task Force on Regulatory Reform, to be chaired by Vice President Bush, aimed at reducing the burden of federal regulations on the economy.

On January 28, one week after we began operations, the President ordered the complete deregulation of petroleum prices, which had been under federal controls for a decade. On the following day, he signed an order eliminating all activities of the Council on Wage and Price Stability—abolishing virtually all vestiges of the federal price controls which had distorted supply and demand in the 1970s and led to ruinous shortages for the country. (Natural gas, under different legislation, was still subject to controls.) The thrust of these actions was both obvious and consistent with the President's pledges—to free the economy from excessive regulation.

The reaction from the Washington establishment was prompt, and loud. Sen. Howard Metzenbaum (D-Ohio) denounced the deregulation of petroleum prices, saying it would raise the price of gasoline to $2 a gallon. The real effect, of course, was just the opposite. Renewed production under decontrol broke the back of the OPEC cartel and drove prices down (they were actually lower in 1991 than a decade earlier). With this stroke of the pen, the President ended the "energy crisis" of the 1970s.

While the President wanted his cabinet in Washington to reflect the one in Sacramento, certain structural and political factors made this impossible. For one thing, the federal cabinet was much bigger, and the range of interests to be covered much more diverse. It would have been a poor allocation of everybody's time, for instance, to have the secretary of state sitting through a discussion of Social Security, or the secretary of agriculture reviewing missile deployments overseas.

The President had discussed with Cap Weinberger and me (both had studied the cabinet system in Sacramento and Washington) the way he wanted to work with the cabinet. At one point he considered the concept of a "supercabinet," which had been suggested by a commission headed by Roy Ash during the Nixon administration. The idea was that certain cabinet members would not only be responsible for their own departments but would also act as coordinators, providing policy leadership to other cabinet members in related areas of concern. But since this was not the basis on which members of the cabinet had initially been recruited, and since it might have caused considerable unhappiness, the President decided against so radical a departure.

As an alternative, I recommended that we devise a series of cabinet councils, which would group various members of the cabinet together in areas where their concerns interrelated, and which would exercise all the powers of the cabinet in advising the President. Reagan agreed with this idea, and cabinet councils became a major feature of the new administration.

Originally, there were five such councils, including economic affairs, natural resources and the environment, commerce and trade, and human resources. The National Security Council served as the fifth cabinet council, on foreign policy and defense, and was indeed the prototype for the others. Later we added three other cabinet councils: food and agriculture, legal policy, and management and administration. The work of these councils was coordinated by the Office for Cabinet Administration, headed by Craig Fuller, under my overall direction.

Also closely involved was Martin Anderson, who served as a member of each of the councils dealing with domestic and economic policy. He served, in a sense, as the President's "quality assurance" representative, raising questions when policy proposals seemed to diverge from Reagan's objectives. As he notes, the councils weren't simply boxes on an organizational chart, but working groups of manageable size that insured a focused effort by people who had knowledge and jurisdiction over policy.

During the first year of the administration, through December 1981, there were no fewer than 112 cabinet council sessions in the White House, many of them chaired personally by the President. Planning sessions of the councils, which the President did not attend, were led by a cabinet member designated as chairman pro tem and were used to obtain factual information, sharpen viewpoints, and formulate options, in preparation for the decision-making council meetings over which Reagan himself presided. As in full cabinet meetings, given the primacy of the economic program, the bulk of these (fifty-seven in all) were meetings of the Cabinet Council on Economic Affairs, of which Treasury Secretary Don Regan was chairman pro tem.

Preferring to err on the side of inclusion rather than exclusion, we let all cabinet members know in advance what the agenda of the councils was going to be, so that if they wanted to participate they were free to do so. Many of them took the President up on the invitation and sat in on matters that weren't specifically under their jurisdiction. This was fine with the President since, as ever, he hoped for the widest possible variety of input from people in his administration.

One of the great managerial problems of the federal government is integrating the cabinet agencies, their leaders, and their vast bureaucracies with the policy-making priorities of the President. Large established entities have a momentum of their own, and even political appointees* who work there tend to take on the viewpoint of the agency—"going native," as the saying has it.

In addition to their other features, the cabinet councils were a method for dealing with this potential problem. By journeying to the White House on a regular basis, cabinet members and their staffs were continuously brought into contact with the President, his policy agenda, and his staff, as well as with others in the administration who were working on related matters.

To reinforce this outlook, we sought to ensure that all political appointees in the agencies were vetted through the White House personnel process, and to have a series of orientation seminars for all high-ranking officials on the various aspects of the Reagan program. We wanted our appointees to be the President's ambassadors to the agencies, not the other way around. In many cases we were successful, in others less so.

In addition to presiding over cabinet and cabinet council meetings, Reagan held innumerable meetings with senior staff, congressional leaders, visiting dignitaries, and others, all the while performing the countless ceremonial tasks that go with the presidency. Not only was he the chief executive in the fullest sense of the term—conceiving and

---

* The term "political appointees" is used to differentiate those officials appointed by the President and his subordinates from civil service or other permanent members of the executive branch.

directing the carrying out of policy—but also its most effective sales-man, carrying the message to the public in speeches, press confer-ences, and televised addresses.*

Besides the cabinet councils, the numerous coordinating, support, and advisory bodies working in and with the White House sought to cut across hierarchical lines, so that everyone would work together, rather than at cross purposes. Examples were the Budget Working Group that pushed for coordinated spending restraints, and the Legis-lative Strategy Group that tried to coordinate the various aspects of dealing with Congress.

Other efforts to encourage team spirit and collegiality included the "management forums" held annually at Constitution Hall, with the President and the cabinet appearing on stage and hundreds of key appointees making up the audience. The object was to expound and clarify administration policies and to build team spirit across depart-ments. As the person in charge of coordinating executive branch activities, I usually acted as master of ceremonies at these gather-ings—one of which featured Secretary of Interior Jim Watt's famous "let Reagan be Reagan" speech.

The most unusual aspect of the White House staffing operation was the so-called "troika"—Jim Baker as chief of staff, Mike Deaver as deputy, and myself as counsellor to the president. Many stories have appeared on how this came about, and particularly on the roles and motivations of different people in Reagan's inner circle.† I don't know all the forces that may have been jockeying for position in the back-ground, but I do know what the President said to me: that the tremen-dous scope of policy and administrative matters converging on the White House required a division of labor.

My wife and I were somewhat ambivalent about whether I should

---

* Some of this public outreach activity was curtailed after the assassination attempt. In particular, there were fewer press conferences, partially to conserve the President's energy but also to shield him from the media—the latter, I think, a mistake. As noted in the Sacramento chapter, frequent press conferences were a tonic for Reagan, both in keeping him sharp in his responses and in raising matters that otherwise might not have come to his attention.

† For contrasting views, see Michael K. Deaver, *Behind the Scenes* (New York: Wm. Morrow, 1987) and Donald Devine, *Reagan's Terrible Swift Sword* (Ottawa, Illinois: Jameson Books, Inc., 1991).

join the Reagan administration at all. I had become involved in the campaign on a full-time basis less than a year before, leaving my personal affairs in considerable disarray to do so. I had been making a comfortable living, enjoyed my work as a lawyer and law professor, and would have had to take about a 30 percent pay cut to go to work for the federal government. On top of this, my family wasn't anxious to move from San Diego to Washington.

On the other hand, we had just come through a presidential campaign aimed at accomplishing some important things, and I wanted to help the President get the job done. Therefore, when he asked me to become counsellor to the president with cabinet rank and with primary responsibility for policy in the White House, I told him I wanted to think about it. Besides the personal aspect, the problems were obvious enough: the possible fragmentation of authority, and the danger of setting up rivalries among the different elements in the White House.

The pluses were less obvious but also important. Certainly there was enough work to do, and then some. From my standpoint, I would not have to deal with such matters as the President's scheduling and personnel matters, two aspects of political life in which you have people constantly importuning you to do things. (I remember one episode while serving as the governor's chief of staff in California. At the funeral of a relative, two people approached me and offered me their resumes, seeking my help in getting them a state job. There is a time and a place for that sort of thing; a funeral is not it.)

I discussed all this with my wife, and the more we considered it, the more we believed the offer made sense. After telling the President I would do it, I sat down with Jim Baker to draw up an understanding, in writing, of who exactly was going to do what. (The decision that my position as counsellor to the president would carry cabinet rank was made by the President, before any of these discussions took place.)

As part of our discussions, it was agreed that Mike Deaver would serve as deputy chief of staff, and a number of responsibilites of that post devolved on him. As it worked out, Mike dealt with matters that directly affected the President personally, such as his schedule, travel, security, the White House residence, and other matters that pertained to the President and the first family.

Baker, for his part, was responsible for the administration of the White House, relationships with Congress and the press, as well as public liaison and political activities. I was responsible for relationships with the departments and agencies, for development of policy, for the administration of the cabinet, and for daily operations of the executive branch.

In matters of personnel, we shared oversight, though this office reported to Jim. We agreed on a review process on presidential appointments, in which Jim, Mike, and I would all participate, before these recommendations went to the President.

Looking back, I think the White House staffing arrangement that we worked out functioned well. There were problems, of course, some of which are touched on later in this narrative. But in terms of daily workload, interaction among the various components of the staff, reaction to events, and policy outcomes—the last being the most important—the "troika" and other staff elements of the Reagan presidency did an effective job.

In part this happened because the different elements of the staffing operation that we worked out suited our different temperaments and aptitudes. My realm was policy coordination on behalf of the President; since I had a strong interest in policy matters and knew the President's views quite well, this was a natural role for me and one that I felt was of the utmost importance for the success of the administration.

Jim Baker, by his own admission, didn't have such an intense interest in policy matters. On the other hand, he knew Washington and the ways of government very well. With his more pragmatic background and outlook, he was both comfortable and effective in dealing with the press or Congress—areas that fell under his jurisdiction in our division of labor. Harnessed to the Reagan program, these skills complemented our efforts in the realm of policy.

Mike Deaver, finally, had a well-honed sense of public relations and knew how best the President should be presented as a personality and leader. He was excellent in staging ceremonial events, photo opportunities, and the like, and in dealing with the scheduling and personal concerns of the President and Mrs. Reagan. Having been with the Reagans for so many years, he had a good understanding of the human side of the equation.

One other positive aspect of this arrangement, in my opinion, was that it afforded the President access to divergent viewpoints and sources of information. Particularly in the early going, there was little danger that Reagan would be isolated from things he needed to know, kept from seeing people he should see, or made dependent on sole-source briefings.

Over time, differences in outlook among members of the senior staff and the administration led to friction. But at the outset, I think the President was well served by such differences, since the mixture of skills and backgrounds melded together to form a highly functional team. The track record of those days, I think, bears out this judgment.

Among other things, the troika arrangement, cabinet councils, and other collegial efforts allowed the administration to move forward quickly and effectively on the President's economic program. Through coordination of policy initiatives, legislative outreach, press liaison, and utilization of Reagan's own tremendous skills in communicating his message to the public, the administration scored impressive victories on tax and economic policy.

At the same time, we were able to make a strong beginning toward the President's goal of rebuilding our defenses, reorienting U.S. policies on arms control, and helping U.S. allies overseas. Doing all these things in the environment of Washington required, first and foremost, the leadership of the President. But it also required a tremendous amount of work by those he had entrusted with key staff and cabinet roles, and a blending of many different skills and aptitudes. I like to think the troika made its contribution to that outcome.

The mettle of our team at a time of crisis was tested early on with the attempted assassination of the President in March 1981. Dating from our days in California, Reagan had been very good at organizing the government in advance for crisis management, as when he planned state support for the local police in the event of a riot or campus disturbance. This had been an important part of my responsibilities while in state service. That training and experience were very helpful on Monday, March 30, 1981, when the President was struck down by John Hinckley's bullet.

At the time the shooting took place at the Washington Hilton Hotel, I was in my office at the White House. The President was addressing a group of labor leaders at a noon luncheon that day. As was usual, one of the troika accompanied Reagan at every event. On this occasion it was Mike Deaver.

When it was discovered that the President had been injured—initially no one knew he had been shot—the secret service agents took him immediately to the George Washington University Hospital. Mike went with him and then telephoned us at the White House. As soon as we learned the full story, I rushed to the hospital, accompanied by Jim Baker and Lyn Nofziger. As we entered the hospital emergency room, the President was being wheeled out to go into surgery. When he saw us—Jim, Mike, and me—he asked, "Who's minding the store?" This typified the humor that he exhibited throughout that fateful day.

In these moments of tremendous stress, the troika pursued its areas of responsibility: Mike took care of the family and assisted Nancy Reagan; Jim kept in contact with the White House and the media; and I established contact with the cabinet, particularly Attorney General William French Smith and Secretary of Defense Caspar Weinberger. At that time, we did not know whether there might be some form of terrorism or organized criminal activity behind the attack on the President. Therefore I talked with Bill Smith to make sure our law enforcement agencies, particularly the FBI, were on the alert and gathering all available intelligence. Cap Weinberger had already recognized the potential national security implications of the attack and had moved the defense condition (known in the Pentagon as "Defcon") one step higher to make sure that all of our military units were on alert.

While Mike, Jim, and I were at the hospital, Dick Allen assembled the cabinet in the White House situation room, both to keep them up to date on what was happening and to have them available if it became necessary to invoke the Twenty-fifth Amendment, temporarily conferring presidential authority on the Vice President (it takes a vote by half the cabinet to do this). Vice President Bush, meantime, was returning to the capital from a trip to Texas.

The President's courage, stamina, and grace during this horrendous episode are well known, showing the nation and the world the true quality of the man. It was a further, if indirect, tribute to him that the team he had assembled worked so well under these conditions. I have mentioned Cap Weinberger's role, Bill Smith's, and Dick Allen's; all performed with resolve and steadiness of purpose.

Someone else whose performance should be singled out was my old colleague from California, Lyn Nofziger. Part of the tragedy of that day was the terrible wounding of Jim Brady, the President's press secretary. In the circumstances, Lyn took over the responsibility at the hospital for briefing the press and the world on what was happening—a role he had filled so well years before in Sacramento. Those who knew Lyn as a fun-loving sort saw in this episode the other side of him, as he handled press queries in a calm, authoritative, and reassuring manner.

One who didn't come off so well in public perceptions at the time was Al Haig—who in my opinion got a bad rap in the media commentary for what essentially was a slip of the tongue. From the Situation Room, Al heard Deputy Press Secretary Larry Speakes in the White House briefing room voicing uncertainty on television about who was running things while the President was in the hospital. Al rushed in to tell the media that the cabinet was on hand, that the Vice President was returning to the city, and that everything was under control.

During these remarks Al said, "as of now, I'm in charge here"—meaning he was the senior cabinet member present—but also suggesting a misunderstanding about the presidential line of succession (which actually goes from the President to the Vice President to the Speaker of the House to the President Pro Tem of the Senate, and only then to the cabinet). Since the President had not surrendered his authority, and since the Vice President was winging his way back to the city, the point was totally academic, but it created a major news flap and subsequently much humorous comment at Al's expense.

There was no plot behind the attempted assassination, and no military threat was looming in connection with it, but nobody knew this at the time. The President fortunately survived the attack, saved by the courage and efficiency of the secret service, who got him to George Washington University Hospital in a matter of minutes, and by the excellent medical treatment he received once he got there. The President has a strong belief in Divine Providence—as do I. As it happened, there was a meeting of emergency treatment doctors at the hospital that very day, and the President received the finest medical attention one could possibly obtain.

(In the midst of this public tragedy and my concern about the President and the others who were shot, even my family was affected, as I later learned. My young daughter, then in the eighth grade, was on her way home from school when she heard the news that the President and some of his staff had been shot. She rode the bus all the way home in fear and uncertainty, not knowing whether or not her dad had been killed.)

All in all, the Reagan team worked together well in this period of stress—the way I would have liked to see it work if we had been involved in a confrontation with the Soviets or any other major crisis. At the end of the hectic week that followed, with the President out of danger and the White House returning to normal, I extended my hand to Jim Baker and said, "It's been a pleasure working with you." I meant it.

As it turned out, the troika as such lasted only a year, since in early 1982 Bill Clark was brought on board as assistant to the president for national security affairs (informally known as the "National Security advisor") and became the fourth member of the White House senior staff reporting directly to the President. This was a natural development inasmuch as Bill not only had his own long-standing relationship with Reagan, dating back to Sacramento, but was well positioned to play a coordinating role among the White House, Pentagon, and State Department.

Reagan had six National Security advisors during his eight years in the White House, testimony to the pressures and difficulties of the job. To be handled to best effect, the post requires a balance between strength in behalf of the President's policies and diplomacy in dealing with the many elements of the national security community, including often strong-willed cabinet secretaries with definite notions of their own.

In this framework the President asked Dick Allen to be his first National Security advisor and have him report through me as counsellor to the president, just as Martin Anderson did on domestic and economic matters. Having served for a time at the NSC with Henry Kissinger, Dick not only understood this outlook but shared it, and in my view did an excellent job at the NSC.

This should have set the stage for a national security decision-making system that would work harmoniously, in keeping with the President's penchant for collegiality among his top subordinates. But during that first year of the administration such was not the case, as will be discussed. Policy differences and personal conflicts occurred far more often than expected. Somehow, the "roundtabling" that had served Reagan in California and in other areas of his new administration didn't seem to work so well when it came to foreign affairs and national security. In frustration, the President decided that a change of players was necessary. He therefore asked Bill Clark to take over from Dick Allen.

Bill Clark served as national security advisor for twenty-one months and did an outstanding job. He was particularly adept at adding a public diplomacy component to our overall national security apparatus, and he initiated steps to gain domestic and international support for the President's foreign policy programs. He helped Reagan establish a strong and effective policy that achieved important successes for the United States—fully comparable, in their way, to those attained in matters of economic policy.

Indeed, as will be shown in these pages, the programs of the Reagan administration were not only successful, they were of immense historical importance, changing the course of human affairs in the United States and around the world. But before those results could be achieved, many obstacles had to be surmounted.

7

THE POWERS
THAT BE

To UNDERSTAND THE TASK confronting the new administration when it got to Washington requires some knowledge of how the system functions. In many respects, the process works quite differently from the approach depicted in our high school civics textbooks.

The established way of doing things in the nation's capital operates in very logical fashion: it suits a tremendous number of people—powerful groups with a professional, financial, or ideological stake in the workings of big government. The influence of such people on politics and policy is immense, far more so than some of us realized before we got there.

First and foremost, at least in terms of numbers, is the huge array of federal government employees—approximately 3 million on the civilian side, roughly the same in the military—whose future is geared to the growth of federal power and spending, whose increase they believe is natural and desirable. Most of these people are decent, honorable, and dedicated. But their self-interest and sense of self-worth depend on doing more of what they have been doing.

Next in line are the many client groups who get official subsidies, as well as vendors, consultants, lawyers, public relations people, and others who receive federal payment for goods and services, studies, projects support, and so on; again, people like everyone else in most respects, but whose self-interest is closely linked to the continued expansion of federal spending. Any effort to stop that expansion, or slow it down, is guaranteed to produce an angry outcry.

Third in line are the lobby groups that have a professional or ideological interest in the further growth of federal regulatory authority, either to protect their financial interest or to advance some cause. These include labor unions and other protected economic interests, environmental groups, and "consumer" organizations, among a host of others. Such groups are vehemently committed to regulating various sectors of our society, as well as to hiking federal outlays.

All of these people had obvious reasons for opposing Ronald Reagan's economic agenda. And they shared one other attribute as well. All are fixtures on the Washington scene, not subject to removal by election. They constituted a kind of permanent shadow government that has seen presidents—and their appointees—come and go. They tend to view an elected chief executive, especially one like Reagan, as a temporary interloper.

Playing an ambivalent role is Congress—an elective body, of course, but in an important sense also part of the permanent government. In the Senate, where members can't be gerrymandered, swings in the popular mood like that which elected Reagan make themselves felt, and the upper chamber accordingly passed to Republican control with the 1980 election.

The House, however, is a different matter, with recent incumbent reelection rates of 98 percent or better. Since most of these incumbents are Democrats, the House stayed firmly Democratic throughout the Reagan era, as it has ever since 1954. The lower chamber, part of the permanent government syndrome, frequently combined with other elements of the establishment in attempting to thwart the Reagan program.*

A fifth element in the system—occupying a special niche—is the Washington press corps. Here ideology was and is a powerful factor; numerous surveys have shown that the "prestige press" of major newspapers, magazines, TV networks, and so on, stands on the liberal side of the ideological spectrum. Thus the philosophical premises of many newspeople prompted a hostility to much of the Reagan program.

Contrary to the usual image, the capital press corps is also very much part of the establishment. The media tend to identify strongly with the outlook of the federal work force, client organizations, and interest groups, particularly those of an environmentalist or regulatory bent. Further, they are dependent on people in government for much of their information. With certain exceptions, therefore, the media tend to function as part of the permanent governing elite.

The odds against change, given all these forces, are thus severe; they are made the more so by some of the curious antidemocratic practices of the federal government. To a degree that is seldom appreciated, much of what happens in terms of federal policy, subsidy programs, and the resultant spending burden is locked in place. Likewise, in terms of personnel, all but a small percentage of the federal work force are "career" employees, not susceptible to removal by an incoming administration.

How these factors combined to inhibit change may be illustrated by looking at a couple of specific cases—one in the realm of domestic affairs, the other in foreign policy. In both categories, as we discovered, the reality of Washington was very different from the civics book description of popular sovereignty over the federal government and policy changes driven by election outcomes.

---

* A further element in the equation—which came vividly to light in the confirmation battle over Supreme Court Justice Clarence Thomas—is the staff of individual lawmakers and congressional committees. While working for elected officials, some of these staff have what amounts to permanent tenure, moving from one office to the next when a member is defeated or retires. They are valued for their "Hill experience" and their contacts with the interest groups and media.

On the domestic side, the biggest barrier to change, by a tremendous margin, was the federal budget itself. Reagan had run on a platform of getting federal spending under control, and heated battles over "budget cuts" continued throughout his eight years in the White House. All of this presupposed that the budget numbers suggested by the President, and voted by the Congress, actually determined the level of federal spending. This, unfortunately, was not the case.

When the administration came to Washington, federal spending and taxation were both essentially on autopilot; sizeable increases were built into the system and occurred of their own momentum. The resulting tax and budget numbers, and what Reagan was able to do about them, will be discussed in chapter 11. At this point, the relevant issue is the *political* problem presented by this largely automatic process.

Issues of spending and taxation are central to our political system, and have been since the American Revolution. In theory, ultimate decisions about such matters are supposed to be made by the people, through the ballot box. In current practice, it doesn't work that way. To understand this, one has to master what might be called "official Washington thinking," which is removed not only from American political theory but from the realm of common sense.

One of the most astonishing things about the federal budget is how much of it is "uncontrollable." This is not an epithet, but an actual technical term. Huge portions of what the government spends— 75 percent or so—are officially described as "uncontrollable" or "relatively uncontrollable" (more recently as "mandatory"). This means that those programs are by definition not subject to the outlay numbers requested by the President, or even to those adopted by Congress.

"Uncontrollables" consist mainly of programs that extend subsidies to people because of their demographic or economic status. Social Security, Medicare, Medicaid, AFDC welfare, unemployment compensation, aid to college students, and farm supports are examples. People get payments from these programs because they qualify by age, income, or other status, and are thus "entitled" to the benefits, based upon authorizations contained in laws passed by Congress.*

This means that, if unemployment goes up, more people will be "entitled" to get unemployment compensation, or food stamps, regardless of the budget totals the President and Congress have agreed to, or how much money is in the Treasury. It also means that so-called entitlement spending is powerfully affected by what is going on in the economy. If there is an economic slump of the type we encountered when Reagan came to office, entitlement spending will naturally trend higher.

During the Reagan years, about 50 percent of the budget—two-thirds of "uncontrollable" or "relatively uncontrollable" spending—consisted of entitlements and was on a constant upward course. (The remainder of "relatively uncontrollable" spending is for long-term procurement, construction projects, and the like, which have been agreed to in previous years but must be partially paid for in the current budget.)

Compounding the problem of uncontrollables and entitlements are cost of living adjustments, or COLAs, which add further automatic increases. These are a pervasive feature of many government programs, adjusting benefit or salary levels by "indexing" them to the estimated rate of inflation. In some cases, we discovered, they were overindexed, and efforts to do something about this were part of our budgetary program.

A final concept that is required to understand the budget is in some ways the most peculiar of all—the "current services" baseline. Under it, the federal budget-makers compute all the increases supposedly needed to provide services next year at a level comparable to those provided this year, including COLAs, other inflation-adjusted costs, assumed growth of populations served, and so on. This "current services" figure, pyramided on top of last year's number, is then plugged into next year's budget as the "baseline."

This way of budgeting not only ensures a lot of built-in increases, it is

* "Entitlements" is a term of art developed fairly recently to give permanence and impregnability to certain types of budget outlays. The term is not found in the Constitution despite the sanctity afforded it by the liberals, and the Founding Fathers would have been astounded by the concept.

also highly useful in keeping taxpayers totally mystified about what is happening to their money. Almost all the budget controversies fought out in the Reagan years revolved around this system of locked-in growth and the confusion generated by the language used to justify it.

Thus, if a particular federal welfare agency was spending $10 billion during the present year, the "current services" approach might conclude that it needed a 10 percent hike to cope with inflation, or increases in number of people served, to stay even—making next year's proposed budget $11 billion. This became the starting point for discussions about next year's budget, usually as a floor beneath still further spending hikes.

To most of us, a 10 percent increase is exactly that, an increase. In Washington parlance, however, this is maintaining "current services"—confusing enough in its own right. It became even more so when Reagan proposed to slow the *rate of increase* of such spending. For instance, our budget might have proposed a $500 million hike for the welfare agency discussed above—making next year's spending $10.5 billion. In common sense terms, this is still an increase, only not so big a one.

But in Washington lingo, this is viewed as a "cut," producing headlines proclaiming, "Reagan Slashes Welfare Spending by $500 Million." With few exceptions (which involved a minuscule portion of the budget) this was exactly what our supposedly draconian "budget cuts" consisted of—attempts to slow the rate of increase of some programs, and of the federal budget generally. Given the fiscal problems we confronted, this seemed a sensible course to follow.

But when the President attempted this, storms of protest broke out from affected interest groups, Congress, and members of the media— many of whom wanted to increase their pet budgets even above their expanded current services levels. The Reagan administration was thus depicted as "slashing" programs, including public housing, nutrition spending, student loans, and countless other seemingly worthy projects—even though no actual reductions were proposed. An image was thus conveyed of people being thrown into the streets, or left to starve, by heartless Reagan policies.

Typically, media stories would pick up some number about an

alleged "cut," without providing any basis for understanding what it meant. The reader or viewer wasn't told the level of spending for the year before, what it would be under Reagan's proposal, or how the process of automatic increases worked. This was true both of individual programs and of the budget in general. The public was thus left totally in the dark as to what was really going on.

The shell game worked on the people would have been a meaty topic for some hard-driving investigative reporter, but the major media showed a curious lack of interest in the topic. The failure to explain the situation to the public—indeed, the tendency to deflect attention from it—suggests the degree to which the major media were part of the problem rather than its "adversarial" critics. The adversarial role was pretty strictly limited to bashing Reagan.

One personal experience may help to illustrate the point. It involved the matter of federal spending for nutrition programs, which according to many liberal groups, members of Congress, and numerous press accounts, were practically being dismantled by the Reagan White House.

In a 1983 radio interview, I attempted to set the record straight about these matters. I noted that, in fact, the federal government was spending billions annually on nutrition programs, and that these outlays were actually rising, not declining. If people were going hungry despite this enormous outlay, I said, the fault must be in the distribution system, not in any "cuts" in spending. For these efforts, I was denounced for my "insensitivity" to the hungry.

The budget data on federal nutrition programs for the years in question, and the preceding decade, are shown in the accompanying table. As can be readily seen, both the long- and short-term trends were on the increase—tremendously so since 1970. There had been a slight dip in food stamp spending in 1982, because of efforts to tighten eligibility (to make sure the benefits went to the truly needy), but even this pause in the upward curve was temporary.

The major media, to my knowledge, never reported these simple facts to the public. Equally to the point, many of them clearly resented my attempts to do so, continuing to insist that there had been drastic "budget cuts" when in fact there hadn't. So we confronted not only a budget problem, but a media problem as well.

FEDERAL FOOD PROGRAMS

Year	Number of people receiving food stamps (millions)	Dollar outlays for food stamps (billions)	Dollar outlays for all federal nutrition programs (billions)
1970	4.3	.53	1.6
1973	12.2	2.31	3.6
1975	17.1	4.65	6.6
1977	17.1	5.42	8.5
1979	17.7	6.89	10.8
1980	21.1	9.13	14.0
1981	22.4	11.08	15.7
1982	22.1	11.05	16.1
1983	23.2	12.79	18.4

Source: Department of Agriculture

All of this translated, in turn, into a *political* problem, not simply for the Reagan White House, but for the American republic. Through this system of locked-in spending, the American people were precluded not simply from controlling outlays through their votes—but from even *knowing* how the system really operated. That state of affairs was not good for our system of self-government, but it was very good indeed for the spending interests who handed out the money and the people who received it.

If the system with respect to federal spending made it hard to bring about changes, the system concerning personnel was a further obstacle. Of the roughly 3 million civilian employees of the federal government, an incoming president can replace perhaps three thousand—one tenth of 1 percent. The rest are all career employees of one sort or another, immune to being fired—except for the most egregious causes, and through laborious procedures.

The rationale for this is that the government should be administered by people who are professionally qualified for the task, avoiding a "spoils system" in which jobs are simply handed out to cronies. These motives are understandable, and the civil service approach has undoubtedly eliminated some of the excesses that existed prior to its creation. But it has also contributed to the locked-in nature of the system.

The assumption is that a professional civil service will administer the government impartially, whoever their elected leaders happen to be. In many cases this is doubtless true. The assumption becomes tenuous, however, when the new elected leadership is intent on changing the settled way of doing things.

With this problem in view, we instituted our series of cabinet councils, frequent meetings with the cabinet and other officials in charge of managing the bureaucracy, and orientation sessions designed to communicate the Reagan program. I think we made significant progress with these measures; but the managerial problems involved in promoting brand-new policies to and through 3 million people accustomed to a different outlook were immense.

Almost any large department of government could serve to illustrate this difficulty. James Q. Wilson, professor of government at Harvard, discusses several in his book, *Bureaucracy*, but gives particular emphasis to the State Department. This is an especially good instance for our purposes since it not only is a case study of the larger problem, but also involves an agency central to many issues of the Reagan era.

For the most part, the State Department is a preserve of the Foreign Service, a cadre of professional diplomats who occupy most of the policy implementation roles in the agency. Like their counterparts in the civil service, the Foreign Service Officers (FSOs) are career employees who continue in government irrespective of who is president. Moreover, to a greater degree than in other agencies, FSOs have historically ascended to positions that are legally open to political appointment—including assistant secretary (and higher) posts, and ambassadorships.

How to deal with the Foreign Service was a continuing issue for the Reagan government. When he began as secretary of state, Al Haig thought it would be a good idea to give FSOs more and more positions, thereby supposedly inducing them to be better supporters of Reagan policy. From our standpoint in the White House, it didn't seem to work that way.

For example, despite his tough rhetorical line on Central America (see chapter 17), Haig for a considerable period retained some of the officials who had been responsible for the Carter policy in that region. It seemed unreasonable, in fact contrary to human nature, to suppose that people who had been carrying out the policies of Jimmy Carter would turn around and carry out, with equal fervor, the very different policies of Ronald Reagan.

One problem at the State Department was similar to that with other agencies of government. Its jurisdiction overlaps with the Department of Defense, and in some cases with the CIA, giving rise to "turf" considerations. Concern about these matters was one reason we didn't adopt, without thorough review, Haig's plan for the NSC, which had been presented on Inauguration Day (while we were still in our morning coats) and would have given predominance to the State Department. It was also a motive behind our attempts to have the President's National Security advisor act as an "honest broker" and coordinator among the various agencies.

The issues, however, went beyond the question of turf. One of the main controversies of the Reagan years, for instance, was whether ambassadorships should go to people from outside of government who were known to support the Reagan agenda, or to career foreign service officers. The President and his staff naturally wanted as many loyalists as possible in these ranks, while the State Department consistently sought to fill them with FSOs. Obviously, the best solution was to have a combination of both, which is what we did. I always thought there should be half of each, but the State Department managed to obtain about twice as many FSOs as appointees favored by the White House.*

The Foreign Service outlook is compounded of several factors. The most obvious is that FSOs view themselves as professionals experienced in foreign affairs, while they assume the President and his appointees generally are not. Such an assumption was particularly

---

* The reason for appointing ambassadors who had a personal relationship to the President went beyond mere commitment to and enthusiasm for his agenda. Those diplomats who knew the President personally and had direct access to him were more credible representatives and therefore more effective in expressing his views to the other nations. Furthermore, the different and often more

false concerning a great number of the Reagan appointees, who had a wide range of foreign experience and expertise. Another element is that FSOs, like career appointees, know they will be in office long after the President and his agents have left. Thus they tend to see themselves as foreign policy mandarins—the true custodians of diplomacy, guarding it from what they view as political meddling. They don't appreciate the view that the foreign service, like the military, should be under the control of an elected leadership.

The essentials of the foreign service agenda, like those of most bureaucracies, derive from its responsibilities: a belief in continuity and stability in working with other countries; a dash of "clientitis," in which some diplomats empathize with the countries or regions with which they deal; and a conviction that the problems of the world can best be handled through diplomacy and negotiation, the agency's stock in trade.

These attributes, whatever their merits otherwise, were not consistent with the kind of foreign policy President Reagan had pledged to bring about. Instead of continuity, in many cases, he wanted change; instead of seeing things from the standpoint of other countries, he wanted to assess them from that of the United States; instead of simply wanting to negotiate at any price, he felt that no agreement was better than a bad one.

There was accordingly a tendency for a State Department "professional" attitude to emerge, in contrast to the attitudes of Reagan. Whether on arms agreements, trade and technology transfer, or dealing with Nicaragua, the State Department tended to favor what it had been doing previously, rather than moving toward Reagan's sharply different policies.

When Al Haig stepped down in 1982 and George Shultz succeeded him, an effort was made to get a handle on the problem. George brought in a distinguished business executive, Jerry van Gorkom,

---

extensive experience—whether in the business, military, or academic field—of such ambassadors provided a perspective different from the usual bureaucratic outlook. To be sure, in some admistrations the only requirement for a diplomatic post has been a hefty campaign contribution or early political support. But most presidents—certainly including Ronald Reagan—have recognized the importance of selecting competent ambassadors.

as his under secretary for management, and van Gorkom tried to make the bureaucracy more responsive to policy leadership. After about a year, however, he resigned, apparently discouraged because he felt the permanent bureaucracy was able to go around him and undo his decisions. No one, he concluded, could manage the State Department.

I should note that many people at State were fine professionals, and a number supported Reagan's outlook. Various of these, however, reported to me that the State Department generally did not support the President, to put it mildly. Too many FSOs disagreed vocally with the President, criticizing him, or condemning his views. By contrast, those who were sympathetic to Reagan had to keep quiet about it if they did not want to jeopardize their future.

Several episodes illustrate the way in which some members of the Foreign Service believed there was a "State Department" policy separate from the policies of the President. A particularly striking example occurred in early 1981, when Navy Secretary John Lehman was reported as saying he would recommend against continued compliance with the expired SALT I and unratified SALT II treaties. Lehman said he was speaking personally, but his comments were fully in line with the President's repeated view that SALT II was "fatally flawed" and shouldn't be binding on our forces.

As soon as Lehman made this comment, the State Department fired off cables to our embassies and issued a press advisory saying Lehman's comments were "not authorized, nor did they reflect administration policy." Instead, according to State, the U.S. would take no action that would "undercut existing agreements" as long as the Soviet Union exercised a similar restraint. (The meaning of "undercut" was not defined.) But no one had consulted the President on whether Lehman was or was not expressing administration policy. When this came to Reagan's attention a few days later, he asked, "Who is sending out these cables?"*[1]

* As it turned out, the State Department and others in the arms control community continued pushing this line successfully within the administration for several years—arguing that the SALT II limits somehow benefited us, and that we couldn't prove conclusively that the Soviets were in violation of them. The President believed that they were in violation, however, and in 1986 announced that we would no longer be bound by terms of this agreement.

The pattern of State Department officials clinging to Carter era policies was most pronounced in matters pertaining to the "Reagan doctrine," chiefly in Central America but also elsewhere around the globe. The President himself, although usually reluctant to criticize, observed that, in his dealings with the communists, he "tried to send out a signal that the United States intended to support people fighting for their freedom against communism wherever they were . . . even though a lot of liberals and some members of the State Department's striped pants set sometimes didn't like my choice of words."[2]

State Department resistance, not only to the President's words but also to the substance of his policy, was frequently apparent when efforts were made to implement the "Reagan Doctrine." In 1982, for instance, Sen. Steve Symms of Idaho introduced a resolution in the Senate restating U.S. opposition to Cuban-Soviet efforts to project military force and spread subversion in this hemisphere, a view that Reagan obviously shared. But when Majority Leader Howard Baker asked the State Department for its view, he was advised that "because of the troubled situation in the Caribbean today . . . we do not find the Symms restatement resolution helpful to our overall efforts in the region now."[3]

Constantine Menges, who worked at the National Security Council as a specialist on Central America, recalls many episodes of this type. One involved Jackie Tillman of the NSC staff, who phoned a State Department official regarding some policy that contradicted a Reagan directive and read the specific directive to him over the phone. According to Tillman, this official answered, "But that is only what the Pres—," then caught himself, realizing he was speaking to "someone who believed that the President's decisions governed the entire executive branch—even the State Department."[4]

Another such episode took place during a Latin American trip by Jeane Kirkpatrick, who had been asked by the President to visit various heads of state, carrying a personal letter from Reagan himself. On this trip, Jeane discovered that the State Department had cabled our ambassadors saying, in Menges' paraphrase, "There is a new Central American strategy coming; it hasn't been formally approved yet . . . so meanwhile, just ignore Kirkpatrick and the letter she is carrying from Reagan."[5]

State Department resistance to "Reagan Doctrine" notions was just as evident in other regions. In 1981, when a legislative effort was launched to repeal the so-called Clark amendment prohibiting aid to Jonas Savimbi's anticommunist forces in Angola, the State Department weighed in against it. In 1985, when Democrat Claude Pepper and Republican Jack Kemp pushed an aid package for Savimbi, George Shultz wrote House Minority Leader Bob Michel: "I understand that Congressmen Pepper and Kemp have introduced legislation which would provide $27 million in nonlethal assistance to Dr. Savimbi's movement, UNITA, in Angola. . . . The suggested legislation should be opposed."[6]

These examples of the intractability of the system, vast and complicated in themselves, were by no means isolated; they were typical in many respects of the problems encountered from various other elements of the establishment. Relations with and battles against Congress, to take the most obvious case in point, were an on-going feature of the Reagan presidency, since nearly everything we set out to do either required the cooperation (or attracted the interest and concern) of the lawmakers. Here again, Reagan's quest for change was met with attitudes ranging from "don't rock the boat" to open hostility.

The press corps, likewise, was a key component of the system and sought to exert its influence on virtually every policy initiative of the Reagan White House. Since the media are the filter through which the public learns about events of government, what they choose to report, and how they report it—as in my encounter on nutrition spending— had a tremendous impact on what the President and his supporters were able to do in terms of mobilizing popular backing.

Understanding these "powers that be" is essential to understanding how Washington works. I cite these matters not to apportion praise or blame, but simply to give as accurate a picture as possible of what the

President had to deal with as he sought to bring about a new direction for the country. Despite these hurdles, as the record clearly shows, he did accomplish major changes, far greater in many respects than most historians have yet acknowledged.

When the administration came to Washington, we knew the goals we wished to attain, as frequently articulated by the President. But we could also see, looming up before us, all the battalions of the established order. The question we faced was how, exactly, to deal with this enormous array of power.

8

GOVERNMENT
BY LEAK

I N SOME RESPECTS, the Reagan presidency was like a coalition
government, albeit a coalition among different varieties of Republicans. One part consisted of the original Reaganites, including those
who had worked for him in California, those who had been involved in
his primary campaigns of 1976 and 1980, and others who identified
with his philosophy of government.

Another part of the coalition consisted of people who, though
Republicans, had not previously identified with Reagan's cause or had
actively opposed it during the primary season, coming on board after
Reagan had won the nomination or—in some cases—after he had
been elected.

The latter group had been brought into the campaign of 1980 in the
interests of uniting the party for the fall election. Many had been
staffers for George Bush, or in some cases for John Connally. Once the
election was concluded, however, another reason for the coalition
approach presented itself. Managing the affairs of the federal govern-

ment is a complex business and most of the California Reaganites had little experience with its workings.

Cap Weinberger had been there, of course, as had Lyn Nofziger, Martin Anderson, and a few others. But to most of the California group, Washington was unfamiliar territory, at least on a daily basis. The President felt we needed to tap the experience of Republicans who had previously served in the federal government—primarily people who had worked in the administrations of Richard Nixon and Gerald Ford. Many of these appointees tended, as might be expected, to be more "pragmatic" than the goal-oriented "Reaganauts," as the President's staunchest supporters called themselves.

The differences between these two elements of the administration were not primarily ideological. Certainly I don't think that many on the pragmatic side were liberals in terms of government philosophy (although perhaps a very few might give rise to such suspicions). Several were in fact fairly conservative in their personal outlook. And a number of them proved to be strongly loyal to the President.

Instead, the main distinction concerned the approach taken to the established way of doing things in Washington. The instinct of most of the Californians was to be wary of the bureaucracy, the media, and the other power centers in the capital. While these Reaganites sought no overt hostilities, they were well aware that attempts at change would not sit well with the ruling elites. The pragmatists, on the other hand, were more comfortable with the existing order, more accustomed to dealing with these forces, and generally more skilled in doing so.

While these two groups often joined together in pursuit of common goals, their outlook when it came to advancing the President's interests tended to have different emphases. The original Reaganites were chiefly interested in changing the existing way of doing things in the direction of Reagan's thinking; the pragmatists were often interested in adjusting Reagan to fit more closely with the existing way of doing things.

The point about these approaches is not that one was right and the other wrong, but that they were different. And, in some respects, both were needed. It was essential that the President have stalwart backers who understood him and his program and were willing to stay the course no matter what. It was also essential that he have people on his team who understood the ways of Washington, Congress, the press corps, and the rest of the establishment.

Though service with Reagan in California was a key to understanding these differences, it was not an infallible indicator. In some cases, people who had not been part of the California group emerged as staunch supporters of the program, while a few who had been with us in Sacramento wound up on the establishment side of things. Nonetheless, granted all the disclaimers, the way things sorted out suggested a pretty definite pattern.

Within the White House, people like Martin Anderson, Dick Allen, Lyn Nofziger (director of political affairs), Edwin Gray, and Robert Carleson (in the Office of Policy Development), and myself would have been described as "policy-oriented," people for whom advancing the Reagan philosophy was the overriding principle.

On the so-called "pragmatic" side, most obviously, were Jim Baker and the staffers he had brought with him, such as Richard Darman (who became staff secretary), David Gergen (communications director), and Frank Hodsel (Baker's assistant).

Two people who were anomalies in this alignment were David Stockman and Michael Deaver. Dave began ostensibly as an ardent tax-cutter and advocate of Reagan economic principles, but soon shifted to the side of pragmatic accommodation of Congress, as will be discussed. Mike was virtually the only original Reaganite from California who seemed to be totally overcome by the power and blandishments of the establishment, so that he basically aligned himself with the pragmatists.

During most of the first term, we were able to blend these approaches in the President's behalf and thus help achieve some of his most important victories. Later, however, the tensions inherent between these differing outlooks became apparent—not only in terms of objectives, but also in methods of operation inside the White House.

One major problem involved "collegiality"—providing information to the President and thereby enabling him to make the best possible decisions. During the time Bill Clark and I served as heads of Governor Reagan's staffs in California, we tried to make sure he heard from the widest possible range of people and had the maximum amount of relevant information. In Washington, we discovered, the more usual procedure was the other way around: some staffers would seek to *limit* the amount and type of information that the President would receive so as to try to influence his decision in a certain direction.

Among the clearest examples of this was the technique employed to pave the way for the TEFRA tax increase of 1982. In this unfortunate episode, Richard Darman and Mike Deaver effectively blocked access to the Oval Office to those who opposed a hike in taxes. The President, in essence, heard the case for but not against the increase. It turned out to be one of the worst mistakes of his administration.

In like fashion, an effort was made to keep Reagan from reading things that went counter to whatever agenda was being promoted. One recurring case was the conservative weekly, *Human Events*, long a favorite periodical of the President. Darman and Deaver tried to make certain the President didn't see *Human Events* or that, if he did, he would have quick rebuttals of its contents.

The flipside of this "access" game, as Bill Clark and I approached it, was to make sure that people *did* get a chance to see the President when they had something to contribute. Bill, for instance, tried to make sure that independent thinkers such as Jeane Kirkpatrick talked regularly with Reagan, which wasn't to the liking of the State Department. In keeping with longstanding practice, Bill wasn't trying to deny access to anyone, but to expand it as much as possible. I did the same.

In one incident, the State Department tried to orchestrate the resignation of several Reaganite ambassadors in various Latin countries. The story had been put out that the ambassadors were resigning voluntarily as part of a normal rotation, which was not the case. Learning of this subterfuge, Constantine Menges, a member of the NSC staff, delivered a memo on the subject to Ken Cribb of my staff, laying out the plot. I saw to it that the President was warned immediately, and he took the necessary steps to prevent a "diplomatic bloodbath."

Another notable difference between our Sacramento experience and standard procedure in Washington was what I would call "government by leak." One of our absolute rules in Sacramento was that nobody leaked to the press—that, in particular, nothing would be said about a forthcoming policy or initiative until the governor was ready to make a statement on it. During the entire seven plus years, from the time Bill Clark became executive assistant to Reagan, through my term in that position, until January 1975 when the governor left office, this rule was scrupulously adhered to.

When we came to Washington, we found a different situation. Leaks were almost a routine way of doing business. The President and the rest of us from California were astonished to discover that leaks were habitually used as a weapon in the political arena, rather than being an occasional problem of somebody running off at the mouth. In Washington, it became quite customary to have some policy discussed in confidence one day and to see it on the front page of the *Washington Post* or *New York Times* the next.

Basically, these political leaks occurred for one of three purposes: to surface something prematurely, either to head it off or to influence policy decisions concerning it; to disparage someone in the administration and bring that person down in the eyes of the press and public; or to curry favor with the media. If you were known to be "cooperative" with reporters, they would downplay what might be detrimental to you and boost your reputation in their stories.

An early example of "government by leak" involved a Social Security reform plan drafted by Martin Anderson and the domestic policy office in the White House. Ultimately, this proposal surfaced, officially and briefly, in a speech by Richard Schweiker. The feeling was widespread in the political shop that Social Security should not be touched by the administration, since it had always been a land mine for Republicans. These concerns were valid; any approach to Social Security had to be handled carefully, with due regard for the public reaction. On the other hand, the problems of the system needed to be addressed; both short- and long-term funding imbalances had to be corrected.

The program developed by Anderson's group did this, in some respects matching an effort then being pursued by Democratic Representative Jake Pickle of Texas. Had we been able to work out an agreement with more responsible members of Congress, then done a proper job of marketing, constructive changes in the system might have been achieved, but this was not to be. Someone leaked the plan before the President and cabinet even had a chance to weigh it properly.

The result was a media flap in which the administration was accused of wanting to damage Social Security, and all the politicians in sight headed for the tall grass. The Republican-controlled Senate passed a resolution, by a vote of 96–0, condemning any efforts to tinker with Social Security. And Democrats in the House were strictly instructed not to cooperate with the administration on the topic, since this would rob them of an explosive issue against the GOP. In the White House, political operatives distanced themselves even further from the issue.

The Social Security episode illustrates how leaks can be used as a preemptive strike. By provoking loud outcry about a contemplated policy before it could be presented in a positive way, a leak could smother the policy in its cradle. The lesson from this early experience, and other cases of preemptive leaking, strongly influenced how we later handled other programs—most notably, the Strategic Defense Initiative.

Another early indication that we were going to have problems in this regard occurred in July 1981, when Lou Cannon of the *Washington Post* called to ask about the impending nomination of Sandra Day O'Connor to the Supreme Court. The President's choice of Mrs. O'Connor had been closely guarded information. The only people who knew about it, supposedly, were the President, Jim Baker, Mike Deaver, and myself, along with Bill Smith and those who had a "need to know" at Justice.

When Cannon called me to discuss the O'Connor nomination, I was completely taken aback that he knew anything about it. It was obvious that someone in a very small circle of people had violated the President's confidence—and I was sure it wasn't anyone at Justice. Cannon tried to divert suspicion by saying that somebody from the *Post* had happened to "see" Mrs. O'Connor in town, but that seemed pretty flimsy. It disturbed me to think that one of my own colleagues in the

White House had breached the rule of confidentiality in such an important matter.

While there were several different kinds of leaks, many of them exhibited a pattern. One recurring feature was that the targets of the leaks, quite often, were the original Reaganites who held more conservative views, those who wanted to "let Reagan be Reagan." Among those targeted in this fashion were Dick Allen, Lyn Nofziger, Bill Clark, Ray Donovan, Cap Weinberger, and myself. Down the line, Faith Whittlesey, a Pennsylvania Republican leader who became a leading advocate of Reagan policies, was also subjected to this treatment.

The nature of these leaks was almost always the same: some staffer of the President was insufficiently "realistic," encouraged the President to pursue his "ideology," catered to the President's "worst instincts," was "ineffective," "losing influence," and so on—usually in contrast to some other staffers who were seen as being "realistic" and "effective."

One story in the *Washington Post*, for example, quoted "White House officials" criticizing Cap Weinberger for the outcome of a committee vote on the defense budget, "blaming him for taking an uncompromising position that turned Republican senators against the administration. 'Cap cost us the committee,' said one White House official . . ." Another story, describing Faith Whittlesey as "the most stiffly conservative of Reagan's top aides," said she "has . . . become an outcast among the President's senior aides . . ."[1] Both Cap and Faith, like many others loyal to the President, were attacked only because they were effective in following his policies and doing what he wanted done.

All of this was very much a case of the self-fulfilling prophecy at work. In Washington, someone repeatedly said to be in trouble, losing influence, or acting ineffectively can suffer such a fate through the mere repetition of the charges in the media. Conversely, someone who is said to be gaining power and influence can in fact do so, for the same reasons. In a city where perception is often more important than reality, carefully planned leaks are a vital part of image manipulation.

In a sense, all this was natural, even though unpleasant and damaging. Large numbers of the capital press corps were unsympathetic to the President and his views, and thus on the lookout for items that would discredit his program and his supporters. There was always a brisk market for "high-level sources" or "senior staff" members who would say that some aspect of Reagan's program was mistaken, that he was getting bad advice from his conservative staffers, and that things had to be altered in the direction of "reality"—as defined inside the Beltway.

The more stalwart Reaganites also seemed less able or willing to play the game, putting them at a disadvantage. Don Regan recalls an episode involving his top staff member Tom Dawson, who was told by a *Washington Post* reporter that if Regan's staff played along with the press, they would get good treatment in return; but if they didn't, they would suffer the consequences. Dick Allen recounts a similar experience in which a prominent columnist suggested they talk frequently about what Dick was doing at the NSC, in which event, "he'd be able to report my views in an informal way."

"In other words," Dick said, "if I fed him, he'd take care of me. I said no, I wasn't interested in the process. And he said, in that case, I wouldn't be interested in the results. . . . Not long after that, the little jabs and barbs—'bad manager,' 'disorganized'—began to appear."[2]

As these examples indicate, one of the most decisive factors in the process was the extent to which those who leaked were creatures of the inside-the-Beltway culture, while the targets of the leaks almost invariably were not. Again, the process was quite logical. In most cases, the issue at hand was whether the government would continue with business as usual. The media could generally be counted on to disparage any attempt at significant change. In numerous cases, that outlook was shared by the leakers inside the government.

I was frequently a target of such leaks. The first that I recall occurred in 1981 in the immediate aftermath of a story in the *U.S. News & World Report* which described me, on the basis of a survey by the magazine, as the second most influential person in the executive branch, after the President. This apparently didn't sit well in some quarters, and the anonymous leakers let it be known that I really wasn't involved at all in the important business of the government.

In the summer of 1982, I got a double-barreled dose of such publicity. Beginning in July, a series of stories appeared alleging that I was losing influence with the President, was being excluded from key decisions, and was too identified with conservative positions on the Siberian pipeline, the Law of the Sea, and other issues. *Time* and *Newsweek* ran virtually identical stories on my asserted decline and fall, as did other media outlets.[3]

A report by Saul Friedman of Knight-Ridder news service summed it up by saying that "Meese, who only a summer ago was being called 'the deputy president,' finds himself beleaguered by reports emanating from others on the White House staff that he has slipped or been pushed from the pinnacle of power and now plays a secondary role in the administration high command." My supposed failings were contrasted with the merits of "super-efficient White House chief of staff James Baker, a smooth and gregarious doer. . . ."[4]

These stories were, of course, false. Indeed, the articles of the previous summer, depicting me as some kind of "deputy president," were greatly exaggerated—as I said at the time. Likewise, later accounts of my imminent demise were inaccurate, as subsequent events proved. This type of backstabbing by leak had a corrosive effect on the President's staff and particularly infuriated the many people inside and outside the White House who supported me and the policies I stood for.

Understandably, when these false stories attacking me appeared, members of my staff became irate. They and others outside the White House urged me to go to the President to complain, or to begin my own campaign of counterleaks. While I appreciated their feelings, I rejected these suggestions. I felt that a spectacle of leaks and counterleaks could only be damaging to the President. Better, I thought, to focus our energies on advancing the President's program and not become involved in an internecine media battle.

To the comment that "everybody does it," therefore, my answer was no, everybody doesn't. I made it a rule not to leak, and not to allow my staff to do so; the proof can be seen in the pages of the Washington and national press, which were rife with stories quoting anonymous sources disparaging me and other Reaganites, but few if any pointing in the opposite direction. In fact, one prominent journalist, Fred Barnes of *The New Republic*, publicly criticized me for refusing to leak—saying I was foolish not to.[5]

In some immediate sense, this might have been correct, since perhaps I would have gotten a more favorable press if I had done some leaking (though pro-Reaganite leaks, for the reasons stated, weren't what the press was after). But in a larger sense, I think such leaking was profoundly wrong, harmful to the cause we were trying to serve, and therefore harmful to what I believed. An administration in which officials attack each other in this fashion is an administration in serious trouble.

The degree to which leaks were a normal part of governing—and the press a major factor in policy outcomes—was perhaps most clearly shown in the battle over taxes and the role of David Stockman, discussed in chapter 10. A close second was the series of events that unfolded in 1981–83 concerning the staffing of the National Security Council. Considering the importance of the position of National Security advisor—because of its confidential status in the White House and the sensitive issues with which it deals—this was an area where leaks were especially damaging.

As it turned out, however, there were a number of such leaks, which had negative impact on the individuals involved, contributed to personnel changes in the post, and thereby affected the course of national policy. From the interaction of these factors, some aspects of the Iran-Contra affair developed. "Government by leak" played a role in determining who would staff the NSC; it also affected the way members of the staff, and others in the government, conducted their activities in their attempts to head off further leaks.

When Dick Allen was appointed NSC advisor, as noted, the President wanted a staffer who would act as an honest broker of policy among cabinet members rather than competing with them. Some Washington pundits tried to portray this as lessening the importance of Dick's role, although actually it was much more in keeping with the traditional (i.e., pre-Kissinger) nature of the position.

In "coalition" terms, Dick was one of the most staunchly conservative of our team and intensely involved in policy matters. Perhaps because of this combination, Mike Deaver took a strong dislike to him, making disparaging remarks about Dick in conversations with, or in front of, the President. In the fall of 1981, leaks about Dick began appearing in the press, saying he was inefficient, wasn't doing his job, and—most damaging of all—was linked to scandal.

An envelope containing $1,000 was found in an NSC staff office safe used by Allen. Because of the low threshold of the Ethics in Government Act, this triggered a preliminary investigation by the Department of Justice. It turned out that the cash had come from Japanese journalists who were interviewing Mrs. Reagan and were tendering it as a gift to her, not understanding that our customs do not permit this. To prevent the First Lady from being embarrassed, Dick intercepted the envelope, put it in his safe, and forgot about it. There was nothing whatsoever culpable on his part, as the Justice Department investigation confirmed. All of this, however, was played up extensively in the press—with the aid of anonymous leakers in the government.

As Suzanne Garment notes, "the journalists on the Allen story, for all their enthusiasm, actually got most of their leaks from inside the government. The scandal grew as big as it did, not simply because of the media's determined nosiness but because players inside the government had decided to manipulate this trait. . . . The anonymous sources . . . spoke to the press more frequently as the scandal wore on, assuring journalists that Allen was going to go. . . . The 'inside' comments gave the press the plot line of the Allen saga."[6]

When Dick left the White House at the beginning of 1982, leaks about the NSC staff continued. Bill Clark, who replaced Allen, was an equally staunch conservative, generally in agreement with Bill Casey and Cap Weinberger on issues such as assisting the freedom movement in Poland, the defense buildup, aid to the freedom fighters in Nicaragua, and the Strategic Defense Initiative.

But then, in the spring of 1983, a profusion of leaks began appearing about Bill, virtual carbon copies of those that had been printed about me the previous summer. Stories appearing in *Time*, *Newsweek*, and the *Washington Post* depicted Bill in various unflattering ways that characterized him as an ideologue who was providing the wrong advice to the President, in contrast to the more knowledgeable and "pragmatic" members of the White House staff. Again, this portrayal of Bill Clark was absolutely false. Widely respected throughout the national security community and by foreign leaders around the world, Bill was doing an excellent job and had the complete confidence of the President.[7]

One story in the *Post* accused Bill, along with Cap Weinberger, of having damaged the President by refusing to accept a compromise defense budget promoted by Jim Baker. This alleged failing on the parts of Cap and Bill was contrasted with the more sensible counsel of Baker and his assistant Darman, depicted as masters of the legislative process.[8]

Newsweek likewise attacked Bill for his "dismal lack of expertise in foreign affairs," for leading the President astray in opposing the Siberian pipeline, for pushing neoconservative Ken Adelman as head of the Arms Control and Disarmament Agency, and for urging the President to be "confrontational" on Central America. The story went on to describe Bill as unpopular with "pragmatic" staffers and quoted one "top level" aide as saying, "There's an attitude of let him fall on his face. . . . It's going to be all the rest of us against Clark."[9]

At about this same time period, Jeane Kirkpatrick recalls, Mike Deaver spoke to her about forthcoming opportunities for the President to improve relations with the Soviets. She quotes Mike as telling her that Reagan had "an opportunity to make peace for our times," and that, "when the time comes that the President has the opportunity to make peace, we can't have you and Bill Clark around raising questions." She says Mike reiterated the point: "We just can't have you and Bill Clark around raising questions."[10]

The leaking problem as it affected the NSC staff became particularly intense in the fall of 1983 when someone gave Lou Cannon of the *Post* a story involving Bill's assistant, Bud McFarlane, and plans for escalating U.S. military activity in Lebanon. Like the story on Sandra Day O'Connor, this information could only have come from a limited number of people, and the source of the leak became a matter of hot dispute within the White House.

Since Cannon was the recipient of the leak, he of course knew its source. While he doesn't reveal this source directly, his discussion of this episode in his most recent book is telling. He comments on the internal dispute about who had been the leaker, noting that he "was known to have good relations with both Baker and Clark, who typically blamed each other for the leak." Cannon goes on to say that Nancy Reagan thought Bill had been the culprit: "At least that is what she told Clark, who *accurately* but unavailingly denied that he had been my source" (emphasis added).[11]

This episode led to yet another clash, a culmination of the long-festering issue of the leaks: the famous "polygraph" dispute, in which Clark wanted to end the problem by having a thorough Justice Department investigation, with use of polygraph tests if that should be deemed necessary. Because of the increasingly serious nature of these leaks, including the possible exposure of Bud McFarlane to attacks by terrorists on his trips to Lebanon, I supported Clark's suggestion.

The move, however, was strongly opposed by Deaver and Baker. Surprisingly, they were joined by George Shultz—who said that if anyone asked him to take a polygraph test he would do it, but only once. This threat to resign—one of several made by Shultz during his tenure—was a major factor in the President's decision to turn down the polygraph proposal, even though an investigation of the matter was conducted by the FBI, with predictably inconclusive results. I was always curious about George Shultz's vehemence on this subject, since he certainly was not suspected of being the source of the leaks.

At this point feelings were running high, and events continued to escalate. I'm not sure to what degree the polygraph episode triggered Bill Clark's decision to leave the NSC position, but it was obviously a contributing factor. Bill had a history of throwing himself intensely into any job he took, and his performance at the NSC bore this out. By the fall of 1983, he was coping simultaneously with the pressures of the job, the problems of coordinating the various contending elements of the national security community, and the efforts of some of his colleagues to undermine him. When Bill Casey learned that Clark was planning to leave the NSC, Casey tried to dissuade him, but to no avail. Casey and I felt that with Bill Clark gone, we would lose a strong force for the Reagan foreign policy agenda.

At the Department of Interior, meantime, Jim Watt had been fighting battles of his own, and in October 1983 he too decided to resign.

As a Westerner and outdoorsman, Bill Clark was interested in the Interior job, and the President decided to appoint him.

Then we got another jolt. We discovered that Mike Deaver and Jim Baker had worked up a plan to switch positions—with Jim assuming the job of National Security advisor and Mike taking over as chief of staff. Mike apparently had the President ready to sign off on this, unbeknownst to the rest of us, and was on the verge of releasing the announcement to the press. This made it pretty clear where the campaign of press leaks against Bill Clark had been leading.

I first learned of the Baker-Deaver plan at a National Security Planning Group meeting in the White House Situation Room, as did Bill Casey and Cap Weinberger. As soon as the NSPG meeting was over, Weinberger, Casey, Clark, and I discussed this proposal with the President. Everyone advised him that it was a bad idea, for several reasons: first, Jim had no background in foreign affairs, which would imply that this office was being made more political than substantive; second, his perceived views and practices would end Bill Clark's effort to have the NSC advisor serve as an honest broker; and finally, as Bill Casey expressed it in his typically blunt fashion, "Mr. President, you can't have the biggest leaker in Washington as your National Security advisor!"

Surprised by the opposition of so many of his top officials, the President decided against the Baker-Deaver switch. With Clark still determined to leave, the question then became who would replace him. Bill Casey wanted Jeane Kirkpatrick, who in my opinion would have been an excellent choice. But she was anathema to the State Department, and the President wanted a harmonious relationship with Foggy Bottom.

Given all this, the natural choice seemed to be Bud McFarlane, who had extensive experience both in military and foreign policy matters and was acceptable to State. Bud therefore got the job, with Rear Admiral John Poindexter moving up to be his assistant. In that post, as is now well known, Bud's involvement in Mideast affairs and his efforts to deal with terrorism led to one of the most problematic episodes of the Reagan era.

In retrospect, this changing of the guard at the NSC—driven by leaks and concern about them—was much more significant than at first appeared. For almost all the first three years of the administration, first with Dick Allen and myself, and then with Bill Clark, the national security process in the White House had been managed by people who were very close to the President. Afterwards, this was no longer the case.

To say this is not to fault Bud, but simply to state a fact—one of which he was acutely conscious and frequently mentioned. In our "coalition," he had not been part of the original team and wasn't familiar with the President's views or methods. This became even more important in 1985 and 1986 when virtually all the original Reaganites had left the White House.

Bad as internal political leaking was, it paled by comparison with a much more serious problem—the leaking of information concerning national security and intelligence matters. This sort of leaking introduced a completely different and more serious set of problems, which also helped to shape White House attitudes and practices. Bob Woodward of the *Washington Post* especially seemed to have a pipeline to somebody on intelligence data, and often broke stories in the *Post* concerning our efforts to deal with terrorism and similar topics. Such leaks were more than inconvenient or politically damaging; they could jeopardize sensitive operations, military plans, U.S. officials, or intelligence sources in other countries.

Leaking of this type (discussed in detail later) had obvious impact on the conduct of policy in several respects. One was that operations were concealed or changed when leaks occurred. Another was that extensive efforts were necessary to keep tight security when military operations such as Grenada were in the making. Yet another was that, when initiatives were being planned in the White House, such as SDI, we had to prevent preemptive leaks that could abort the project before it started.

Most significant of all, in view of later events, leaks of this type caused suspicion of the intelligence committees on Capitol Hill, leading Casey and others to believe that data supplied to Congress would wind up on the front pages of the *Post*. As a result, Bill and others became extremely reluctant to provide such material to Congress if it could be avoided.

In my own view, the American people are entitled to full and accurate information about what their government is doing. Indeed, I would argue that one of the problems with the media is that they don't really provide such information on a regular basis. I believe this from a standpoint of principle, and also from one of political interest: I never thought Ronald Reagan would suffer politically from a free flow of accurate information about the issues and the policies of the federal government. On the contrary, I believed—and still believe—that such information would, and did, incline the public in his favor.

There are, however, some obvious limits to providing information to the media. The most important is to protect military, intelligence, and national security secrets that could jeopardize the defense of the country or the lives of our servicemen, citizens, or hostages held overseas. I don't accept the theory that the rights of the press are more important than the security of the nation or the lives of innocent people. Efforts to prevent the leakage of information on this score—as in the liberation of Grenada—had my support.

A second limit is that the President and his staff are entitled to reasonable confidentiality in the internal discussion of policy issues, a position recognized in the doctrine of "executive privilege." If the contents of White House staff meetings are to be spread over the front pages of the morning paper, then all concerned will be inhibited in voicing their opinions. Still less excusable is one-sided, sole-source leaking that seeks to put a "spin" on what occurred, or tear down an individual, to benefit one side against another.

Unfortunately, our efforts to stop the leaks were largely unavailing. The President, and the rest of us, would pay a heavy price for this continued hemorrhaging of confidential data to the press.

9

HIT THE GROUND RUNNING

WHEN PRESIDENT REAGAN arrived in Washington, he brought with him a sweeping agenda touching virtually every aspect of domestic life and foreign policy. Dealings with the Soviet Union and other foreign states, defense, the growth of the federal budget and taxation, so-called social issues, and numerous other topics vied for attention. All these matters had to be addressed, even as the new administration was sorting itself out, making key appointments, and preparing to deal with a divided Congress.

Given the many problems that demanded attention, the President realized the need for clear-cut priorities. Not everything could be done at once, especially since he hoped to modify if not reverse entirely the conventional workings of the federal city.

As already noted, the President's economic program was high on the list of priorities. In early 1981, few people doubted that the country was in serious trouble. Inflation and unemployment had been steadily on the rise—contradicting the standard Keynesian view of a trade-off between these economic evils. The Consumer Price Index had risen at a rate of 12.5 percent in 1980, after rising 13 percent in 1979. And joblessness in the second half of 1980 had risen to 7.5 percent, up from 6.3 percent the preceding March.

In the 1976 contest with Gerald Ford, the Carter campaign had invented a statistic called "the misery index"—the combined inflation and unemployment rates—to show the depths of economic hardship. Under Ford, that number had been 13.5. Under Carter, the comparable figure was over 17 percent (see Chart A). Also in double digits was the prime interest rate banks charged their best customers (topping out at 21.5 percent in the latter part of 1980). Taxes on the average citizen, meantime, were high and rising. As Professor Lawrence Lindsey recalls:

"The real wages of American workers plunged by 9 percent in just the two-year period 1979–81, offsetting nearly two decades of growth and reducing real wages to their 1962 level. With the enormous tax increases accumulated over that period, workers in 1979 were far worse off than their counterparts in 1962. American workers had not taken such giant steps backwards since the 1930s."[1]

Adding to the nation's woes were the petroleum and natural gas shortages of 1978–79, which saw people shivering for lack of fuel supplies and enduring huge gas lines at service stations in many areas.

CHART A   MISERY INDEX (UNEMPLOYMENT RATE PLUS INFLATION)

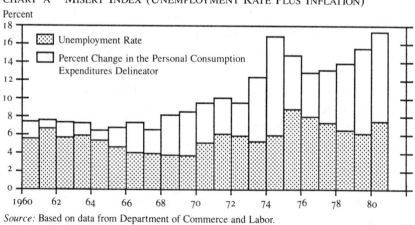

Source: Based on data from Department of Commerce and Labor.

The conventional wisdom had no answer to such problems—except to promise more of the same. President Carter and other spokesmen for the *status quo* said, resignedly, that this was just the way it was. We had, it seemed, reached the era of "limits," running out of energy supplies and suffering "stagflation," with no alternative but to hunker down and bear it.

The outlook of Ronald Reagan and his team was dramatically different. In the President's view, the ills we suffered were the result of faulty policies by the federal government: runaway spending and taxation, excessive expansion of the money supply that fueled inflation, and intensive regulation of the economy which stifled investment and production. Such ideas were not, of course, new to Reagan, who had been preaching the virtues of free enterprise, limited government, and lower taxes since the early 1960s. During the 1980 campaign, the message had not materially changed, but the country had. The American people had become more receptive to what he had to say.

In trying to correct the nation's problems, the Reagan administration faced not only economic but political constraints. Our stated hopes of making significant changes in the traditional Washington way of doing things went against the grain of many powerful interests. We were up against the "establishment"—a Congress whose senior members ranged from skeptical to overtly hostile, the media who considered the President's ideas strange, if not bizarre, and a vast array of groups who had a stake in keeping things the way they were.

To overcome all this, we needed to hit the ground running. The President's victory, popular support, and communications skills gave us a powerful impetus coming out of the election. And a Republican Senate and the potential support of the "boll weevil" (conservative, mostly Southern) Democrats in the House gave us hopes of winning majorities for our legislation in Congress. Most important—the flipside of all these developments—was the widespread belief that the system was not working, that some kind of change was urgently needed.

This configuration of forces by no means guaranteed victory. But it did give us a "window of opportunity." We knew the President's strength with Congress and the public would be greatest at the outset;

historically, it has been harder for a chief executive to get his policies adopted later in his tenure. To succeed, we needed coherent policies to address the underlying problem; an effective communications strategy to inform the public of what we were doing and why we were doing it; and a series of skillful negotiations with a wary Congress.

Looking back, I think we did a number of these things well, others not so well. On net balance, the program was a success, and one of historic dimensions. Indeed, I think Ronald Reagan worked enormous changes for the good, not only in America, but in the world at large.

The major domestic accomplishment of the Reagan years, bar none, was getting tax rates down, and—despite slippage, confusion, and bitter opposition—keeping them down. When Reagan became president, the top marginal rate on individual income was 70 percent. When he left office, it was 28 percent. The evidence shows that this and related changes, such as a monetary policy that would halt or dampen inflation, contributed powerfully to the recovery of the economy, which was a necessary prerequisite to the other benefits brought about through Reagan's leadership.

The net effect, of course, was to restore incentives to work, produce, save, and invest. With dramatically lower marginal rates and extra dollars of purchasing power, both individuals and businesses worked harder and produced more. With substantially lower inflation, individuals were not pushed up so rapidly into higher tax brackets and were thus less tempted to divert resources from investment to tax-and-inflation shelters. And businesses were better able to recover their investment in the capital equipment that increased productivity.

But these changes were not achieved without tremendous difficulty. The Reagan Revolution of 1981 was not the cakewalk depicted in some histories of the era. Had it not been for the tenacity of the President against doubters, both within and without his administration, the whole thing could have died aborning—and nearly did. The pitfalls, however, were pretty much the opposite of those that are usually cited.

What the Reagan government did (and did not do) concerning economic policy, was, from my standpoint, quite distinct from the prevailing orthodoxy on such matters. Indeed, many accounts of how the economic agenda was devised, and what was done in terms of tax and budget policy, portray quite a different picture from the one I saw during my tenure with the President.

A stream of books and articles about the Reagan presidency have propagated countless misconceptions about "Reaganomics." Many contended that the economic program was invented by a small group of supply-side theorists who foisted their untested notions on the President—a variation on the well-worn theme of Reagan, the passive figure with no policy of his own.

As a consequence of accepting supply-side theory, the pundits continue, the President and his advisors believed the tax rate reductions would "pay for themselves." Instead, it is claimed, the reductions caused a tremendous loss of revenue, and this accounted for the budget deficits that grew in the 1980s. On the spending side, the administration supposedly fought for stringent budget cuts that deprived the needy but were not sufficient to make up the hemorrhage of revenue.

Almost all these notions, and many others that have been spun about "Reaganomics," are incorrect. The most obvious and easily refuted is the idea that anybody had to, or could have, foisted off an economic theory on Ronald Reagan. In plain fact, it was the President's strong commitment that drove the process from start to finish—and at times it needed plenty of driving. This applied both to the general philosophy of lower spending and taxation, and to the specifics of the program eventually adopted by Congress.

Reagan's interest in lower taxation was spurred not only by his philosophy of limited government and by his extensive reading on economic subjects, but also by his personal experience. He frequently stated that exorbitant taxes were not only wrong as a matter of principle, but a drag on production. In this respect, he was a "supply-sider" long before the term was invented.

His famous speech on behalf of Barry Goldwater in large part spoke about the perverse incentives created by a high-tax, big-subsidy welfare state. "No nation in history," Reagan said in 1964, "has ever survived a tax burden that reached one-third of its national income.

Today, thirty-seven cents out of every dollar earned in this country is the tax collector's share, and yet our government continues to spend 17 million dollars a day more than the government takes in."[2]

During his years in California politics, Reagan continued to hammer on these themes. Having had to accept a tax hike immediately after taking office in Sacramento, he determined to return state surpluses to the taxpayers—and he did so. He used his line item veto (943 times in all) to hold down excessive spending and pushed hard for budget and welfare reforms. And in his second term, as noted, he sponsored a tax limitation state amendment that was narrowly defeated but became the precursor of the successful "tax revolt" of 1978.

The President (again contrary to the usual image) was also a voracious reader and would frequently come up with out-of-the-way items that vividly made a point. One such was a statement that he often quoted to me and others, from the Muslim scholar Ibn Khaldoon on the dynasties of ancient Egypt: "At the beginning of the dynasty, taxation yields a large revenue from small assessments. At the end of the dynasty, taxation yields a small revenue from large assessments."[3] In other words, as costs of government rise and the economic base contracts, higher and higher taxes yield proportionately less revenue.

Also important to the President was the question of marginal tax rates—the tax imposed on an extra dollar of earnings—which in a steeply progressive system could be exorbitant. He frequently told of his peak earning years in Hollywood, when he was in the 94 percent tax bracket. As he put it, it was not logical to work for six cents on the dollar, so after making three or four pictures a year he and others in his bracket would go on vacation.

When this happened, he would continue, it affected many other people in the lower brackets, hundreds and sometimes thousands of crew members, extras, electricians, cameramen, and make-up people who could have had employment in those unmade pictures.

The logical conclusion, in an era of "stagflation," was that a tax cut was needed to spur production—the essence of supply-side theory. In fact, the President even anticipated the "Laffer curve," the idea of a dynamic feedback effect on receipts, since the lower tax rate would be applied to an expanding economic base. In an October 1976 column, for example, Reagan wrote:

"Warren Harding did it. John F. Kennedy did it. But Jimmy Carter and President Ford aren't talking about it. The 'it' that Harding and Kennedy had in common was to cut the income tax. In both cases, federal revenues went up instead of down. . . . Since the idea worked under both Democratic and Republican administrations before, who's to say it couldn't work again?"[4]

As the history of the 1980s demonstrated, the feedback effect and the increase of revenues were both quite real. This is different, of course, from saying that tax cuts "would pay for themselves"—that tax cuts standing alone could somehow balance the federal budget.

Reagan's economic statements, years before the campaign against Jimmy Carter, make hash of the notion that supply-side theory was imposed on a passive Ronald Reagan by Kemp and others. In Dave Stockman's version, Kemp was thinking of running for president himself in 1980 until a January meeting in Los Angeles when he sold Reagan on supply-side tax cuts. This meant, the Stockman story spins on, that since the revolution could be accomplished through Reagan, Kemp no longer needed to be a candidate.

Such tales circulated freely after the administration came to office. One version was promoted by Jude Wanniski, former editorial writer for the *Wall Street Journal* and author of an exposition of supply-side theory called *The Way the World Works*. In Wanniski's story, set forth in an interview with the *Village Voice*, a battle raging within the administration for "Reagan's mind" pitted supply-siders against more traditional economists.[5]

All these stories are fantasies. (At the time, my comment on Wanniski's account was that "a cease-fire has been declared in the war for Reagan's mind.") The President knew his own mind very well; he knew exactly where he stood on tax cuts. Indeed, as events were to prove, he was by far the staunchest tax cutter in the executive branch—far more so, to pick the obvious example, than David Stockman.

In fact, the idea of pressing not only for lower taxes but specifically for a three-year phased reduction to spur recovery was official doctrine in the Reagan camp well before Kemp's visit to Los Angeles. I was present at the discussions with Kemp, and I can testify that the President needed no persuading at all to adopt a tax reduction program. The President liked Jack, and Kemp's support for Reagan was naturally welcome. But far from having to convert Reagan to anything, Jack was basically pushing on an open door.

A pretty good blueprint for cutting taxes had been prepared for us by Martin Anderson back in August 1979. Marty's formulation was so close in all respects to what emerged as policy two years later that it deserves citation at some length:

> We must speed up economic growth to increase the take-home pay of workers and to provide new jobs. . . . This can be done if we:
>
> (a) Reduce federal tax rates. . . . We must have a program—of at least three years' duration—of across-the-board tax cuts. The personal income tax rate must be cut by a specific percentage every year for three years, especially the higher, incentive-destroying marginal rates. The capital gains tax, and the corporate income tax must be cut by a commensurate amount. Tax rates that are too high destroy incentives to earn, cripple productivity, lead to deficit financing and inflation, and create unemployment.
>
> (b) Index federal income tax brackets. The most insidious tax increase is the one we must pay when inflation pushes us into higher tax brackets. While inflation is with us, taxes should be based on real incomes, not government-inflated ones. Federal tax rate brackets, as well as the amount of exemptions, deductions, and credits, should be adjusted to compensate for inflation.
>
> (c) Reduce and eliminate counterproductive federal government regulation of business, education, and the professions. . . . Deregulation should be pursued vigorously on a broad front. . . . The aggregate cost to business of complying with federal regulation in 1977 was over $75 billion . . . and these costs are passed on to the consumer in the form of higher prices—higher prices of homes, of food, of gasoline, of virtually everything we buy. . . .
>
> (d) Federal spending must be controlled. It is not necessary to cut federal spending from its current levels, but it is necessary to reduce the rate of increase in federal spending . . . [and to] seek a constitutional limitation on the percentage of the people's earnings that can be taken and spent by the

federal government. Give the President line-item veto power over the budget . . . [and] transfer certain federal programs, along with the tax resources that finance them, back to state and local government. . . .

   We should add a balanced budget amendment to the Constitution. "Economic policy must be consistent, dependable, with no abrupt change . . . the 1978 report of the Federal Reserve Bank of Minneapolis states: 'What policy makers must do to fight inflation is to eliminate, whenever possible, surprises in fiscal and monetary policies.' "6

Similar ideas were expressed routinely in the inner circles of the campaign. While my notebooks are usually telegraphic in style—topic headings, scheduling matters, staffing, and so on—they also refer to substantive discussions that took place among the candidate and his advisors. Here are excerpts from a meeting on June 14, 1980, of Reagan, George Shultz, Bill Casey, and myself:

   "Economic Program. Unemployment may rise to 8½% and become double digit by end of year. . . . Long term strategy: Less taxes, less Fed spending, more sensible regulation. Sooner we start the better. Also increased defense spending. Priority effort even if means temporary budget imbalance.

   "Tax cuts. Ind. Tax burden appro. $270B . . . Kemp-Roth cuts would be about $27B in first full year.

   "Entering recession by a monetary policy which represents most abrupt change in post-war world. Increase in taxes of gigantic proportion.—Bracket creep.—Increase in social security rates. 'Windfall profits' tax.

   "Social Security. Stretching point at which working people are willing to support, through payroll taxes, those not working.

   "Money supply. (Milton Friedman analysis.) M1-B. Too big an increase in money supply for long time and then sudden decrease. Abrupt changes—plus and minus—have occurred. Monetary authorities should have monetary supply increasing at a constant rate consistent with growth in the economy."

   Concerning these notations, a couple of points. First, this was a meeting not of economic advisors per se, but of the candidate himself, his campaign manager, and two of his senior staff. Of the four of us, only George Shultz was there specifically because of his economic expertise. Second, the meeting occurred before the Republican nomination, before the fall campaign started, and obviously before the election. Yet it concerned not campaign tactics—what was good for Ronald Reagan the candidate—but national policy—what was good for the country.

This was characteristic of Reagan. It was something his critics, alternately deriding his abilities and amazed at his persistence in sticking with his program, seldom grasped. Had they understood it, they would not have been so consistently baffled by his success.

As discussed in chapter 4, these basic ideas were elaborated by Reagan in his major speech at the Chicago Economic Club on September 9, 1980; in it he laid out his rationale for cutting federal spending and taxation, and the need for steady, moderate monetary growth and an extensive program of deregulation. He also supplied the background data to show how the various elements of the program would work together to foster economic growth.

Thus the building blocks of the economic program were in place for many months—in fact, for years—before President Reagan arrived in the Oval Office. There was no need to invent something after the fact, or to accept the conventional wisdom of the establishment, as was the practice of many newly elected chief executives.

A resulting novelty about Reagan was that the ideas spelled out in the campaign—and in all the years preceding it—were, essentially, the program. There wasn't the usual disparity between election rhetoric and governing agenda; what you heard was what you got. This also meant that the President and his team were ready to go as soon as the election was won.

And the President did not let up. He continued to sound these themes, and repeatedly. In his inaugural, for instance, the President said Americans were being "denied a fair return for their labor by a tax system which penalizes successful achievement and keeps us from maintaining our full productivity. . . . But great as our tax burden is, it has not kept pace with public spending. . . . In the present crisis, government is not the solution to our problem; it is the problem."[7]

In his televised economic message on February 5, he emphasized that "we must increase productivity . . . that means above all bringing government spending back within government revenues. . . . [A]t the same time we're doing this, we must go forward with a tax relief package. I shall ask for a 10 percent reduction across the board in personal income tax rates for each of the next three years. Proposals will also be submitted for accelerated depreciation allowances for business to provide necessary capital so as to create jobs."[8]

A few days later, in his February 18 message to Congress, the President summarized his economic program under four main headings:

"A budget reform plan to cut the rate of growth in federal spending;

"A series of proposals to reduce personal income tax rates by 10 percent a year over three years to create jobs by accelerating depreciation for business investment in plan and equipment;

"A far-reaching program of regulatory relief;

"And, in cooperation with the Federal Reserve Board, a new commitment to a monetary policy that will restore a stable currency and healthy financial markets."[9]

All these statements, and the program they embodied, were the culmination of a lifetime of thought and advocacy.

While the basic ideas of the program were vintage Reagan, the particular shape that they assumed owed a great deal to the economic advisors on whom he called, both during the campaign and in the White House. Prominent among them were George Shultz and Bill Simon, both former secretaries of the treasury, Paul McCracken, Michael Boskin of Stanford University, Murray Weidenbaum of Washington University in St. Louis, Martin Feldstein of Harvard, and numerous other experts.

Of special importance among the academic advisors was Professor Milton Friedman, the Nobel Laureate and master of monetary policy. Friedman, who is able to translate economics into comprehensible language for the public, was a particular favorite of the President. His staunch advocacy of private enterprise, the free market, and tax limitation (dating back to California), and his extensive knowledge of monetary matters were invaluable to the administration.

Don Regan at Treasury was a businessman, not an economic theorist, as he freely acknowledges, but he was in tune with the President's ideas and became a loyal battler for the Reagan policies. Pen James and I interviewed him for two hours at the University Club during the transition, and I came away thinking he would fit in well with the President's economic program. I was not disappointed, nor was the President. (Don's difficulties once he moved from Treasury to the White House as chief of staff were something else altogether.)

Don was backed up at Treasury by a first-rate team of economic experts, including Undersecretary Norm Ture, Assistant Secretary for Economic Policy Paul Craig Roberts, and Deputy Secretary Steve Entin. All of them were veterans of economic battles on the Hill, and knew the supply-side catechism backwards and forwards. All of them kept fighting for the Reagan program, even when others dropped by the way. Craig Roberts has given his own account of these battles in *The Supply-Side Revolution.*

On budgetary matters, the central figure, of course, was Stockman, director of the office of management and budget. Though not quite the lone ranger he made himself out to be, Stockman had the "black books" full of budget figures and number crunchers at OMB, and he was thus the one we relied on for data. But, as he later admitted, he was using the numbers in rather singular ways. This and other Stockman practices had some painful consequences down the road.

Also involved in promoting the Reagan program was the "other side" of the White House, the side under Jim Baker. This included the outreach and implementation functions, bureaucratese for press relations, public liaison, and dealings with Congress. Theoretically, our end of the operation would formulate policy, and the Baker shop would sell it. Among those working with Baker were his principal aide Richard Darman, Communications Director David Gergen, press secretaries James Brady and Larry Speakes, and legislative liaison Max Friedersdorf, assisted by Powell Moore and Ken Duberstein.

Since policy and legislation are not assembly line products but the results of a lot of give and take, the way communications and liaison are handled can have a powerful impact on the policy itself. For example, since nearly everything in national policy involves Congress, legislative negotiations can powerfully affect its course. By the same token, handling the press, which influences public perception of the policy, can strongly influence its chances of adoption.

In the legislature itself, we saw both problems and opportunities. The Senate, for the first time in a generation, was in Republican hands, its twelve new GOP members having ridden into victory with the President—a favorable omen. On the other hand, the more senior Republican members, the committee chairmen, were not necessarily attuned to Reaganomics. A number of them, most notably Finance Committee Chairman Bob Dole of Kansas and Budget Committee Chairman Pete Domenici of New Mexico, were skeptical of the Reagan tax cut program.

Then there was the Senate Republican leader, Howard Baker, who was not a Reagan partisan—he had in fact competed for the 1980 Republican presidential nomination—but he was a good team player and an honest broker with Congress. Baker always gave the President a dispassionate reading of the Senate and worked hard to get the President's plan adopted, as did Bob Michel of Illinois in the House.

In the lower chamber, we faced a formidable adversary in Speaker "Tip" O'Neill, a welfare stater of the old-fashioned type, who was backed by a substantial Democratic majority. But as some counterbalance there were the forty or fifty boll weevil Democrats who were more conservative than O'Neill and who represented districts the President had carried in the fall election. These were people with whom we could do business.

Aside from the formal leadership, individual members had important roles to play. One such was Sen. Paul Laxalt of Nevada, a friend of the President dating back to the days when both were governors. Another was Kemp, a tireless missionary for the supply-side gospel and coauthor with Sen. William Roth of Delaware of the Roth-Kemp tax bill, which embodied the tax rate reductions the President wanted to see adopted.

Four other names that became prominent in the legislative battles of 1981 were Kent Hance (D-Texas), Barber Conable (R-New York), Phil Gramm (D-Texas), and Del Latta (R-Ohio). They were the principal sponsors of the legislation eventually adopted, which contained large segments of the Reagan program. Kent Hance was a youthful boll weevil Democrat from Texas, and Barber Conable a veteran Republican from upstate New York and a specialist in tax issues. Their names were attached to the tax-cutting legislation that finally passed the House on July 29, 1981. Gramm, another boll weevil Democratic congressman, later became a Republican senator, while Del Latta was one of the staunchest antispending Republicans in the House. They led the way in getting our first round of spending cuts through Congress.

Again, contrary to the usual image, the personal leadership of the President was indispensable to the program's success. When the effort was launched, worries about lost revenue dominated Hill discussions—particularly from Dole and Domenici on the Republican side, but also, of course, from the Democratic leadership in the House. In the spring and early summer of 1981, doubts were rampant as to whether the program could be adopted at all.

But when Democratic prophecies of defeat were brought to the White House by the legislative team, or by Howard Baker, the President always gave the same answer: "Do what is necessary to get the program adopted. Don't back off. Find out what needs doing and do it. Period." In White House meetings day after day, that message came through loud and clear. The President had supplied the conceptual basis of the program, and he was now throwing into the battle his communications skills to explain it to the public and the political will to stay the course until the plan was adopted.

Given his courage and steadfastness, which I have witnessed in many similar circumstances, I am certain the tax reduction program would not have been adopted under any other President in recent memory. Ronald Reagan, working through his aides and directly with Congress, showed again that behind the pleasant demeanor there was a tough and determined man.

The tax and budget battle was affected, of course, by the attempted assassination of the President on March 30. A surge of sympathy for the President, and deep admiration for his pluck and humor at a moment of mortal peril, swept the country. But his absence from the political fray for almost a month further delayed the cumbersome legislative process. By the end of April, when the President returned to the battle, the program's future was debatable.

While the President was in the hospital, moreover, various press leaks from "senior White House aides" suggested a willingness to compromise his tax program in order to ease the deficit and relieve the "disarray in the markets." In May, Senator Dole announced that he might have trouble getting the package out of the Finance Committee, and Howard Baker joined the doubters by opining that, if we insisted on the full tax package, we would have a problem getting a vote on the budget resolution.

As a result, a case began to take shape for delaying the first phase of the rate reductions. Finally, in response to repeated suggestions from Stockman and his worries about the deficit numbers, the President agreed to change the first year cut to 5 percent, instead of 10, and to have it take effect October 1 rather than retroactively to the first of the year. The second phase, a full 10 percent, would take effect July 1, 1982, with a final 10 percent reduction scheduled for July 1, 1983.

The theory was that reducing and postponing the first tranche of the tax cuts would minimize revenue loss for 1981 and the first half of 1982, while willingness to compromise would help consolidate support from the Republican leadership in the Senate. In addition, since the legislation was not signed into law until August, having it take effect October 1, the beginning of the fiscal year, seemed plausible.

When the smoke had cleared, we had not gotten everything we had hoped for, but we had achieved a great deal. We wound up with an effective rate cut of about 23 percent—the first 5 percent applied to one quarter of 1981 and each of the 10 percent reductions thereafter applied against a progressively lower income base. Still, measured against what had been happening to income taxes under Carter, and what would have happened without Reagan, it was quite a feat, as the ensuing prosperity proved.

In addition, the final legislation included an indexing feature, adjusting brackets beginning in 1985 so that taxpayers would not have to pay higher rates on purely nominal income gains. Indexing, part of the original Reagan program, had been dropped in a conciliatory gesture to Congress. The President was accordingly delighted (though some were not) when Sen. William Armstrong (R-Colorado) offered indexing as an amendment, which carried by a substantial margin in the Senate.

The package also included a number of tax relief provisions for businesses, most notably accelerated cost recovery depreciation features which allowed them to retain the funds needed for new equipment and other capital investment. In fact, tax-cutting on Capitol Hill became so popular that a "bidding war" developed, with members offering a plethora of new tax breaks and the Democrats proposing a tax reduction package that rivaled our own.

In the event, the President carried the day for Conable-Hance with a televised address explaining our three-year approach and indexing. In a gibe at the Democrats, he said their program would work out pretty well "if you're only planning to live two more years." Pointing to charts, he showed their tax line going down, then curving up again, while ours went down and stayed down. (See Chart B)

The calls and letters came pouring in, and on July 29, a coalition of Republicans and boll weevils voted down the Democratic package in favor of Conable-Hance. The Republican Senate followed suit on August 5, and on August 17, 1981, the President signed the Economic Recovery Act (ERTA) into law. The centerpiece of Reaganomics was on the books—a logical extension of the themes that Ronald Reagan had been preaching for two decades. How long it would stay there was another question.

CHART B   KEEPING TAXES DOWN

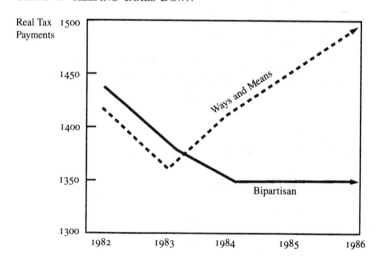

10

TAXES AND
TREACHERY

LOOKING BACK on the legislative battles of 1981, it seems strange to recall that we initially thought spending cuts would be more easily attainable than tax reductions. Our reasoning was that cutting tax rates went against the grain of both liberal Democrats and conservative Republicans who believed we should not be reducing taxes when the federal budget was already in deficit.

As it turned out, it was the other way around: cutting income tax rates was irresistibly popular; candidates who seemed to want to raise them again were swimming against a powerful tide of public feeling— as Walter Mondale discovered in 1984 and Michael Dukakis reconfirmed in 1988. Lowered tax rates on individual income turned out to be an enduring political as well as economic legacy of the Reagan era.

On the spending side, however, the story was different. The power of the spending advocates is enormous, and to mobilize public opinion against them on a piecemeal basis almost impossible. In any battle over a specific program in such fields as welfare, housing, agriculture, or education, the dynamics favor spending; those who benefit from the program are a concentrated bloc with high stakes, while taxpayers are a diffuse group, with relatively low degrees of interest in any individual spending measure. In addition, as discussed, a tremendous percentage of federal spending is locked in through "entitlement" programs and other so-called "uncontrollables."

As a result, we were not nearly so successful in reducing spending as we were in cutting tax rates. While we did in some ways reduce the growth of government expenditure, its built-in nature ensured continuing large deficits—which in turn threatened the tax cuts.

Those of us from California, having come from a state where spending was more susceptible to executive control, were, I think, a little naïve about the tremendous difficulty of reining in the federal budget. When our initial steps were largely negated by the surge of spending during the 1982 recession (a vestige of the previous administration's economic policies), the deficit numbers began to spiral. In very short order, the politics of the deficit dominated the attention of the media, Congress, and the administration itself.

In this respect, the most important player by far was David Stockman—though just *how* important we came to realize only after the fact. To many of us, Stockman was, and remains, an enigma. He is unquestionably brilliant, and an indefatigable worker. These qualities made him, at the beginning of the administration, an invaluable member of the Reagan team. Unfortunately, he had some other attributes as well.

I have alluded to our naïveté about the tremendous thrust of federal spending, and the difficulty of controlling it. Related to this, on my part as well as on the President's, was the assumption that everyone on the Reagan team had a similar view of the problems we faced and a similar commitment to solve them, whatever the difficulties. My approach was that we all knew what the President wanted and that our job was simply to go out and do it.

But as later became apparent, various members of the team thought otherwise. Foremost among these was Stockman, who, increasingly frustrated with the difficulties of our situation, secretly decided that we should give up on the Reagan program. His feelings were not expressed in cabinet meetings, but became abundantly plain as events unfolded. From a fairly early point, Stockman decided it was his mission, not to support Reagan's tax reduction program, but to maneuver the President into backing away from it.

Stockman had not been a member of the Reagan campaign operation and, as he acknowledged, was not a particular fan of the President. At the time of the 1980 election, he was a youthful two-term congressman from Michigan who had made common cause with Kemp's band of supply-siders in the House and had impressed them with his intelligence and zeal. He had been mentioned to us by Kemp (my notes refer to May of 1980) and had helped draft the Republican platform at the Detroit convention.

We did not really become acquainted with Stockman, however, until September, when at Kemp's suggestion he was called in to help us prepare for the first presidential debate, which pitted Reagan against independent candidate John Anderson, a moderate Republican ex-congressman from Illinois. Stockman, a former staffer for Anderson at the House Republican Conference, knew his mental processes and argumentative style. He was ideal for the job, and later played a similar role in preparing Reagan for his even more important debate with Jimmy Carter.

Stockman's quick mind and mastery of detail made a favorable impression on a lot of people, including then-candidate Reagan. He reinforced this by authoring a postelection memo, "Avoiding a GOP Economic Dunkirk," on the crisis confronting us and the steps needed to solve it. [1] This all led to his being nominated as director of the office of management and budget, a post from which Stockman believed he could orchestrate a grand supply-side revolution.

Stockman at the outset fought valiantly to get the budget under control. While economists such as Martin Anderson and Bill Niskanen could analyze the vast complexities of the budget, Stockman was one of the few political types—the only member of the cabinet—who understood it. Accordingly, the rest of us relied on him in budget matters—which had both its good and bad sides.

The good side was that Stockman became a prolific source of ideas for cutting spending. He knew, or learned, the ins and outs of countless federal programs, the overlaps among them, the inequities in their benefit levels, and so on. Often, he knew as much about the programs as the bureaucrats who ran them, which meant he knew far more than virtually all members of Congress and certainly more than the senior members of the administration who were enmeshed in countless other issues.

But there was another side to Stockman that we came to see clearly only toward the end of 1981 and that haunted the administration for many months to come. For one thing, when it came to budget-cutting, he had a "not invented here" mindset, rejecting approaches other than his own.

Sens. Pete Domenici (R-New Mexico) and Ernest Hollings (D-South Carolina), for example, were upset about entitlements and came up with a plan to defer and cut back cost of living adjustments (COLAs) on pensions, such as Social Security and similar federal programs, that could have saved billions of dollars in future years. In like fashion, Rep. Jake Pickle (D-Texas) had a plan to raise the retirement age for Social Security beneficiaries.[2]

Stockman actually *opposed* these efforts since they didn't fit his own budgetary master plan. As he explained it, he first wanted a series of cuts in discretionary programs (amounting to $41 billion in fiscal 1982), to be followed by even tougher cuts in Social Security and other entitlements. Since the Domenici-Hollings and Pickle efforts did not fit this plan Stockman successfully maneuvered to get the administration to oppose them.

At the time, and even more so subsequently, I thought this a mistake. In the first place, given our "window of opportunity," the notion of taking easier cuts first and harder ones later was strategically backwards. If we could not make cuts in the early days when the President's strength was greatest, we would hardly be able to make them later.

Also, the Domenici-Hollings and Pickle proposals had an important and helpful political attribute: both were being sponsored (or cosponsored) by Democrats. Given the trouble Republicans have had with benefit programs in general, and Social Security in particular, Democrat participation was indispensable if we were to move Congress. Had

a similar plan only surfaced from a conservative Republican administration, it would inevitably have drawn political flak—which is exactly
what happened when our program for reforming Social Security was
leaked in May of 1981.

Third, Stockman's thinking was of the all-or-nothing type: If we
rejected partial savings plans, he thought, the situation would become
so bad that something far more sweeping would eventually have to be
adopted to avert enormous deficits. It didn't work out that way, of
course. The implicit lesson is that it is better to take attainable smaller
savings now rather than gamble everything on bigger savings you
might not (and we did not) get in the future. Stockman's strategy made
the best the enemy of the good.

Similar attitudes toward concepts not invented at Stockman's OMB
surfaced in his reaction to the Grace Commission report, a private
survey conducted at the President's behest by a team of two thousand
specialists under the leadership of businessman J. Peter Grace. The
Grace Commission identified some 2,478 specific examples of government waste, ranging from unneeded programs to antiquated management practices, elimination of which could have saved up to *$135
billion annually*. Stockman had nothing but disdain for the Grace
report and did nothing to implement its recommendations.

Likewise, Stockman was contemptuous of our cabinet-wide effort to
reduce the number of federal jobs by 75,000, chiefly through the
process of attrition. Even though this effort, to which several of us gave
constant attention, was worth some $5 billion a year in direct savings to
taxpayers and even more as a symbol of belt-tightening by the government, Stockman treated it as a meaningless exercise. But then no idea
was worthwhile if it did not originate in the OMB.

There was one other problem, unknown to the rest of us—and
particularly alien to those of us accustomed to the openness and
collegiality of the Reagan cabinet in California. That was Stockman's
secretive and brooding nature. As he himself has admitted, he did not
always level with the President or with members of the administration.
There were things he knew, or thought, that he did not tell us—even
though, as we would soon discover, he was not so bashful in talking to
William Greider of the *Washington Post*.

Part of the reason for this, as Stockman complains, was that too many other things were occurring while he was fighting the early battles of the budget. Tax and deregulatory issues, defense and foreign policy, the administration of justice and the courts, staffing the government, all competed for the attention of the President and his cabinet. Getting all the key budget participants to sit down and listen to the voluminous matters Stockman wanted to talk about was often difficult, although more cabinet and presidential time was spent on this subject during the early days than on any other. It would have been much better all the way around if Stockman had spent Saturday mornings with us in the cabinet rather than tape-recording sessions with Greider.

Compounding this problem was Stockman's low opinion of the people he was working with; most of us were not budget specialists and did not have his grasp of all the minutiae of federal programs. This led to what he later described as intellectual arrogance—the assumption that he was making a revolution virtually by himself, aided only by a handful of supply-side allies (from whom he eventually became estranged as well). It also led to one of the most remarkable reversals in the annals of our politics—Stockman's transformation into a tax-hike mole in a tax-cutting government.

Even before the tax cut legislation was passed, Stockman began his litany—the projected reductions were too large, and would lead to huge deficits. We would have to reduce the size of the rate cuts, delay them, cancel part of them once they were in effect, or adopt other tax increases.

Stockman played endless variations on these themes in cabinet meetings, conjuring up bigger deficits, leading to more inflation and higher interest rates (both of which warnings turned out to be wrong). These ideas were presented as if in support of the President's program—trying to make sure that it was not derailed by the deficit problem.

But behind the scenes, Stockman had already crossed his personal Rubicon on the way to increased taxes. This was evident in the Greider interviews, but even more so in what Stockman was doing and saying on a confidential basis outside the cabinet room. This was revealed both in Stockman's memoir, *The Triumph of Politics*, and in Laurence Barrett's chronicle of the early days of the administration, which was obviously written with cooperation from Stockman and Dick Darman.

In his book, *Gambling with History*, Barrett quotes from confidential memoranda prepared by Stockman and Darman in 1981-82 and from agenda items and minutes of legislative strategy meetings. He also makes liberal references to the statements, motivations, and tactical planning of Stockman, Darman, and the "Baker group" throughout this period. This account shows Stockman and Darman becoming convinced by the late summer of 1981 that tax rate reductions would be calamitous for the economy and setting to work surreptitiously to change the program.

Barrett reports members of the "Baker group" as believing the President needed to be "educated" on the folly of reducing tax rates and the need for increased revenues to "reassure the markets." He also discusses the methods by which the Stockman-Darman axis tried to keep people who supported the tax rate reductions from talking to the President.

At one point, Barrett notes, "supply-siders were still getting through to the President," so suitable measures were taken. "This was not difficult because Deaver and Darman between them controlled most of the traffic, human and documentary, that reached Reagan. Important business leaders who favored compromise were brought in for private conversations. Supply-siders like Jack Kemp, who opposed any tinkering with taxes, were excluded." When some visiting economists actually supported the President's view, "Baker and Stockman concluded that this session was a net loss in their effort to turn Reagan around."[3]

Stockman himself more or less confirms all this. The time factors are particularly striking, since the attempt to derail the Reagan program preceded the date when the rate reductions actually took effect. Stockman says, for instance, "I finally understood that the war was over. . . . *On Friday, September 18, Darman and I met in my office to try to design the retreat*" (emphasis added).[4]

The significance of this date is that the first (and very small) reductions had not yet been implemented—and would not be for another twelve days, thanks to the delays we had accepted. Stockman and Darman, that is, had already given up on a three-year tax rate reduction that had not even gone into effect.

The contrast between the public and private Stockman came vividly to attention when William Greider's article appeared in the December 1981 issue of *The Atlantic*. Among other things, Stockman told Greider that "supply-side is just trickle down"—a way to get tax breaks for the wealthy while supposedly helping others in the long run—and the Reagan program was a "Trojan horse" way of accomplishing this. When the President read these words, he was stunned, and, as described in the press, took Stockman on a "trip to the woodshed."

Staff reactions were even more emphatic. Most of us thought Stockman should have been fired outright—not only for his disloyalty in leaking, but because of his obvious lack of belief in the Reagan program. Worse still, many of his comments about the intent and impact of the program were absolutely untrue and severely damaging to the President. All good reasons, I thought, for firing him.

Among the senior staffers, only Jim Baker thought Stockman should be kept on. He had a talk with Stockman and then arranged a private luncheon for him with the President. The line that Jim suggested, and Stockman followed, was that the Greider interviews were a blunder for which he was profoundly sorry. The President, as generous as ever, accepted Dave's apology and allowed him to stay on. (To my recollection, this was the only case in our long association when the President did not accept my advice to fire someone. I still wish he had.)

While the "Trojan horse" and "trickle down" statements got most of the attention, other things Stockman said were even more significant—and more indicative of things to come. Greider, for instance, recounted Stockman's growing obsession with the deficit and the resulting desire to cut back on the tax reductions. Stockman, Greider wrote, "wanted a compromise on the tax bill which would substantially reduce its drain on the Federal Treasury and thus moderate the fiscal damage of Reaganomics."[5] This proved to be an accurate summary of Stockman's thinking from there on out.

Ed Meese, Ronald Reagan, Martin Anderson, and Jim Lake prepare for Reagan's official 1979 announcement of his candidacy for the presidency.

Briefing session for the New Hampshire debates during the February 1980 campaign. L-R: Campaign Director William J. Casey; (partially hidden) Monroe Browne; LTG Daniel Graham; Robert Carleson; Campaign Chief of Staff Ed Meese; the Candidate; Richard Allen; Gary Jones; Jeffrey Bell; Congressman Jack Kemp.

Ed Meese being welcomed to the White House by President and Mrs. Carter during the transition visit of President-elect Ronald Reagan. 20 November 1980.

Speaker of the House of Representatives Tip O'Neill talks with prominent Washington representative Tom Korologos; Chief of Staff James Baker; and Counsellor Edwin Meese during preinaugural visit in 1980.

President Reagan and his staff celebrate his inauguration in the Oval Office. L-R: Michael Deaver, James Baker, Edwin Meese, James Brady, Richard Allen. 20 January 1981.

Counsellor to the President Edwin Meese makes a point at the first staff meeting in the Oval Office on the day after Inauguration. L-R: Meese, Deputy Chief of Staff Michael Deaver; National Security Advisor Richard Allen, Press Secretary James Brady; and (seated) Chief of Staff James Baker. The President has his back to the camera. 21 January 1981.

The Meese family after the Counsellor to the President was sworn in on 21 January 1981. L-R: son, Scott; daughter, Dana Lynne; wife, Ursula; Meese; and son Michael.

Edwin Meese greeting British Prime Minister Margaret Thatcher during her official visit on 20 February 1981.

The President and his colleagues enjoy a story while toasting the retirement of Walter Cronkite from the CBS Evening News. 3 March 1981.

The Meese family with President Reagan in the Oval Office, 24 March 1981. R-L: Counsellor Edwin Meese III; his daughter, Dana; the President; brother, Myron Meese; mother, Leone Meese; and father, Edwin Meese, Jr.

President Reagan meets with Egyptian President Anwar Sadat at the White House. 5 August 1981.

The "Troika": James A. Baker III, Chief of Staff; Edwin Meese III, Counsellor to the President; Michael K. Deaver, Deputy Chief of Staff. In the Colonnade outside the Oval Office. 2 December 1981.

President Reagan and Ed Meese on board "Marine One," the presidential helicopter. 24 March 1982.

Ronald Reagan addressing the British Parliament at Westminster, 8 June 1982. This was where he talked about "consigning Communism to the ash-heap of history."

Counsellor Edwin Meese shares a light moment with the President at his desk in the Oval Office as Aide David Fisher enters to escort Reagan to his next appointment. 16 September 1982.

National Security Adviser William P. Clark briefs President Reagan aboard Air Force One. 29 June 1983.

Ed Meese and Ronald Reagan talk at the President's ranch near Santa Barbara, California.
27 November 1982.

President Reagan meets with Prime Minister Eugenia Charles, of Dominica, who represented the Organization of East Caribbean States, just prior to the military operation that liberated Grenada. 25 October 1983.

A young girl kisses the runway at the Charleston Air Force Base as she and her companions arrived from the island of Grenada. The medical students were the first ones to leave the island which was taken over by U.S. forces. 25 October 1983.

Treasury Secretary Don Regan jokes with the President as he prepares to trade jobs with White House Chief of Staff James Baker. L-R: Michael Deaver, Baker, the President, Edwin Meese, and Regan. 8 January 1985.

A farewell photo with the President for Ed Meese's White House staff. L-R: John Richardson; Edwin Meese; Carol Hallene; Dorothy Kuhn; Kim Riley; Cathie Appleyard; Cynthia Duncan; John Marion; Marilee Melvin; Kenneth Cribb; Neil Hammerstrom; and Bruce Chapman.

For Stockman never did change back to his original jersey. He had not, apparently, apologized so much for the views expressed to Greider as for the fact that they had gotten into print. He was now a committed partisan of raising taxes, and continued working behind the scenes against the Reagan program.

"Government by leak," meantime, swung into action. Both before and after the Greider interview, a flow of press leaks was being used to get the President to back off from his no-more taxes stand. Daily stories filled the media, quoting various "aides," "senior officials," and "advisors to the President" to the effect that he would have to change his course if the nation was to avert disaster.

In a three-day span in December, for example, the *New York Times* quoted a White House aide as saying that "a full-scale battle" was under way "for the soul of the Reagan administration and the mind of Ronald Reagan"; Joseph Kraft wrote in the *Washington Post* that members of the President's staff were trying to bring him out of his "dream world"; and columnists Evans and Novak asserted that the President had "to fight better than two-thirds of his economic team to save his program."[6]

On December 17, the President decided to scotch such talk in a nationally televised address, saying he would not, repeat not, reverse his stand on taxes. "You can balance the budget by robbing the people," he said, but "you will find you have torpedoed the economy. The only proper way to balance the budget is through control of government spending."[7] This statement had a curious aftermath, as reported by Howell Raines of the *New York Times*:

> Privately, the President complained, according to aides, that his staff was not resisting the effort of the budget director, David A. Stockman, to maneuver him into calling for higher taxes. Publicly, he contradicted senior advisers who back Mr. Stockman by saying on Friday that he was "against increasing taxes in any way." This led to an extraordinary spectacle. Minutes after Mr. Reagan's press conference, James A. Baker 3d, the chief of staff, dispatched the White House spokesmen, David R. Gergen and Larry Speakes, to tell reporters the President had not really meant what he said. . . .[8]

During this period, Stockman tried to implicate me in his plans. As he recounts in his book, after he and Jim Baker agreed that the second and third phases of the tax cut would have to be postponed to bring the budget closer to balance, they decided to make a run at me for support before broaching it to the President. Stockman accordingly met with me to present his enormous deficit projections and argue that the President should suspend the rate reductions.

Stockman's figures were alarming, and I agreed that the facts should be presented immediately to the President. This was in keeping with my view that the President should always be aware of all relevant opinions before making a decision: it did not mean I favored the proposed option. I was, of course, concerned about the deficit projections, but I also believed that the tax cuts were vital for our economic recovery and long-range expansion.

It did not take long for the issue to be decided. Stockman had barely finished presenting his analysis of the deficit and his proposal to postpone the tax-cut schedule for the next two years when Don Regan exploded, saying that this would kill the Reagan economic program. Despite my misgivings about the deficit, I agreed. The President needed little urging from us. Being opposed to any further dilution of his tax relief plan (he felt he had already compromised enough when he agreed to halve the first year's cut), he rejected Stockman's plan and stated that the tax reductions were to go forward as scheduled.

History has proved Reagan correct, for his program halted the recession and began the longest peacetime economic expansion in history. But Stockman was angry and, in his memoir, treats my siding with the President as some sort of betrayal, which it was not. I believed the President should get all the facts, not that his staff should gang up to make him accept a specific choice. In this respect, Dave Stockman and I had very different views about our obligations to the President.

This instigated a campaign of leaks against the President, led by some of his most senior officials—so far as I know, an unprecedented maneuver. For a period of months, as Stockman puts it, he and others were engaged in an "open conspiracy" to force the President to change his mind.[9] Those involved included Stockman, Baker, Darman, Mike

Deaver, powerful Republicans in the Senate, and a substantial portion of the Washington press corps.

If ever there was a time of testing for Ronald Reagan's commitment to tax reduction, this surely was it. Yet the President never wavered, once more refuting the view that he was a docile puppet of his staff. The episode did demonstrate, however, a weakness in the Reagan management style: his continued confidence in Stockman even after so systematic a betrayal. If any Reagan vulnerability was displayed in this episode, it was excessive kindness to those who had abused his trust.

In his State of the Union address, January 26, 1982, the President gave a definitive answer to the Stockman tax-hike crusade. "The doubters," he said, "would have us turn back the clock with tax increases that would offset the personal tax-rate reductions already passed by this Congress. Raise present taxes to cut future deficits, they tell us. Well, I do not believe we should buy their argument. Higher taxes would not mean lower deficits. . . .

"Raising taxes won't balance the budget. It will encourage more government spending and less private investment. . . . So I will not ask you to try to balance the budget on the back of American tax-payers. . . . I will seek no tax increases this year and I have no intention of retreating from our basic program of tax relief. . . . I will stand by my word."[10]

That seemed to have settled the argument. Stockman and Company had failed. Mike Deaver, for one, was contrite. "I learned something from the process," he said. "Never try to talk any man who holds deep convictions out of them for reasons of political expediency because it will destroy him. We almost destroyed Ronald Reagan, and I was one of the people arguing for this."[11]

The campaign to reverse the tax cuts, however, did not stop; in fact, after a brief hiatus, it accelerated—though on a slightly different track. Having failed in the direct approach, the tax hike forces decided to go by another route.

In the spring of 1982, numerous senators and congressmen contin-ued to agitate for an increase in taxes. Sen. Robert Dole had proposed a $105 billion, three-year package which would repeal the third year of the rate reductions; the Democrats countered with a proposal for $165 billion in added taxes over three years, also canceling the third-year tax cut. Although the President had stated he would not go for this, there was continued interest in seeking a compromise with Congress.

This effort at compromise, which did in fact culminate in higher taxes, began innocently enough—or so it seemed. Early in 1982 it was suggested—both by the administration and Congress—that representatives from Capitol Hill and the White House meet in bipartisan discussions to seek agreement on a deficit reduction plan. The reasons given were appealing: it would show both parties cooperating to solve an urgent economic problem; it would build confidence among the business community; it would reassure the stock markets; and it would encourage the Federal Reserve to lower interest rates. So, in mid-March the President authorized the White House to participate in the negotiations. It seemed harmless at the start, because no agreements were to be binding until they were approved by President Reagan and the Republican legislators on the one side, and by House Speaker O'Neill, Senate Majority Leader Byrd, and the Democrats on the other. So began what, in my opinion, became the "Debacle of 1982."

The members of the negotiating group soon became known as the "Gang of 17"—the number of participants. The House team included such fiscal policy heavyweights as Richard Bolling, Dan Rostenkowski, and Jim Jones, while the Senate group was led by Bob Dole, Pete Domenici, and Ernest Hollings. The executive branch was represented by David Stockman, Jim Baker, Dick Darman, and Ken Duberstein (who had become head of legislative liaison early in the year, succeeding Max Friedersdorf). Since the mission was supposedly limited to exploring options with the Congress, it was handled as a strictly legislative matter, and none of us from the policy side of the White House was included. I had been assured that we, along with the President, would be thoroughly briefed on any proposals that might emerge.

In retrospect, not having a policy perspective in the discussions contributed to the unfortunate outcome. The Gang of 17 negotiations were a good example of how "process" can shape policy—rather than the other way around. From the outset, the basic idea of the GOP participants was to trade some kind of concessions on the tax front for a Democratic agreement on spending cutbacks. (Ironically, almost the same situation occurred eight years later, in 1990, when taxes were again unwisely raised. The arguments for that year's "budget summit" and even some of the participants were the same as in 1982.)

The Gang conducted its meetings at Blair House, at Jim Baker's home, at the residence of Vice President Bush, and at other unusual locations to conceal the meetings from the press, and also from others in the administration and Congress. By the time the package was finally presented to the President, it was treated virtually as a *fait accompli*—something to which "the process" had committed us. The President, along with cabinet members and senior advisors not in the Gang, was briefed on the TEFRA proposal and participated in decision meetings with congressional leaders; but the legislative package was rolling ahead with such momentum—in the news media and among both parties in Congress—that it would have been virtually impossible to stop or even modify it.

The negotiators recognized that Ronald Reagan would be hard to sell on any tax increases. So they included the one ploy they felt might overcome his resistance: a large reduction in federal spending in return for a modest rise in business (but not individual) taxes. The proposal as presented to Reagan by Stockman and Baker called for three dollars of budget reductions (composed of both spending cuts and debt interest savings) for every dollar of tax increases.

The resulting legislative package was called the "Tax Equity and Fiscal Responsibility Act of 1982," or TEFRA. This measure—a series of increased business and excise taxes, removal of business tax deductions, and stepped-up enforcement activities—was estimated to bring in $98 billion in a three-year period, and $228 billion over a total of five years.

This proposal, presented to the President and the concerned cabinet members, including myself, sounded persuasive at the time. Believing it the only way we could bring the spending side of the budget under control, I agreed that we should pursue the compromise, as did most of my colleagues. While the President remained concerned about the tax increases, he also accepted the package. As he expressed it:

To win congressional approval of additional spending cuts and show the financial community we were serious about reducing the deficit, I made a deal with the congressional Democrats in 1982, agreeing to support a limited loophole-closing tax increase to raise more than $98.3 billion over three years in return for their agreement to cut spending by $280 billion during the same period. [12]

Still relying on Dave Stockman's deficit projections, and the supposed need for a compromise with the Democrats, Reagan not only went forward with the agreement but strongly defended it against its critics (including some of his closest supporters), repeatedly stressing the three-to-one ratio of spending cuts to tax increases. But Reagan's good faith was not matched by Congress.

The Democrats' strategy was simple—let the Republican party take the lead in raising taxes—with Dole becoming the point man in Congress. Thus, despite our alleged deal, not a single Democrat voted for TEFRA when it passed the Senate. And when it came time for the package to be voted in the House, the Democratic leadership waived the usual procedure of hearings and let the Republican Senate bill sail through.

This step was particularly unusual because the Constitution provides that "all bills for raising revenue shall originate in the House of Representatives." The concept goes back to the ancient English and later the American colonial tradition, holding that taxes on the people should originate in the legislative body closest to them (at least in theory); i.e., the House of Commons in England and the House of Representatives in the United States. That the Democrats in the House were willing to waive their constitutional prerogatives in order that the tax hike bear a Republican label testified to the political motives at work.

As it turned out, the ultimate fate of the TEFRA package involved more than just political game-playing. The basis of the agreement was almost totally negated by subsequent congressional action. While the tax increases were promptly enacted, the promised budget cuts never materialized. After the tax bill passed, some legislators of both parties even claimed that there had been no real commitment to the three-to-one ratio. It was a sadder but wiser President who wrote, "the Demo-crats reneged on their pledge and we never got those cuts."[13] In fact, spending for fiscal year 1983 was some $48 billion higher than the budget targets and no progress was made in lowering the deficit. Even tax receipts for that year went down—a lingering effect of the reces-sion, which the additional business taxes did nothing to redress.

I believe that the TEFRA compromise—the "Debacle of 1982"—was the greatest domestic error of the Reagan administration. It was a complete departure from our tax-cutting mandate, failed to reduce the growth of government spending, did not decrease the deficit, and divided the President from some of his most ardent supporters. Judged by the results, TEFRA was not only a mistake, it was an object lesson in how *not* to reduce the deficit. (We did learn that few members of Congress can be counted on when you try to cut federal spending.) It also contributed greatly to what Ronald Reagan considered one of his biggest disappointments as President: the inability to do more to cut federal spending.

But there was one redeeming feature: it left intact the individual income tax rate reductions that had been passed the previous year.

11

THE TRIUMPH OF REAGANOMICS

P OPULAR AND MEDIA MISCONCEPTIONS about the origin of "Reaganomics," bad as they have been, are relatively minor compared to those about the economic and fiscal impacts of the program. Of the scores of books and hundreds of articles that have poured out about the Reagan years in Washington, only a handful provide any comprehensible data on this subject.

Since the economic agenda was the centerpiece of the Reagan program, an accurate understanding of what it meant in terms of taxes, budgets, deficits, and other outcomes is essential to any judgment of the President's place in history. The economic program was the first matter the administration tackled, and it dominated discussion of domestic politics for years. It was the most consistently attacked and most ardently defended of all the President's initiatives.

The facts concerning the Reagan tax and budget record must therefore be reviewed with care. At the risk of swamping the reader with numbers, this chapter will attempt to do just that. The charts and tables printed here are admittedly not as entertaining as talk of astrology, or dress designers, or even "gaffes," but they are essential to an understanding of what did and didn't happen in the Reagan era.

Foremost among the prevailing misconceptions is that Reagan's "massive tax cuts" sharply reduced the revenues of the federal government. Although this idea is repeated time and again, those making the assertion seldom bother to cite the fiscal record. The "lost revenues" of the Reagan era have assumed a mythological status akin to that of the lost Continent of Atlantis.

A close second in the array of misconceptions, as noted, is that the President imposed stringent "budget cuts" that harmed the poor, the homeless, and the hungry. Even these economies, however, were allegedly not sufficient to make up for the "gargantuan tax cuts." Reagan supposedly depleted federal receipts so much that even his skinflint budget policies could not keep spending down enough to fit the shrunken revenue.

The only exception to this policy was the "trillion dollar defense buildup." While cutting back on everything else, the critics continue, the Reagan government squandered billions on the Pentagon, further contributing to our deficit problems.

Such were the major features of the Reagan program, as portrayed in countless articles, books, and television news accounts. But a survey of the tax and budget data shows this picture to be at total variance with the truth.

As the accompanying graphic (Table I) shows, federal revenues did *not* decrease in the Reagan era. On the contrary, they increased dramatically—almost exactly *doubling* in the decade of the 1980s. This increase was well in advance of the rise in median family income for the period. Any family that doubled its income in a decade would think it had done rather well. But for Uncle Sam, it was claimed, this was an era of "lost revenues."

As this table also shows, federal taxes as a percent of Gross National Product were virtually identical when Reagan left the White House in 1989 as when he ran against Carter in 1980 (19.2 vs. 19.4). On average, federal revenues were slightly *higher* in the Reagan era than during the four Carter years (18.9 vs. 18.8).

TABLE I

FEDERAL SPENDING AND TAXATION IN BILLIONS OF $ AND AS % OF GNP

	Taxes	% GNP	Spending	% GNP
1977	356	18.4	409	21.2
1978	399	18.4	459	21.1
1979	463	18.9	503	20.6
1980	517	19.4	590	22.1
1981	599	20.1	678	22.7
1982	617	19.7	745	23.8
1983	600	18.1	808	24.3
1984	666	18.1	851	23.1
1985	734	18.6	946	23.9
1986	769	18.4	990	23.7
1987	854	19.3	1,004	22.7
1988	909	19.0	1,064	22.2
1989	990	19.2	1,142	22.2

Source: Office of Management and Budget

The same was true, only more so, in terms of federal spending. While receipts were going up from $517 billion to $1.03 trillion in the decade of the 1980s, a hike of 99.4 percent, federal spending increased still more—growing by 112 percent. As a share of GNP, federal outlays were 22.1 percent in 1980 and 22.2 percent in 1989—having risen as high as 24 percent in 1983.

Simply looking at these numbers refutes the standard misconceptions. On the face of it, in the aggregate, there were neither tax nor budget cuts in the Reagan era. Both trend lines continued to grow, although the spending line grew faster than the taxing line. How, then, is it possible for Reagan critics to argue that he presided over "massive tax cuts" that deprived the federal coffers of hundreds of billions of dollars in revenues? On the other hand, how is it possible for Reagan backers to claim that he brought about substantial changes that benefited the average taxpayer?

To answer these questions, it is necessary to recall how the tax and budget system works, and in particular how it had been working under Jimmy Carter. This information—a matter of public record—is one of the best-kept secrets of the liberal welfare state.

The secret, in a nutshell, is that the system runs itself, and does so at a constant upward angle. The federal fiscal machinery, as discussed in chapter 7, operates on autopilot, with huge increases built into the very structure of the budget. Thus, the spending interests harvest sizable revenue hikes each year simply by letting the machinery run of its own accord. As we in the Reagan White House discovered, it is enormously difficult to get these processes under control.

On the taxing side, the built-in increases we inherited were of three types: those resulting from the growth of the economy, providing a larger base from which to draw receipts; already legislated increases in the Social Security tax, which had been voted in 1977 to be phased in over a span of years; and so-called "bracket creep," which pushed tax-payers to higher nominal income levels and thereby to a higher percent-age of taxation even if their purchasing power remained the same.

Neither President Reagan nor his advisors had any objection to the first of these; a natural revenue rise through expansion of the economy was a supply-side effect expected from recovery. And the Social Security increases, whatever their economic merits, were openly de-bated and voted by Congress, as befits our system of representative government.

But the effects of bracket creep were far more insidious, for they allowed the federal government to profiteer secretly from inflation. This process punished taxpayers not once but twice—debasing the purchasing power of their dollars, then hitting them with higher taxes as their (nominal) incomes moved up the tax scale. As Federal Reserve economists Stephen Meyer and Robert Rossana described the process, as it existed prior to adoption of the Reagan program: "Husbands and wives who filed joint returns in 1980 and who earned a $30,000 taxable income paid $6,238 in federal income taxes for that year. Now suppose that all prices rise 10 percent. If taxable income also rises by 10 percent (enough to preserve purchasing power), these households would pay $7,348 in federal income taxes—an increase in tax payments of *nearly 18 percent.*"* ¹

This process, combined with increases in Social Security levies, was driving taxes relentlessly higher. And these hikes were more than matched by corresponding hikes in spending—also largely automatic. As a result, federal outlays grew from 19-plus percent of GNP in the early 1970s to 22 percent under Carter, again with prospects of becoming even larger. What the American people confronted in 1980, therefore, was an escalating system of built-in tax and budget hikes for the benefit of the spending interests.

The Washington establishment, for obvious reasons, wanted to keep this system in place. As matters stood, it could secretly transfer billions of dollars from the taxpayers to the government without the public realizing what was happening, and without any inconvenient votes on taxes.

Unsurprisingly, the response to all of this by the Carter administration had been—more of the same. The 1980 Economic Report of the President, for instance, explicitly embraced the concept of bracket creep as a method of increasing revenues: "Since individuals will be moving into higher brackets as their incomes increase, the share of personal income taken by federal income taxes will rise. Social Security liabilities are scheduled to increase in January 1981 by $18 billion." The report concluded that this rise in taxes combined with limited growth of federal outlays would bring the budget into balance. † ²

The bland assumption that this was a proper way to balance the

---

* This is exactly what happened to millions of taxpayers as federal spending and inflation accelerated in the 1970s. In 1965, before the onset of the Great Society, a four-person median-income family was in the 19 percent federal tax bracket; in 1980, a family in the same relative income position was at the top of the 28 percent bracket, fast approaching a 32 percent marginal tax rate. A family at two times the median income in 1965 was in the 22 percent bracket; by 1980, it faced a top rate of *49 percent.*

† Carter projections envisioned federal taxes rising to 22 percent of GNP by 1984, at which point they would have equaled the then current level of federal spending. As economist Micky Levy notes, "in President Carter's last submitted budget, spending was projected to rise at a 10.3 percent annual rate during 1981-84, and to remain above 22 percent in each year. *A whopping 54.9 percent budgeted rise in revenues from 1981 to 1984 (15.7 percent annually), driven by inflation-induced bracket creep, was expected to eliminate the deficit and generate a large surplus in 1984*" (emphasis added).

budget ignored the terrible burden on the taxpayer; it also implied that there was no connection between the downward drift of the economy and the upward thrust of spending and taxation. President Reagan and his team saw matters otherwise: piling on still more taxes would be a disaster for the economy.

The constant emphasis of Stockman and others on "lost revenues" notwithstanding, the Reagan program was actually a fairly modest effort to *keep the situation from getting worse*. Sizable tax hikes had already kicked in against American taxpayers in the 1970s and would continue to do so in the 1980s. What the Reagan reductions amounted to was a *partial rollback of this continuing increase*. As the *National Journal* put it, projecting the impact of the Reagan program: "Tax increases between 1977 and 1981 more than offset the coming tax cuts. No category of taxpayer will have a significantly lower tax burden in 1984 than in 1977."[3] (See Table II)

As it worked out, because the Reagan tax cuts were diluted and delayed, they were scarcely able to keep pace with the automatic hikes. Bracket creep would continue until 1985, when indexing eliminated it,

TABLE II
PER CENT OF INCOME FOR FEDERAL TAXES, FAMILY OF FOUR

1977 Income	Old Law—'77	New Law—'84
$ 5,000	− 0.2%	5.9%
$10,000	10.2	13.6
$20,000	16.7	17.7
$30,000	20.0	21.2
$50,000	23.8	25.5

PER CENT OF INCOME FOR FEDERAL TAXES—SINGLE TAXPAYER

$ 5,000	11.3	14.4
$10,000	17.8	17.5
$20,000	20.9	22.0
$30,000	22.9	24.4
$50,000	27.9	28.3

Source: *National Journal*

and the scheduled Social Security tax hikes (with some others added in 1983) continued as well. The rate reductions for 1981 amounted to only 1.25 percent, which subtracted less than $4 billion from federal revenues. This was easily overwhelmed by the continuing tax hikes for the year. As Don Regan noted, "We have not had major tax cuts . . . bracket creep and Social Security tax increases produced roughly a $15 billion tax increase for 1981."[4]

In short, the revenue "lost" by the Reagan tax reductions was actually a further huge, unlegislated hike that didn't happen. Instead of an aggregate decrease in revenue, there was a sizable net increase— but not *as big* an increase as the spending forces had been expecting. In the topsy-turvy world of Washington, as noted, such lesser increases translate into massive "cuts."

As to how much revenue was lost, even in this way of thinking, the standard version also needs correction. Contrary to popular belief, Reagan never thought—or stated—that the rate reductions would "pay for themselves" in the sense of providing sufficient revenues to fund all federal spending at prevailing levels. In all our discussions on the subject, I never once heard the President or any of his advisors say anything of the sort. What he did say was that tax reductions would spur economic growth, and that a revenue feedback would accompany an expanded economy.

There is considerable evidence that this is exactly what occurred. As the economy grew and personal incomes recovered from stagflation, the new lower rates brought in a steadily mounting flow of federal income. Research by Professor Lindsey and others indicates that two-thirds to three-quarters of the revenue "lost" by the rate reductions was recaptured in this manner.

Part of the problem in assessing revenue feedbacks is the difficulty of measuring something hypothetical—namely, what would have happened *in the absence* of the Reagan program. The critics, in essence, argue that the economy would have expanded anyway, even without the Reagan rate reductions, thereby providing both a bigger economic base *and* higher tax rates. Recalling the performance of Carternomics, this prospect seems remote. The more likely outcome would have been a continued decline of the economy under the burden of taxes and inflation.*

The fixation on "lost revenues," moreover, considers the matter exclusively from the standpoint of the government. This is typical of the establishment, which tends to view the economy and individual taxpayers chiefly in terms of how much they contribute to the Federal Treasury. From the standpoint of the taxpayers, however, the notion of lost revenues sounds rather more attractive; "lost revenue" is money they don't fork over to Uncle Sam.

Another major change of the Reagan era was the rapid decline in the rate of increase in consumer prices. Stockman and liberal spokesmen such as Walter Heller claimed the Reagan reductions would lead to runaway inflation. This, of course, never happened. On the contrary, the rate of increase in the Consumer Price Index fell from double digits in 1979–80 to an average rate of 3.3 percent in 1981–86, the lowest level since the early 1960s.

The sudden collapse of inflation took everyone by surprise, including our own economic forecasters. From a fiscal standpoint, this was not an unmixed blessing, since the lower rate of nominal GNP increase meant lower than anticipated revenues, contributing to the deficit. Again, however, this viewed the matter from the standpoint of the government. For the average taxpayer, lower inflation meant that

---

* This point is explored by Lindsey in his book, *The Growth Experiment* (New York, Basic Books; 1990). Using tax returns from 34,000 taxpayers over a six-year period, Lindsey and his associates tracked economic and fiscal patterns before and after the rate reductions. Their conclusion was that there was in fact some revenue loss, but that feedback from economic growth made this much smaller than suggested.

Under "static analysis," Lindsey notes, the five-year loss from the Reagan program would have amounted to $324 billion. This assumes that the reductions had *no* effect whatever in spurring economic growth, and that the constantly mounting tax rates and inflation of the Carter era (which had generated the previous decline) would have produced a boom like that which followed the 1981 reductions.

Factoring in economic growth from supply-side effects, Lindsey and his colleagues came up with a very different reading. All told, they estimated net losses for the period amounted to $80.5 billion— meaning that $240 billion or so of the static analysis shortfall was made up as a result of the recovery. In this computerized analysis, feedback effects recouped three-quarters of the receipts assumed to have been forfeited by the cuts.

dollars earned were not losing purchasing power at such an alarming rate.

While control of the money supply and hence inflation is vested in the Federal Reserve Board, the President was steadfast in supporting the Fed's stance of monetary restraint—too much so in the thinking of some of his staff. He never wavered, even in the dark recession days of 1982. I was frequently involved in meetings with Federal Reserve Board Chairman Paul Volcker, and the message was always the same—the President backed the board's approach.

Reagan policies helped relieve inflation in another way as well. Since inflation is a ratio between dollars and output, restarting the economic engines and getting greater production can also contribute to price restraint. In both respects, the Reagan program was the opposite of Carternomics, which featured high rates of money growth and stagnating output.

The Reagan policies contributed to recovery in three obvious ways: first, by leaving more purchasing power in the hands of private citizens; second, by cutting marginal tax rates on extra dollars of income, encouraging additional investment, work, and entrepreneurial risk; and third, by helping to slow the rate of increase in government spending.

Thanks to lower tax and inflation rates, American citizens were able to keep more dollars of their income, and those dollars were depreciating less rapidly in terms of purchasing power. As a result, for the first time in a decade, the average citizen had a substantial increase in disposable real income.

In 1973, as Table III shows, per capita disposable income (measured in constant dollars) was $9,042, which rose to $9,829 by 1979. During Carter's latter years, this number actually began to fall, and in 1982 it was $9,725—little net change in the span of a decade. Beginning in 1983, however, the numbers started moving in a positive direction. By 1990, per capita real income measured on this scale hit $11,793—more than $2,000 higher than it had been when Reagan ran against Jimmy Carter.

In terms of marginal tax rates, as noted, average citizens were being moved into higher brackets by inflation, and would have been stuck in

TABLE III
DISPOSABLE PERSONAL INCOME IN
CONSTANT (1982) DOLLARS

Year	Per Capita Income
1973	9,042
1974	8,867
1975	8,944
1976	9,175
1977	9,381
1978	9,735
1979	9,829
1980	9,722
1981	9,769
1982	9,725
1983	9,930
1984	10,419
1985	10,625
1986	10,929
1987	11,012
1988	11,337
1989	11,680
1990	11,793

Source: Tax Foundation

those or even steeper brackets had the Carter policies continued. The top rate was at 70 percent when Reagan came in. The 1981 package cut the top rate to 50 percent and the average marginal rate to 34 percent, reversing the long-term upward push of this important economic hurdle. The effects of such changes on economic effort should be apparent.*

For a variety of reasons, the spending numbers of the federal government are even more important for the economy than are the

* Under the assumptions used by Carter economic planners, as Professor Lindsey observes, "the average marginal tax rate would have been roughly 44 percent instead of just 34 percent. . . . Critics of ERTA . . . must believe that we could have imposed a 44 percent marginal tax rate on the tax base, instead of a 34 percent rate, without affecting the size of the base." (In the 1986 tax package, of course, the top rate was reduced to 28 percent.)

taxing numbers; and, as discussed, this was an area where we had considerable trouble. The continued upward arc of spending while the tax line continued as before was the principal reason for the deficit.

On the other hand, Reagan's refusal to let the tax line continue soaring contributed to restraints on outlays. Sen. Daniel Moynihan of New York theorized that the Reagan rate reductions were a cynical ploy designed to bloat the deficit, thus barring the addition of more programs to the budget. This attributed levels of cunning to the administration to which not even David Stockman or Richard Darman would lay claim.

There was, of course, no such scheme, and certainly no welcoming of the tremendous deficits that loomed. No one who knew anything about our discussions in the White House could have believed the Moynihan theory for a minute. Still, the premise behind Moynihan's thinking contained a grain of truth: the refusal to expand available revenues inevitably put a damper on further extravagance by Congress.

This is confirmed by the fiscal record when attempts were made to cut the deficit by raising taxes. TEFRA was a prime example, but only one of several. All told, there were a half-dozen such "budget summits" in the period 1982–90 aimed at "reducing" the deficit through increased taxes. In every case, as shown in Table IV, the budget results were just the opposite.

The reason for these outcomes is fairly plain: when Congress knows more money is being made available, its reflexive impulse is not to curtail spending, but to increase it. Thus, instead of the three-to-one budget cuts in exchange for TEFRA, Congress (and the recession) gave us stepped-up spending. In like manner, when a $158 billion tax hike was negotiated with Congress in 1990, the immediate response of House appropriations committees was to jack up the spending bills an average of 12 percent. There always is, and always will be, far more demand for spending than there is money. Making more money available simply feeds the spenders' appetite.

The clearest expression of this logic surfaced in the second Reagan term with the adoption of the Gramm-Rudman-Hollings Budget Act of 1985. Deprived of still more tax revenue, Congress moved to enact a series of mandatory deficit reductions, to be reached through auto-

TABLE IV
NEGOTIATED DEFICIT TARGETS VS. ANNUAL DEFICITS

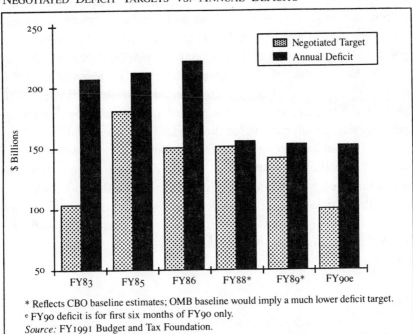

* Reflects CBO baseline estimates; OMB baseline would imply a much lower deficit target.
e FY90 deficit is for first six months of FY90 only.
Source: FY1991 Budget and Tax Foundation.

matic cuts, if targets were not met by statutory deadlines. While Gramm-Rudman limits could be and were evaded, they acted as a general restraint on the spending impulse.

As Table I shows, federal spending continued its steady upward march as a share of national output through 1983–85, topping out at about 24 percent of GNP. In 1986, when Gramm-Rudman first took effect, this particular trend line was reversed and started moving downward. Because more money was not being made available, the spenders were forced to slacken the pace of outlay increase.

The net result was that growth of domestic spending was slowed dramatically. After rising at rates of 10 percent a year, and more in the period 1982–85, the pace of federal outlays declined in the latter years of Reagan: 4.7 percent in 1986, 1.3 in 1987, 6.1 in 1988. Having plateaued at 24 percent of GNP in 1983–85, spending declined to slightly more than 22 percent in 1987–88.[5]

Some of this downturn was due to the slackening of increases for defense. But it was also due to an overall slowdown in the growth rate of domestic outlays. As Stephen Moore of the Cato Institute observes, "although Ronald Reagan was thwarted in his effort to cut government spending (real domestic spending grew by 1 percent per year during his two terms), one of the central budgetary achievements of the Reagan years was to halt the creation of new domestic spending programs."[6] In fact, this 1 percent rate of annual real growth for such spending was a historic low for the modern era. (See Table V)

The effect of lowered tax rates in curtailing outlay growth is important, because the ultimate burden on the economy is, precisely, the total amount of government spending. Fixation on the deficit tends to ignore this crucial fact. If the government spends it, then one way or another it has to be paid for—either through taxes or through the credit markets. Agitation on *how the burden is to be financed* distracts attention from this larger point.

TABLE V

ANNUAL REAL DOMESTIC SPENDING INCREASES BY PRESIDENT, 1946–91

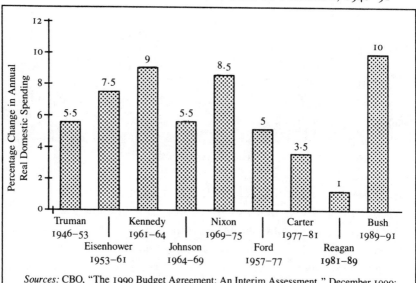

Sources: CBO, "The 1990 Budget Agreement: An Interim Assessment," December 1990; OMB, *Historical Tables of the United States Budget: Fiscal Year 1990*, Cato Institute.

For instance, Stockman, along with tax hikers in Congress and numerous commentators in the media, was constantly warning that deficit financing would "crowd out" private borrowers when the Treasury went into credit markets—absorbing funds for lending and driving up the rate of interest. This "crowding out," for the most part, did not happen in the 1980s, thanks chiefly to the influx of capital from overseas.

Nonetheless, federal deficits *can* crowd out, generating pressures for creating more credit by the Federal Reserve, thereby leading to inflation. To guard against this was, supposedly, why we needed a substantial hike in revenues. But if government pressure on credit market crowds out the private sector, what is the effect of ever-increasing *taxes* on individuals and businesses? This factor is routinely ignored by the crowding-out theorists.

It follows that concentrating on a balanced budget, as such, also misses the point. The concept has appeal to most Americans, and to conservative Republicans in particular. But the budget can be balanced in two very different ways (or combinations thereof)—by raising taxes to equal the burden of spending, or by reducing spending to fit the level of taxation. It would be possible to balance the budget at a point where federal spending and taxation both equaled 50 percent of GNP, but no economic theorist I am aware of considers this desirable.

The approach the President favored—holding the line on taxes while also trying to bring down spending—was not a total success. But the numbers show that, in rough fashion, the policy worked. Had the alternative course been followed—raising taxes to match the level of spending increase—all the budget numbers would have been substantially higher.

Conversely, if higher taxes had been used to seek a balanced budget, all the positive numbers for the economy would have been substantially lower. As noted, the long stagnation and decline of personal incomes reversed itself in 1983, just as the Reagan policies of tax relief and lowered inflation began to have their impact. This phenomenon was followed by a general surge of economic growth that dominated the remainder of the 1980s.

When the first of the Reagan 10 percent reductions took effect in

July 1982, the nation's economic problems had been evident for more than two years. While the rate cut did not cancel many other tax hikes, it was the first hint of major tax relief the average citizen had experienced in a decade, and taxpayers knew another 10 percent reduction was coming in 1983. The ensuing turnaround in the economy, after so long a period of stagnation, seems more than a coincidence.

In August of 1982, for instance, the stock market finally ended its long decline and began a period of record expansion which continued uninterrupted for the next five years. From 1982 to 1987, the Dow Jones Industrial Average went from 776 to 2,722; it has since gone on to top 3,000—despite two intervening major slumps in 1987 and 1989. This was matched by corresponding growth not only in personal incomes, but also in jobs, output, and productivity. It was one of the longest and most dynamic expansions in American history, and by far the most substantial in a time of peace.

As Alan Reynolds of the Hudson Institute sums it up: "The 92-month economic expansion that began in November 1982 and ended July 1990 was 3½ times as long as the average peacetime expansion since 1919, and second only to the record of the 106 months in 1961–69. From trough to peak, real GNP rose 32%, or 4.2% per year. . . . The Federal Reserve's index of manufacturing grew faster still—by 6.3% a year—yielding an awesome total increase of 48.3%."[7]

Tax and budget figures tell only part of the story. The real point about changes in economic policy in the 1980s is that the American people—in all income brackets—were better off because of Reagan's leadership. As the President himself observed: "We knew the program was a success when they stopped calling it 'Reaganomics.' "

12

THE MAN WHO WON
THE COLD WAR

F ROM THE PERSPECTIVE of the 1990s, it may be hard to recall how
the Soviet system was viewed for years in American academic, media,
and governmental circles.

The Soviet approach, it was said, may have been flawed, unfree,
and very different from our own—but, somehow, it "worked." Such
comments ranged from fervent statements of enthusiasm by left-wing
visitors to the USSR in the 1930s to more guarded but still respectful
assessments after the onset of the Cold War. Across the years, we were
treated to numerous statements about five-year plans, "growth rates,"
improving health care, and the like, allegedly provided by the Soviet
regime.

In 1984, for instance, liberal economist John Kenneth Galbraith
paid a visit to the USSR and wrote: "That the Soviet Union has made
great material progress in recent years is evident both from the statistics (even if they are below expectations) and, as many have reported,
from the general urban scene. One sees it in the appearance of solid

well-being of the people on the streets, the close to murderous traffic, the incredible exfoliation of apartment houses and the general aspect of restaurants, theaters, and shops—though these are not, to be sure, the most reliable of indices."[1] Similar comments from other sources could be duplicated across a span of decades.

Accordingly, the total economic collapse of Soviet communism that occurred soon after Galbraith's assertions about "great material progress" and "solid well-being" came as a jarring surprise to many. Who, it was asked, could have known the Soviet system was so weak? Who could have expected what was about to happen?

At least one person did expect it—and he repeatedly said so. That person was Ronald Reagan, who throughout his career had made a point of emphasizing the errors of the Soviet approach, the resulting vulnerabilities of communist rule, and the inevitable breakdown of the Marxist system if it were ever seriously challenged.

This view, moreover, was not simply a theoretical analysis used to counter the academic notions of such as Professor Galbraith. It was the essence of Reagan's real-world strategy toward communism—a point he emphasized consistently while in the White House and on which he based his major initiatives in defense and foreign policy. Reagan was more than simply "anticommunist"; he was an anticommunist with a game plan.

Reagan's analysis of communism was spelled out repeatedly in his major speeches, and in numerous press conferences and responses to questions about the Soviets. There was nothing secretive about it. The usual response to his comments on the subject, however, was to dismiss them as "Cold War rhetoric," or the comments of an "ideologue," since they did not fit the conventional view of things in Washington.

While many of Ronald Reagan's statements might be cited to make the point, four sources in particular set forth his view of communism, the Soviet system, and the required free world response in comprehensive fashion. These were, in chronological order, his June 1982 address to the British Parliament; his speech to a gathering of Evangelical Christians in 1983; his appearance at the Brandenburg Gate in June 1987; and his talk at Moscow State University in May 1988.

The theme most people remember from Reagan's foreign policy speeches was his assertion (before the Association of Evangelicals) that communism was "the focus of evil in the modern world," and that the Soviet Union was an "evil empire."[2] These comments were derided at the time as mere rhetorical posturing. But to people living under the yoke of Soviet communism, his words were all too obviously accurate—and they were words of hope. They showed that the American President understood their plight and was not about to accede to their subjugation.

Today, after the people of Eastern Europe and the former Soviet Union have thrown off the shackles of communist rule, few doubt that the Soviet system was indeed an "evil empire," and that the world is better for its passing. If Reagan had done nothing more than proclaim this truth, while fashionable opinion was ridiculing it, he would stand vindicated before history. But the President did a great deal more than this.

In addition to stressing the *evils* of communism, Reagan stressed its inherent *weakness*. In his view, the two were related, since in denying freedom the communists not only engaged in tyranny, they also crippled the creative potential of the human spirit. Reagan firmly believed that freedom was both morally and materially superior to communism, and constantly linked these themes in his speeches. In addressing the British Parliament in 1982 at Westminster, he said:

"The decay of the Soviet experiment should come as no surprise to us. Wherever the comparisons have been made between free and closed societies—West Germany and East Germany, Austria and Czechoslovakia, Malaysia and Vietnam—it is the democratic countries that are prosperous and responsive to the needs of their people. And one of the simple but overwhelming facts of our times is this: Of all the millions of refugees we've seen in the modern world, their flight is always away from, not toward, the communist world."[3]

In 1983, in his speech to the Evangelicals, Reagan pushed this analysis even further. After the famous quote about the "evil empire," he asserted that the free world must avoid the hazards of "moral equivalence" thinking that balanced the actions of the United States with those of the Soviet Union. The communist evil, he said, must be resisted. He then went on: "I believe we shall rise to the challenge. I believe that communism is another sad, bizarre chapter in history whose last pages even now are being written . . ."[4]

At the Brandenburg Gate, Reagan again expanded on these themes. "In the 1950s," he recalled, "Khrushchev predicted, 'We will bury you.' But in the West today, we see a free world that has achieved a level of prosperity and well-being unprecedented in all human history. In the communist world, we see failure, technological backwardness, declining standards of health, even want of the most basic kind—too little food. Even today, the Soviet Union still cannot feed itself.

"After these four decades, then, there stands before the entire world one great inescapable conclusion: Freedom leads to prosperity. Freedom replaces the ancient hatreds among nations with comity and peace. Freedom is the victor."[5]

Finally, at Moscow State University, Reagan put it this way: "It's hard for government planners, no matter how sophisticated, to ever substitute for millions of individuals working night and day to make their dreams come true. . . . We Americans make no secret of our belief in freedom. . . . Freedom is the right to question and change the established way of doing things. It is the continuing revolution of the marketplace. . . . It is the right to put forth an idea, scoffed at by the experts, and watch it catch fire among the people."[6]

Obviously, then, Ronald Reagan was not surprised by the economic and political collapse of communism in the years 1989–91; on the contrary, he clearly saw the vulnerabilities of the Soviet system and accurately predicted what must result from them.

As Reagan's view of communism differed from the accepted orthodoxy, so did his strategy for dealing with the Soviets. In the standard approach, the proper way of handling the USSR was to "ease tensions," seek accommodation, build bridges, and so on. This outlook embraced everything from arms control agreements such as SALT and SALT II, to economic credits and technology transfer, to exclusive reliance on negotiations with the Marxist leaders in places such as Nicaragua and El Salvador.

While Reagan was not opposed to negotiations (conducted in his own fashion, from a position of strength), he thought that this approach to Marxist expansionism was basically wrong, for very practical reasons: accommodation eased the economic and technical pressure on the communist system. Confronted by a declining U.S. military, restraints on American technology, and a general Western posture of retreat, the Soviets could postpone the day of reckoning between their inherent domestic weakness and their globalist ambitions.

Confronted by a different kind of policy, he thought the Soviets would find all these factors reversed. Faced with refurbished American defenses, American technology set free to achieve new advances, and a U.S. policy that didn't back off from protecting Western security interests, the Soviets would be forced to choose: either stand down from their continuing confrontation with the West, or face increasingly devastating pressures on the home front.

These points, too, were frequently stated by the President in his addresses, in his cabinet councils, and in his memoirs. "How long," the President wondered, "can the Russians keep on being so belligerent and spending so much on the arms race when they can't even feed their own people?"[7] Commenting on intelligence updates about the condition of the Soviet economy, he said:

"The latest figures provided additional evidence that it was a basket case, and even if I hadn't majored in economics in college, it would have been plain to me that communism was doomed as a failed economic system. The situation was so bad that if Western countries got together and cut off credit to it, we could bring it to its knees."[8]

If economics were a major weakness of the Soviet system, he reasoned, it was a huge advantage for our own. "The great dynamic success of capitalism," he said, "has given us a powerful weapon in our battle against communism—money. The Russians could never win the arms race; we could outspend them forever. Moreover, incentives inherent in the capitalist system had given us an industrial base that [meant] we had the capacity to maintain a technological edge on them forever."[9]

This viewpoint dictated a strategy in which we would *utilize* our economic and technological strength, rather than unilaterally restraining it; hence, the Reagan defense buildup, SDI, and other measures to be discussed. In this analysis, the President was strongly backed by

Cap Weinberger, Bill Clark, and myself, and also by Don Regan. Regan took his lumps for his involvement in the summits with Gorbachev in 1985 and 1986, on the grounds that he had no foreign policy expertise. Such criticisms ignored the fact that Regan contributed powerful understanding of the economic factors involved, and their significance in the East-West contest.

As Regan recalls it, "Gorbachev's motives in seeking a reduction in nuclear arms seemed to me to be almost entirely economic. . . . The Soviets could not spend more on arms without running the risk of bankrupting the state. . . . To stay in the arms race, the Russians had to spend a lot more money because President Reagan had committed the United States, with all its wealth and all its technical capacity, to developing SDI, a defensive system that made the entire Soviet missile force useless. . . . This meant that Reagan had been dealt the winning hand."[10]

The other side of the equation was for the United States and other Western powers to stop bailing the Soviets out of their economic difficulties through subsidized credit, one-sided business deals, and technology transfer. As Reagan observed, he wanted a coordinated Western policy in which "none of us would subsidize the Soviet economy or the Soviet military expansion by offering preferential trading terms or easy credit, and to restrain the flow of products and technology that would increase Soviet military capabilities."[11]

This was the principal motive behind the battle over the so-called Siberian pipeline, and also behind the systematic effort of the Pentagon's office on technology transfer, to impede the flow of Western computers, precision machinery, microelectronics, and other militarily useful systems to the East. The coordinated effort at the Department of Defense (headed up by Stephen Bryen) to curtail such transfers, both from the United States and from third countries receiving our technology, was one of the great unsung successes of the Reagan era.

From Reagan's many statements on this topic, and from the various policies initiated on his watch, a clear, coherent, and comprehensive Cold War strategy emerged. Though there were occasional setbacks along the way, the main elements of this strategy never altered:

1. In the Cold War confrontation between East and West, there was

no "moral equivalence." At the level of ultimate values, we were right, and they were wrong. Freedom was in every way superior to tyranny. This did not mean that we were perfect, that we wanted war, or that we wouldn't negotiate. But it did mean that we should never blur the key distinctions between a free society and the regimented system of our adversaries.

2. Given the totalitarian and expansionist ambitions of the Soviets, converging in their huge military establishment and worldwide program of subversion, it was essential that we vigorously defend ourselves. Wishful-thinking strategies—seeking peace through weakness and accommodation—only encouraged the expansionism of the communists. America, and the West in general, needed a policy of peace through strength.

3. Despite its armed might (and in part because of it), the Soviet system was inherently weak—it could not command the allegiance of its captive peoples, and its economic system could not produce the goods required to shelter, feed, and clothe them. A free society was superior to communism on both these counts.

4. Communism was accordingly torn by fatal contradictions—its global and military ambitions on the one hand, its internal economic and political problems on the other. In any full-scale competition with the United States and other Western powers, therefore, communism would be forced to choose between maintaining its global empire and solving its domestic problems.

5. It followed that the United States and the Western world in general should stop retreating before the communist challenge, stop imposing artificial limitations on themselves, and begin competing in earnest against the Soviets; this meant refurbishing our defenses, assisting anticommunist resistance forces around the world, and giving greater emphasis to the scientific/technological strength afforded by the free society.

6. It further followed, finally, that the West should stop bailing the communists out of their technical and economic difficulties. This implied an end to one-sided arms agreements that tilted the strategic balance toward the Kremlin; it meant no longer giving the Soviets and their proxies a free hand in subverting Third World countries; and it

meant cutting back on technology transfer from East to West, on strategic trade that helped to build the Soviet war machine, and on economic credits that eased the problems of the communist system.

On this basis, the President believed, the Soviets would have to come to terms on authentically peaceable agreements, not because they were trustworthy (although he eventually came to have a relatively high regard for Soviet President Gorbachev), but because they had no other choice. The "objective factors," to use a communist phrase, would lead inexorably to a stand-down from the Cold War.

A vivid example of the Reagan strategy in action was the liberation of Poland, which presaged the disintegration of the other communist regimes of Eastern Europe. This was among the earliest of test cases for the President's effort to coordinate economic, technological, and diplomatic factors against the Soviets and their clients—and it turned out to be a momentous success.

In December 1981, the government of Gen. Wojciech Jaruzelski declared martial law in Poland, cracking down on the protests of the Solidarity labor union headed by Lech Walesa. Here, indeed, was the face of the "evil empire," and it prompted a strong response from Reagan. The nature of that response was twofold: to provide material and moral support to Walesa's freedom movement, and to put the economic squeeze on Jaruzelski and his Soviet mentors.

As has now been made public by Carl Bernstein in an article for *Time*, Reagan conducted this effort in concert with Pope John Paul II, himself a native of Poland, whom the President greatly admired and with whom he saw eye-to-eye concerning the Jaruzelski crackdown. The administration shared intelligence data on the situation with the Vatican, making certain that our policies were on the identical wavelength. The President conferred directly with the Pope, while others in the administration worked closely with Catholic Church officials.[12]

The main elements of this strategy were to keep Solidarity alive through financial aid, clandestine radios, underground newspapers, and the like. Much of this was done jointly with the AFL-CIO, which had a strong and obvious interest in helping sustain the Solidarity union. At the same time, sanctions against the Polish regime—and against the Soviets—added to the pressure on the communists. Administration opposition to the Siberian pipeline, and to other economic dealings with the Soviets, were integral to this campaign.

It was, as Bernstein notes, a carefully calibrated effort, designed to keep the opposition viable and the communists on the defensive, without provoking the kind of violent clashes that had previously led to tragic outcomes in Poland, East Germany, Hungary, and Czechoslovakia. The object was to bring irresistible forces to bear that would exploit the political and economic weakness of the communist regime—exactly as Reagan had envisioned in his many statements on the topic.

In the end, Solidarity did survive, and the Jaruzelski government backed down in stages from its hard-line posture. In 1987, the Pope traveled to his native land, where he was acclaimed by millions of his coreligionists and countrymen, to give his personal backing to Solidarity. The days of communist rule in Poland were numbered, and the other tottering dominoes of Eastern Europe would soon follow in its wake—as would, eventually, the dictatorship of the USSR itself.

Key players in the Polish drama, from the administration side, included Bill Casey, Dick Allen, Bill Clark, and Richard Pipes, and it is good to see them receive some credit, along with the President and the Pope, from such an unlikely source as *Time*. As noted below, this magazine has not always been so ready to acknowledge the President's grasp of Cold War issues, or the degree to which his strategy exploited the vulnerabilities of the communist system.

The economic and technological weakness of the Soviets, as noted by Don Regan, were also prime factors in the battle over SDI. The President was convinced that Moscow couldn't compete with us at this level, that if we unleashed the capabilities of our technology, the communist system would be unable to keep pace. The resulting cost, he believed, would lead the Soviets to abdicate the struggle.

This is essentially what happened. Even though Gorbachev himself attempted to contend otherwise (as in his book, *Perestroika*), considerable testimony from the Soviet standpoint confirms the President's judgment. Some of this appears in the reporting of Don Oberdorfer of the *Washington Post*, who closely tracked Soviet attitudes on Cold War issues in the period 1983–87.

On a 1984 trip to Moscow, for instance, Oberdorfer reports that when asked what were the most important questions facing the country, "nearly all of the twelve Soviet officials or journalists whom I met, named the internal management or economy of the USSR." He quotes a former KGB official, assailing Reagan's policies, as saying, "You are trying to destroy our economy, to interfere with our trade, to overwhelm and make us inferior in the strategic field . . . "[13]

Oberdorfer similarly quotes Soviet Foreign Minister Andrei Gromyko as telling former Sen. George McGovern that Reagan and his aides "want to cause trouble. They want to weaken the Soviet system. They want to bring it down."[14] Such concerns became more acute, Oberdorfer notes, when Gorbachev succeeded to power the following year: "Gorbachev and his new team were more conscious than their predecessors of the economic troubles of the country, induced in large part by massive military spending."[15]

These concerns were made official and overt at the Twenty-Seventh Party Congress of the Soviet Communist Party in March 1986, which declared that "without an acceleration of the country's economic and social development, it will be impossible to maintain our position on the international scene."[16]

The final straw for the Soviets, as Don Regan and the President foresaw, was SDI. Oberdorfer quotes Gorbachev advisor Aleksandr Yakovlev as saying: "We understood that it was a new stage, a new turn in the armaments race." If SDI were not stopped, "we would have to start our own program, which would be tremendously expensive and unnecessary. And this [would bring] further exhaustion of the country."[17] For this reason, SDI became the focal point of U.S.–Soviet negotiations—at Geneva in 1985, and at Reykjavik in 1986.

These Soviet reactions obviously tracked closely with Reagan's analysis of the situation. How this worked in the realm of arms control and defense is discussed in chapter 14. In terms of conventional arms, the process was capped by Gorbachev's December 1988 announcement at the United Nations that he was ordering a unilateral cutback of 500,000 men from the Soviet armed services and the withdrawal of some tank divisions from Eastern Europe.

As *Newsweek* observed, this initiative by Gorbachev "was surely a move forced by his economic woes, but it was also a brilliant way to play a losing hand."[18] Gorbachev himself put it this way in a luncheon with President Reagan and President-elect Bush: "I'm not doing this for show . . . I'm doing this because I need to. I'm doing this because there's a revolution taking place in my country."[19]

From a post-Cold War perspective, the main principles of the Reagan program may seem self-evident. Given accurate data about the communist system, indeed, they are the very essence of common sense. Viewing the rubble of the Berlin Wall, the upheavals that have transformed Eastern Europe, and the internal collapse of the Soviet regime, hardly anyone can doubt that communism was indeed an "evil empire" and a failed economic system. Such points have been affirmed by the former leaders of the communist world itself.

Yet at the time Reagan was making these statements and pursuing these policies, there was nothing self-evident about it. On the contrary, he was roundly attacked both for his general analysis of the situation, and for nearly all the specific steps he took in carrying out his policy— the defense buildup, INF deployments, aid to anticommunist resistance forces, curtailment of technology transfer, SDI, and so on.

In fact, even in the aftermath of the communist collapse Reagan critics were reluctant to credit the President with the accuracy of his vision or the correctness of his policy. Many discussions of the communist debacle completely ignore the impact of the Reagan strategy, attributing the demise of the evil empire to a change of heart on the part of the communists, or to unnamed forces that somehow brought about the toppling of the system.

Perhaps the most famous example of this tendency was the issue of *Time* magazine celebrating the virtual end of communism and proclaiming Mikhail Gorbachev "Man of the Decade."[20] The role of Ronald Reagan in all of this was scarcely mentioned, nor was much notice given to the fact that the establishment view had been mistaken at every step along the way. Instead, *Time* concluded that the collapse of communism proved the "doves" had been right all along! Margaret Thatcher provided a more accurate view at a 1991 Heritage Foundation dinner in Washington, when she summed up the President's accomplishments abroad: "He won the Cold War without firing a shot."

13

REBUILDING OUR DEFENSES

AT THE TIME of the 1980 elections, there was widespread agreement that America needed to spend substantially more on its defenses. Candidate Reagan emphatically agreed with this analysis; he voiced it forcefully in his campaign and acted on it once he was in office. The reason for this "defense consensus" is apparent from the budget figures. Over the decades, the share of federal dollars going to the military had been in a state of free-fall. (See Table I)

In 1961, when John Kennedy was president, defense took almost exactly half the federal budget. In the ensuing years, this fraction steadily declined, falling to 37.5 percent of total spending in 1971. By 1981, when Reagan came to office, it was down to 23.2 percent—less than a quarter of all outlays.

This curtailment of relative spending for defense was due to the surging budgets for social welfare that began with the Great Society of Lyndon Johnson and accelerated in the 1970s. The Soviets were in the meantime devoting even greater resources to their own strategic arse-

174

TABLE I

DEFENSE AS SHARE OF FEDERAL BUDGET

Year	%	Year	%
1961	50.8	1971	37.5
1963	48.0	1973	31.2
1965	42.8	1975	26.0
1967	45.4	1977	23.8
1969	44.9	1979	23.1

Source: Office of Management and Budget

nal, not to mention the billions they were spending to encourage revolution around the globe.

One of the paradoxes of this record is that the fraction of the budget going for defense continued to fall even while we were spending billions on the Vietnam War. Under the double pressure of the Vietnam commitment and a declining share of the budget, outlays for long-term military development relentlessly contracted. Modernization of strategic weapons, including our aging bomber force, had been indefinitely postponed. Our Minuteman missiles were state of the art in 1960, but by 1980 lagged far behind the Soviet's offensive weapons. Our naval forces had been cut in half. And pay raises for the military were put off, and then put off again.

To these constraints, another had been added: the heavy emphasis on arms control throughout the 1970s. In a sense, this policy sought to make a virtue of necessity; since we weren't upgrading or even maintaining our military forces, we tried to get the Soviets to follow suit. Unfortunately, they didn't. As a result, while we restrained our strategic power and technology, they continued to forge ahead with a vast military buildup.

The decline of our defenses and the disparity between the arsenals of the U.S. and USSR were frequent Reagan themes, featured in several major speeches to the nation—most notably in November 1982, and again in his SDI address in March of 1983. Among the specifics he laid before the American people:

"[T]he United States introduced its last new intercontinental ballistic missile, the Minuteman III, in 1967, and we are now dismantling our even older Titan missiles. The Soviet Union has built five new classes of ICBMs, and upgraded them eight times. As a result, their missiles are now much more powerful and accurate than they were several years ago, and they continue to develop more, while ours are increasingly obsolete. . . .

"Over the same period, the Soviet Union built four new classes of submarine-launched ballistic missiles and over sixty new missile submarines. We built two new types of submarine missiles and actually withdrew ten submarines from strategic missions. The Soviet Union built over two hundred new Backfire bombers, and their brand-new Blackjack bomber is now under development. We haven't built a new long-range bomber since our B-52s were deployed about a quarter of a century ago, and we've already retired several hundred of these because of old age."[1]

Indeed, as Reagan noted, many of the B-52s were older than the pilots who flew them. When he arrived at the White House, he said, he was appalled to discover we had planes that couldn't fly and ships that couldn't leave port because of a lack of spare parts and a shortage of crew members. The deterioration of our navy, recalls Reagan Secretary of the Navy John Lehman, was particularly serious:

"I was aghast to find in my first briefing that we had less than a week's supply of most major defensive missiles and torpedoes. Though the fleet had been cut in half since 1969, we could not even fill out the 479 ships' magazines even once, let alone refill them. In ships and aircraft spare parts, we had a third of the minimum requirement."*[2]

It was this alarming shortfall that Reagan and Cap Weinberger set out to correct—recommending budgets, that, if adopted, would have raised defense to about a third of total spending. These funds would

---

* Lehman adds that "by 1979 the backlog of ships requiring overhaul that could not be fixed for lack of funds had grown to seventy-five . . . The Navy budget declined 22 percent in real terms between 1973 and 1980 . . . Enlistment retention rates dropped by 1979 to the lowest ever recorded . . . [B]y 1979 the fleet was manned at only 91 percent, four ships could not sail because of undermanning, and the CNO, Admiral Thomas Hayward, testified that we had a one-and-a-half ocean Navy for a three ocean commitment."

have gone to modernize our strategic triad, acquire new ballistic missiles, replace the B-52, rebuild the navy, upgrade tactical weapons systems, and adjust pay to improve the condition, morale, and reenlistment rates of our armed services.

Despite the defense consensus, this was no easy task, and the level of outlays Reagan sought was never fully attained. Table II shows the trend of military spending in the 1980s. Under the impact of Reagan's advocacy, the number moved up gradually to about 28 percent of the total budget in 1986-87, only to decline again thereafter. (Defense as a percent of total spending was actually lower by 1991 than it had been in 1980.)

TABLE II
DEFENSE AS SHARE OF FEDERAL BUDGET

Year	%	Year	%
1980	22.7	1986	27.6
1981	23.2	1987	28.1
1982	24.8	1988	27.3
1983	26.0	1989	26.5
1984	26.7	1990	23.9
1985	26.7	1991	20.1

Source: Office of Management and Budget

As these figures clearly show, laments that the Reagan defense buildup robbed domestic programs, or was chiefly responsible for the deficit, were spurious. Reagan's defense outlays never moved very far above one-fourth of federal spending—below the levels that obtained under Kennedy, Johnson, Nixon, and Gerald Ford, and only a couple of percentage points higher than with Jimmy Carter.

This was a reallocation of resources toward defense—urgently needed after a decade of neglect—but hardly a massive realignment of priorities, or even the level requested by Reagan in his initial budgets. As for the deficit: if defense were responsible for only a quarter of the budget, then logically it could be responsible for only a quarter of the deficit.

In pushing for his defense policy, Reagan was bucking continued demands for more domestic spending amid continuing concern about the deficit. This led not only to battles with Congress, but to struggles within the administration, often pitting David Stockman against Cap Weinberger. Dave was looking strictly at the deficit numbers, while Cap concentrated on our defense requirements and force levels for the services.[3]

Throughout 1981, as a spin-off from the tax and budget battles, a series of confrontations took place between Cap and Dave concerning the level of military outlays. Dave, backed by Jim Baker and some others, believed we needed to curtail our requests for increases in defense spending; Cap said the levels he sought were needed to restore our forces to minimal effectiveness.

A noteworthy episode occurred in August 1981, during the congressional recess, when members of the National Security Council met with the President in California. Cap, Al Haig, and Deputy Defense Secretary Frank Carlucci were very strong on building up the Pentagon budget, with Stockman opposed. My role was to attempt to work out a compromise, and I asked Cap and Frank to see if they could come up with numbers that would accommodate Stockman's objections.

As it turned out, Cap and Frank weren't able to make much headway, but Jim Baker nevertheless issued a statement to the press saying the defense number would be reduced—which hadn't been agreed to. I remember calling Jim and asking him why he was going public in this way. In retrospect, I'm sure he did it at Stockman's request, in order to exert leverage on the process. It was a portent of things to come.

Here again, these showdowns revealed the quality of Reagan's leadership. In political terms, it would have been relatively easy to back off on defense, since Congress and many in his own administration were pushing him in that direction. But the President just would not do it.

As he frequently put it in cabinet and National Security Council meetings: "I am concerned about the deficit, but nothing can take precedence over rebuilding our defenses. If we have to put up with a deficit to protect our national security, that's what we're going to do."[4] As a result, we got far more by way of military improvements under Reagan than we would have under any other President in recent memory.

But rebuilding our defenses was more than just a matter of allocating money. Above all, it was what was done with the money in acquiring and modernizing specific weapons systems, something to which the Reagan team had given considerable thought both during the campaign and in the transition. Studies conducted by transition task forces under Dick Allen were passed on to Cap when he became secretary of defense, and he in turn drew on and evaluated the funding and modernization requests received from the different branches of the military. This was not simply "throwing dollars" at the Pentagon.

The culmination of the process occurred in the early fall of 1981 when Cap came to the White House to present his plan for rebuilding our strategic forces. Dick Allen and I joined the President as he was briefed by Cap and his deputy, Frank Carlucci. It was a warm day, so we sat outside on the patio, directly adjacent to the Oval Office. Cap's plan consisted of five main elements:

1. Strengthening our land-based missile capability with the MX missile, which had far more striking power and could carry more warheads than the Minuteman;

2. Improving the sea-based missile program with the D-5 (Trident) missile to be carried aboard our nuclear submarines—far more capable than the missiles on our Polaris and Poseidon subs;

3. Refurbishing our airborne capability, which included the B-1 bomber (canceled by Carter), and moving ahead with the development of a Stealth bomber, the B-2, that could evade enemy tracking and surveillance;

4. Strengthening our air defense capabilities and civil defense, particularly the command and control elements and the ability of the government to survive in the event of attack;

5. Improving our command and control system generally so that we would have proper interconnection among civilian authority, military command, and operating forces in the event of a nuclear attack.[5]

These measures were important on three levels: (1) to protect the United States from aggression by the Soviets (or by others, an increasing possibility in view of the proliferation of nuclear weapons in the 1980s); (2) to tell the Soviets we were going to renew our strength to keep the peace; and (3) to use the resulting leverage to obtain authentic arms reduction rather than a continuing Soviet buildup.

The results of this retooling were evident in Grenada in 1983, in our confrontation with Libya in 1986, and even more so, in the showdown with Saddam Hussein in 1990-91. It was from the Reagan buildup that we achieved "smart" bombs and radar suppression, Tomahawk cruise missiles and Patriot defenses, Aegis cruisers and Abrams tanks, Apache helicopters, night-fighting capability, and other military advances that were exhibited in the Persian Gulf.

In the aftermath of the Gulf fighting, Carter partisans claimed that many of these weapons had been in the pipeline, or at least designed, before Reagan came to office. This was true in certain cases. But being designed or in the pipeline is very different from being produced and deployed. (In the case of the Tomahawk cruise missile, for example, the technology had been in existence for a long time, but deployments would have been banned by a protocol to Jimmy Carter's SALT II treaty.)[6]

What the President and Cap achieved, against great opposition, was to make these systems operational. For such weapons to work, they had to be in the field long enough for pilots, tank commanders, and other personnel to discover and correct any problems, train with the weapons, and develop an ability to use them. We also needed spare parts, delivery capability, and backup systems—all the things that make for a successful fighting force. It is not enough to have something invented. It has to be out there in quantity, where the troops are using it. That is what the Reagan buildup accomplished.

As noted by former Assistant Secretary of Defense Lawrence Korb: "By the middle of the decade, U.S. military expenditures exceeded those of the Soviet Union for the first time since the late 1960s. . . . In his first six years in office, Reagan purchased nearly 3,000 combat aircraft, 3,700 strategic missiles, and about 10,000 tanks."[7] These procurement levels were roughly double those of the 1970s; and, of course, the weapons being brought on line in the 1980s were much more sophisticated than their predecessors.

Nor was the President's effort to restore the military simply a program of acquiring hardware. He was equally concerned about the morale of our forces, beginning with respect for the military as an institution. During the campaign, he talked about how, too often, the military wouldn't wear their uniforms off post because they feared public reaction. He wanted to change this from an inspirational as well as from a practical standpoint.

To this end, he spent a good deal of time visiting with the armed services and expressing pride in what they were doing. In the summer of 1981, for example, he went to Long Beach to visit the aircraft carrier *Constellation*, meeting with the personnel aboard the ship. I went with him on that visit and well recall his electrifying remarks to the seamen and the inspiration he received in return.

He did this sort of thing innumerable times—visiting bases, addressing military gatherings, meeting with military personnel, insisting on respect for the uniform—as well as inviting the winners of the service academy football games to the White House to receive a trophy from their commander-in-chief. All in all, he developed a sense of patriotism in the people, and a sense of pride in the military services.*

Beyond all this, of course, lay the question of how best to use our increasing strength in dealing with the Soviet Union, including disputes about the deployment of our forces, both those in being and those we were moving to develop. Among the most urgent, which dominated discussion in the period 1981-83, was upgrading the defense of Western Europe.

For a generation and more, that defense had been linked closely to the nuclear deterrent of the United States. Should the Soviets launch a massive ground invasion or otherwise attack the NATO countries, the U.S. would supposedly respond with a missile fusillade on the USSR. But over the years, this guarantee became decreasingly credible to Europeans, and they began to agitate for further upgraded deterrent forces in the region.

* In his book, *Fighting for Peace*, Cap Weinberger tells a particularly inspirational story about Master Sergeant Roy Benavidez, who had been awarded the Congressional Medal of Honor for heroism in Vietnam. The Carter administration, Cap recounts, had not wanted to have a White House ceremony for Sergeant Benavidez, since this would have reminded people of Vietnam. When the Pentagon raised the question to Cap and Reagan, the President not only approved the ceremony immediately, but personally read the citation and awarded the medal.

One option that had been considered by the Carter administration was the "neutron bomb," or enhanced radiation warhead, which would have provided war-fighting capability against Soviet tanks without destroying the countryside that was being defended. The "neutron bomb" would have utilized the radiation effects of nuclear weapons, rather than their massive blast effects, to attack the enemy formations, thus providing a more controllable and credible deterrent.

But when Carter talked of deploying such weapons, he was hit by a massive propaganda campaign from the Soviet Union and its friends, claiming the neutron bomb was especially fiendish since it destroyed people instead of property. This propaganda line proved particularly effective in Western Europe (though why weapons that killed people *and* destroyed property were somehow more desirable was not made clear).[8] In the end, Carter backed off from the proposal.

By the time Reagan arrived at the White House, the neutron bomb was on the back burner; Cap Weinberger wanted to proceed with it, but the issue had been superseded by one considered even more important—the problem of the Euromissiles. In the latter 1970s, as part of its general military expansion, the Soviet Union had positioned increasing numbers of intermediate-range nuclear missiles, targeting Western Europe, in the Warsaw Pact countries. These MIRVed missiles bore three warheads each, and among them had sufficient firepower to obliterate every major target in West Germany, France, Italy, the United Kingdom, and other countries of the Western alliance.

"In 1978," as Reagan noted, "the Soviets had 600 intermediate-range nuclear missiles based on land and were beginning to add the SS-20—a new, highly accurate, mobile missile, with three warheads. We had none. . . . By the end of 1979, when Soviet leader Brezhnev declared 'a balance now exists,' the Soviets had over 800 warheads. . . . By last August [1982], their 800 warheads had become more than 1,200. . . . The Soviets are still adding an average of three new warheads a week, and now have 1,300. . . . We still have none . . . So far, it seems the Soviet definition of parity is a box score of 1,300 to nothing, in their favor."[9]

These Soviet deployments understandably made the West Europeans nervous, and since they had come to doubt our guarantees of long-range retaliation, they wanted intermediate missiles on their territory. The principal advocate of this view was West German Chancellor Helmut Schmidt, who agitated for upgraded intermediate forces in Europe and got NATO to concur. The fact that the impetus for these deployments came from the Europeans, not the United States, was conveniently forgotten when the issue became a source of intense political dispute.*

This was the situation that the Reagan administration inherited when it came into office in 1981. For the next two years, deployment of INF forces in Europe would dominate discussion of defense, dividing the U.S. and Europe as well as the Reagan administration. It was a time of testing for President Reagan, gauging both his willingness to reverse the previous drift of U.S. policy, and his new approach to arms control.

In an effort to duplicate the success of their neutron bomb campaign, the Soviets and their allies in the "peace" movement of the West worked diligently to head off the new deployments. In 1982, these efforts began to sway the parliaments of the West, raising doubts about deployment. They culminated in the nuclear freeze campaign that was waged intensively in the fall of 1982.[10]

The thrust of this campaign was to focus attention on the Pershing and cruise missiles to be deployed by NATO, completely ignoring the fact that Moscow already had one thousand warheads targeted on Western Europe. Such reversals of logic were not unusual in discussions of arms control and relations between East and West.

The inequity of not deploying INF while leaving all the Soviet SS-20s in place was obvious to everyone but the most fervent members of the "peace" brigade and some of their allies in the media. What to do about it was less clear; it became a source of disagreement within the alliance as well as within the Reagan government. On the one side

---

* As Zbigniew Brzezinski commented in 1982: "I was personally never persuaded that we needed [the INF deployments] for military reasons. I was persuaded reluctantly that we needed [to deploy] to obtain European support for SALT. This was largely because Chancellor Schmidt made such a big deal out of the so-called Eurostrategic imbalance that was being generated by the Soviet deployment of the SS-20. To keep him in line we felt that some response in Europe on the intermediate level would be necessary."[11]

were some of the Europeans, the U.S. State Department, and members of the arms control community who wanted to cancel or downgrade the U.S. deployments in return for a partial limit on the SS-20s—leaving an imbalance in favor of the Soviets but a smaller one.

On the other side was the so-called "zero option," favored by the President, by Cap Weinberger and Richard Perle at DOD, by many members of the military, and also by me. The essence of this view was to confront the Soviets with a choice of all or nothing: either dismantle their SS-20s entirely (including those stationed elsewhere that could be moved rapidly to Europe), or face a go-ahead with U.S. deployments.

While some conventional histories suggest the "zero option" was foisted on the President by his advisors, I know for a fact that it was his own idea; he frequently discussed it at National Security Council meetings. It was central to his view of arms control, notwithstanding that Al Haig and the State Department dissented, arguing that, since the Soviets wouldn't agree to such a proposal, it was "not negotiable." They thought we should come up with something the Kremlin was more likely to accept.[11]

From Reagan's standpoint, letting Soviet intransigence dictate our position was not the right way to negotiate. He preferred to stake out the case for zero-zero, telling the Soviets that if they wouldn't agree we would simply proceed with our deployments. Only by bargaining from strength, he said, were we likely to get any movement from the Kremlin.

As he explained it: "[T]ogether with our NATO allies, we decided . . . to deploy new weapons, beginning this year, as a deterrent to their SS-20s and as an incentive to the Soviet Union to meet us in a series of arms control negotiations. . . . At the same time, however, we're willing to cancel our program if the Soviets will dismantle theirs. The Soviets are now at the negotiating table and I think it's fair to say that, without our planned deployments, they wouldn't be there."[12]

Accordingly, when the Soviets refused to move on zero-zero we made plans to go ahead with the deployments—whereupon the Soviets walked out of the negotiations in Geneva. This was universally deplored by the arms controllers and liberal media; it showed, they lamented, that the President was not really interested in arms control. But of course the President was proved right: Four years later, the INF agreement of 1987, in which both sides agreed to dismantle Euro-missiles, was signed; it was the "zero option" by another name.

This outcome showed that the President knew a good deal more about how to negotiate with Moscow than did his critics. Clearly, if the Soviets could have blocked the Western deployments while keeping some or all of their SS-20s, they would have done so. That episode spoke worlds about the President's adherence to his principles—not only against the "peace" brigades, but against a firestorm of criticism in the media. The pattern would be repeated.

14

ARMS AND THE MAN

O F ALL THE DIFFICULTIES the President had to deal with in refurbishing our defenses, none was more complicated than "arms control." The complexities were magnified by the fact that different people meant different things by the expression.

The President himself had very definite ideas about arms control, based on two guiding principles: (1) the security of the United States must be protected from any possible attack by keeping our defenses strong and properly utilizing our technology; and (2) the idea of nuclear war and reliance on nuclear weapons was abhorrent and should be repudiated. From these two premises flowed all his initiatives in the realm of strategic arms, intermediate missiles, defensive systems, and negotiations with the Soviets.

Again, the President's foes, betraying their own lack of vision, have twitted him on this topic—for lack of technical knowledge concerning throw-weights, the attributes of individual weapons, and the like— while failing themselves to grasp the significance of what he did in fact accomplish. He brought to the table a strategic vision that far surpassed the micromanaging concerns of his opponents, and he never wavered throughout his eight years in the White House.

What most puzzled Reagan's critics was his deep aversion to nuclear weapons and even the remotest prospect of a nuclear war. But as Reagan recalls, when he was inaugurated, he took on the largest responsibility of his life—"of any human being's life": "The plastic-coated card, which I carried in a small pocket of my coat, listed the codes that I would issue to the Pentagon confirming that it was actually the President of the United States who was ordering the unleashing of our nuclear weapons."[1]

Such a decision, the President reflected, would mean the incineration of millions of innocent people in the Soviet Union—in response to a similar holocaust in America. "As long as nuclear weapons were in existence, there would always be the risk that they would be used, and once the first nuclear weapons were unleashed, who knew where it would end? My dream, then, became a world free of nuclear weapons. . . . [F]or the eight years I was president, I never let my dream of a nuclear-free world fade from my mind."[2]

This hardly bore out the conventional image of the President as a trigger-happy cowboy who liked to pile up weapons and lavish billions on the Pentagon, and who yearned to slug it out with Moscow. If anything, Reagan's antipathy to nuclear bombs was far greater than that of his adversaries on the left. But he drew sharply different conclusions from his revulsion.

For thirty years and more, the established view on atomic weapons had been basically schizophrenic. On the one hand, their destructive power made them horrible and dangerous and their actual use should never be considered. On the other hand, we had to rely on them and plan our defenses *as if* we were prepared to use them. We should, moreover, develop and deploy them to cause the greatest possible death and suffering, if used, by targeting them exclusively on civilian populations.

This latter doctrine, called "mutual assured destruction" (MAD), was particularly repugnant to the President. Under MAD theory, the very horror of nuclear weapons was their most useful feature; nothing, therefore, should be done to relieve it. If each side in the Cold War could blow the other to smithereens, neither, supposedly, would dare launch an attack; a "balance of terror" would ensure the peace. This theory dictated that each side have sufficient offensive weapons to wreak destruction on the other, and that neither have defenses that could deter the carnage.

From the 1960s forward, U.S. weapons development, targeting doctrine, and strategic planning were governed by this doctrine. The SALT agreements between America and the Soviet Union negotiated in the 1970s by Richard Nixon and Jimmy Carter were constructed within its framework. These agreements sought to limit, but not eliminate, offensive weapons, while barring development of anti-missile defenses against them (accomplished in the ABM accord of 1972). The civilian populations of both countries would thus be exposed to "assured destruction."

To President Reagan, this thinking was illogical, dangerous, and immoral, and he was determined to reverse it. He had little use for arms agreements, such as Carter's SALT II treaty, that simply sought to limit the rate of increase in offensive arsenals, thereby legitimizing and making provision for such increases in the future. Instead, he wanted agreements that would reduce the number of weapons, or eliminate them, and he wanted these reductions strictly verified.

(Actually getting rid of offensive weapons, by both sides in the Cold War, was the basis for his "zero option" approach in Europe and his proposals for strategic arms reductions talks (START) concerning long-range missiles.)

Even more revolutionary, and more disconcerting to the establishment, was Reagan's belief that we should develop defenses against these destructive weapons, unless and until they were abolished. In his opinion, this was both an ethical and a strategic imperative, as well as a policy that would play to American technological strength in computers, lasers, microelectronics, and other areas where the Soviets lagged behind us.

"I came into this office," he recalls, "with a distinct prejudice against our tacit agreement with the Soviet Union regarding nuclear missiles . . . the idea of deterrence providing safety so long as each of us had the power to destroy the other with nuclear missiles if one of us launched a first strike. . . . It was like having two Westerners standing in a saloon aiming their guns at each other's heads—permanently. There had to be a better way."[3]

Apart from the immorality of MAD doctrine, many strategic problems had evolved from arms control as practiced on this basis. The ABM treaty, for example, barred development of antimissile defenses on the assumption that, since both sides adhered to MAD neither should seek to threaten the strategic deterrent of the other. With invulnerable long-range missiles on both sides, neither would dare launch a surprise first-strike attack.

But it hadn't turned out that way. While we had stopped work on our ABM defenses—and made cutbacks in air defense, civil defense, and radar warning systems—the Soviets had forged ahead with their offensive buildup. As a result, by the latter 1970s, both our civilian population *and* our deterrent were at risk.

In particular, the Soviets had developed "heavy" SS-18 ICBMs, equipped with multiple warheads and upgraded accuracy, which provided "missile busting" power far in excess of anything supposedly required by MAD. This raised the specter of a preemptive strike by Moscow, with enough strategic weapons left to nullify any American effort at retaliation. This was the "window of vulnerability" that worried defense experts in the 1970s and that Reagan stressed in his campaign.

From Reagan's standpoint, such dangerous outcomes under prevailing concepts of arms control meant new approaches were needed. In fact, the President believed the textbook on arms control negotiations with the Soviets needed to be rewritten, from start to finish. In the establishment view, arms discussions with the Kremlin were virtually an end in themselves. The very process of negotiating was looked upon as positive, as a way of maintaining contact and building confidence, while any actual agreement—no matter its contents—was hailed as a major breakthrough.

This outlook dominated the political and media attitudes toward the President, who was graded on *whether* negotiations were proceeding rather than on *what* was (or wasn't) being negotiated. The President was constantly attacked for not reaching agreements with the Soviets, not having summit conferences with Brezhnev or Andropov, not consummating a deal to head off INF deployments, and so on.

In Reagan's view, the process of negotiation was subordinate to *what* was being negotiated, and *no* agreement was preferable to a bad one. He was quite willing to walk away from the bargaining table if indicated, and did so. He also believed in negotiating from a position of strength. If the Soviets knew we would accept an agreement no matter what, he frequently said, they would obviously hold out for one most disadvantageous to the United States.

On analysis, it became increasingly clear that many of the strategic problems we faced resulted from MAD doctrine theories of arms control. One such was the "MX" missile controversy, which first arose in the Carter administration and continued throughout the Reagan years. The object of the MX, which Reagan strongly supported to replace the Minuteman, was to have a powerful weapon that could threaten hard targets in the USSR, not simply civilian populations.

The problem with the MX was the "basing mode," since these missiles were vulnerable to (and attractive targets for) a Soviet preemptive strike. This led to various schemes—including multiple protective shelters, race track designs, and truck and rail transport—to hide the missiles from the Soviets. It also led to a concept called "dense pack" (grouping our missiles close together so that attacking Soviet ICBMs would knock each other out through "fratricide").

In 1983, the President appointed a commission under General Brent Scowcroft to address the MX controversy. The commission approved the idea of deploying the MX in existing Minuteman silos, which gave us added offensive power, but didn't solve the problem of vulnerability. (After repeated battles in Congress, the last of fifty MX missiles were deployed in this fashion in 1989—more than a decade after the Carter administration had first suggested going forward with them.)

One obvious but neglected reason for the MX predicament was that we had no "point" defenses to protect our missiles in their silos and therefore had to resort to exotic measures to conceal them. At the time, and even more so later, evidence suggested that such defenses were feasible and would have enhanced the survivability of our Minuteman, or the MX, against a Soviet onslaught. This fact was noted in 1981 congressional hearings by Sens. Jake Garn, Paul Laxalt, Harrison Schmitt, and others, and was confirmed in lengthy testimony by technical experts from the U.S. army's Office of Ballistic Missile Defense.[4]

Deployment of such defenses had stopped, however, in obedience to the ABM treaty—including the dismantling of our one permitted base in Grand Forks, N.D., in 1976. The "arms control" establishment wanted nothing to do with antimissile defenses, even when these would have "enhanced stability" by protecting our deterrent. Thus, by a strange jiu-jitsu, MAD doctrine turned against itself. Because we had no antimissile protection, our deterrent was perceived as vulnerable—which undercut a basic tenet of MAD.

This situation also fed the controversy over INF deployments. Because the Europeans saw our vulnerability, they doubted our guarantee to "risk our cities" to save theirs, as John Kennedy had phrased it. Such a promise seemed credible when U.S. forces could attack the Soviets without a retaliatory strike on the American homeland. But it seemed less so when the Soviets had huge missiles that could not only strike the U.S. but take out our deterrent as well.

Thus a whole knot of problems traced back to the doctrine of Mutual Assured Destruction, arms control as practiced by its guidelines, and the ABM accord that made it a permanent feature of our policy. These difficulties underscored the President's belief that sole reliance on offensive killing power was a mistake—that we had to move forward toward development of defenses.

Long before these specific wrangles had reached the realm of national policy, the President had been concerned about MAD doctrine. "During the spring of 1981," the President recalls, "the arms race was moving ahead at a pell-mell pace based on the MAD policy . . . [A]s far as I was concerned, the MAD policy was madness. For the first time in history, man had the power to destroy mankind itself. . . . I wondered if it might not be possible to develop a defense against missiles other than the fatalistic acceptance of annihilation that was implicit in MAD policy." He wanted, he adds, to develop a system that would allow us to change from "a policy of assured destruction to one of assured survival."[5]

In my conversations with him, the President frequently noted that there had never been an offensive system for which there wasn't some kind of countervailing defense. When warriors used bows and arrows, shields were developed; when tanks were invented, antitank weapons were devised; when aerial warfare loomed large, anti-aircraft weapons were designed. To say we couldn't do the same with ballistic missiles, the President thought, was both dangerous and defeatist.

A key influence in Reagan's thinking on such matters was Dr. Edward Teller, head of the Lawrence Livermore laboratory at Berkeley. Teller had a long history of bucking fashionable opinion, having crossed swords with liberal favorite Robert Oppenheimer on U.S. nuclear policy and having been a longtime advocate of the peaceful uses of nuclear power.

Teller and his colleagues at Lawrence had been considering new technologies that could be used to intercept ballistic missiles in the earth's atmosphere and above. He had the scientific knowledge and the philosophic commitment to use it in a patriotic cause. In addition, he was known to Reagan from his days as a regent at the University of California and had been an advisor to the President in the campaign of 1980.

But while Teller was in favor of the idea, the arms control establishment was adamantly against it. Arms controllers disparaged the idea of ABM defenses, and the military, for reasons of its own, was divided on the question; the ABM treaty of 1972 had virtually institutionalized MAD doctrine in official thinking. Given all that, the idea of strategic defense against nuclear missiles could hardly have surfaced if the President had relied on standard, bureaucratic methods.

In the early days of the administration, when we were enmeshed in tax and budget battles, we didn't have the leisure to review the question of ABM defenses in detail. But the President never lost his interest in the topic, nor did Dick Allen, Martin Anderson, or I. We were in contact with Dr. Teller, defense expert Karl Bendetsen, General Daniel Graham of High Frontier, and others who believed in the concept, and also with those members of the "kitchen cabinet" who were most sympathetic, such as Joseph Coors, Jack Hume, and William Wilson.

In mid-September 1981, with the initial battle over tax reductions behind us, the time seemed right to revisit the question of developing such a system. Accordingly, I hosted a small meeting in my office in which we discussed the feasibility of pushing ahead with plans for an ABM defense in keeping with the President's wishes, and the kinds of emerging technologies available for such a task. Present were Teller, Bendetsen, Graham, George Keyworth (the President's science advisor), Martin Anderson, and myself.

The consensus of the discussion was that such an approach was indeed possible. We met again to draw up provisional plans, and I then arranged a meeting with the President on January 8, 1982.* The tenor of this discussion was highly favorable. The President directed the National Security Council Staff to look into this matter and develop a proposal for a strategic defense program. Bill Clark personally made sure this happened, even though some thought it to be a futile task.

A crucial turning point in these continuing discussions was a meeting between the President and the Joint Chiefs of Staff in January 1983. For a variety of reasons, as noted, the concept of SDI was not an automatic winner in military circles. There is always a fair amount of competition among the services concerning roles and missions, as well as established ways of doing things inside the Pentagon, and SDI didn't fit very comfortably with any of these (one reason it eventually was administered by a separate agency). A spin-off of this problem was the vigorous competition for available funds. This intensified questions about a project that, at this point, was more in the realm of science than military feasibility.

As a result, getting a favorable reaction to SDI from the Joint Chiefs was hardly a foregone conclusion. But when the President met with them in January, the circumstances were unusual: the problem of the MX basing mode was still—and would remain—unsolved. "Dense

---

* That meeting included Bendetsen, Hume, Wilson and Teller from the outside group, and Bill Clark, George Keyworth, Martin Anderson, and myself from the White House.

pack" having recently been defeated in the Senate, the military was troubled by the vulnerability of our deterrent. All of which pointed to renewed consideration of antimissile defenses of some sort.

Thanks, moreover, to recent advances in microelectronics, lasers, guidance technology, and computers, the technical success of such defenses seemed to be increasing exponentially. The work being done by Teller and his colleagues, and by others, strongly indicated that the job of knocking down incoming missiles was within our capability.

Several members of the Joint Chiefs of Staff—including the chairman, General John Vessey, and Admiral James Watkins, felt strongly that SDI was a moral as well as a military necessity. Thus, when the President tasked them with looking into it, the chiefs came up with a largely positive analysis. Backed by these military findings, and by the scientific researches of Teller and Jay Keyworth, the President resolved to push ahead. Accordingly, he had a passage inserted in his defense budget speech of March 23, 1983, in which he said:

"Wouldn't it be better to save lives than to avenge them? Are we not capable of demonstrating our peaceful intentions by applying all our abilities and our ingenuity to achieving a truly lasting stability? . . . Let me share with you a vision which offers hope. It is that we embark on a program to counter the awesome Soviet missile threat with measures that are defensive. . . . Current technology has attained a level of sophistication where it's reasonable to begin this effort . . . to give us the means of rendering these nuclear weapons impotent and obsolete."[6]

The preparations for this announcement were kept in utmost confidence. Given the aversion to missile defenses in the arms control community, the hostility of many in the State Department, and the skepticism of some in the military, the possibility that information on the program would be leaked was extremely high. So too was the likelihood that bureaucratic resistance would be mounted inside the government to kill the project off entirely.

This called for confidentiality—and dedicated leadership by the President. And, again, the President gave it. Had it not been for his perseverance and personal commitment, based on his study of the matter over a span of years, I don't think the program would have ever been born. Had it worked its way through the bureaucratic system, it almost certainly would have been stifled somewhere along the line.[7]

Although most objections to SDI were phrased in technical terms, the strongest reason for opposing it was political. The real problem was not that it might not work, but that it would—and thus go directly against the theory of MAD. And though research on it up to a certain point could be conducted within the limits of the ABM treaty, the basic idea was directly contrary to what the treaty was all about.

Once SDI was on the table, therefore, numerous discussions took place at the National Security Council on how to reconcile it with the ABM accord. Abe Sofaer of the State Department came up with a "broad" construction of the treaty, which would permit extensive testing of components of such a system, but no actual deployment. This provoked considerable criticism in Congress, and also in the USSR, on the grounds that it was simply a ruse to circumvent the treaty.

True or not, the effort to reconcile SDI with the ABM accord was essentially an effort to square the circle. If SDI was desirable, then homeland defenses were desirable as well. And if homeland defenses were desirable, the ABM accord was not. My own view was that since the treaty itself provided for termination on six months' notice, and since the treaty and SDI appeared to be in conflict, we should be prepared to invoke this clause. For the time being, however, the "broad" construction view prevailed.

Of special interest in all this was the reaction of the Soviets, who suddenly became devoted advocates of the ABM accord (though plentiful evidence existed showing that they were in violation of it). Thus they contended that any move to develop SDI would violate the treaty, which they proposed to extend and strengthen even further. Obviously, if the Soviets hadn't thought that SDI would work, they wouldn't have tried so hard to head it off.

Nothing could have better illustrated the importance that both Reagan and the Soviets attached to SDI—for diametrically opposite reasons—than the October 1986 summit at Reykjavik, Iceland. As became crystal-clear at the end of these proceedings, Gorbachev had carefully crafted his presentation to induce the President to abandon such defenses. Eliminating SDI was Gorbachev's main objective, and he gambled everything on its demise.

As his performance made plain, the Soviets not only thought SDI would work, they feared—above all—competition in this area of U.S. expertise. Economically and technically, as Reagan had foreseen, keeping up with America in such an enterprise was far beyond their means. And with SDI developed and deployed, all the strategic factors stemming from our vulnerability—such as the MX muddle or the INF dispute—would have been reversed. In all respects, SDI must have looked to Gorbachev like the trump card of the West.

He was accordingly willing to risk, or promise, whatever it took to bottle up the program. In this, he had some cards of his own to play: the hunger by many in the West and the United States (including Reagan) for deep reductions in offensive weapons; the deep hostility in our arms control community to ABM defenses; and the various people in our government (not including Reagan) who viewed SDI exclusively as a bargaining chip.

Gorbachev's actions at Reykjavik were artfully designed to play on all these motives and thereby induce the President to give up SDI in return for an alleged arms control utopia—INF cutbacks, slashes in strategic weapons, even limits on conventional forces. Thus Gorbachev front-loaded the proceedings by agreeing to reduce by half—and eventually eliminate entirely—all intercontinental and intermediate missiles, leading the President, George Shultz, and others on the scene to believe an historic breakthrough was in the making.

Then, having created near-euphoria, Gorbachev sprang his trap: All these good things could be achieved, he said, but at a cost—the elimination of SDI. By all reports, a number of officials in the U.S. delegation were more than willing to make the trade. And had Reagan been the passive creature popularly depicted, the offer would have been accepted on the spot. SDI would have been eliminated.

But Gorbachev—and just about everyone else—had badly underestimated Reagan's comprehension of, and perseverance on, this issue.

The President understood the relevant factors concerning SDI just as well as, or better, than Gorbachev, and he was not about to trade it away, even for so enticing an offer as that extended by the Soviet leader. Since SDI threatened no one, Reagan realized that there was nothing incompatible with maintaining it as a defense while eliminating offensive weapons. So why insist on its removal?

Reagan also knew the Soviets had a lengthy history of evading arms agreements. In a world devoid of missile defenses, and with everyone else disarmed, this meant that a power possessing even one offensive missile could exert irresistible blackmail. SDI was an insurance policy against that possibility, and Reagan was not about to give it up. As he put it:

"[A]fter everything had been decided, or so I thought, Gorbachev threw us a curve. With a smile on his face, he said, 'This all depends, of course, on you giving up SDI.' I realized he had brought me to Iceland with one purpose: to kill the Strategic Defense Initiative. He must have known from the beginning he was going to bring it up at the last minute. 'The meeting is over,' I said. 'Let's go . . . we're leaving.' "[8]

Though many inspiring episodes have marked Ronald Reagan's career, in global-strategic terms this was his finest hour—and arguably the one that conclusively won the Cold War for the West. The President, going one-on-one with Gorbachev, not only avoided the trap set for him, but effectively turned the tables—strengthening rather than weakening the U.S. commitment to SDI. Gorbachev at this point must have known that he had gambled, and lost.

It wasn't treated that way, of course, by the media, the arms control community, or other establishment spokesmen. Taking their cues from a lugubrious briefing by George Shultz, the press treated Reykjavik as something close to a disaster: a blundering Ronald Reagan had refused to get an historic arms agreement because of his "ideological" hang-up with SDI. How foolish, ran the commentary, not to trade away this pet project for the deal proposed by Gorbachev.

But the public saw it differently—to the amazement of the pundits and the politicians. Post-Reykjavik polls showed strong support for Reagan's position and rising approval for SDI itself, suggesting that the common sense of the American people was far superior to the theories of the arms control establishment. And, as it turned out, the Soviets came back to the bargaining table to sign the INF agreement the following year. Clearly, Ronald Reagan knew more about this subject—and about how to bargain with the Soviets—than did the voluble chorus of his critics.

15

THE QADDAFI
CONNECTION

A CHRONIC PROBLEM of the modern era has been terrorism, with its many facets, and it presented many challenges to the Reagan government. The issue had absorbed the public in 1979–80 because of the long captivity of fifty-two Americans at our embassy in Tehran. In the early 1980s it subsided, only to revive in 1985 with the seizure of TWA flight 847, the kidnapping of individual Americans in Lebanon, the hijacking of the *Achille Lauro*, terrorist bombings in Vienna and Rome, and other episodes.

The most prominent replay of the terrorist-hostage melodrama, of course, was the "Iran-Contra" dispute of 1986 (more on which in due course), turning against the Reagan White House the issue that had plagued the government of Jimmy Carter.

The underlying dilemma in all such incidents is much the same—the danger posed to innocent parties when action is taken against terrorists, balanced against the costs incurred if action is not taken. In the obvious case, the rescue of people held hostage can result in the death of the hostages themselves. Terrorists also often conceal themselves among, or near, civilian populations or institutions (such as schools or hospitals), creating the possibility of "collateral damage" in any strike against them.

How to handle problems of this sort was a top priority of the Reagan administration. First as counsellor to the president and then as attorney general, I had occasion to address them many times. (The law enforcement aspects of the issue, which were one of our major considerations at the Department of Justice, are discussed in chapter 22.)

Of special concern to U.S. policymakers was the matter of state-sponsored terrorism, and how to deal with nations that promoted it. Contrary to the popular impression, acts of terrorism are not always or even usually isolated episodes by individual fanatics, but more often part of a much larger scheme, promoted by countries hostile to America and the West.

There was considerable evidence, for example, that the Soviets and various of their satellites were involved in training, subsidizing, and otherwise encouraging terrorists. As intermediaries, they supported or used such countries as Syria, Libya, East Germany, Bulgaria, and Cuba, as well as the Palestine Liberation Organization. We had intelligence data on each of these, showing how they sponsored, trained, financed, and facilitated the movement of terrorist groups. (At the same time, numerous terrorist organizations had their own causes, objectives, and targets.)

Logically, this suggested the need to go after the sponsors of state terrorism, and we formulated a variety of approaches for doing just that. But a number of impediments were raised, both within the intelligence community and in the State Department, against such action.

One aspect of this disagreement became public in the 1991 Senate hearings weighing the nomination of Robert Gates to head the CIA. Some Soviet analysts within the agency doubted the evidence that the USSR was involved in promoting terrorism—evidence persuasive to Bill Casey and many other terrorism experts—on the grounds that there was no "smoking gun" to pin the guilt conclusively on Moscow. Even more bitter disagreements had arisen within the CIA on the specific question of whether the Soviets and their Bulgarian agents had been involved in the attempted assassination of the Pope.[1]

Such uncertainties meant that a retaliatory strategy against states responsible for terrorism, while easy to propound in theory, was harder to execute in practice. These factors lent special importance to the case of Libya's Muammar Qaddafi, the most active and visible promoter of state-sponsored terrorism in the 1970s and early 1980s and one on whom we had the most extensive information.

Bill Casey had long been keeping an eye on Qaddafi, who was closely linked to the PLO and to Abu Nidal (mastermind of the attack on the Rome and Vienna airports). Western intelligence had broken the Libyans' code, which enabled us to track many of their activities. In addition, Qaddafi often spoke on open phone lines, and we received good intelligence on Libya from the Israelis.[2]

Qaddafi had a theatrical streak that led him to posture on the world stage, bragging of his plans and exploits. In particular, he seemed to relish the idea of going head to head with Ronald Reagan, apparently viewing this as the way to become a "Third World" revolutionary leader. This combustible mix of elements produced a series of clashes with the United States across a five-year period during the Reagan era.

The principal site of these collisions was the Gulf of Sidra, off the North African coast in the Mediterranean, an area where the United States has long maintained a major naval presence. Every year, the U.S. Sixth Fleet conducts extensive exercises in this region, recognized as international waters, to test its battle-readiness.

In the late 1970s, in his role as would-be challenger to the United States, Qaddafi decided to extend the coastal claims of Libya to the waters where these maneuvers were conducted. The entire Gulf of Sidra, extending up to one hundred miles from Tripoli and Benghazi, was proclaimed by Qaddafi to be a Libyan lake, off limits to our forces. The Carter government, unfortunately, had meekly rescheduled our maneuvers to stay outside the prohibited area.

In 1981, with Reagan in the White House, the situation predictably arose again—but with a different outcome. Apprised of Qaddafi's claims as the time for these annual exercises approached, the President let it be known that the United States would not be buffaloed or bullied. He gave the order for the maneuvers to proceed, saying that if the Libyans attempted to interfere, our personnel had orders to defend themselves as needed.

To insure this outcome, the Joint Chiefs established rules of engagement for our forces, which were then reviewed and approved directly by the President. At a briefing of the President and the National Security Council on these rules, the admiral responsible for the naval forces asked whether our response to any attack included hot pursuit into Libyan territory. The President answered: "All the way into the hangar," if necessary.

On the evening of August 18, 1981, two navy F-14s flying escort for our ships were challenged by a pair of Libyan MIGs, one of which fired on the American planes. Our pilots immediately launched heat-seeking missiles and downed the Libyan fighters. So ended Qaddafi's military pretensions—for the moment.[3]

Having failed in this straightforward military challenge, Qaddafi resorted to his favorite tactic—terrorism. Our intelligence sources informed us that, in conversations with an African leader, Qaddafi had vowed to bring about the assassination of President Reagan. Shortly thereafter, we received intelligence that Libyan "hit" teams were making their way to the United States, with the President and others in our government as their targets. Security measures were mounted and no assassinations were attempted.*

In March 1986, having obtained Soviet SA-5 anti-aircraft missiles and other more advanced weapons, Qaddafi was ready for another military showdown. This time he declared that the Gulf of Sidra was a "zone of death" and vowed to destroy any American forces that ventured into it. Again we proceeded with our exercises, which brought on a series of engagements between U.S. and Libyan forces, in which we destroyed two Libyan missile boats and knocked out the radar for the SA-5 sites. This time the Libyan MIGs stayed prudently in their own air space, and the U.S. maneuvers went on as planned.

So, once again, Qaddafi fell back on the terrorist option. On March

---

* I remember this one very well, since I was one of the people on the list, along with the President and Vice President, the secretary of state, Jeane Kirkpatrick, and others. As a result, for a period of several months, Secret Service men went with me everywhere and watched our house.

28, he called on Arabs everywhere to attack anything and everything American, "be it an interest, goods, ships, plane, or person." Based on past experience, and on information we were receiving at the time, we knew the threat should be taken seriously.

Specifically, we had intelligence that Qaddafi was planning a terrorist act against American interests, most probably in Germany— although we did not know exactly when, or where. That act occurred on April 5, when a bomb exploded in a West Berlin discotheque frequented by the U.S. military; one serviceman was killed and fifty others injured, along with even larger numbers of civilians. From messages we had picked up out of Tripoli and Berlin, there was no doubt that Qaddafi was behind the bombing.[4]

The President never hesitated. He gave the order for a swift and sure response. He directed Cap Weinberger and the Joint Chiefs to come up with a very specific and highly focused plan to punish Qaddafi's terrorism. The essence of the plan was to go after military, support, and training assets directly linked to Libya's terrorist activities, while avoiding collateral injury to civilians.

Despite tremendous logistical difficulties, the retaliatory strike was conducted almost exactly as the President directed. Our combined forces performed brilliantly, knocking out the selected targets and totally discomfiting Qaddafi and his henchmen. In military terms, it was a great success; politically speaking, there was the usual quota of dissension.

Our biggest political/logistical problem had been the refusal of the French president, François Mitterrand, to allow our planes to use French air space to reach Libya. The French refusal added about a thousand miles to the distance covered by our planes, which had to be refueled four times in flight (at night and under radio silence). Mrs. Thatcher, in contrast, readily assented to having U.S. F-111s take off from England.

At home, dissenters complained that Reagan was engaging in unnecessary violence (including unproved charges that U.S. bombs had killed Qaddafi's adopted child), that the raid really had not accomplished anything, and that our retaliation would only spur Qaddafi on to greater acts of terrorism. Oddly enough, it did not work out that way. Qaddafi faded from view, seldom seen or heard from again during the remaining Reagan years.

Reagan's actions against Qaddafi were of key importance in breaking the "Vietnam syndrome." Not only did the President move against one of the world's most notorious troublemakers, he did so in a situation where the Carter government had shown visible signs of weakness. The contrast could hardly have been lost on Qaddafi—or his allies in the Kremlin.

The Libyan episode of 1981 was the first time President Reagan authorized the use of military forces in defense of U.S. interests—and the President never flinched. His message was loud and clear: No longer could Third World despots challenge the United States and depend on America's post-Vietnam guilt complex, or its uncertainty about its global role, to bind our hands. No longer would we act as a "pitiful, helpless giant," crippled by internal divisions or ideological confusion.

Vital to this success, as to many others, was the personal leadership of the President. His critics tried hard to obscure this point—using me as their instrument. This had to do with the flap about "letting the President sleep" when we were informed about the engagement between our F-14s and Libyan MIGs. In the total scheme of things, this sidebar is hardly crucial, but since it has been distorted to portray the President as snoozing while U.S. forces were in combat, the record should be set straight.

Of key importance, as noted, the rules of engagement for our forces in the Mediterranean had been personally approved by Reagan—and strengthened by his personal order that our pilots engage in hot pursuit as needed. The significance of this instruction can hardly be overstated, particularly in view of the experience of the military in Vietnam and before that in Korea. The President did not want American pilots to have any doubt about what they could or couldn't do if they were attacked by Libyan forces.

At the time of this episode, the President was at the Century Plaza Hotel in Los Angeles with members of the senior staff for a series of meetings on the budget. On the evening of August 18, I had retired at about 10:00 or 10:30 P.M. only to be awakened around 11:00 by Dick Allen who was in communication with Cap Weinberger, now back at the Pentagon. Cap had informed him that U.S. planes had been fired upon over the Gulf of Sidra and that our pilots had responded.

This was only a preliminary report. Two Libyan planes, Cap said, had been shot down. There was speculation that other planes had been downed as well and that a Libyan patrol boat had been involved in the fighting; more details were to follow. I told Dick we needed to get the story together accurately before informing the President.

As it happened, we did not get the complete report from Washington until about 4:00 A.M. when Dick and I talked with Cap Weinberger from my room. At that point, at 4:28 A.M. to be precise, we roused the President and gave him the complete report. And that, believe it or not, is the extent of the story, a story that administration critics have tried to use to the discredit of the President (and mine as well).

This episode is a good example of what I have called "gotcha" journalism, which has little to do with substance but a lot to do with trying to discredit something or someone. In this case, the action had gone according to the President's instructions, no further presidential decision was required, and it didn't matter a whit when the President was awakened. Yet this episode became a whirlpool of media charges and political innuendos.[5]

In the 1986 retaliation against Qaddafi, the President's direct involvement was equally pronounced, though you would hardly know it from the conventional treatment. I vividly remember the Joint Chiefs of Staff assembled in the Oval Office, showing the President maps of Tripoli and getting his direction about targets. A great deal of care was taken in the planning, with the President insisting on precision bombing of military targets. In some cases, because these were close to civilian populations, they were excluded from the target plan at the President's command. It was a further example of the complexities involved in dealing with terrorists—and of the President's hands-on involvement in the direction of our policy.

If Libya was a strong plus for America in the battle against terrorism, Lebanon was the opposite. The Reagan administration inherited a host of problems in this strife-torn country and made little headway in resolving them. Nor, on the record, is it likely that anyone else is going to do much better in the foreseeable future.

Events in Lebanon also had repercussions in other areas—most notably for the Reagan government, in the Iran-Contra affair. In the dialectic of Mideast politics, action and reaction have a way of compounding that no one can foresee. This dynamic—pushed partly by our adversaries, partly by our own decisions—led to the most searing tragedies of the Reagan era.

When the Reagan government arrived in Washington in 1981, Lebanon had been involved in fratricidal conflict for years. Internally, the country was split between Maronite Christians (most prominently headed by the Gemayel family) on the one hand, and an array of Muslim forces on the other. In addition, Lebanon had become the unwilling host of the Palestine Liberation Organization and a sizable contingent of troops from neighboring Syria.

The countryside was ruled by various militias, both Christian and Muslim, which fought among themselves and controlled different sections of Beirut. Their constant infighting meant the central government, headed by Bashir and then Amin Gemayel, had only nominal authority. It also provided the pretext for Damascus to keep forty thousand to fifty thousand troops in Lebanon, which Syria had long claimed as part of its domain.

These circumstances were made to order for terrorism, and Lebanon's Bekaa Valley was a training ground for terrorist factions from around the world—principally the PLO, but also the Japanese Red Army, the IRA, and many others. The PLO and its allies, moreover, controlled entry to and exit from Beirut airport, which meant that terrorist groups could come and go at will.[6]

As if all this were not enough, the forces deployed in Lebanon included groups of Shiite extremists, opposed to both the Christians and Sunni Muslims of the country. The Shiites were virulently anti-American and looked for inspiration and support to the government of the Ayatollah Khomeini in Iran.

The Soviets and the Eastern bloc, as might have been expected, were in the thick of these events, principally by supplying the Syrians, but also through their direct involvement with terrorist groups in the Bekaa. During the fighting of 1982, huge quantities of East-bloc ordinance were captured by the Israelis, as were PLO guerrilla fighters with identity cards attesting that they had been trained in Bulgaria, Hungary, and the USSR itself.[7]

Numerous acts of terrorism traced back to this complex of forces. Intelligence data on hijackings, bombings, assassinations, and hostage-takings repeatedly pointed to Lebanon, often implicating Syria, Iran, and Libya along the way. If there was such a thing as terrorism central, Lebanon was obviously the place.

All of which meant Lebanon was a dangerous spot for Americans, and we made a concerted effort to keep our citizens from going there. But there were professors and administrators at the American University in Beirut, religious missionaries, journalists, diplomats, and other officials—all stationed in the country representing Western interests. They were obvious targets for harassment by extremists and, in 1984 and 1985, for hostage-taking and other acts of terrorism.

Flashpoint for these antagonisms was the hostility of the Palestinians, the Shiite and other Muslim militias, and the Syrians, toward Israel. A constant series of guerrilla raids and terrorist acts crisscrossed the Israeli border, principally involving the PLO, which, in uneasy alliance with the Syrians, had virtually become a state within the Lebanese state.

In attempting to cope with this chaotic scene, the Israeli strategy was to work with Maronite Christians to shore up the power of the central government. But this was obviously impossible, unless the power of the Syrians and PLO were broken. In retrospect, this was exactly what the Israelis wanted all along—although they did not say so at the time.

In June of 1982, the Israeli ambassador to London was injured in a terrorist attack linked to the PLO. On June 6, after a preliminary exchange of air and artillery attacks, the Israeli Defense Force rolled into southern Lebanon with the avowed intent of suppressing the PLO guerrillas in the vicinity. As the fighting continued, however, it became clear that the Israeli goal was to force the PLO out of the country altogether.

When the Israelis laid siege to Beirut, political and media protests rapidly mounted. Televison featured reports of civilians, including infants, allegedly killed by the Israeli forces. State Department and White House policymakers were increasingly worried by these reports. They were also attempting to maintain a delicate balance in the region, fearing the Soviets might be drawn into the fighting on the Syrian side.[8]

Most people in the administration—Cap Weinberger, Bill Clark, and nearly everyone else in the defense and foreign policy loop, including the President—were aghast at the accounts of the Lebanon conflict and what was perceived as the intransigent stance of Israeli Prime Minister Menachem Begin. The chief exception was Al Haig, who was more inclined toward the Israeli viewpoint.

Al, however, was in the process of resigning—and by June 25 his resignation had been accepted. But since George Shultz was not yet confirmed as his successor, Al continued to administer the department in a lame-duck capacity. In these circumstances, Phil Habib, a career diplomat and the President's special emissary to the region, came to the forefront. He devised a plan to halt the fighting with a multinational peacekeeping force, including U.S. Marines, along with troops from Italy and France, to oversee the resulting truce. This course was followed, and the MNF presided over the PLO's evacuation of Beirut.

Seemingly successful at the time, this proved to be a fateful decision. The Marines remained in Lebanon for over a year (after a brief two-week withdrawal in September 1982*), in an increasingly untenable situation. Cap Weinberger argued strenuously against keeping the Marines in place. Since they were there only as a "presence" and buffer among warring factions and were not a viable military force, Cap contended, they could become a sitting duck for hostile forces.

This disquiet became even more pronounced when the Israelis, under a May 1983 agreement worked out by George Shultz, agreed to withdraw their forces on condition the Syrians do likewise. But the Syrians refused. When the Israelis pulled back anyway, our Marines

---

* The Marines withdrew after the evacuation of the PLO, but returned when Bashir Gemayel was assassinated in a bombing attack that our intelligence indicated was inspired by Syria.

were left in an even more exposed position. Most worrisome militarily, they were billeted on the low ground at Beirut airport, while Syrian and Muslim militia forces occupied the mountainous positions above.[9]

Despite Cap Weinberger's repeated warnings, the State Department insisted that the marines be left in place. And so, in the absence of any other policy, and with a deceptive lull in Lebanon, they were. Then, on the night of October 23, 1983, a suicide bomber drove his truck through the perimeter defenses of the U.S. installation and exploded a bomb that destroyed the building and killed 241 marines. Within three months, the remaining marines were "redeployed" out of Lebanon.

That was the most tragic of our experiences with terrorism in Lebanon, but not the only one. In 1984 and early in 1985, though it received little notice at the time, extremist groups began kidnapping Americans (and other Westerners) and holding them hostage, usually demanding the release of some arrested terrorist or prisoners from the Lebanese fighting. By mid-1985, the score had reached seven American hostages. While their plight perturbed us, it had not yet been sensationalized by the media. That would soon change dramatically.

In June 1985, a group of Shiite terrorists hijacked TWA flight 847 out of Athens bound for Rome and wound up seeking refuge at Beirut airport; the thirty-nine Americans on board were held captive. This hijacking was directly linked to the Lebanese fighting of 1982–84, as the terrorists demanded the release of seven hundred Shiite prisoners captured by the Israelis, and blamed the U.S. hostages for American actions in the conflict.

The terrorists flaunted their brutality by beating and killing a passenger on flight 847, American navy diver Robert Stethem, and dumping his body on the airport tarmac. This gruesome episode and the armed standoff around the plane once more riveted the attention of the American nation on the issue of terrorism and hostages. For two weeks, dramatic footage of the TWA crew and American passengers with their armed captors dominated television news.

Bud McFarlane, who had been actively involved in the Lebanon situation in 1983, conducted intensive negotiations to free the captives. Bud dealt mainly with the extremist Amal militia of Lebanon, which held most of the prisoners, and with the government of Syria, widely known to have influence over the Lebanese group. Less publicized help was also provided, according to Bud, by representatives of Iran, which had influence with another Shiite group, the Hizballah, holding some of the American captives.

After seventeen days of negotiations, the TWA hostages were set free, with most of the public credit going to President Hafez al Assad of Syria. Similar thanks were quietly extended, however, to the government of Iran, though what role exactly it had played was unclear at the time. Suffice it to say, the intervention of these third parties in the airport crisis was recognized by President Reagan and others in the administration.

This episode had many repercussions. It served to focus much greater public attention on the seven other U.S. hostages then being held in Lebanon, raising the question of why they could not be released as well. And it intensified efforts within the administration to strengthen our counterterrorism program with a task force at the National Security Council, including representatives of the CIA, FBI, Defense, and State. The coordinator from the NSC staff, operating under the direction of Bud McFarlane, was marine Lt. Col. Oliver North.

On October 7, 1985, North, Charles Allen of the CIA, and the U.S. military were put to the test in another sensational episode—the hijacking of the *Achille Lauro*, an Italian cruise ship in the Mediterranean. I learned of the situation at about ten o'clock that evening, Washington time, when Ollie North phoned me to help enlist the cooperation of the Italian interior minister, with whom I had previously worked on antiterrorism matters. The minister was very helpful and his government gave some cooperation, though not as much as we would have liked.

The hijackers, as it turned out, were henchmen of Abul Abbas, a key lieutenant of Yassar Arafat of the PLO. They demanded the release of fifty Palestinians jailed by the Israelis on charges of terrorism. To prove they meant business, they murdered an invalid American passenger named Leon Klinghoffer and pushed his body overboard.

When the terrorists sought asylum in Egypt, Abul Abbas attempted to sneak them out on an Egyptian commercial flight. Through radio intercepts and intelligence supplied by the Israelis, North and the antiterrorism team were able to pinpoint the airbase, flight time, tail numbers, and other specifics of the journey. North and others at the NSC, working with Admiral Art Moreau, coordinated a remarkable midair interception, in which F-14 Tomcats from the USS *Saratoga* forced the Egyptian plane to land in Sicily. The four original terrorists were eventually tried and convicted, although the Italians allowed Abul Abbas himself to escape.[10]

This daring interception showed once again that the U.S. government, under Reagan, was ready to use military assets to protect its interests. When news of this exploit was broadcast around the world, it signaled another high point in our struggle against terrorism—for which Bud McFarlane, Ollie North, Art Moreau, and the courageous military personnel who executed the intercept deserve the utmost credit.

Still, the underlying problems of terrorism remained. We had gotten a relatively clean shot at Qaddafi's military forces, after irrefutable proof of his involvement in the disco bombing, and our military had been able to catch the *Achille Lauro* hoodlums in midflight. But we seldom had a chance to get the perpetrators in the open without endangering civilians. The hostage problem continued to gnaw at all of us.

Out of this jumble of events there grew a series of relationships, precedents, actions, and reactions that would ultimately play out before the world in the Iran-Contra controversy. Three developments in particular foreshadowed what would become the most serious crisis of the Reagan government:

—Terrorists in the region continued to torment the United States with hostage-taking and other hostile actions, demanding concessions from the U.S., other Western nations, or the Israelis. And the glare of publicity heightened concern about the ordeal of the hostages.

—McFarlane, North, and others at the National Security Council were drawn into the maelstrom of Mideast politics, the problems of Lebanon, and terrorism, which among other things meant dealing with regimes in Syria and Iran that supported and influenced the hostage-takers.

—McFarlane and North, in attempting to disentangle all these problems, as in the *Achille Lauro* episode, came increasingly to work with and rely on Israeli officials, whose intelligence about the Middle East and terrorist groups—and whose experience in acting on such matters—far surpassed our own.

We would all hear more about these topics in the days to come.

16

CONFLICT IN THE
CARIBBEAN

"I T WAS THE BEST OF TIMES, it was the worst of times." That passage
from Dickens aptly describes American foreign policy in the turbulent
days of October 1983.

On the third weekend of that month, U.S. efforts to establish peace
in Lebanon were shattered by the tragic death of our Marines, victims
of a terrorist bomb attack. But on that weekend, too, the President
showed the quality of his leadership by the way he handled the crisis in
Grenada. His resolve was the more remarkable for coming in the wake
of the sickening blow to America's servicemen in Beirut.

We had been aware for many months of trouble brewing in Grenada,
a tiny island nation in the southern Caribbean, and of the threat it
posed to the region. This was yet another country that had fallen under
Marxist-Leninist domination in the late 1970s, and though it received
less notice than Vietnam, Afghanistan, or Nicaragua, we viewed it
with great unease.

The strategic significance of Grenada can be grasped by viewing a map of the Caribbean. As Cuba sits astride the northern sealanes to the region, so Grenada sits athwart the southernmost. With Nicaragua adjacent to the Panama Canal, the Marxists could easily threaten all our vital sea routes in the region, through which passes something like 50 percent of American foreign commerce and military traffic.

Grenada had fallen under the control of a Marxist group called the New Jewel Movement, under Prime Minister Maurice Bishop, through a coup d'état in 1979. As was evident then and became even more so later, Bishop and his party were closely linked to Cuba, and through Cuba to the Soviet Union and the entire Eastern bloc. In 1983, he was himself the target of a coup by a still more radical faction, and in October he and his closest followers were murdered.

The civil war raging on the island and the rule by violence deeply disturbed the governments of the small neighboring island nations. Threatened by the deteriorating situation in Grenada, leaders of these countries, operating through the Organization of Eastern Caribbean States (OECS), called on the United States for help. As did Sir Paul Scoon, Grenada's British governor general, who constituted the last vestige of any kind of lawful authority on the island (and was himself under house arrest).[1]

The gravity of the situation to the United States was underscored by the presence on the island of some one thousand U.S. citizens—about eight hundred of whom were students at St. George's Medical College, a branch of an institution headquartered in New York. As martial law was imposed, with a shoot-on-sight curfew, we became increasingly worried about these Americans.

We also knew that there were Cubans on Grenada—mostly a "construction" battalion building a 10,000-foot jet aircraft runway at Port Salines on the southern part of the island. (These "construction" battalions, it turned out, were heavily armed paramilitary forces.) The runway, far larger than anything Grenada might need for peacetime use, was obviously intended for Soviet and Cuban military aircraft. As the President had put it in his March 23, 1983, defense address:

"On the small island of Grenada, at the southern end of the Caribbean chain, the Cubans, with Soviet financing and backing, are in the process of building a 10,000-foot runway. Grenada doesn't even have an air force. Whom is it intended for? The Caribbean is a very important passageway for our international commerce and military lines of communication. More than half of all American oil imports pass through the Caribbean. The rapid buildup of Grenada's military potential is unrelated to any conceivable threat to this island country of 100,000 people and totally at odds with the pattern of other Eastern Caribbean states, most of which are unarmed."[2]

Also noteworthy, Grenada had close ties with almost all the Soviet bloc and slavishly followed the Moscow line on global affairs. The Marxist government of Grenada voted more than 90 percent of the time with the Soviets at the United Nations, even opposing a UN resolution condemning the USSR's invasion of Afghanistan. It had military aid agreements with Moscow and Havana, and trade agreements with the Soviets, East Germany, Bulgaria, and Czechoslovakia. Bishop and other Grenadians were also in regular contact with the Soviet KGB under Yuri Andropov, and with Vietnam and North Korea, in search of training, arms, and indoctrination. Bishop himself had visited Cuba, Moscow, and Eastern Europe.

This ought to have established Bishop's hard-line Marxism, but to New Jewel dissidents it was not enough. Either fearing that Bishop might moderate his course, or simply for internal power purposes, a group under Gen. Hudson Austin moved against Bishop. On October 12, Bishop was placed under house arrest, and a week later he and his immediate followers were put to death. The thought that people even more fanatical than Bishop were now in charge and ruling by "shoot on sight" martial law was hardly reassuring.

All of this was more than confirmed by papers captured during the liberation of Grenada (see below). But for the time being, the evidence of violence on the island, and the potential threat to U.S. citizens was sufficiently compelling. The urgency of the situation came crashing in on us that third weekend in October. It demanded—and received—immediate action by President Reagan.

Just about everything, it seemed, happened on that weekend. For the only time in his presidency that I can remember, Reagan had decided to take a golfing weekend, and had gone to Augusta, Georgia, to play a few rounds with George Shultz, Nick Brady, and Donald Regan.*

Early Saturday morning, the request came from the Organization of Eastern Caribbean States, signed by Mrs. Eugenia Charles, the prime minister of Dominica and chairman of the OECS, asking for U.S. military assistance to help deal with the threat in Grenada. This request was relayed to George Shultz in Augusta at the golfing cottage where he was staying with the President; the message arrived at 2:45 A.M. on Saturday morning, while the President was asleep. Shultz conferred with Bud McFarlane, who was with the traveling party, and both of them talked by secure phone with Vice President Bush and others in Washington, gathering more information.

At 5:15 A.M. Shultz and McFarlane decided to wake the President and inform him of the situation—the request for assistance from the OECS and the danger to the American students. The President immediately decided we should honor the OECS request, while also assuring the safety of the students, and called for a National Security Council meeting. Four hours later, these matters were discussed over a secure speaker phone with the rest of us on the National Security Planning Group, who had gathered in Washington, at a specially constructed conference room in the Old Executive Office Building. Within hours, military plans were being drawn up and further information sought concerning the Americans on the island.[3]

While this was going on, the terrorists in Lebanon were preparing their attack on the Marines. That evening (actually, early Sunday morning), word was received that the Marines had been killed. The President, who had previously determined not to come back to Washington so as not to alert the Grenada regime of our impending plans, decided now to return immediately, and arrived at about eight o'clock on Sunday morning.

Again he conferred with the NSPG, this time in the Situation

* On Saturday afternoon, while the President was on the golf course, an apparently deranged person invaded the pro shop, took Dave Fisher, a member of the President's traveling party, hostage, and demanded to talk to the President. The assailant was captured and no one was harmed. But the incident was unsettling for everyone—especially as it raised the specter of the assassination attempt of 1981.

Room, where he was briefed on the tragedy of the Marines and brought up to date on the Grenada operation. It was a grim and serious time for all of us, but especially for the President. The combined weight of these two crises would be a heavy burden on any leader.

It may seem hard to remember now—after successful actions in Panama and the Persian Gulf—but the negatives arrayed against decisive action in Grenada were almost too numerous to count. Not only did the operation proceed in the very wake of the disaster in Beirut, it flew in the teeth of fashionable opinion about the uses of American military power. From the standpoint of 1970s ideology, Reagan was planning to throw America's weight around, using our military to stand up for our interests and our allies. This was heresy, and plenty of people were prepared to say so.

Given this thinking, the President knew he wouldn't get much by way of bipartisan backing, though he dutifully briefed the leadership of Congress on what was about to happen. I vividly remember Tip O'Neill listening in silence as the President explained the situation, then saying, "Well, Mr. President, it's your show." The implication, all too clearly, was that if the effort misfired, Ronald Reagan would be the one responsible. The President accepted that.

As if domestic opposition weren't enough, a further element weighed against the President's decision: his closest international ally, Prime Minister Margaret Thatcher, opposed the action.

Grenada was part of the British Commonwealth and had a British-appointed governor general, but the British were too far away to take any immediate measures. With this in mind, the President talked to Mrs. Thatcher to brief her on the crisis and our impending action. For whatever reason, she was against it. The President was deeply disappointed, but he stood firm, telling her that we intended to go ahead.

Meanwhile, in National Security Council meetings on Sunday, we were aware that public revulsion to the killing of the marines would argue against committing our forces in Grenada; the President gave the go-ahead to the planning and said he would make his final decision on Monday. On Monday afternoon, he met with the Joint Chiefs, who presented him with the final plans for the operation.

Again the political factors came into play. In the course of the military briefing, Gen. John Vessey, chairman of the Joint Chiefs, gave voice to the NSC's apprehensions when he said, "Mr. President, we think we ought to bring up, even though it is not a military matter, the fact there is a potential public opinion downside to this because of what happened to the marines."* He and his colleagues thought too much of their commander-in-chief not to at least raise the question.

The President asked one question: "Is there any military reason for not going ahead with the operation?" The chiefs answered no; militarily, the plan was feasible. The President thereupon gave the order to proceed; he signed the official authorization at 6:55 P.M. on Monday evening.[4]

The Joint Chiefs were right, of course, about the political outcry. The uproar was nearly deafening. In Congress and the media, and in the forums of "world opinion," the President was denounced for reviving gunboat diplomacy, practicing imperialism, and the rest of the familiar litany. The head of St. George's Medical School was quoted as saying the students were in no danger, and assertions were made that, in fact, the students were merely a ruse on Reagan's part to justify belligerence. The alleged security concerns of other nations in the area were viewed with a similarly jaundiced eye.

Predictably, the far Left was outraged by Reagan's action. Jesse Jackson accused Reagan of "unjustly occupying" Grenada, George McGovern denounced the action as "utterly irresponsible," and Sen. Alan Cranston attacked the President as "trigger happy." Rep. John Conyers went so far as to file suit in federal court—supported by the ACLU Foundation of Southern California, the National Lawyers Guild, and others—seeking an injunction against the presence of our forces in Grenada.[5]

More mainstream liberal voices were just as critical. Sen. Daniel P.

---

* Another factor that helped stir resistance, but was necessary to the success of the mission, was the decision not to take the press along. Some of the press corps viewed any such action by the United States as a media event, and were outraged that they weren't allowed to have reporters and camera crews along on the initial landings. From the President's standpoint, this would have been a distraction and a military hazard, with the added danger that anything known in advance to the press could all too possibly be leaked.

Moynihan called the Grenada operation "an act of war," which the United States "does not have a right to do." And Tip O'Neill, initially noncommittal in tone, compared Reagan's action to Soviet aggressions. The *New York Times* unhesitatingly took a similar line: "The cost is the loss of the high moral ground, a demonstration to the world that America has no more respect for laws and borders, for the codes of civilization, than the Soviet Union."* 6

Especially (and predictably) negative was the response of the United Nations, which voted overwhelmingly to deplore the "armed intervention" of the U.S. The Security Council vote was 11 to 1 against us, while in the General Assembly it was 108 to 9—with only El Salvador and Israel joining America and the six small Caribbean countries who sought our help. (Among those who voted against us, sad to say, were France, Australia, and Ireland, plus eight members of NATO; such usually stalwart allies as Britain, West Germany, Japan, and Canada abstained—while issuing public criticisms of our action.)7

Thus, the United States under Ronald Reagan stood virtually alone on the question of Grenada. If "world opinion" had won the day, the citizens of Grenada and the Americans there would have been consigned indefinitely to the mercy of the murderous regime of General Austin. That says a great deal about the United Nations. It says even more about the determination of Ronald Reagan.

Given the welter of charges and countercharges, the average American could have been forgiven for not knowing who, or what, to believe. On the one hand, President Reagan, plus some Republicans in Congress, declared the Grenada action was urgently needed. On the other, the massed forces of the liberals—congressional critics, the media, "world opinion"—excoriated it. In the battle of the sound bites, it was hard to know who was telling the truth.

But as events unfolded, the battle tipped decisively toward Reagan,

---

* Such comparisons, of course, blandly ignored the fact that the Soviets invaded, say, Afghanistan, to control it, and that their entry was bitterly contested by the local population. Americans went into Grenada to liberate it, to protect U.S. citizens, and to restore order, were joyously welcomed by the local population, and left as soon as the job was completed. Surveys after the Grenada operation showed 90 percent of the people there in favor of the U.S. action.

making the Grenada operation one of the watershed developments of the era.

The first turning point was the appearance of Mrs. Charles at Reagan's side in an early morning press conference on Tuesday, October 26, where she calmly and forcefully explained the threat in Grenada, and the fears of other nations in the region. She was an impressive leader in her own right, as I discovered when I breakfasted with her early on the morning of the conference. Her words made plain that the danger of Marxist violence in Grenada was not a figment of Reagan's imagination.

The second event, even more dramatic, took place when the American students from Grenada were flown back to the United States and appeared before a skeptical press corps and a public that had been told they were in no danger. On live television at Charleston Air Force Base, a crowd watched curiously as the first of them descended from the plane; before he could reach a microphone, he walked over to the runway tarmac, dropped to his knees, and kissed the soil of the United States.

With that simple gesture, the debate about Grenada was effectively over.

The most conclusive proof of all, however, was still to come: the 35,000 documents that showed in detail the despotic character of the Grenada government, its suppression of dissent, its linkage to the communist movement around the world, its massive (relative to its size) arms buildup, and its threat to its neighbors in the region. The memoranda of the government also revealed tentative plans by the Grenada military to seize the U.S. medical students as hostages—something we had foreseen and feared.

Of particular interest was the material about arms acquisitions by the Grenada regime and the contracts and treaties that promised more of the same. A State Department analysis notes that "Soviet, Cuban, North Korean, and Czechoslovakian agreements included the following items, which were to have been delivered by 1986":

—approximately 10,000 assault and other rifles
—more than 4,500 submachine guns and machine guns

—more than 11.5 million rounds of 7.62 mm ammunition
—294 portable rocket launchers with more than 16,000 rockets
—84 82 mm mortars with more than 4,800 mortar shells
—12 75 mm cannon with 600 cannon shells
—15,000 hand grenades, 7,000 land mines, 60 armored personnel carriers
and patrol vehicles
—more than 150 radio transmitters, 160 field telephone sets, approximately
23,000 uniforms, and tents for about 7,700 persons.[8]

These data fully confirmed the OECS' alarm about the possibility
of aggression by the Grenada Marxists. As the State Department
analysis adds:

By the U.S. Department of Defense estimates, equipment found on the
island (not all of it had arrived) would have been sufficient to equip a
fighting force of 10,000 men. Furthermore, there evidently were some plans
for special forces, since the Soviets promised to provide an airplane capable
of transporting 39 paratroopers, as well as other special equipment.

All of this made Grenada a real military threat to its neighbors, most of
whom had only local constabularies rather than standing armies. And there
was little question that the airport was going to be used for military purposes, since General Hudson Austin's military deputy, Liam James, reported on his notebook on March 22, 1980, "The Revo has been able to
crush Counter-Revolution internationally, airport will be used for Cuban
and Soviet military."[9]

Grenada was a pivotal episode, and it is hard to overemphasize its
importance in restoring the security, strength, and self-confidence of
the United States. This was the first such use of military force by
America since Vietnam. Given the mood of retreat that engulfed
America's elites in the wake of that debacle, going into Grenada was a
tough call to make. And it was made all the tougher by the tragedy of
the Marines in Lebanon.

The shootdown of the Libyan planes in 1981 had signaled Reagan's
determination that America stand up and be counted, but that was a
brief skirmish. Sending ground forces into another country was a far
different matter, and it transmitted a far sterner message. We know for

a fact that it was heard loud and clear by the communists in Nicaragua and El Salvador, and we may be sure that it echoed in Moscow as well. If there were any doubts that America was back as a major power prepared to defend its legitimate interests, Grenada pretty clearly erased them.

Beyond this, there was the geostrategic significance of Grenada. For the first time ever, a country that had been drawn into the communist orbit had been liberated by force of arms, and by American willingness to assist the forces of freedom. This in essence repealed the Brezhnev Doctrine, which held that once a country had gone communist, it could never revert to noncommunist status. In place of the Brezhnev Doctrine, Grenada gave us a sampling of what was increasingly known as the Reagan Doctrine.

Grenada also demonstrated the solicitude of Ronald Reagan and the U.S. government for the well-being of American citizens in foreign nations. President Reagan anguished over the fate of Americans who were in danger anywhere in the world, and wanted to do whatever he could to assure their safety. This attitude was to feature prominently three years later in the Iran-Contra affair, but to a less enthusiastic response. The urge to protect American citizens abroad, however, is not exactly a character flaw in an American president—as could be attested by the students who kissed the ground at Charleston Air Force Base.

The battle against communist aggression that occurred with lightning quickness in Grenada was fought out on a more protracted basis in other sectors of the Caribbean.

Ever since Fidel Castro had taken control of Cuba in 1959, Marxist-Leninist forces had sought to subvert the hemisphere, a development of which Ronald Reagan and his advisors had long been acutely conscious. The Latin revolutionaries, and their Soviet sponsors, had scored a double breakthrough in 1979—first with the New Jewel takeover in Grenada, then with the Sandinista victory in Nicaragua.

While some early efforts had been made to depict the Sandinistas as wide-eyed reformers, by the time the Reagan administration came to office the reality of the situation was apparent to any knowledgeable person. The Sandinistas had lost or were in the process of losing their more moderate allies who had joined them in the overthrow of Anastasio Somoza; even the Carter administration had become uneasy about the government in Managua.

The misdeeds of the Sandinistas, from a U.S. perspective, fell into three main categories, all common to Marxist-Leninist regimes: (1) internal repression, denying the democratic freedoms of the Nicaraguan people and dragging down the economy of the country; (2) close alignment with Castro and the Soviets, converting Nicaragua into an integral part of the worldwide communist network; and (3) use of Nicaragua as a base for exporting further revolution in the hemisphere, most systematically in El Salvador, but also, on a sporadic basis, in Honduras, Costa Rica, and Guatemala.

From the standpoint of President Reagan and the U.S. government, the third of these interrelated problems was of the most immediate importance. Not that the President was indifferent to the internal repression in Nicaragua—far from it. But the voluminous evidence showing that the country had become a launching pad for aggression against its neighbors was a matter of urgent concern for U.S. foreign policy.

Latin and Central American affairs had long been of interest to Reagan and his backers in the Republican party. As governor of California, which shares a common border with Mexico, he was attuned to developments in the region, as were Reaganite Republicans from Texas and the Southwest generally. This concern had sparked Reagan's opposition to surrendering sovereignty over the Panama Canal, a major issue in his 1976 campaign.

As the President frequently pointed out, the countries of this region were far closer to major population centers in the United States than some of these centers were to one another. "El Salvador," he noted, "is nearer to Texas than Texas is to Massachusetts. Nicaragua is just as close to Miami, San Antonio, San Diego, and Tucson as those cities are to Washington. . . ."[10] This seemed not to be appreciated in the nation's capital, or other points to the north and east.

There was also the strategic significance of the Caribbean, and the fact that Nicaragua was well positioned to help with communist force projections in the region. All these matters were repeatedly addressed by Reagan in cabinet and National Security Council meetings and in his communications with Congress and the public. As the President summed it up:

"Almost half of U.S. exports and imports, including close to half our essential petroleum imports, travelled through the region. Two out of three ships transiting the Panama Canal carried goods to or from the U.S . . . There was security of our borders to think about, and the question of our economy's ability to absorb an endless flow of refugees. . . . If the Soviet Union and its allies were allowed to continue subverting democracy with terrorism and fomenting so-called 'wars of national liberation' in Central America, it wouldn't stop there: It would spread into the continent of South America and North to Mexico."[11]

The issue reached a climax when the communist insurgents of El Salvador decided to launch a "general offensive" in January of 1981— a well-coordinated effort that had been planned for months. The idea of the offensive, apparently, was to get the job done before Reagan came to office, or at least to push matters so far that the new administration would have difficulty mobilizing an effective response. The offensive, fortunately, failed, but it augured other problems to come.

As we monitored the situation in Grenada, we also followed events in Nicaragua, El Salvador, and the rest of the Central American isthmus. In addition to our usual intelligence operations, from time to time we received a windfall of captured documents when a convoy or safehouse of the communist guerrillas was taken by governments in the region. These documents highlighted the pattern of subversion at work, leaving little doubt about what we were facing in the Caribbean.

One compilation of such papers, captured in November 1980 and January 1981, was published by our State Department barely a month after Reagan's inauguration. These documents not only mapped out the preparations made for the "general offensive," they also revealed the guerrillas in El Salvador as ardent Marxist-Leninists, heavily backed by the global communist network.

In particular, the documents showed how the guerrillas were being supplied with weapons, logistical support, and intelligence backing through Nicaragua, with plentiful help from Castro's Cuba. Indeed, one of the most striking things about these materials was how often Nicaragua was mentioned, as indicated by the following excerpts from the State Department summary:

—July 23, 1980—"Comrade Bayardo" (Bayardo Arce of the FSLN* Directorate) met in Managua with a delegation of the Salvadoran guerrilla Joint General Staff. Arce promises ammunition to the guerrillas and arranges a meeting for them with the FSLN "Military Commission."

—July 22, 1980—Guerrilla military leadership meets in Managua, Nicaragua, with PLO leader Yassar Arafat.

—July 27, 1980—Guerrilla General Staff delegation departs from Managua where Cuban "specialists" add final touches to their military plans.

—September 24, 1980—Guerrillas receive and distribute $500,000 logistics donation from Iraq. Funds are distributed to the Nicaraguan FSLN and within El Salvador.

—September 26, 1980—Guerrilla logistics committee informs its joint General Staff that 130 tons of arms and other military material supplied by the Communist countries have arrived in Nicaragua for shipment to El Salvador.

—End of September 1980—Nicaragua FSLN suspends its weapons deliveries to El Salvador for one month after the United States government protests to the Nicaraguan leadership over the supply activities.

—End of October 1980—The Nicaraguan FSLN provides the Salvadoran guerrillas a new delivery schedule and resumes weapons deliveries.

—November 1, 1980—The guerrilla general staff is informed that there are approximately 120 tons of military equipment now in Nicaragua ready for shipment to the Salvadoran guerrillas.[12]

These revelations were unwelcome to certain members of Congress and the media, who preferred to take the Sandinista denials of subversion at face value. The State Department report was accordingly subjected to a withering critique by both the *Wall Street Journal* and the *Washington Post*—on such spurious grounds as that a comment attributed to one guerrilla leader had actually been written by another.[13]

But the evidence showing the nature of the communist insurgency in

* Acronym for the Spanish version of "Sandinista National Liberation Front."

El Salvador and Nicaragua's role in fomenting it was too voluminous for such nitpicking. The data demonstrated not only that the Sandinistas were helping move arms into El Salvador, but that the Salvador guerrillas were actually headquartered in Managua. Even more damaging, the guerrillas were being directed at every step along the way by Nicaraguan comandantes. In 1984, the Defense and State departments published a joint report on these activities that noted:

> The subversive system that seeks to destabilize neighboring democratic governments includes communications centers for Salvadoran guerrillas, safehouses, arms depots, vehicle stops, training camps for guerrillas, and assistance in transporting military supplies to Salvadoran guerrillas via air, land, and sea. El Salvador has been the principal target of guerrilla and Nicaraguan-sponsored subversion, but Costa Rica and Honduras have also been subjected to armed attack, bombing, attempted assassinations, and other violent activity.[14]

As far back as May 1979, the CIA had prepared a memorandum detailing Castro's assistance to the Sandinistas, his coordination of their different Marxist elements, and the movement of East-bloc aid to the Marxist rebels via Panama and other routes—much as later happened in El Salvador.[15] In addition, our intelligence showed that Nicaragua, like Grenada, had been provided by its Soviet and Cuban mentors with weapons far in excess of anything needed for self-defense. This military machine, which dwarfed all the other armies of the region, was managed with the aid of thousands of East-bloc personnel who had swarmed into the country after the Sandinista victory.*

* As the Defense-State report observed: "In less than five years the Sandinistas have built the largest and best equipped military force in Central America. About 240 tanks and armored vehicles, surface to air missiles, 152 mm howitzers and 122 mm rocket launchers give it a mobility and firepower capacity unmatched in the region. (Honduras, for example, has a total of 15 armored vehicles.) Nicaragua has a 48,800-man armed force. A total of about 100,000 men have been trained and could be mobilized rapidly.

"The rapid growth of Nicaraguan military strength could not have been possible without the help of about 3,000 Cuban military advisors, some of whom have been deeply involved in the decision-making process in Nicaragua. In addition, the Soviet Union, East Germany, Bulgaria, Czechoslovakia, Poland, Hungary, and Libya have military and/or civilian advisors in Nicaragua. Also, international groups, including the PLO, Argentine Montoneros, Uruguayan Tupamaros, and the Basque ETA all have offices and representatives in Nicaragua."

The similarity to Grenada was striking. In both cases, a communist takeover engineered with Cuban assistance was followed not only by internal repression, but by the arrival of numerous Cuban and other East-bloc "advisors," the militarization of the country, and the infusion of vast quantities of weapons far in excess of any possible defensive needs.

These signs pointed, in both cases, to preparations for further military adventures against other countries—the OECS nations in the case of Grenada, Central America in the case of Nicaragua. The major difference was that the Nicaragua threat was considerably larger, much closer to the United States, and already operating at full tilt.

This was the situation the Reagan administration confronted in the early 1980s. The burning question was, what, exactly, we should we do about it. The issue divided official Washington for the whole of the Reagan era and presented the President with one of his most persistent, and difficult, foreign policy challenges.

17

"DEAR COMANDANTE"

AL Haig was seldom in doubt about any subject, and on the topic of Central America he was especially emphatic. In dealing with the problems of subversion and conflict in the region, he asserted that we needed to "go to the source"—meaning the communist regime in Cuba.

Al made the point in cabinet and National Security Council meetings, and in frequent public statements. He wanted a tough line against Castro, as well as against the forces that Cuba was supporting in the Caribbean. (This was not always a typical State Department view.)

Haig's statements were widely reported by the media and sparked debate within the government. They were interpreted as meaning that he, and the administration, wanted to take military action against Castro, impose a blockade, or engage in some kind of overt hostilities. As Al himself explained, what he meant was a campaign of diplomatic and economic pressure against Cuba, and a strengthening of anticommunist military assets in the hemisphere. The President and his other advisors didn't necessarily disagree with this, but they believed the issue had to be handled in the context of other pressing foreign policy matters.

Though we might not have done everything Al wanted, the President and the rest of us shared in his unease, and a variety of measures were taken regarding Cuba, as well as El Salvador and Nicaragua. Naval carrier groups were sent to maneuver in the waters around Cuba, amphibious exercises were staged in the region, a Caribbean Command was established at Key West, and so on. These actions, and our communications to Havana, made clear how seriously we viewed the Cubans' role in fomenting violence in the area.[1]

As for the problem on the ground in Nicaragua and El Salvador, all of us from the President on down agreed that firm resistance had to be mounted against communist aggression. One obvious and continuing problem, however, was that any long-term policy would have to be supported by Congress. As Grenada demonstrated, this was hard to come by even in a blitzkrieg operation, where the lives of American civilians were reportedly at risk; in something that might have to be sustained for months or years, legislative backing would have been well-nigh impossible.

Intensifying these concerns were the lingering impact of Vietnam and the fear that U.S. forces would be bogged down in a foreign war—something the Reagan administration was frequently accused of planning. All of this, of course, was on top of the ongoing agitation about "Yankee imperialism," a ritual outcry from the Marxists and many others in Latin America, as well as from the left intelligentsia in the United States.

President Reagan was well aware of all these factors, and—despite the charges—never had any intention of sending U.S. forces into Nicaragua. He knew that neither public opinion nor Congress would support it; nor was a Vietnam-type commitment on the ground compatible with his own philosophy, which rejected the notion of having U.S. forces fight foreign battles that others could be fighting for themselves.

As Reagan put it, "I never considered sending U.S. troops to fight in Latin America. [I realized] that neither our people nor those south of the border would want to use American forces to repel Communist advances. . . . Hovering over everything, I think, was the old fear of the Great Colossus of the North—the apprehension that we'd try to dictate and dominate Latin American affairs."[2]

What the President wanted was to help the people of the region defend themselves from communist oppression. That was the genesis of the Reagan Doctrine, which held not only that people threatened with communist takeover should be given U.S. assistance, but that countries already under communist rule should receive our aid in lightening the yoke of domination.

Strategically, the problems of El Salvador and Nicaragua were linked to the point of being one and the same. Diplomatically and politically, however, they were very different and susceptible to different kinds of action. In El Salvador, we inherited a policy of supporting a recognized government against a communist-led insurgency, and our approach was therefore rather obviously to continue to strengthen it, which we proceeded to do as rapidly as possible.

Among the first acts of the administration with regard to El Salvador was to provide $20 million in military aid from emergency funds, and to increase the numbers of U.S. advisors in the country from thirty-four to fifty-four. This was necessary to assist with the training of the Salvadoran armed forces and to provide better intelligence coordination against a highly sophisticated enemy. It too was denounced as portending "another Vietnam," which was never contemplated and never happened.

In Nicaragua, where the insurgency was being supported and was actually based, we faced a different diplomatic-political situation, in that the recognized government was the source of the trouble. It was also a government in which many left-liberal spokesmen in the United States, and elsewhere around the world, felt a vested ideological interest—and for which many in the Democratic party seemed to have an almost bottomless reservoir of tolerance.

This emotional-political commitment dated to the regime of Jimmy Carter. The Carter administration had cut off aid to the Somoza government at a crucial point in the fighting of 1978–79, prevented the Israelis from supplying weapons to Somoza, withdrawn diplomatic recognition, and orchestrated Somoza's abdication—all on the basis of unkept promises from the Sandinistas. Then, once the Sandinistas were in power, Carter had pushed through $150 million in U.S. aid as start-up money for their experiment.

(Carter's appeasement of the Sandinistas was part of an overarching pattern in the region, as also in the world: ceding the Panama Canal to the dictatorship of Omar Torrijos and Manuel Noriega; acquiescing in the huge military buildup of Cuba and suspending aerial surveillance off Cuba as a "gesture of good will"; adopting a do-nothing posture toward the communist takeover of Grenada; moving to destabilize the anticommunist government of Guatemala in the name of "human rights," and so on.[3])

Confronted by mounting evidence of Nicaragua's involvement in the El Salvador fighting, Carter had finally broached the matter to the Sandinistas and attempted to negotiate a peaceful settlement. These protests caused the Sandinistas to slow down their arms shipments— for about a month. During this month—specifically, on October 17, 1980—the Carter administration actually signed a formal aid agreement with Nicaragua, after receiving assurances from the Sandinistas that they would cease their subversive activities.

One of the most obvious things the Reagan government could do on assuming office was to suspend any remaining aid to the Sandinistas, and the President did so (about $15 million; $118 million had already been delivered).[4] Cutting off aid was not, however, a policy in itself, nor did it end our attempts to find a just solution to the conflict.

In August 1981, newly appointed Assistant Secretary of State Thomas O. Enders traveled to Managua and offered to restore aid if aggression against El Salvador were suspended, the military buildup abated, political pluralism restored, and the Cuban-Soviet connection severed. The offer was rejected by the Sandinistas on the (untruthful) grounds that they weren't aiding the Salvador guerrillas anyway.[5]

As that 1981 proposal shows, Reagan was attempting to deal peacefully with the Sandinistas. Similar efforts and proposals were made intermittently throughout the Reagan years, but to no avail. The record amply reveals that the Sandinistas and their Cuban mentors were bent on exporting revolution and were not about to be negotiated out of it by offers from the U.S. State Department.

While our government couldn't or wouldn't directly go after the Sandinistas, plenty of others were ready to do the job. For the most part, these were people who had been allied with the comandantes against Somoza, had trusted Sandinista promises of democracy, and were appalled by the reality of what was happening in Nicaragua.

The comandantes, among other things, had seized control of communications and heavily censored *La Prensa*, the nation's leading newspaper; belittled the Catholic Church—in a country 85 percent Catholic—and shouted down the Pope; persecuted the Indian populations on the Caribbean coast; confiscated private property for collectivized farming (and offical gain); and turned the schools into vehicles of Marxist-Leninist indoctrination.[6]

These actions, plus the presence of the Cubans and other East- bloc functionaries, caused numerous defections from the Sandinistas. These included Catholic Archbishop Obando y Bravo; Violeta Chamorro, widow of the murdered publisher of *La Prensa*; Eden Pastora, the "Commander Zero" who had fought for Somoza's downfall; Alfonso Robelo and Arturo Cruz, both former members of the ruling junta; Adolfo Calero, a longtime opponent of Somoza and former Sandinista supporter; and many others.[7]

Just as important, many of the Nicaraguan rank and file also went into opposition. The confiscation of property for collective farms, the war on religion, the conscription into military service, and the politicization of the schools were not to the liking of the Nicaraguan peasants and other working people. As a result, in 1980 and 1981, political and military resistance began to take shape.

As this background clearly indicates, indigenous and widespread resistance to the Sandinistas existed well before a Reagan policy of military backing for such forces. Repeated statements that "Reagan created the Contras" are thus untrue; what created the Contras was the despotic character of the Sandinista government.

As it happened, the idea of providing U.S. assistance to noncommunist forces was not new. Within six months of the Sandinista takeover, Jimmy Carter himself had signed a finding which provided clandestine political aid to noncommunist elements in Nicaragua in the hope of sustaining political pluralism—while also aiding the

Sandinistas. (Ever since the inception of the Cold War, U.S. help had been supplied to noncommunist elements around the world.)

Not long after the Reagan administration came to office, in March 1981, Bill Casey, director of the CIA, proposed a more comprehensive program of political assistance—including covert support to elements in Afghanistan, Cambodia, Cuba, Grenada, Iran, Laos, Libya, and Nicaragua—and the President executed a written finding to this effect, duly reported to the intelligence committees of Congress.

In military terms, the original source of outside support for the Nicaraguan resistance was Argentina. Because the Sandinistas were hosting and abetting the Montoneros, an Argentine terrorist movement, they were looked upon with hostility by the Galtieri regime, and Buenos Aires began to provide help and training to a small group of Nicaraguan resistance fighters, based in Honduras, who were bent on harassing the Sandinistas.

By the fall of 1981, the failure of our diplomatic approaches and the growing internal resistance to the Sandinistas prompted Casey and Enders to propose a U.S. effort to help these anti-Sandinista military forces. On December 1, at a meeting in the Sit Room, Casey sketched the outlines of a "covert" operation to do just this, envisioning an outlay of $19 million by the CIA to develop and train the fledging opposition armies. The clearly stated purpose of this activity at the time—and thereafter—was to hinder the Sandinistas' ability to supply the revolution in El Salvador. That afternoon, the President signed a written finding to this effect, and it was duly communicated to Congress. Thus was the "Contra" program set in motion.[8]

A strategy of helping the indigenous resistance had obvious appeal, first of all on its merits, but also because it averted the bugaboo of U.S. policy in the region—the notion of the United States, Yankee imperialist, inflicting itself on a tiny neighbor. Far better to have the Nicaraguans themselves carry forward the resistance.

The policy had the further benefit of actually being approved by Congress, which received official notification of the finding and appropriated money (on an intermittent basis) to support it. If Congress would not openly declare a state of war against Managua, it would fund an effort behind the scenes to help the forces of the resistance.

This fact of record was conveniently forgotten in the heat of later partisan battles.

On the other hand, covert activities have obvious negatives; they cannot, for one thing, be advertised and explained to the public. All the initial moves to organize U.S. government support for the resistance in 1981 and 1982 occurred with zero publicity from the administration and became a matter of public outcry only when *Newsweek* wrote about it in November 1982. The administration was immediately on the defensive—both because we appeared to have been "caught" at something, and because the policy had never been spelled out to the public.9

Thrown off balance at the outset, the administration never succeeded in gaining the rhetorical initiative, despite valiant efforts by the President and some of his key supporters. Instead, the liberal Democrats and their allies in the media successfully defined the issue—the Sandinistas as the injured party, the Contras as evil "Somocistas," and the CIA conducting a "secret war" on their behalf.

Such problems fueled and were in turn intensified by divisions within the administration. Viewpoints once again sorted out between the Reaganites on the one hand, and the more establishment-minded on the other.

On the Reaganite side were Casey, Bill Clark, Cap Weinberger, Jeane Kirkpatrick, and myself, all favoring a policy of helping the resistance and launching full-scale public diplomatic efforts to muster backing for the policy.

Predominating on the other side were elements of the State Department, supported much of the time by Bud McFarlane (who became National Security advisor in October 1983), and by the political side of the White House, primarily Jim Baker and Mike Deaver. In the State Department view, post-Haig, nearly all conflicts could be or should be settled by negotiation, and a quest for some kind of agreement with the Sandinistas was relentlessly conducted out of Foggy Bottom.

To Casey, Kirkpatrick, and Co., the problem with the proposed agreements which were continually floated was that they amounted to trading one rabbit for one horse: we would suspend aid to the resistance and cease hostility toward the Sandinistas; they would agree to reforms, or to stop aiding El Salvador rebels, but with no guarantees that the promises would be kept.

On the political side of the White House, where policy as such was not taken all that seriously, it seemed obvious that we should go along with State. Once we got behind the public opinion curve, the issue was perceived to be a loser; the polls were against helping the resistance. Association with the cause could only tarnish the President's popularity, and repeated votes on Contra aid in Congress ran the danger, from a public relations standpoint, of posting "losses" instead of racking up "wins."

For this reason, the political shop was averse to having the President go on television to fight for Contra aid, particularly in 1983–84, and supported the State Department approach, which basically promised to "negotiate" the Sandinista problem under the rug until after the election. To this end, according to the records, Mike Deaver helped arrange over ninety private sessions between George Shultz and the President, without Cap or Bill Casey present.[10]

The net result was that we did a great deal less to sell the cause of the resistance than we might have done. I personally think we should have come out fighting sooner, and much harder. Once locked into a format of compromise with Congress, we found ourselves being squeezed into tighter and tighter corners, subjected to more and more restrictions, and pushed all the harder by the State Department and the political shop to come up with gestures to show we weren't war mongers. Calling the issue a loser became a self-fulfilling prophecy—because we didn't do what it would take to win.

Though Alexander Hamilton and Thomas Jefferson disagreed on many things, they concurred in stressing that the Constitution placed authority over the conduct of foreign policy in the hands of the executive.

These Founding Fathers also agreed that our basic law had made this allocation of power for very good reasons: A nation can't be effectively represented in its dealings overseas by a legislative body consisting of scores, or hundreds, of people. The essence of the legislative process is diversity, a stress on local interests, public debate, cumbersome procedures, and ultimate compromise. These are not necessarily bad qualities in themselves, but they are ill-suited to the conduct of diplomacy.*

These common sense precepts were systematically violated in our dealings with Nicaragua and El Salvador. In large measure this was part of the backlash against Vietnam, which increased congressional constraints on military matters and attempted to direct or limit our overseas policy through the appropriations power. (A particularly egregious case occurred in 1986, when the House conditioned military funding on continued adherence to the SALT II treaty, which the Senate had refused to ratify. This notwithstanding that the House has no constitutional authority over treaties.)[11]

In part also, this drive was fueled by strictly political and ideological motives. In the 1980 election, the Democrats had lost the presidency and the Senate, but still controlled the House. Though they had to come to terms with the Reagan Revolution in some respects, they still could make trouble for the President—and in Central America, they had both means and motive.

Since the preceding Democratic administration had virtually midwifed the Sandinistas into power, the issue was ultrasensitive for Democrats. It was hard for them to acknowledge the true nature of the Sandinista regime, or to do much of anything about it if they did. Also, the ideology of détente had a powerful grip in certain liberal quarters, which looked with favor not only on the Sandinistas, but also on Castro, the Marxists of Grenada, and the guerrillas of El Salvador.

---

* Hamilton described the impact of the legislature in foreign affairs this way (in *Federalist* No. 22): "The fate, the reputation, the peace of the whole union, are thus continually at the mercy of the prejudices, the passions and the interests of every member of which it is composed. Is it possible that foreign nations can either respect or confide in such a government?"

Jefferson, as our nation's first secretary of state, reiterated the point in the affair of Citizen Genet: "The transaction of business with foreign nations is executive altogether. It belongs, then, to the head of that department, except as such portions of it are specially submitted to the Senate. Exceptions are to be construed strictly."

John Marshall, the great Chief Justice of the Supreme Court (and often a Jefferson antagonist), put it even more explicitly: "The President is the sole organ of the nation in its relations, and its sole representative with foreign nations."

The new Attorney General is congratulated by President Reagan after
informally taking the oath of office in the White House on 25 February 1985.
A formal ceremony followed two weeks later. Ursula Meese and the
Vice President look on.

Edwin Meese is installed as
Attorney General by Chief
Justice Warren Burger as
his wife, Ursula, holds the
Bible and his predecessor,
William French Smith,
looks on. 14 March 1985.

President Reagan conducts a meeting of the National Security Council in the White House Situation Room. L-R: William Webster, Director of the Federal Bureau of Investigation; Gen. Jack Vessey, Chairman of the Joint Chiefs of Staff; Caspar Weinberger, Secretary of Defense; the President; George Shultz, Secretary of State; Edwin Meese, Attorney General. 7 August 1985.

Director of Central Intelligence William J. Casey meets with President Reagan in the Oval Office. 22 October 1985.

Edwin Meese, Chairman pro tem of the Domestic Council, briefs the
President prior to a meeting of the Council. L-R: Donald Regan (Chief of
Staff to the President); Al Kingon (Cabinet Secretary Domestic Policy
Council); Malcolm Baldrige (Secretary of Commerce). 11 March 1986.

The President shares a joke with Vice President Bush and Attorney General
Meese. 16 April 1986.

The Reagans and the Meeses at a State Dinner. 23 September 1986.

Attorney General Edwin Meese briefs the Congressional Joint Leadership in the Cabinet Room just prior to his public announcement of the Iran-Contra discovery. To the President's right are Senate Majority Leader Robert Byrd and Minority Leader Robert Dole. To the President's left are House Minority Leader Robert Michael and Speaker Jim Wright. 25 November 1986.

President Reagan discusses the Iran-Contra affair with members of the
National Security Council. 25 November 1986. L-R: Caspar Weinberger,
George Schultz, Ed Meese, Don Regan and the President.

Ursula Meese (right) with Barbara Bush and Nancy Reagan.

President Reagan greets Judge Robert Bork just prior to announcing his nomination to the Supreme Court. 1 July 1987. In the background are Chief of Staff Howard Baker, Communications Director Tom Griscom, Attorney General Ed Meese, and Deputy Chief of Staff Ken Duberstein.

Attorney General Edwin Meese testifies at the Iran-Contra hearings. 28 July 1987.

Attorney General Edwin Meese participating in a panel with Dan Rather at the Ford Library, Ann Arbor, Michigan (1987).

Edwin Meese presenting report of National Drug Policy Board to
President Reagan. 30 July 1988.

Ronald Reagan's first Cabinet.

The Cabinet in 1984.

The Cabinet in 1987.

A wild card in this equation was House Speaker Tip O'Neill, more an old-line welfare stater than a fire-breathing leftist. But on Central America, by most accounts, he bought the radical position almost entirely because of an aunt who was a Maryknoll nun. The Maryknollers, in the thick of promoting "liberation theology" in Central America, had lined up with the Sandinistas and Salvador guerrillas, and their attitudes had rubbed off onto O'Neill. (According to Bob Woodward of the *Washington Post*, O'Neill told an aide after a two-hour meeting with one Maryknoller: "I believe every word.")[12]

For all these reasons, congressional obstructionism was an ongoing feature of the conflict. Aid to El Salvador was hedged with numerous legislative conditions—certifications of progress on human rights, "land reform," and democratic elections. Much energy and time, in a country wracked with warfare, terrorist violence, and threatened takeover by communist insurgents, were expended on complying with these requirements. (No one can argue with protecting human rights in El Salvador, or anywhere else. But I found it ironic that many of the people who talked the loudest about these rights looked benignly at Communist China, Mozambique, Romania, Zimbabwe, and other Marxist countries where political freedoms were far less secure than in El Salvador.)

With respect to Nicaragua, the micromanaging was even more intense and, just as bad, completely inconsistent. Congress alternately voted for and against aid to the resistance forces through the so-called Boland amendments, conditioning aid on various provisos, changing these from year to year, and passing legislation that seemed to conflict with other enactments. (The legal intricacies of all of this are examined in a later chapter.)

Nor was this confusion limited to the halls of Congress. Numerous congressmen and senators journeyed to El Salvador, Nicaragua, and other Caribbean countries, conferred briefly with officials, and then made "informed" pronouncements about our policy. The net effect was to generate a mass muddle about what our policy was at any given time, what it might be a few months hence, and who in fact was running it.

An extreme example emerged from the captured archives of Grenada. In 1982, Rep. Ron Dellums (D-California) made a "fact-finding" trip to Grenada to check up on administration charges that the 10,000-foot runway at Port Salines had military implications; a follow-up internal memo of the Grenada government spoke of the report that Dellums was going to file in Washington:

"Ron Dellums. His assistant Barbara Lee is here presently and she brought with her a report on the International Airport that was done by Ron Dellums. *They have suggested that we look at the document and suggest any changes we deem necessary. They will be willing to make changes*" (emphasis added).* 13

Less sensational but in some ways even more disturbing—since it involved the Democratic leadership of the House—was the famous "dear comandante" letter of 1984, addressed to Sandinista dictator Daniel Ortega. The signers were then Majority Leader (later Speaker) Jim Wright of Texas, House Intelligence Committee Chairman Edward Boland, Reps. Lee Hamilton of Indiana and Stephen Solarz of New York, and six others—all influential in legislation on and funding of U.S. foreign policy. This letter to Ortega said, among other things:

As members of the U.S. House of Representatives we regret the fact that better relations do not exist between the United States and your country. We have been, and remain, opposed to U.S. support for military action directed against the people or government of Nicaragua.

We want to commend you and the members of your government for taking steps to open up the political process in your country. . . . We support your decision to schedule elections this year, to reduce press censorship, and to allow greater freedom of assembly for political parties. Finally, we recognize that you have taken these steps in the midst of ongoing military hostilities on the borders of Nicaragua.

We write with the hope that the initial steps you have taken will be followed by others designed to guarantee a fully open and democratic electoral process [including, specifically, participation by exile groups in the election]. . . .

* When Maurice Bishop came to Washington the following year, Dellums arranged for an appearance by him before a subcommittee of the House Armed Services Committee. Dellums, a main congressional defender of the Grenada regime, asserted that "nothing being done in Grenada constitutes a threat to the United States or its allies."

If this were to occur, the prospects for peace and stability throughout Central America would be dramatically enhanced. Those responsible for supporting violence against your government, and for obstructing serious negotiations for broad political participation in El Salvador would have far greater difficulty winning support for their policies than they do today.[14]

In floor debate, Representative Solarz defended this letter as simply an appeal for free and fair elections. But on the face of it, it was a great deal more than that. By totally omitting any reference to Sandinista repression, killing, or expansionism, it conveyed the notion that the Sandinistas were essentially on the right course—at least in the eyes of the Democratic leadership.

More than this, the letter sent the message that other cosmetic measures would undercut the Reagan administration in domestic U.S. politics, both in funding the Nicaraguan resistance and in preventing the Marxist guerrillas of El Salvador from shooting their way to power. In essence, the letter advised the communists of Nicaragua on how to manipulate opinion in the United States.

While defending this letter, Solarz conceded that members of Congress could not enter into diplomatic negotiations with other governments. "We understand full well," he said, "that negotiations with a foreign government are the responsibility of the executive branch, and not of the Congress. . . . It was not an offer to negotiate. It certainly did not bespeak an intention or a desire to negotiate."[15]

Even this slim distinction was obliterated, however, when Jim Wright ascended to the Speaker's chair in 1987. In fairly short order, Wright had set up shop as a surrogate secretary of state—meeting with Ortega, negotiating with Central American leaders, conferring with Obando y Bravo. Wielding the congressional power of the purse, Wright sought not merely to influence but to dictate the content of policy in the region.

From the administration side, we saw the results of this in our dealings with Wright, struggles on the floor of Congress, and reports we received about his various meetings. What it looked like from Wright's standpoint and what he thought he was trying to accomplish are indicated in a remarkable book by John Barry, *The Ambition and the Power*, that chronicles Wright's activities and attitudes, on almost an hourly basis, at this time:

"He was indeed running Central American policy, and he intended to force both the Sandinistas and Contras toward peace . . . Wright informed Shultz of his meeting with Ortega, adding, 'They want me to have people assist them in negotiations, probably oversee them'. . . . *If the administration stood in the way of this peace process, then by God someone had to push it forward.* . . . If he proceeded it would be a great breach of power that violated the institutional integrity of the State Department and the White House. . . . He would not only have defeated the administration's foreign policy, but would have substituted his own" (emphasis in original). [16]

Wright's over-reaching not only tampered with the constitutional balance of powers, it inhibited the ability of the President to conduct foreign policy, creating uncertainty among our personnel, our allies, and other nations in the region. And it led precisely to the sort of debacle our Founding Fathers had foreseen.

Adding to the problem was the covertness of the policy, which not only clouded public understanding but allowed the liberal Democrats to have it both ways at once. "Covert" in this case meant that while the existence of the policy generally was public knowledge, details concerning it were not. Congressmen and senators were briefed in secret, many particulars of what was done (or not done) were classified, and many understandings behind the scenes were never aired.

Given these factors, the worst potential of legislative foreign policy-making became reality: *the exercise of power without accountability.* The liberal Democrats wanted to combat Reagan on the issue and have a major hand in shaping policy, but they did not want to be blamed for any unhappy outcomes. They could use their power to hamstring, condition, deny, authorize, or consent to certain lines of conduct—then walk away from the debris if things went wrong.

This happened early on when aid to the resistance first became public and when it was revealed that the CIA had been involved in the mining of Nicaraguan harbors; and at the end, when Ollie North was coordinating help for the resistance out of the White House. The comment on the mining episode by Sen. Patrick Leahy (D-Vermont), himself a vehement critic of Reagan policy, is to the point:

"One advantage of a covert operation is that it allows an awful lot of people who knew about it to say they didn't. It will be fascinating to see the number of senators who will object to the mining during the coming week when virtually the whole of the Senate had a chance to vote on the issue of covert operations against Nicaragua last week and most members knew the mining was part of it."[17]

Such Democratic schizophrenia pervaded congressional lawmaking on the subject. The following is an excerpt (one of many such examples) from a 1983 report of the House Intelligence Committee, chaired by Representative Boland, concerning the conflict in El Salvador and Nicaragua's role in it:

A major portion of the arms and other material sent by Cuba and other Communist countries to the Salvadoran insurgents transits Nicaragua with the permission and assistance of the Sandinistas.

The Salvadoran insurgents rely on the use of sites in Nicaragua, some of which are located in Managua itself, for communications, command-and-control, and for logistics to conduct their financial, material, and propaganda activities.

Nicaragua provides a range of other support activities, including secure transit of insurgents to and from Cuba, and to the insurgents in planning their activities in El Salvador. . . .

Another area of serious concern to the committee is the significant military buildup going on within Nicaragua . . . . Within the Central American isthmus, it poses a potential threat to its neighbors.[18]

And more of the same. All of this, obviously, confirmed the view set forward by the administration. Yet these findings were in a Democratic report that *opposed* providing assistance to the anti-Sandinista forces.

Thus, congressional Democrats officially went on record (1) affirming that the Sandinistas were a serious military-strategic problem in the region, while (2) refusing to supply the resources needed to resist them. It was in the vise of that have-it-both-ways paradox that Marine Lt. Col. Oliver North of the National Security Council staff set out to muster other backing for the freedom fighters.

18

DISCOVERING
A CRISIS

T HE OLD EBBITT GRILL is a Washington restaurant on 15th Street, Northwest, across the street from the Treasury Department and a block from the White House, famous primarily for its chili. It has always been one of my favorite restaurants in D.C. But on the afternoon of November 22, 1986, it took on a new significance for me—and even more so for the Reagan administration and the country.

I had been attorney general since 1985 and I was meeting at the grill that Saturday with three members of my staff from the Department of Justice—Assistant Attorneys General Charles Cooper and William Bradford Reynolds, and my chief of staff, John Richardson. They had been helping me over the weekend with a review of a hitherto secret administration initiative toward Iran. This covert activity had burst into public print two weeks before through an item in *Al Shiraa*, an obscure publication in Lebanon, apparently inspired by anti-U.S. elements in Iran.

I had first learned of this project in January of 1986 at a White

House meeting with President Reagan and other members of the National Security Council. The object of the plan was twofold: to obtain a strategic opening to Iran, and to seek Iranian help in freeing the U.S. hostages held by extremists in Lebanon. One component was to sell limited quantities of defensive arms to dissident elements in Tehran.

Because the initiative toward Iran had to be kept secret, it was compartmentalized; many people in the administration knew only parts of it, some knew nothing at all, and few if any knew the whole story. (For example, I knew some of the legal and policy background but none of the operational details.) As a result, the administration was speaking in many different voices, inaccurate media speculation was rampant, and congressional foes of the administration were exploiting the situation for partisan ends. The President himself had held a press conference on Wednesday, November 19, in which he had misspoken about one of the crucial aspects of the initiative.

Concerned about the fallout from the situation, and in possession of some new information, I had suggested to the President on Friday, November 21, that someone needed to review all aspects of the matter so the administration could present a comprehensive and accurate account. The President asked if I would undertake the assignment myself, and I accepted. Because of the need to work rapidly over a weekend, I called on members of my Justice Department staff who I knew would be available on short notice.

Beginning on Friday, Cooper, Reynolds, Richardson, and I began contacting key members of the administration, including Secretary of State Shultz, officials of the CIA, and the staff of the National Security Council. We conducted personal interviews and asked to see documents relevant to the Iranian initiative. Our approach at this point was not a criminal investigation, but an administrative inquiry seeking to pull together all the relevant details, so that a coherent and accurate presentation could be made to the public and to Congress—which was already planning to hold hearings on the subject.

The purpose of our Saturday luncheon was to compare notes on the work of the previous twenty-four hours, which had included an examination of documents at the National Security Council. The routine nature of our inquiry suddenly changed when Reynolds and Richardson informed us of an unexpected discovery. They had reviewed the files and papers of NSC staffer Lt. Col. Oliver North, who had been involved in implementing the Iran initiative. North had also, as noted, supervised aid to the anticommunist forces in Nicaragua. If the information was correct, it meant that actions had been taken by NSC staff members which connected these two secret and highly volatile projects. The effect for the administration could have been the political equivalent of a nuclear bomb.

In North's files, Reynolds had found a memo describing a plan to direct profits derived from the arms transactions with Iran to support the Nicaraguan freedom fighters. The memo said that, out of "residual funds" from the arms sales, "$12 million will be used to purchase critically needed supplies" for the Nicaraguan resistance forces.[1] While it was unclear whether this had actually happened, or whether it had simply been proposed, I viewed it as something that could dwarf any previous problems of the administration.

Support for the Nicaraguan resistance was one of the most hotly disputed topics in our politics; Iran was also a touchy subject in its own right, and while arms sales were only one component of the Iranian initiative, they were guaranteed to be intensely controversial. The combination of these necessarily secret ventures into one explosive issue would provide tremendous ammunition to opponents of the administration. We had to find out exactly what had happened.

We accordingly stepped up our inquiries over the next two days, interviewing North, NSC Staff Director John Poindexter, former NSC Staff Director Bud McFarlane, and several others. Our key discovery, confirmed by North and Poindexter, was that "diversion" of Iranian arms money to the Contras had in fact occurred. We were also told that only three people in the U.S. government had known about it—North, Poindexter, and McFarlane.

Of the three, the person who obviously knew the most was North; he gave us a fairly explicit account of the situation on Sunday afternoon. (I subsequently found out from Poindexter that he had known about the diversion and had done nothing to stop it because of his outrage at Congress for "selling out" the freedom fighters in Nicaragua.) With this verification, it was imperative that the President learn about the matter as soon as possible.

On Monday morning, even before meeting with Poindexter, I phoned Chief of Staff Don Regan and asked him to arrange a private meeting with the President. Don and I met with the President briefly that morning, then more extensively in the afternoon, and I told the President of our discovery. He decided that we should immediately make a complete disclosure of our findings, and this resulted in a full-scale press conference the following day at noon.

The revelation that arms sale money from Iran had made its way to the Nicaraguan freedom fighters was, as expected, a Washington sensation. The matter quickly became the subject of three official investigations—one by the Tower Commission appointed by the President, one by Congress, and one by Independent Counsel Lawrence E. Walsh. While these inquiries unearthed some specific data that had not emerged from our initial inquiry, in major respects they confirmed the story that my staff and I had been able to piece together in less than seventy-six hours.

The Iran-Contra affair, as it became known, was treated then, and has been since, as an enormous crisis for the Reagan White House. I never doubted its potential gravity, especially if the administration itself had not moved quickly to uncover the story of the fund diversion. Had this information been dragged out piecemeal, another Watergate-type scandal could all too easily have ensued.

Some media accounts have in fact treated the affair as if it *were* another Watergate, replete with questions about what the President knew and when he knew it and the quest for a "smoking gun" that would prove his complicity in some plot. One best-selling book on the matter was subtitled, *The Unmaking of the President*—a wishful thinking judgment shared by many of the President's critics in Congress and the media but not borne out by history.

Too often, such accounts have depicted Iran-Contra as a criminal matter, in which the administration and various of its officials "illegally" dealt with the government of Iran, "illegally" sought to help the Nicaraguan freedom fighters, and then "illegally" yoked these ventures together. This notion undergirded the proceedings of the House and Senate committees and the activities of Independent Counsel Walsh and provided themes for numerous books and articles.

As the person whose inquiry discovered the diversion, who participated in the response of the administration, and who was privy to information about the development of the Iran initiative and the legal issues pertaining to it—information not known at the time to the general public—I think I can speak with some authority on the topic. And I have no hesitation in saying the conventional treatment of this issue is almost totally wrong—that administration's policy in both these cases was founded on a solid legal basis.

It is possible, of course, to question the wisdom of the policies involved on substantive grounds, and many have done so—including some within the administration itself. Both situations involved a number of tough and very controversial decisions, and mixing them together was admittedly a grievous error. But saying that is quite different from contending that either the Iran initiative or the effort to help the Nicaraguan freedom fighters, taken on its merits, was illegal.

To understand what really happened in the Iran-Contra affair, and why the conventional treatment is so far off base, it is necessary to review the history, legal status, and policy impacts of these initiatives separately, before the wires got crossed.

Sorting out such matters is important for historical reasons, to make sure the record is straight, and even more so for human reasons. Careers were shattered as individuals were dragged before committees and courts; life savings were depleted in an effort to mount defenses; and enormous opprobium was heaped on people who were branded criminals after having devoted long and faithful—and law-abiding— service to their country.

In addition, Iran-Contra was a tremendously significant episode in the political life of the Reagan administration, with far-reaching impact in terms of our constitutional system and its balance of powers.

Accordingly, this and the following chapter will review the history of the Iran initiative, how it came about, and how well-laid plans of the administration went awry. A succeeding chapter will review our policy toward Nicaragua's freedom fighters, what the administration did (and did not do), and the legal framework in which that policy was carried out.

In many commentaries, the administration's covert dealings with Iran during 1985 and 1986 are viewed as a direct "arms-for-hostages" swap, which would have violated the relevant law on arms trade with Tehran and the President's statements about getting tough on terrorists. Critics accuse Reagan of paying ransom to Iran and dismiss the idea of strategic objectives, such as encouraging the "moderates" in the regime and other geopolitical goals, as window-dressing. All these charges, as the record clearly shows, are false.

First of all, contacts with Iran predated not only the Iran-Contra affair, but the Reagan administration itself. Though the point has received surprisingly little attention, the effort to establish some kind of dialogue with the Iranian regime dated back to President Jimmy Carter and the hostage crisis of 1979-80. During the 1980 election year, the Carter White House was in continuous communication with the Iranian government, trying to secure release of the U.S. hostages held at our embassy in Tehran.

This effort was known in a general way in the Reagan camp, and provides some necessary background to our concern that Carter was trying to arrange an "October surprise" to strengthen his chances in the election.

For some reason, the fact that Jimmy Carter was dealing directly with the hostage-holding government of the ayatollah excites no comment from people who roundly criticize the Reagan White House for having any traffic whatsoever with anybody in Iran. But for the moment the relevant point is that contacts with Tehran were already an ongoing feature of national policy in 1980 and were not invented by Ronald Reagan.

An interesting if biased view of the Carter contacts has been provided by Abol Hasn Bani-Sadr, a former ally and protégé of the ayatollah and the first elected president of revolutionary Iran. Among other data, Bani-Sadr supplies the text of a "draft agreement" between the Carter administration and Iran concerning the release of the hostages. The key ingredients of this agreement were to institute proceedings against the shah, then in exile in the United States; to take measures to recover the shah's assets in the United States, estimated at tens of billions of dollars; and to appoint a UN fact-finding commission to hear Iranian grievances and resolve the U.S.–Iran crisis.[2]

Bani-Sadr also provides details on asserted offers of arms to Iran by Carter if Tehran would release the U.S. hostages quickly. This verifies Bill Casey's thesis that an "October surprise" was in the making— including approaches to Iran through West Germany, Switzerland, France, and Algeria, among others. The problem from Carter's standpoint was that he could not pull it off before election day, but on Bani-Sadr's (and other) evidence, it was not from lack of trying.

Noteworthy in these revelations is Carter's focus on arms in dealings with Tehran, then in the midst of a military crisis. In September 1980, Iraq had attacked Iran, and desperate fighting was in progress. Iraq's army had been heavily supplied by the Soviet Union and the Eastern bloc in general, and was far larger than Iran's. The Iranian army, equipped and trained by the U.S. under the shah, was lacking spare parts and armaments and needed defensive weapons to counter Iraqi tanks and planes.

Iranian dealings with other nations were accordingly governed by a desire for military hardware. Among those who accommodated this concern was the state of Israel, which had its own geopolitical reasons for helping Iran against Iraq. Not that Tel Aviv and Tehran had anything but mutual loathing, insofar as the public record went; but they now had a common enemy in Saddam Hussein.

From the Israelis' standpoint, Saddam was their most powerful and determined adversary in the region. If he should triumph over Iran, he would be free to turn his attentions, and his weapons, westward. Far better a stalemate between two Islamic states, with no clear victor. Thus in 1981 and 1982, Israel sold defensive weapons to Iran, as did a number of West European states.

Within the Reagan administration, meanwhile, a different but congruent set of motives was at work, stemming from concern about our long-term relationship with Tehran. Iran was, after all, by far the largest of the Gulf states and an important strategic factor in the Middle East. In addition to its own petroleum reserves, its location athwart the Persian Gulf and Straits of Hormuz made it a potential threat to oil supplies in transit to Europe and Japan.

In addition, Iran shared a 1,000-mile border with the USSR, which at the time posed a real threat to its neighbors. Moscow has always coveted a path to the warm water ports of the Gulf, and the most obvious route runs through Iran. In the early 1980s, there were ominous signs that the Soviets were massing forces near the border and cultivating assets within the country.

As a result, the idea of developing a strategic opening to Iran was frequently talked of in administration councils. In January 1984, for instance, Geoffrey Kemp of the National Security Council staff sent a memorandum to Bud McFarlane suggesting that the U.S. start planning for a post-Khomeini situation, including work with Iranian exile groups. And in August 1984, McFarlane requested an interagency analysis of how the U.S. could best influence a post-Khomeini Iran.

The following spring McFarlane requested an intelligence update from the CIA concerning the situation in Tehran. The assessment, drafted by Graham Fuller, the national intelligence officer for the Middle East, stated that "the Khomeini regime is faltering. . . . We will soon see a struggle for succession. The U.S. has almost no cards to play. The USSR has many. Iran has obviously concluded that whether they like Russia and Communism or not, the USSR is the country to come to terms with . . . Iran has in fact now begun moving toward some accommodation with the USSR."[3]

Fuller's memorandum said the "twin pillars" of U.S. policy toward Iran—denying arms to the regime and denouncing its support for terrorism—were entirely negative, and did nothing to prepare us for the future. It was imperative, he added, "that we perhaps think in terms of a bolder—and perhaps slightly riskier policy which will at least ensure greater U.S. voice in the unfolding situation."[4]

On June 11, 1985, Don Fortier and Howard Teicher of the National Security Council staff presented a draft of a National Security Decision Directive (NSDD), which reinforced the analysis of the Fuller memorandum and suggested that the U.S. work with conservative elements in Iran and with the regular army to block the development of Soviet influence there. To this end, the NSDD suggested encouraging Western allies to provide "selected military equipment as determined on a case-by-case basis."[5]

This proposal did not receive the usual NSC review, but was circulated only to the secretaries of State and Defense and the director of Central Intelligence. It drew strongly negative comment from Caspar Weinberger and George Shultz, while Bill Casey and Bud McFarlane were for it. This disagreement in the highest circles of the government was to persist over the next year and a half and became a major topic of comment when the Iran-Contra affair broke into the headlines. Be that as it may, this background and chronology make it clear that the notion of an initiative to Iran, including the provision of arms to dissident elements, was being discussed inside the administration *before* the Lebanese hostage situation engrossed the public.

As noted in our discussion of terrorism in Lebanon, individual hostages had been seized over a period of months in 1984 and 1985. Though the object of official concern and efforts to obtain their freedom, these hostages were not highly publicized or treated in terms of national crisis. Lack of publicity was in keeping with standard policy on terrorism, which holds that notoriety and psychological paralysis of the target nation are what the captors generally seek and should if possible be denied.

This low-keyed approach and lack of obvious focus on the hostages under Reagan was a source of complaint by relatives of the hostages, one of whom charged in early 1985 that "U.S. newspapers and television have given little attention to the issue," and that the administration also wasn't paying enough attention to the subject. As it developed, the hostage in question, Jeremy Levin, was released about a month later, through back-channel efforts in which the help of Syrian President Hafez al Assad was acknowleged.[6]

Official attempts to treat the hostage question quietly were completely torpedoed, however, in June of 1985, as events spun beyond control and hostages in Lebanon became the most sensational topic of the day. This was the hijacking of TWA Flight 847, which wound up at

Beirut airport and for two weeks was the subject of nonstop television drama. The holding of Americans by hooded terrorists, the televised press conferences of the hostage-holders and their prisoners, and the murder of Robert Stethem burned the issue into the consciousness of the nation.

As it happened, this spectacular and sickening event began on June 14, three days *after* the Fortier-Teicher NSDD proposal, and of course well after the memorandum by Graham Fuller concerning a possible opening to Iran. Efforts to seek such an opening therefore could not have been prompted by public-political fixation on the problem of the hostages, which developed as a consequence of this episode. Moreover, even in the case of Beirut airport itself, as with Jeremy Levin, the major player in our efforts to free the captives was not Iran, but Syria.

Nonetheless, as has since been made public, the Iranians did assist at Beirut airport—playing a bit part, as it were. As Bud McFarlane indicated at the time, Iranian Speaker Rafsanjani helped out with Hizballah, the terrorist group that was holding some of the U.S. captives. It was this fact that prompted Bud to ask the President to thank Rafsanjani, and established the notion that the Iranian Speaker was someone who might be worked with.

Given all the publicity lavished on Assad, and the generally secret character of Bud's negotiations, nobody paid much attention to Rafsanjani's participation at the time. In retrospect, however, this was obviously the most crucial factor in the whole equation, since it established a strong precedent for the dealings that were to follow. This was publicly confirmed to the *Washington Post* by some of the relevant officials in early 1992:

"[Hizballah leader Imal] Mugniyah participated in, and may have planned, the hijacking in June 1985 of TWA Flight 847, the first high visibility hostage episode of the Reagan administration. After most of the hostages were released, a small group kept behind by Mugniyah was let go only after personal intervention by Ali Akbar Hashemi Rafsanjani, then Speaker of the Iranian parliament and now President of Iran. This demonstration of Iran's influence with the Hizballah captors was the starting point of the secret U.S. efforts in 1985–86 to negotiate with Iran for the release of the Americans being held in Lebanon, according to anti-terrorist officials who were in the government at the time."7

All of this, to reiterate, took place after proposals by Graham Fuller, Casey, and others to develop a strategic opening to Iran, showing clearly that the idea was not concocted after the fact to cover up for hostage-dealing. Once Rafsanjani came into the picture, however, and appeared more helpful and reasonable than others in Iran, he became a natural focus for efforts at improved relations.

On the home front, meantime, Beirut airport was having further consequences. On June 28, the President met with the families of some of the airport captives in Chicago. At this meeting, relatives of a previously seized hostage, Father Lawrence Jenco, demanded to know why the President was not trying to obtain his freedom, along with the captives from the airport. Those who observed the President agreed he was deeply moved by the distress of the hostage families and frustrated at his inability to help them.

Three main outcomes thus emerged from Beirut airport: (1) the hostage issue became a major concern of the public and in the thinking of the President; (2) the Iranians showed they could indeed exert influence on the Hizballah extremists in Lebanon; and (3) the Iranians could be worked with in respect to certain common, if limited, objectives—including the release of hostages.

By coincidence or otherwise, the developments that led to Iran-Contra followed hard on the heels of the airport crisis. On July 2, the President laid a wreath on the grave of Robert Stethem at Arlington National Cemetery, then proceeded to Andrews Air Force Base to welcome home the captives from Beirut. The very next day, Bud McFarlane met at the White House with David Kimche of the Israeli Foreign Ministry.

Kimche told McFarlane that Israel had contact with moderate elements in Iran who were interested in working with the United States in the post-Khomeini era. He added that these Iranians could prove their good faith by helping obtain the release of other U.S. hostages held in Lebanon, including CIA station chief William Buckley. In return, the Iranians wanted small quantities of defensive weapons as a token of good faith. This obviously fit with Bud's desire, and that of Bill Casey, to pursue an opening to Iran. Bud and Don Regan discussed the general idea with the President ten days later when he was in Bethesda Naval Hospital for abdominal surgery.[8]

By early August, the proposition had become concrete: the Israelis wanted to ship TOW missiles to Tehran, on the understanding that they would be replenished from U.S. stocks. In return, the Iranians would use their influence to seek the release of one or more U.S. hostages. The Israelis wanted Reagan's approval for this transaction, and the idea was debated on August 6 at a White House meeting attended by the President, the Vice President, Shultz, Weinberger, McFarlane, and Regan. The President made no decision at that time.

According to McFarlane, however, the President subsequently gave his approval and Bud communicated this to the Israelis. Ninety-six TOW missiles accordingly were shipped on August 24, and another 408 on September 14. The following day, one American hostage, Rev. Benjamin Weir, was released near the U.S. embassy in Beirut.

This success, though limited, encouraged both the Israelis and McFarlane to continue the initiative. But these efforts were complicated by our official diplomatic stance in the Iran-Iraq war. Basically, the State Department was "tilting" toward Iraq. In 1983, the department had launched a program called "Operation Staunch," aimed at cutting off global arms shipments to Iran. That policy created serious problems in the next phase of the operation.

This occurred in November 1985, when the Israelis proposed a transfer of HAWK anti-aircraft missiles to elements in Iran, on the understanding that the Iranians would again try to secure the release of U.S. hostages. (The situation was further complicated by the fact that President Reagan, along with Secretary Shultz, McFarlane, and other top White House officials, were totally involved in preparing for and then conducting the first summit talks with Soviet General Secretary Gorbachev in Geneva, Switzerland.) Israeli Defense Minister Yitzhak Rabin contacted MarFarlane on November 15 and asked if the President would approve such a transaction. Bud, viewing it essentially as a continuation of the activity begun in August, indicated he would, and the Israelis prepared to go ahead.

As revealed by subsequent investigation, the HAWK shipment ran into tremendous difficulties. The Israeli plane carrying the missiles could not fly directly into Iran and was supposed to land in Portugal for transfer of the cargo. But because of Operation Staunch, the Portuguese were highly suspicious of any shipments to Iran and would not allow the plane to land. The Israelis asked McFarlane to intervene, and because he was in Geneva and preoccupied with the summit, he passed the assignment along to Oliver North.

When repeated efforts failed to get the necessary clearance, McFarlane asked North to make other arrangements. Acting through Maj. Gen. Richard Secord, who had been helping North with the Nicaragua effort, North contacted CIA official Dewey Clarridge, who referred Secord to a CIA proprietary called St. Lucia airlines. (A "proprietary" is a company maintained by the CIA for its purposes, but which can also do commercial work for other people.) In this case, St. Lucia agreed to carry the arms on a commercial basis and was paid $127,000 (out of Israeli money transferred to Secord) to transport eighteen HAWK missiles to Iran.[9]

Bill Casey had been out of the country while all this was going on, but when CIA Deputy Director John McMahon learned of even this minimal involvement by the agency, he requested a written presidential "finding" to approve the CIA's actions; this was signed by the President on December 5. During 1985, the entire subject of these dealings with Iran was so closely held—understandably—that even several of us on the NSC knew nothing about it. But the controversy among those who did know continued during December, and finally the whole venture stalled. Thus, it was not until early January 1986 that I first learned about the matter.

Just after the first of the year, a representative of the government of Israel, Amiram Nir, came to the United States and met with Bill Casey and John Poindexter (who had become head of the NSC staff when Bud McFarlane resigned in December 1985), among others. Nir encouraged a new effort to develop a rapport with moderate elements in Iran because of the strategic importance of that country to the West. Thus a meeting was held in the Oval Office on January 7, 1986, which I was asked to attend.

At this gathering, the full pros and cons of an opening toward Iran were discussed, with an eye to making it a full-fledged American, rather than an Israeli, policy. As before, Cap Weinberger and George Shultz opposed any such initiative, while Bill Casey and John Poindexter wanted to proceed. When it came my turn to speak, I declared it to be a 51-49 proposition, with the balance tipping narrowly in favor. I felt that tentative overtures could be made; if successful, they could be developed further; if not successful, they could be scrubbed with minimal losses.

From my standpoint, the potential gains were two: the possibility of a strategic opening, and the possibility of getting back our hostages. The dangers were that we would have transferred a small quantity of defensive arms to Iran, and that a covert activity always entailed the danger of exposure and political embarrassment.

My principal reason for being at the meeting was to address the legal issues involved, which were complex. I still was not privy to the August-September and November 1985 Israeli shipments. This meeting concerned not what had happened previously, but a prospective program in which an opening to Iran would be made official U.S. strategy; it would involve using U.S. assets and selling U.S. weapons. This introduced a set of legal issues concerning arms transfers and covert activities, and the appropriate statutory basis for such transactions (see chapter 19).

One legal issue raised was the question of notifying Congress. As previously noted, there were grave concerns about leaks and whether these would endanger the lives of the hostages and/or the people with whom we were dealing in Iran. The tenor of the discussion was that once arrangements were concluded and the hostages had been freed— or were on their way to freedom—Congress would be notified. From Poindexter's explanation, the time-frame for this was thirty to sixty days. Our research suggested that such deferral was legally permitted.

As spelled out in our NSC discussions, the policy we would adopt had four main objectives:

1. To establish communication with moderate elements in Iran, in order to improve relationships with a post-Khomeini government

2. To help bring an end to the Iran-Iraq war, preferably with neither a clear-cut winner, lest the war continue and ignite still further conflict in the Middle East

3. To influence the Iranian government to discontinue or at least diminish its support of terrorism

4. To get the Iranians to use their influence to obtain freedom for the hostages held in Lebanon.

In pursuit of these goals, the U.S. would make limited sales of defensive weapons to elements in Iran, operating through an "authorized agent" which was unspecified, but in context presumably would be Israel. All four points were of key importance; in my opinion, if there had not been such a comprehensive set of objectives, the President would not have agreed to the negotiations.

After the substantive and legal issues had been reviewed, Stan Sporkin drafted a finding for the President's signature, which was forthcoming on January 17. At that point, having provided the legal information that was requested, I returned to my duties at Justice. Because it was a covert activity, I was not apprised of the operational details, and I did not feel I should ask. Once the President had made his decision, I no longer had a "need to know."

Except for a brief inquiry in the summer of 1986, to verify that a pending legal question had no relation to the Iranian initiative, the next time I heard about the matter was when everybody else did—in early November 1986 with the article appearing in *Al Shiraa*. As the story reverberated in the U.S. media, the members of the National Security Council were convened on November 10 and given a briefing by John Poindexter. There I discovered that, far from being concluded in a month or two, the Iran initiative had dragged on for the better part of a year. I also learned about the 1985 transactions involving Israel.

Poindexter further informed us that, under the January 1986 finding, a shipment of TOW missiles had been made in February 1986, and Bud McFarlane and Ollie North had traveled to Tehran in May in an unsuccessful effort to secure the freedom of the remaining hostages.

The following week, the President gave a press conference on the ballooning controversy, trying to set the record straight while still protecting the initiative. It was at this press conference that he misspoke about the involvement of a "third country" (Israel) in the transactions, prompting me to call Poindexter to express my concern. The next day, I took Chuck Cooper with me to a meeting to go over testimony Bill Casey was going to give to the intelligence committee, and I discovered that there was considerable confusion among the people there as to what exactly had occurred.

Casey had a document that had been prepared by the CIA, but Ollie North suggested modifying it and adding a chronology of the various transactions. Subsequently, I learned from Chuck Cooper that George Shultz and Abe Sofaer, the counsel to the State Department, had still another version. The jumbled evidence convinced me that someone needed to do a comprehensive inquiry to gather all the facts of this highly compartmentalized and complex activity. Fortunately, the President accepted my suggestion, which led to the discovery of the diversion by our administration so that immediate remedial action could be taken.

I have presented this brief chronology on the Iran initiative, not only to establish what happened when—something not often done in Iran-Contra accounts—and my own degree of knowledge and participation, but also to highlight some key issues that need to be examined. These issues are chiefly four in number: (1) Was the administration paying ransom to hostage-takers, in defiance of the President's frequently stated opposition to such dealings? (2) Was the strategic opening to Iranian moderates merely a ruse to cover up arms-for-hostages transactions? (3) Did the administration ignore the requirements of the law in conducting these activities? and, (4) Was the failure to notify Congress of the initiative a legal violation?

President Reagan's critics have repeatedly made all four of these assertions, hurling countless charges of illegality, usurpation of power, and unconstitutional behavior. The facts of the case are altogether different, as the next chapter will reveal.

19

THE IRANIAN
INITIATIVE

W AS THE PRESIDENT simply paying ransom to hostage-takers?
Few notions about the complex events of the Iran-Contra dispute have
been more frequently repeated, yet few are more obviously refuted by
the evidence.

Throughout the Iran initiative, both in 1985 when it was being
handled by the Israelis and in 1986 when the United States handled it
directly, the President stressed that we were dealing, not with the
Hizballah extremists who had seized the hostages, but with third
parties who had influence on them. He repeated this statement, over
and over, but his opponents chose just as doggedly to ignore it.

In this respect, as discussed, the example of the Beirut airport crisis
of June 1985 is instructive. In that episode, the United States dealt with
the governments of Syria and Iran to obtain the release of hostages
held by extremist groups on whom these countries had some sort of
influence. Those efforts ultimately proved successful—the hostages
were released, the governments of Syria and Iran were thanked, and

no one accused the President of dealing directly with the hostage-takers.

The President's experience in that episode clearly shaped his response to the negotiations of 1985 and 1986. In these later cases, the contacts of the United States were not with the people who took the hostages, but with people who presumably had some leverage over them—that is, the exact same configuration as at the Beirut airport. When he was in the hospital in July 1985, Don Regan recalls, the President raised the issue of the remaining hostages, "asking whether I thought Syria and Iran might be helpful."[1] Since these were the two governments that had just finished assisting us at Beirut airport, the train of thought is apparent.

The Hizballah extremists who held the hostages in Lebanon were Shiite Muslims who looked to the ayatollah for leadership and were friendly to Iran. But they were not controlled outright by Iran, and, in fact, often seemed to have a different agenda from Tehran. This point was made, not only by the President, but by some of his severest critics. The Democratic majority of the Iran-Contra committees said, for example:

"The Hizballah, a loosely structured movement centered in the Shiite clans of the Bekaa Valley, emerged as the principal opponent of the United States presence in Lebanon. The use of force—particularly terrorism—against Western interests in Lebanon was viewed by the more militant members of the Hizballah as religiously sanctioned. From the outset, U.S. intelligence recognized that the Hizballah was composed of competing political interests, not all of whom were controlled by Iran."[2]

Lack of direct control by Iran came up repeatedly in the dealings of McFarlane, North, et al, with the Iranians. North's notes show an Iranian spokesman complaining that "we are negotiating . . . we cannot make the final decision on when they will be released." Theodore Draper, who has done the most thorough journalistic work on this issue, adds that "in one last exchange with [CIA official George] Cave, the Iranians admitted that the hostages were not under Iranian control."[3]

This point occurs over and over again in the narrative supplied by

Draper, who, though frequently critical of the administration, none-theless provides supporting data on this score. Draper writes, for instance, that the American hostages "were in Lebanon, not under direct Iranian control. Just what hold Iran had on the Lebanese who held the hostages was never satisfactorily established." And again: "The demands of the Lebanese captors put the problem of releasing the hostages in an altogether different light. . . . The Americans had to negotiate with the Iranians, and the Iranians with the Lebanese. The latter had their own demands, which went far beyond the mere pay-ment of arms to Iran."[4]

The evidence is strong, therefore, that the President was doing exactly what he said he was doing—dealing, not with the hostage-takers, but with third parties who had a degree of influence over them. This stance of President Reagan was substantially different from that assumed by Jimmy Carter in 1980, a point frequently overlooked. In dealings recounted by Carter NSC official Gary Sick and Iranian ex-President Bani-Sadr, Carter was conducting negotiations *directly* with Iranian officials at a time when Iran itself was holding U.S. citizens captive.

Under these circumstances, according to Sick, Carter offered to the Iranians far more than anything proposed under Reagan. Sick writes that on October 11, 1980, "a draft message was prepared for President Carter's approval offering a military package of about $150 million (including the aircraft spares) that would be made available upon release of the hostages. . . . The President approved the draft, and it was sent out that evening."[5]

Bani-Sadr confirms and amplifies that Carter was ready to trade arms for hostages, dealing directly with the hostage-takers. He says that "on September 3, [1980,] the ambassador of the Federal Republic of Germany handed me an offer from Jimmy Carter, which seemed very favorable." He adds that "Carter was offering the arms we had purchased under the Shah's reign; they were paid for and we desper-ately needed them."[6]

In late September, when Iraq attacked Iran, the need became even more urgent. Bani-Sadr says that "unexpected proof of Carter's good will arrived on October 7, 1980. . . . The second part of Carter's message [via the Swiss ambassador to Tehran] was of vital importance. He assured me that, for geopolitical reasons, the United States would never accept Iran's defeat. He even suggested providing us with all the arms we wanted if we would quickly resolve the hostage problem."[7]

From these disclosures, it appears that Carter not only was willing to trade arms for hostages, but that he made definite—and quite generous—proposals to that effect. Morever, he was willing to provide these arms, and other inducements, directly to the people who had seized the hostages. That was something President Reagan never did, even though his critics have persisted in saying otherwise.

But if we were not dealing with the hostage-takers, whom were we dealing with? President Reagan contended that we were trying to get an opening to "moderate" or anti-Khomeini forces in Iran rather than trafficking with hard-line terrorists and extremists. This explanation, too, has been dismissed as a subterfuge on the grounds that "all the moderates in Iran are dead." Again, the evidence strongly supports the President's view.

As our chronology makes clear, the idea of seeking an opening to Iran—of trying to identify and deal with moderate elements there—predated the events that brought the hostage issue to the forefront. This theme emerged time and again in early statements from the NSC and CIA and were prominent in administration thinking throughout the Iranian initiative. And the President himself consistently stressed that he sought an opening to moderate elements in Tehran.

Reflecting on the August 1985 decision to approve the Israeli TOW shipments, for instance, the President wrote: "The transaction was to be solely between Israel and the Iranian moderates and would not involve our country, although we would have to waive for Israel our policy prohibiting any transfer of American-made weapons to Iran."[8]

Bud McFarlane's recollection of this decision tells the same story. "The President's points," he testified, "were foremostly that he could imagine that these people in Iran were legitimate in their interest of changing Iranian policy, and were against terrorism, that to provide them with arms would not be at variance with his policy, since he wasn't providing arms to Khomeini, but to people opposed to Khomeini's policy."[9]

In early 1986, before the official U.S. Iran initiative had gone very far, the President gave an interview to journalist Dale Van Atta on the understanding that Van Atta observe the necessary security requirements until the operation was concluded. Asked about the nature of our dealings with Iran, and about trying to free the hostages in particular, the President responded:

"We have to remember that we had a pretty solid relationship with Iran during the time of the Shah. We have to realize also that that was a very key ally in that particular area in preventing the Soviets from reaching their age-old goal of the warm water ports. . . . And now, with the take-over by the present ruler, we have to believe that there must be elements present in Iran that—when nature takes its inevitable course—they want to return to different relationships. . . . We have to oppose what they are doing. We at the same time must recognize that we do not want to make enemies of those who today could be our friends."[10]

As noted by the minority report of the Iran-Contra committees, references to such considerations—the Soviet presence in the region, the need for a strategic opening, approaches to more moderate elements, and so on—were rife in the testimony of administration spokesmen and official documents of the Reagan government, both before and during the Iran initiative. That the administration was authentically trying to deal with more moderate elements in Iran as part of a long-term strategic program, with hostages or without, is apparent from the record.

How realistic were such efforts? Despite frequent statements that the President was deluding himself about the existence of dissident elements in Iran, plentiful data suggest he was correct. Iran under the ayatollah was not a monolithic place, with everyone marching in lockstep to a common policy, but a cockpit of warring factions. There were a number of competing groups, with different political views and conflicting attitudes about the long-term relationship with America.

As described by Bani-Sadr, for example, these differing elements included his own faction, which was relatively moderate but anti-

American; the army inherited from the shah, which was American-trained and American-equipped and presumably less fanatic than the followers of the ayatollah; the Revolutionary Guards the ayatollah had raised up to act as his personal army; the mullahs who followed the ayatollah; Rafsanjani, the Speaker of the Parliament with whom we were attempting to work (a process that is continuing today), and others.

The existence of these factions, the competition among them, and the shifting alliances that resulted made it difficult for us to know with whom we were dealing, whether they were reliable, and whether they could deliver what they promised. The difficulty was compounded by our lack of intelligence from Iran, a weakness that had blindsided us to the uprising against the shah and made us dependent on the advice of such middlemen as Manucher Ghorbanifar, whose contacts inside Iran were recommended by the Israelis.*

Complexities notwithstanding, these different elements did exist, and some of them wanted a better relationship with America. It was therefore hardly outrageous to seek out some kind of opening to them, however difficult the problems of intelligence.

A factor that powerfully affected this subject, as noted, was our tilt toward Iraq in its conflict with Iran. Though officially we were neutral, many factors reflected this tilt. Operation Staunch, for example, was in effect pro-Iraqi, since weapons were thereby denied Iran but not Iraq; Saddam Hussein was getting all the hardware he needed from the Soviet Union and the Eastern bloc. Besides allowing weapons and high technology to go to Baghdad, we shared intelligence with the Iraqi army. Trading arms to Iran, irrespective of the hostages or moderates, went counter to this policy.

This tilt continued to be the official posture of the foreign policy establishment well into the era of George Bush—right up, in fact, to

---

* Many points are suggested by this chaotic scenario. One is that we urgently needed to rebuild the intelligence capability that had been degraded in the 1970s. Another is that operations of this sensitivity and complexity should not be undertaken on an operational basis by people such as McFarlane and North whose experience in such matters is limited, but by experts from the CIA. The first point is a reproach against the Carter administration, the second against our own. Both are arguments against a debilitated CIA.

Saddam Hussein's invasion of Kuwait. George Shultz and Cap Weinberger, for what they considered good and sufficient reasons, strongly supported this viewpoint and battled within the administration against any effort to counterbalance it. Bill Casey and Bud McFarlane, on the other hand, argued for a correction toward Iran for long-term strategic reasons.

As often occurred when his advisors disagreed, the President sought for equilibrium. He certainly had no desire to see Iran win the Gulf War or have Khomeini fundamentalism sweep the Middle East. On the other hand, he was no fan of Saddam Hussein and did not want him to emerge the victor, either. The President believed that planning for a post-Khomeini Iran and contacting moderate elements was worth attempting. And if this could help get American hostages out, as at Beirut airport, so much the better.

Looking back, it is obvious that media and official horror over any proposed initiative to Iran in 1985-86 was strongly affected by then-prevailing attitudes that we should favor Saddam Hussein—the supposed good guy in the Persian Gulf—as opposed to the bad guys in Tehran. Nowadays, after our shooting war with Saddam, we have a slightly different perspective. Saddam, it appears, was not such a good guy after all, and the President's decision not to put all our eggs in that particular basket looks pretty sound.

But, whatever its merits as policy, was such an initiative legal? By far the most serious accusation against the President was that his attempted dealings with Iran, the arms sales in particular, were unlawful. Such a charge is far more serious, of course, than a simple policy disagreement. Yet it has been lightly bandied about in our political debates, with precious little to back it up.

The notion that there was something illegal about the initiative stems largely from two factors: (1) It was a covert activity. This meant it was never debated fully or clearly explained to Congress or the American public and gave rise to suspicions that there was something disreputable about it. Such accusations were frequently made in the aftermath of the November 1986 disclosures. One of my chief regrets was that, in its defensive reaction, the administration never made the legal and policy basis for the initiative clear; (2) The initiative was linked, via Ollie

North, to the diversion of funds to the Nicaraguan resistance. (Views differ about whether the diversion itself involved criminal liability; and to date, no one has been convicted of such an offense.)

These accusations of illegality, plus repeated assertions that the administration was violating the law with respect to the so-called Boland amendments, strongly biased public perceptions of the Iran initiative. (Both the diversion and the Boland amendments will be examined in the following chapter.)

In point of fact, the conduct of the White House in carrying out the Iran initiative was legal at every step along the way. To understand this, it is necessary to consider the laws applicable to the situation, something the critics of the administration seldom bother to do. These topics were carefully discussed in the Oval Office on January 7, 1986, and at subsequent meetings, and subjected to considerable research by CIA counsel Stanley Sporkin and myself. In addition, prior research on these matters had been conducted by Davis Robinson, legal counsel to the State Department, and by my predecessor at Justice, William French Smith.

Two kinds of statutes were relevant to the situation: those pertaining to the transfer of arms by the United States and countries who were recipients of U.S. weapons, and those pertaining to covert activities by the CIA. In the first instance, the Arms Export Control Act (AECA) required that any direct or indirect transfer of U.S. arms (as, for instance, by Israel), amounting to $14 million or more in terms of acquisition costs, required submission of an unclassified notice to Congress before the shipment could go forward.

An alternative route to arms transfers lay in the so-called Economy Act, which allowed the CIA to obtain weapons at cost from the Defense Department for subsequent resale in pursuit of covert activities. This triggered the requirements of the 1974 Hughes-Ryan Amendment to the National Security Act, which says that before the CIA engages in such activity the President must find it in the national interest and report the finding "in timely fashion" to the relevant committees of Congress.

In our discussions of the 1986 Iran initiative, we concluded that the Economy Act was the way to go, because it did not involve the advance, unclassified notification that would have jeopardized the security of the operation. The legality of this approach was confirmed by the researches of Davis Robinson and Bill Smith, as well as by Stanley Sporkin and myself.

One point of confusion on this subject (among many) is the suggestion that the August-September and November 1985 Israeli shipments to Iran, on the understanding that these supplies would be replenished by the United States, violated either the AECA or the Hughes-Ryan requirement on presidential findings. In fact—though this particular subject was not raised in our January 7 meeting—neither of these transactions was illegal under the relevant statutes.

Under the AECA, U.S. approval was required for Israeli shipments of U.S.-origin equipment to Iran. As determined by all investigations of this topic, such approval was given orally by President Reagan (as will be discussed more fully in a moment), which satisfied this requirement of the law. As for notification, neither shipment amounted to a value of $14 million in terms of acquisition costs and therefore was not covered by the statute.

Under Hughes-Ryan, the Israeli transaction that raised the most concern was the November 1985 HAWK shipment in which the CIA was very marginally involved. This consisted, as noted, of making phone calls and sending cables in an effort to get clearance for the Israeli plane to land in Portugal, and then referring General Secord to the "proprietary" St. Lucia airways to make commercial delivery of the missiles.

Since there was no operational involvement by the CIA, Deputy Operations Director Ed Juchniewicz, who made the referral, did not consider the matter significant enough to require a finding. But Deputy Director McMahon felt that even this peripheral involvement should be backed up with written authorization from the President, and a "retroactive" finding was duly authorized on December 5.

The Hughes-Ryan amendment says that CIA funds may not be expended on covert operations, as opposed to intelligence activities per se, "unless and until the President finds that each such operation is important to the national security of the United States." The involvement of the CIA in this activity included no operational role and the expenditure of no intelligence funds. Against that backdrop, it is questionable whether the help provided by the CIA rose to the level that would require a presidential finding.*

Yet even if it *did* require a finding, the requirement was already satisfied in terms of the substance and intention of the law. One reason for confusion on this score was the widespread assumption that Hughes-Ryan required a *written* finding by the President. But under the law as it then stood, there was no such stipulation. All that was mandated was that he "find" the operation in question to be important to the national security of the United States.

The point of Hughes-Ryan was to ensure that agents of the CIA did not roam around on their own inventing plots, planning coups, or conducting other covert activities without the knowledge and approval of the President. That was the object of the statutory language pinning responsibility directly on the chief executive, but it said nothing about the matter of *written* determinations on the subject.

As for the HAWK shipments—though discussions on the matter were conducted in the hurried atmosphere surrounding the November 1985 summit—we have good evidence that the President approved the initiative in question, a point on which Bud McFarlane and Don Regan, for once, emphatically agreed.

Concerning the November 15 visit from Rabin inquiring about the HAWKs, for example, Bud said the deal was okay from the President's standpoint, "based upon recent questions and reaffirmations by the President that I have received."[11] According to Don, McFarlane told the President about the developing HAWK transaction shortly before they left on November 17 for the Geneva summit.[12] The President's reaction, McFarlane testified, was "cross your fingers and hope for the best, and keep me informed."[13]

According to Bud, the President viewed the November HAWK

---

* In an opinion letter I wrote as attorney general on February 18, 1987, to the Tower Review Board, I indicated that if the CIA had actually participated in the November HAWK shipment and if the object of this involvement was to "influence the policy of a foreign government," the Hughes-Ryan Act would require a finding. Whether the marginal nature of the agency's involvement amounted to such an attempt to "influence" would have to be resolved as a factual matter to say conclusively whether a finding was required.

shipments as a continuation of the initiative begun in August with the TOWs. In essence, therefore, the entire series of Israeli transactions with Iran, on the understanding that the arms would be replenished by the United States, was orally approved by President Reagan. Under the requirements of Hughes-Ryan, he "found" these activities important to the national security. Any peripheral involvement of the CIA was covered by such findings.

The Juchniewicz opinion that a finding was not required is therefore understandable; but so too is the very different reaction of Deputy Director McMahon, who secured the retroactive written finding. Having gone through the savaging of the CIA that occurred in the 1970s, when it was roundly accused of "rogue" activities, McMahon wanted to make sure the CIA involvement was covered in every possible fashion. The written finding of December 5, on top of the oral findings already made, was analogous to wearing suspenders with your belt— just to be on the safe side.

That a written finding under Hughes-Ryan was not needed is noted (regretfully) by the Iran-Contra committees majority and was the basis for legislation (passed August 14, 1991) that *now does require* that covert activity findings be in written form. The passage of such legislation obviously acknowledges that the Hughes-Ryan amendment, at the time of the 1985-86 transactions, included no such requirement.*

All these considerations were superseded, of course, on January 17, 1986, when the President signed a written finding that set forth the goals and methods of the Iran policy, making it an American rather than an Israeli initiative. From that point forward, there could be no question about the degree of presidential authorization for the initiative as such.

---

* As it happens, I am in favor of written findings; the absence of them in these cases, while certainly not illegal, was a substantive and procedural error. When initiatives of such importance are undertaken, the legal and policy basis for them should be established clearly. Also, at the time of these activities, there was an executive order, signed by the President himself, setting out guidelines for written findings. This is further evidence of bad procedure, but not of illegality; since such an order was issued within the discretion of the President, it could be rescinded or modified by him if he believed such action appropriate.

Still another legal question that has been raised concerns the failure to provide notification of this finding to Congress. To understand the issue of disclosure, it is important to note the environment in which these activities were occurring, and the constitutional-legal obligations of the President in dealing with that environment. It is no exaggeration to say that during this period a veritable Niagara of "leaks" threatened our intelligence activities, particularly those pertaining to terrorism in the Middle East and our attempts to cope with it.

Perhaps the most notorious was the leak to Bob Woodward of the *Washington Post* concerning a CIA plan to harass Libyan dictator Muammar Qaddafi. The plan showed up on the front page of the *Post* on November 3, 1985, just two weeks before deliberations on the HAWK missile transaction. Previously, a plan to organize preemptive strikes against terrorists had also leaked to the *Post*. So had a covert finding to provide assistance to Jonas Savimbi in Angola, and a secret trip by Poindexter and Fortier to Egypt to coordinate Mideast strategy.

And there was more: Sen. David Durenberger of Minnesota, chairman of the Senate Intelligence Committee, was undergoing a series of well-publicized personal problems; Sen. Patrick Leahy of Vermont, the vice chairman, had gone on television in October 1985, divulging details of our intelligence knowledge concerning Egypt; and two listening devices were discovered in the office of Sen. Barry Goldwater, a staunch friend of the administration and former chairman of the committee.[14]

Obviously, leaks had become a way of life in Washington and the probability that anything provided to Congress would *not* wind up on the front page of the *Washington Post* was remote. For those who say, "too bad, the President has to provide the notification anyway," the short answer is "no, he does not." The President takes a solemn oath to protect and defend the United States and is not required, either constitutionally or legally, to countenance the hemorrhaging of national security secrets.

Such considerations, as it happens, are recognized even in the disclosure provision of Hughes-Ryan, which says that notification must occur "to the extent consistent with due regard for the protection from unauthorized disclosure of classified information and information relating to intelligence sources and methods." Such unauthorized disclosure was exactly what we had been seeing with respect to plans concerning Qaddafi, and antiterrorist actions generally, and it was exactly what we were trying to prevent in the case of the Iran initiative.

To my mind, these factors never suggested that congressional notification should not occur at all. They did suggest that measures should be taken to protect premature disclosure; that is, to delay notification until the danger had elapsed. This was why the transfers could not occur under the Arms Export Control Act, which required unclassified notification prior to shipment.

The disclosure requirement under Hughes-Ryan, on the other hand, explicitly envisioned the possibility of notification *after the fact*. It states that the President shall inform the intelligence committees "in timely fashion" concerning covert activities "for which prior notice was not given." This language obviously contemplates the need for secrecy before or during the course of such activity with *ex post facto* notification to Congress, while leaving the question of timeliness open to construction.

Exactly these considerations applied in this case and weighed heavily in the thinking of Stanley Sporkin, general counsel to the CIA. In a paper prepared for Bill Casey on the subject, Sporkin spelled out the rationale for going via the Economy Act and CIA to conduct the arms transactions, and for deferring notification.

"The key issue in the entire matter," Sporkin wrote, "revolves around whether or not there will be reports made to Congress. . . . While the National Security Act provides for a certain limited reporting procedure, it is my view that there may be other ways of making a suitable report by exercise of the President's constitutional prerogatives. One such possibility would be not to report the activity until after it has been successfully concluded and to brief only the chairman and ranking minority members of the two Oversight Committees. This would maximize the security of the mission and reduce the possibility of its premature disclosure."[15]

In the framework of a short-term operation, designed to test the waters and succeed (or fail) within a brief time, such as thirty to sixty days, we concluded that such withholding was legally justified. Of course, when the operation dragged on inconclusively for another eight or nine months, the nondisclosure appeared quite different, and the administration paid heavily for it.

In retrospect, I believe that when it became apparent that the Iranian initiative was not succeeding, it should have been dropped and Congress should have been notified of what had happened. I therefore do not defend the protracted failure to disclose—but it was a policy error, not a crime. And it is worth recalling that when much the same thing happened under Jimmy Carter, the public reaction was very different. As the minority report of the Iran-Contra committees observes:

"According to Admiral Stansfield Turner, who was Director of Central Intelligence at the time, there were three occasions, all involving Iran, in which the Carter administration withheld notification [from Congress] for about three months until six Americans could be smuggled out of the Canadian embassy in Tehran. . . . Notification was also withheld for about six months in two other Iranian operations during the hostage crisis. Said Turner: 'I would have found it very difficult to look . . . a person in the eye and tell him or her that I was going to discuss this life-threatening mission with even half a dozen people in the CIA who did not absolutely have to know.' "[16]

The fact that the Carter administration withheld notification for a protracted period does not, of course, justify the Reagan administration in doing so, or vice versa. But why was Reagan's case treated as a terrible offense, demanding congressional hearings, evoking fulminations about the fall of our democracy, and culminating in countless hostile books and articles? And why, when the same thing was done by Carter, was there no slightest murmur of protest?

Exactly the same double standard prevailed on the questions of trading arms for hostages and dealing directly with hostage-takers. In both of these, the Carter administration was clearly *more* culpable than the Reagan administration, but it received not even a fraction of the abuse heaped on President Reagan and his staff. That discrepancy may not tell us very much about Carter or Reagan, but it tells us a great deal about the prevailing standards of our discourse.

20

THE BOLAND
AMENDMENTS

Iᴠ ᴛʜᴇ Iʀᴀɴɪᴀɴ ᴘᴀʀᴛ of the Iran-Contra affair was marked by legal complexities and policy ambiguities, the part involving the freedom fighters who became known as the Contras was even more convoluted. Again, the reality was very different from the image conveyed by the administration's critics.

In what has become the conventional view the story is this: Congress in its wisdom had banned all assistance to Nicaragua's anticommunist resistance (the Contras) through the strictures of the so-called Boland amendments, named for Rep. Edward Boland (D-Mass.), then chairman of the House Intelligence Committee. The Reagan administration then supposedly flouted the Boland amendments by illegally soliciting private and third-country assistance for the Contras through Lt. Col. Oliver North—culminating in the diversion of the Iranian arms sale money.

Lou Cannon of the *Washington Post*, for example, asserts in his history of the Reagan era that aid from Saudi Arabia solicited by the

272

White House "was . . . outlawed by the second Boland amendment."[1]
Sen. John Kerry (D-Mass.), for his part, said the Boland amendments
prohibited "any support for the Contras, direct or indirect," and that
"during fiscal year 1985, no U.S. official was permitted to provide any
form of assistance, direct or indirect, to the Contras."[2] These notions
concerning the legal aspects of the matter became ingrained in media
reports.

Such statements, echoed by many other sources, are widely believed and account for numerous denunciations of the Reagan government and its policy toward Nicaragua. But they are quite untrue. This
becomes immediately evident to anyone who takes time to study the
history of Contra aid and the relevant legislation.

The substantive problem of Nicaragua under the Sandinistas and its
place in the evolution of the Reagan doctrine are discussed in chapter
17. From the President's standpoint (and intermittently that of Congress as well), the Sandinistas were a clear and present danger to their
Central American neighbors, El Salvador in particular, and to the
security of the hemisphere. Helping anticommunist resistance forces
in Nicaragua was a way to defend hemispheric security interests and
collaterally those of the United States.

The more liberal Democrats on Capitol Hill, however, felt differently. They believed that, rather than assist the anticommunists, we
should simply bargain and negotiate with the Sandinistas. From this
they slid to the conclusion that the United States was somehow the
"aggressor" in Nicaraguan affairs, and if only we would stop assisting
the Contras peace would once again reign in the region. The United
States, they said, should clear out of Central America and let the
people there "decide things for themselves."

This view, of course, downplayed or ignored entirely the fact that
the Soviet Union, Cuba, and various elements in the Eastern bloc were
pouring supplies in to the Sandinistas. To cut off aid to the Contras
would have been tantamount to disarming one side but not the other.
Rather than letting the people of the region "decide things for themselves," such a policy would have let the Soviets, Cubans, and Sandinistas do the deciding.

Because assistance to the Contras was allegedly "covert"—

arguably the most openly debated covert operation in our history—it would in the usual course of events have been handled by the CIA. Thus the authorization and appropriations bills for the CIA—and other intelligence agencies—became perennial battlegrounds over U.S. policy toward Nicaragua, and it was to these bills that the various Boland amendments (ultimately five in number) were attached.

In these battles, it should be noted, the liberal Democrats could not—and did not—simply work their will. In the first place, they could not constitutionally deprive the President of his inherent power to conduct the foreign policy and protect the security of the United States.

In the second place, the liberal Democrats did not have total control of the legislature. While the House was under Democratic control, the Senate was not. During the period of repeated battles over Contra assistance, the Republican Senate stood basically with the administration. Thus the House could not unilaterally make *legislative* decisions on the issue, much less perform the functions of the executive.

In the third place, the House itself was bitterly divided on the issue, with not only Republicans but many moderate Democrats sharing the administration's concern about Nicaragua and inclined to help the Contras. This led to a series of closely contested votes in the lower chamber, most of which—but not all—were won by the liberal Democrats.

All these factors inevitably meant that the policy emerging from the legislative process, and from the tension between the legislature and the executive, was a series of blurred compromises. And since some who opposed support for the freedom fighters did not want to take the blame should the U.S. pull out and the Marxists take over in Central America, compromises became a linguistic way to obscure the issue. Ambiguous policy approaches were devised which accommodated the conflicting viewpoints of the various governmental branches. This was the legal framework in which the Boland amendments were adopted and the administration's Nicaragua policy carried out.

The result, as the Tower Commission drily observed, "was a highly ambiguous legal environment." Contrary to the image of a single sweeping Boland amendment that once and forever barred all aid to the anticommunist resistance, what developed was a series of changing enactments that allowed some things, barred others, allowed some things that had been barred, barred something else that hadn't been, and so on. The administration, rather than flagrantly ignoring the law, was highly sensitive to the ambiguities and nuances of the situation and constructed its policy as best it could to fit them.

The nature of this process is well illustrated by the very first Boland amendment, adopted in December 1982, which was so (purposely) ambiguous that it meant whatever the differing parties wanted it to mean. This measure barred the use of funds from the CIA or Department of Defense "for the purpose of overthrowing the government of Nicaragua or provoking a military exchange between Nicaragua and Honduras."

Since the official purpose of the United States was not to overthrow the Nicaraguan government but to interdict its aggression against El Salvador and other neighbors, the administration found this language acceptable. Accordingly, the formulation was approved by the White House legislative team, and all Republicans voting in the House supported it. The amendment passed unanimously, by a vote of 411-0.

The significance of this initial Boland language was underscored by the defeat of a motion by then-Rep. Tom Harkin (D-Iowa), which would have barred assistance to any group or individual "in carrying out military activities against Nicaragua." This much more categorical prohibition—barring military aid regardless of its purpose—was voted down in favor of the more open-ended Boland language.

The meaning of this change is spelled out by the Congressional Research Service of the Library of Congress in a summary of the various Boland amendments and their legislative history (compiled at the instigation of the administration's critics). In its discussion of the first Boland amendment, the CRS observes:

"This restriction represents a compromise between legislators who desired no limitations on U.S. assistance to the Contras and those who favored broader restrictions. *It was clearly understood at the time of enactment that the compromise would not cut off all direct or indirect assistance to the Contras.* At that time the administration had been asserting that U.S. assistance was intended for use to confine the Sandinistas to Nicaragua and not for the purpose of overthrowing them" (emphasis added).[3]

It was the compromise nature of this language, of course, that caused the administration and all Republicans voting in the House to go along with it. Had such a compromise not been reached, a bitter fight would have ensued, rather than a unanimous vote. It is thus completely disingenuous of administration critics to claim the original Boland amendment barred all military aid to the Contras. It did not—and they know it.

The ambiguities evident in the first of the Boland amendments continued to surface in subsequent legislative battles. The following year, the Boland restrictions were tightened—but only slightly: Contra aid was voted, but capped at $24 million. Then, in intelligence appropriations for fiscal year 1985 (voted in October 1984), the most restrictive of the amendments (usually called Boland II) was adopted. It stated:

"During the fiscal year 1985, no funds available to the Central Intelligence Agency, the Department of Defense, or any other agency or entity *involved in intelligence activities* may be obligated or expended for the purpose or which would have the effect of supporting, directly or indirectly, military or paramilitary operations in Nicaragua by any nation, group, organization, movement or individual" (emphasis added).[4]

According to such as Cannon and Kerry, it was this language that made illegal any and all attempts to muster backing for the Contras, most specifically the activities run by Oliver North out of the White House. In their view, North's attempts to coordinate private and third-country aid for the resistance and to provide advice and communications support, and the related fundraising efforts of Elliott Abrams at the State Department, were categorically forbidden by this measure.

This construction, however, is flatly wrong—unequivocally so on the face of the language, its legislative history, and contemporaneous actions by Congress. Most obviously, Boland II did not, and could not, bar private or third-country aid to the Contras, or the solicitation of such aid by the White House. The Boland prohibitions affected only *appropriated U.S. tax funds* expended by the CIA or other intelligence agencies—not private or third-country funds.

Representative Boland himself alluded to this distinction in House floor debate in June 1985, opposing a motion by Minority Leader Bob Michel (R-Illinois) to extend some $27 million in U.S. humanitarian aid to the Nicaraguan resistance. Boland commented: ". . . the Contras, who haven't received $1 from the U.S. government for more than a year, are doing just fine. They continue their military operations in Nicaragua and they have increased in numbers. *They have done this with funds provided by private groups, mostly from the United States.* Those funds have helped purchase weapons, ammunition, food, clothing—everything the Contras would have needed to maintain themselves as an army in the field.

"Now comes the Michel amendment and provides humanitarian assistance on top of that. . . . Is this a policy of restraint by the U.S. government? *Hardly, in light of the fact, as we all know, that private groups will continue to provide money for arms and ammunition.* The effect of the Michel amendment, and that private aid, is going to be more money for the Contras than they have ever received in the past" (emphasis added).[5]

In this colloquy, Representative Boland nowhere suggested that such private aid was in any way illegal, and most conspicuously did not suggest it was barred by the amendment that bore his name. Nor could he accurately have done so, since its language was directed at appropriated tax funds, not private funds. Yet the fiction persists that such assistance was outlawed by the language of Boland II.

A similar logic would apply, of course, to third-country funds, which were provided to the Contras by Saudi Arabia and Taiwan. Boland II could not and did not bar provision of such funds; third countries are not under congressional control, and their funds are not U.S. tax funds. Nor could Congress constitutionally bar the President or his designates from soliciting such assistance, as long as it was not recycled U.S. tax money or a quid pro quo for U.S. government-provided funds.

Equally important, the only legislation Congress passed contemporaneous with the Boland amendments touching the subject of third-country aid solicitation explicitly *approved* it—at least for "humanitarian" purposes. Thus the Intelligence Authorization Act, adopted in December 1985, said that "nothing in this section precludes . . . activities of the Department of State [one of the covered agencies in the legislation] to solicit . . . humanitarian assistance for the Nicaraguan democratic resistance."[6]

Further illustrative of the twilight zone created by the legislation of the time were other elements of the 1985 act, which specifically sanctioned tax-supported provision of communications, communications equipment, and "advice" for the Contras. In addition, Congress voted that nothing in the law "shall be construed to prohibit the United States from exchanging information with the Nicaraguan democratic resistance."[7]

As the House conferees on this measure explained: "The conference committee discussed, and the Intelligence Committes have clarified, that none of the prohibitions on the provision of military or paramilitary assistance to the democratic resistance prohibits the sharing of intelligence information with the democratic resistance."[8]

All of this language was adopted, it bears repeating, at a time when the most restrictive Boland amendment was in effect. Obviously, then, this amendment not only did not prohibit private or third-country aid to the Contras, it did not even bar all forms of *official* U.S. aid. Explicit provision was made, instead, for communications assistance, communications equipment, "advice," and the sharing of intelligence information.

Against that backdrop, the notion that the Boland amendment was a clear-cut total prohibition of any and all aid to the Contras, public or private, dissolves into absurdity. What existed instead was a legal setting in which direct arms aid from intelligence agencies was barred, but private aid concededly continued, third-country aid for humanitarian purposes was explicitly authorized, and various kinds of official assistance other than tax-funded military aid were legislatively approved.

Further complicating the situation was the fact that Congress, while at various times expanding and contracting limits on aid to the Contras, was simultaneously condemning the Sandinistas for aggression and declaring them to be in violation of the charter of the Organization of American States (OAS), to which the United States is a signatory.

In 1983, as noted, Congress found that the Nicaraguan government was "providing military support (including arms, training and logistical, command and control, and communications facilities) to groups seeking to overthrow the government of El Salvador and other Central American governments," and thus was in violation of Article 18 of the OAS charter prohibiting aggression against neighboring countries.

In 1985, while the most restrictive of the Boland amendments was in effect, Congress repeated this finding, asserting that the Nicaraguan government "has committed and refuses to cease aggression in the form of armed subversion against its neighbors" in violation of the OAS charter and other international treaty commitments.[9]

The significance of these findings, as noted by the Iran-Contra minority report, is that the OAS charter defines an act of aggression against one member as an act of aggression against other members, including the U.S. In effect, therefore, Congress was branding the Sandinista government as an aggressor and outlaw against whom the United States was committed by treaty obligation, as well as by its own security interests, to respond.

By adopting so many countervailing measures while placing limits on Contra aid, Congress was sending a double message: condemning the Sandinistas for aggression and authorizing certain means of defense against them, while simultaneously constraining official U.S. military aid to the forces resisting the Sandinistas in the field.

In political terms, it was an effort to have it both ways at once: to be on record as opposing the Sandinistas, but to hobble assistance to the forces that were actually combatting them. In legal and policy terms, it said to the administration: The Sandinistas are committing aggression and need to be resisted; but *do not* resist them by channeling arms aid to the Contras through the CIA or other intelligence agencies.

As the record shows, the Reagan administration carefully navigated its way through these confused, and confusing, waters—withdrawing the CIA from the field of action when the Boland restrictions were in effect, no longer providing direct arms aid through the agency, but attempting to keep the Contra opposition alive by methods other than the transfer of U.S. taxpayer-provided funds.

Given this history, the activities to support the Contras conducted by Oliver North from his position on the National Security Council staff, other than the diversion of the Iranian arms funds, were clearly within the confines of the controlling statutes. The things that North was doing—coordinating private and third-country aid, providing communications, intelligence, and so on—were precisely the things that *were* permitted, not prohibited, by the Boland amendments and accompanying legislation. Even had the NSC staff been covered by the Boland amendments, there are substantial grounds for concluding that North's activities were legal.

There is the further point, however, that the NSC staff was *not* so covered. The most restrictive of the amendments barred the use of "funds available to the Central Intelligence Agency, the Department of Defense, or any other agency or entity involved in intelligence activities" to help the Contras. Critics of the administration have assumed or stated that this phrasing included the National Security Council staff at the White House.

Yet the legislative history of the language argues otherwise. The phrase "agency or entity involved in intelligence activities" is a term of legislative art that has a very definite meaning and has been spelled out on several occasions in some detail. Such exegesis makes it plain that the National Security Council staff is *not* one of the entities included.

This point was made, interestingly enough, by the Carter administration, when the Intelligence Oversight Act was being drafted and adopted in 1980. At that time, some in the Senate wanted to include the NSC and its staff within the definition of an intelligence agency, and thus within the strictures of the act. But the Carter White House and Justice Department objected, and the NSC was accordingly excluded.

Senate Intelligence expert William Harris, who was closely involved in drafting this legislation, recalls the circumstances. Harris himself wanted to include the NSC in the definition of an "intelligence" agency. But, he notes, "specific requirement of reporting by the National Security Council raised constitutional issues relating to 'executive privilege' and separation of powers. . . . Any change of the nature I was proposing would reopen constitutional issues of concern to the Attorney General and the Counsel to the President [Carter]. . . . The President would not permit, I was advised, the conduct of covert operations by the NSC staff itself."[10]

As a result, the legislation adopted by a Democratic Congress and a Democratic president did *not* include the NSC or its staff in its definition of "intelligence" agencies. The agencies covered by the act were said to be the following:

"The Office of the Director of National Intelligence; the Central Intelligence Agency; the Defense Intelligence Agency; the National Security Agency; the offices within the Department of Defense for the collection of specialized national intelligence through reconnaissance programs; the intelligence components of the military services; the intelligence components of the Federal Bureau of Investigation; the Bureau of Intelligence and Research of the Department of State; the foreign intelligence components of the Department of Treasury; the foreign intelligence components of the Department of Energy; the successors to any of these agencies; and any other components or departments, to the extent determined by the President, as may be engaged in intelligence activities."[11]

While the NSC was excluded from this roster, the President could have designated the NSC to be an "intelligence" entity, if he had so chosen, under the final category listed. But President Carter clearly did not so choose; neither did President Reagan. In an executive order issued on December 4, 1981, President Reagan, in his official definition of "agencies within the intelligence community," essentially recapitulated the list above—not including the NSC, and also not including the final elastic clause.[12]

In the Intelligence Authorization Act of 1985, including by reference the then-current restrictions of Boland II, Congress revisited the issue of what was or was not an "intelligence" entity. This act set forth the agencies of the U.S. government involved in "intelligence and intelligence related activities," which were essentially those defined in the 1980 act, plus the Drug Enforcement Administration. The NSC, again, was nowhere mentioned.

As this history distinctly shows, the NSC was excluded from the definition of an "intelligence" agency, both at the time the intelligence law was being drawn up and at the time the Boland amendment, using the same term of art, was being adopted. It is hard not to conclude that the "intelligence" prohibitions not only failed to include the NSC, but did so quite deliberately. As Harris observes in his discussion of the original 1980 legislation:

"Proposals in 1980 to extend the scope of 'entities' to include the National Security Council and its staff were expressly rejected. . . . The linked reference to a 'department, agency or entity' engaged in intelligence activities developed a meaning widely understood in the executive and legislative branches. This phrase of legislative art applied exclusively to the intelligence agencies or specialized intelligence collection components of the U.S. intelligence community. This definition did not include within its scope other entities of government that supervised the 'intelligence' entities or summarized and disseminated their products."[13]

The reason for such exclusion, as suggested by the Carter objections, is the separation of powers within our constitutional system. Administration critics contend that the Reagan White House was subverting the constitutional order by trying to do with nonappropriated funds what Congress had forbidden via the appropriations process. The truth is more nearly the reverse. If Congress were to control the actions of the NSC by way of the appropriations process, it would be doing indirectly what it could not, in constitutional terms, achieve directly: that is, exercise the institutional prerogatives of the executive.

While the President in many key respects operates in tandem with Congress, and most particularly in the matter of appropriated funds, it must be remembered that the executive is an equal and coordinate branch of government, with its own inherent constitutional powers, and may not be prohibited by Congress from performing functions vested in the office by our fundamental law.

The Congress could not, for example, directly forbid the President to veto a bill that it had passed, or prevent him from discharging executive employees under his authority, or forestall him from meeting and conversing with other heads of state, and so on. Such steps could not be overtly taken under the Constitution. By the same token, they could not be done by resorting to the appropriations process, even though the President and other executive branch officials have their salaries paid with money appropriated by the Congress.

This point is of particular relevance in the Iran-Contra affair. Some critics argue that since the salaries of Oliver North and other NSC officials were paid with appropriated funds, their activities necessarily fell within the prohibitions Congress attached to its appropriations. This is not, however, the case. Just as Congress could not forbid the President to veto a bill because his salary is paid with appropriated funds, so Congress can not constitutionally interfere, by way of the appropriations process, with his authority over members of his own executive staff.

It was precisely to avoid such problems that the NSC was not included in the original definition of intelligence agencies. And if it had been included, it would have been unconstitutional. It follows *a fortiori* that Congress could not retroactively make the Boland strictures applicable to the NSC when it had not previously been designated as an "intelligence" agency. The conclusion: North *et al* were not covered by the amendment. (Their coordinating activities assisting the Contras would, of course, have been legal even had the amendment applied.)

These and related points have been made and documented by Brett Sciaroni, the former White House Intelligence Oversight Board counsel, and by legal counsel to the minority members of the Iran-Contra committee. It is interesting to note, however, and rather appalling, that they were also made by members of the staff of special prosecutor Lawrence Walsh, who brought indictments against North, Poindexter, and others for their role in the Iran-Contra affair.

This was revealed in a 1991 book by Jeffrey Toobin, a youthful lawyer on Walsh's team. Toobin's inside account discloses that the prosecutorial staff itself had serious doubts on all issues cited. His treatment of the matter is worth citing at some length:

". . . I heard Danny Coulson, the chief FBI agent assigned to

Walsh's team, muttering after an early staff meeting: 'The Boland amendment?' he said. 'What the hell kind of crime is that?' . . . Coulson's grumbling was my first clue of a deep split within the [team]. A criminal charge based on the Boland amendment divided us not only by political inclination but by professional background. By and large, the professional civil litigators and full-time defense lawyers . . . wanted to bring the Boland case. The experienced prosecutors did not. . . . Like Coulson, the experienced prosecutors . . . believed the office should select discreet criminal acts for prosecution. . . . Charge crimes, they urged—lying, cheating, stealing—not policy disputes. 'Hell,' said Coulson, 'I don't even know if North did violate the Boland amendment.' The Boland amendment was actually a series of laws that prohibited only the expenditure of funds for military aid to the Contras. What government money did North spend?

"True, Coulson conceded that North used his considerable influence on behalf of the Contras, but the law banned expenditures. 'We can say that North spent his own salary to aid the Contras,' Keker answered. [John Keker was the Walsh deputy who argued the case against North in court.] Then he laughed. 'I know that's not a hell of a lot of money.' Coulson sniffed, 'Don't forget the price of the paper clips he used.'

"Coulson noted that Boland applied to 'the Central Intelligence Agency, the Department of Defense, or any other agency or entity of the United States involved in intelligence activities.' North worked at the NSC. Was the NSC 'involved in intelligence activities' and thus covered by Boland? 'Berman says yes,' Keker answered. [Geoff Berman was another apprentice attorney on the staff.] . . .

"History, I thought, would see the Boland amendment violations by North and the others as their most significant misdeeds. . . . But was a Boland charge too technical? Did it belong in a criminal court? . . . One office wit summed up the concerns well when he promised us that we would never hear the cry: 'Officer, arrest that man—he's violating the Boland amendment!' "[14]

21

RESPONSIBILITY AND REFORM

I T WOULD BE a mistake to conclude from my discussion of Iran-Contra that I approve of everything that was done; I do not. Plenty of errors were made, both in substance and procedure, and their net impact was profoundly harmful to the Reagan government and the country, as well as to many individuals who were involved, some only indirectly.

The most obvious error—the by-product of several others—was the diversion of the Iranian arms sales proceeds to support the Nicaraguan resistance. Most discussion of this development treats it as if it were self-evidently a criminal act—a perception that is then erroneously transferred to the whole of both the Iranian and Nicaraguan initiatives.

The possibility that Oliver North's use of the Iran arms money for the Contras might be illegal certainly occurred to me and to others at Justice. In fact, when we made this discovery in our initial inquiry, I instructed Chuck Cooper to examine the question of criminal

liability, and—on the basis of his preliminary analysis—directed the
Criminal Division of the Justice Department to look into the matter. It
was the diversion, and it alone, that turned what had basically been a
fact-finding inquiry into a potential criminal investigation.

This does not mean, of course, that the diversion was *ipso facto*
illegal, but merely that it might have been. The point turned on
whether the excess proceeds from the arms sales, after the weapons
had been sold to the Iranians, belonged to the U.S. government. If they
were U.S. property, then Secord and Co. could not simply allocate
them at will. If they were not, then the funds resembled private or
third-country support for the resistance, and such use would arguably
have been legal.

Despite all the rhetoric expended on this issue, it has never been
settled in a court of law. The legal verdicts against North and Poindexter, which were subsequently overturned on appeal, were based
on other, collateral issues. Likewise other convictions that were obtained, generally on minor offenses, involved peripheral charges that
had more to do with the *investigation* of the Iran-Contra affair than
with the matter itself. To this day, the remaining funds from these
transactions are impounded by the Swiss authorities, subject to competing claims from General Secord and the U.S. government. Thus,
it is far from certain that the diversion was illegal—and still less
certain that any other parts of the Iran-Contra affair were criminal
activity.

Whether it was technically legal or not, however, the fund diversion
was a tremendous error that should never have been allowed to happen.
That it did happen was a failure of the administration—for which it
paid dearly—as well as a consequence of the legal twilight described
in the preceding chapter. And, like many efforts to go outside the
bounds of correct procedure, it wound up doing grievous damage to
the cause that it was meant to serve.

In terms of intelligence doctrine, the diversion represented one
of the most fundamental errors in the book: crossing or combining
two different covert operations. By doing so, it created the danger
that problems with one—always a possibility in such high-risk
ventures—would have repercussions on the other. Which, of course,

is exactly what happened. This aspect of the Iran-Contra affair will undoubtedly be cited in future intelligence annals as a case study of how *not* to do it.

Politically speaking, crossing the initiatives was equally foolish—as the results show. Given the intensely controversial nature of both projects, the political hazards involved should have been readily apparent. However much North and Poindexter thought they were serving the President and his policies, the effect of the diversion in terms of political support and general credibility for Reagan policies was just the opposite.

The merging of the initiatives followed, all too naturally, from the fact that both were being managed out of the White House by the same individual, North, who was juggling them on an improvisational basis while handling a number of other things as well. The temptation to take from one project to help another was all but inevitable.

Moreover, the closely held nature of what North was doing—first under McFarlane and then under Poindexter—meant there were inadequate safeguards in vetting the policy. In the usual way, these would pass through people with the experience and expertise to spot the legal, intelligence, and political dangers involved. In this respect, it is noteworthy that McFarlane, Poindexter, and North were all career military men—highly distinguished in their field and intensely patriotic, but untrained in spotting legal and political pitfalls.

This problem was apparent when Poindexter destroyed the December 5, 1985, retroactive finding that covered the November 1985 HAWK missile shipment, and even more so when he decided to go along with the fund diversion while withholding information about it from the President. The motive in both cases was to distance the President from a controversial decision and thereby presumably shield him with "plausable deniability."

The actual effect of these decisions, however, was to undercut the legal basis of the policies in question. Under the relevant laws, as discussed, a decision by the President was the proper legal basis for covert activity. As I told Bud McFarlane when I interviewed him that November weekend, it could well be that the earlier the President knew about key events the better—one reason among many that all concerned should not try to "outthink" the situation, but simply tell the truth.

A related problem with running such operations on an *ad hoc* basis through the NSC staff was that there was no paper trail establishing when something was done, why, and by what authority. When national policy is conducted in a deliberate and regularized fashion, such as through approval at a formal meeting of the National Security Council, where an issue is clearly presented in all its alternatives, the President can sign off one of these, or a combination of them— providing a clear-cut executive decision.

Under these circumstances, you have documentation of what was done, and the particulars can be disseminated in a structured way to those who need to know. The one advantage of working through bureaucracies, cumbersome as they may be, is that they operate through regularized procedures; no one can doubt what policy is being followed or who is responsible for it.

What was happening in the White House with regard to Iranian and Nicaraguan policy was very different. In part because of the President's illness in the summer of 1985, and also because of the burdens placed on the NSC staff by congressional restrictions on aid to the Contras, regular procedures were frequently ignored. People were gathering around the President's sick bed making suggestions and getting answers, staffers were not keeping formal records, general policies were being decided upon without follow-through on specifics, and so on.

A further and more generic point—applicable to many other issues—was the inadvisability of the President's staff trying to make decisions for him, keeping information from him, or otherwise attempting to manipulate policy. Without exception, in my experience, when people attempted such maneuvers in the Reagan White House, or in Sacramento, the result was serious policy error. Given all the relevant information, Reagan made excellent decisions. When information for whatever reason was withheld from him, proper decision-making was obstructed.

That information about the diversion *was* withheld from him is, I think, established beyond all possibility of doubt. Despite conspiracy theories to the effect that the President knew of or condoned the diversion, there is not a scintilla of evidence to support that view. On the contrary, Oliver North stated very clearly that only three people in the U.S. government knew about the diversion—himself, Poindexter, and McFarlane. Likewise, Poindexter's testimony on this point (which concurred with his initial statement to me on November 24, 1986) should be dispositive, since the admiral would hardly have accepted the whole responsibility if the diversion had been based on presidential authority.

Equally convincing, to me at least, was the President's absolute shock and surprise when I informed him of the diversion. I think I know Ronald Reagan pretty well, and in my experience deep-dyed duplicity is not in him. His astonished reaction when I informed him of this matter was completely genuine—a judgment confirmed by Don Regan, who was present at the interview.

Similar considerations apply to Bill Casey, who according to the Iran-Contra committee majority and other critics was supposedly the mastermind of the diversion. Again, the evidence for this ranges from slim to nonexistent. Interestingly enough, the only real authority for this view is Ollie North—which makes this one of the few topics I can think of where congressional Democrats were ready to take Ollie at his word.

My principal reason for doubting this accusation against Casey is that when I confronted North with evidence of the diversion, he did not say Casey was involved, even though he did say McFarlane and Poindexter knew about it. At that point, North urgently needed to show higher authority for what he was doing. He unhesitatingly mentioned McFarlane and Poindexter, and was emphatic that only the three of them were involved. If Casey had approved it, what reason would North have had not to tell me at the time?

At that point, it should be recalled, Bill was still alive. It was only after his death the following spring that Ollie suddenly began saying that Casey had approved of the diversion. Since Bill could no longer defend himself, the facts of what he knew and did not know went with him to the grave. The only other "evidence" we have about this point is the alleged death-bed confession given to Bob Woodward—which has been expertly dissected by Casey's biographer, Joseph Persico. Woodward has a pattern of claiming—after people are dead—that he had at some point obtained a sensational interview from them. Necrojournalism?

In addition to interviewing North over the period November 21–25, 1986, I talked with Bill Casey, not once, but twice, the first time on Saturday afternoon, November 22, 1986. Bill knew I was gathering information on the Iran-Contra matter and wanted me to know about a recent development. A few weeks previously, he said, he had been approached by a former business acquaintance named Roy Furmark with a story about some businessmen who had been involved in the Iranian transactions.

These businessmen, according to Bill, alleged that they had not been paid for their services. If they were not reimbursed, they said, they would go public with accusations that money from arms deals was being used by the U.S. and the Israelis for "other purposes." At the time this sounded like an effort to pressure the U.S. government into coming up with money rather than any information concerning what we later found to be a diversion. My second conversation with Casey occurred three days later, on Tuesday morning, and will be related in detail below.

In both instances, nothing indicated that Casey himself had knowledge of North's diversion. Nor, in my experience, would Bill Casey have been involved in any such activity. Beginning with the 1980 campaign, I had worked fairly closely with him for almost seven years, and while there was naturally a lot I did not know about his conduct of the CIA, the notion that he would have encouraged or even condoned something like the diversion strikes me as implausible.

This is so, above all, because Bill had an acute awareness of two key factors ignored in the diversion effort, even if it were in some technical sense acknowledged to be legal: bad tradecraft in covert operations, and the political calamity latent in crossing controversial policies. Whatever his critics say about Bill Casey, nobody questioned his knowledge of intelligence matters, or his political horse sense. Even if he thought such activity were legal, he would have been too savvy to risk so much for the marginal gain involved in the diversion.

A further element in the equation is the attitude adopted by the CIA during this time period. Once the most restrictive of the Boland amendments went into effect, all CIA station chiefs were advised to stand down—to withdraw from contacts with the Contra "account," steer clear of the Nicaragua situation, and in general distance themselves from involvement in this area.

Given the state of the law, this might well be viewed as an over-reaction. After all, what was prohibited by the Boland amendments was *spending intelligence funds to help the Contras*. Nothing was done to limit intelligence activity concerning the Contras; on top of which, at various times certain kinds of assistance by the CIA itself were authorized by statute. Notwithstanding, the directives that went out from the agency were to observe accepted practice about compartmentalization and the need to know, and this implied a deliberate effort *not* to inquire too closely into what was going on regarding NSC staff efforts related to Nicaragua.

This outlook accounts for some of the "averted-gaze" approach that led to cover-up charges involving CIA officials such as Alan Fiers and Clair George, and that were later pressed at Robert Gates' confirmation hearings. The whole mindset of the CIA during the period 1985-86 was to stay as far as possible from the situation, to let the NSC staff handle the Contras.

Thus, to take the obvious example, when private donors who wanted to help the Contras approached Bill Casey, he would tell them he could not help them—that they would have to talk to Oliver North. Under the law, as I read it, this was not necessary. Bill could legally have told such donors to help the Contras without violating restrictions on the expenditure of CIA *funds*. Yet he insisted on distancing himself and the agency from the operation.

Under the circumstances, it defies credulity that Casey would have turned around and secretly issued instructions to North, masterminded the Contras' supply effort, and ordered the Iranian fund diversion. That scenario fits neither the knowledge we have of Bill Casey in general, nor the specific data we have about his behavior in this period and the policies he was pursuing at the CIA.

This distancing by experienced hands at the CIA, as well as by Shultz and Weinberger (for different reasons), left the matter almost entirely in the hands of North and, to a lesser extent, Poindexter. In their defense, and that of the administration, it is worth recalling that this situation was imposed on them by the contradictory policies of Congress. Faced with the dual imperatives of resisting the Sandinistas and withholding direct CIA assistance to the Contras, the administration thrust the NSC staff into an operational role that it was ill equipped to handle.

In discussing the activities of Bill Casey, attention must also be given to more recent assertions that he orchestrated an effort during the 1980 campaign to delay the release of the U.S. hostages held in Tehran so as to deny the Carter administration the political benefit of their return. This "October surprise" story, resurfaced by Carter NSC official Gary Sick in April 1991, is totally contrary to the facts of the situation. Such theories, indeed, get the essential details of the matter almost entirely backwards.

As noted, the term "October surprise" was a phrase developed by the Reagan-Bush campaign team to describe anticipated activities of the Carter election effort, not our own. We worried that President Carter and his staff, having control of the American end of the negotiations, would try to manipulate the matter so that the hostages would be returned immediately prior to the election, creating a kind of euphoria that would revitalize his lagging fortunes.

As subsequent research has shown, evidence points to just such an effort being waged by the Carter White House, involving very generous offers of arms and other benefits if only the hostages could be released prior to the election. By talking about an October surprise, we were trying to inoculate the public to this eventuality. If it happened, we could say, "This is exactly what we've been talking about all along." Obviously, it would be more than coincidence if the hostages, after their long captivity, were to be released just a day or two before the voting.

Put another way, if the Reagan-Bush campaign had arrived at a secret agreement to keep the hostages from being freed, the prospect of such a surprise by Carter would not have concerned us and we would have taken no preemptive measures. The continued anxiety in the Reagan camp about this subject, right up to election day, does not fit with Gary Sick's scenario.

Nor did the repeatedly stated attitudes of candidate Reagan about getting the hostages out. Throughout the campaign, Reagan assumed a posture that was designed to accelerate their release. First, he said in a statement September 13, and steadfastly maintained thereafter, that he would abide by whatever terms the Carter government arrived at to secure the freedom of the hostages—even though he did not particularly agree with the way the negotiations were being conducted.

Second, Reagan warned the Iranians that they could not get any better conditions from him than from Carter. As indicated by considerable evidence at the time, and confirmed by Bani-Sadr and others since, the Iranians viewed Reagan as someone who would have been much tougher to deal with than was Carter, and our campaign did nothing to dispel this notion. Thus the attitude of the Reagan forces was directly contrary to that suggested by Sick and others charging Casey with cynical manipulations.

As to the details of Casey's supposed meetings with Iranians in Paris or Madrid in the summer and fall of 1980 (along with George Bush, among others), these charges have been completely refuted by former congressional investigator Herbert Romerstein, the conservative weekly *Human Events* and the liberal *Village Voice*, as well by both *Newsweek* and the *New Republic*.

As it turned out, of course, the Carter administration did make a deal to get the hostages, involving the release of Iranian assets held in the United States. These protracted dealings dragged on through the end of 1980, well after the completion of the November voting, and finally resulted in the freedom of the captives on January 20, 1981, the day of President Reagan's inauguration.

How and why these negotiations went on so long is not totally clear. It should be evident, however, that any electoral motive the Reagan camp might have had for delaying the release of the hostages, in even the most cynical interpretation, would have ended on November 4, 1980. Whatever problems the Carter government had in dealing with Iran from early November 1980 to late January 1981, they obviously cannot be traced to the election campaign of Ronald Reagan, who in this period had already been elected and was waiting to take office.

As our own later experience was to show, dealing with people in Tehran involved all kinds of difficulties. Accounts by members of the Carter administration who took part in the 1980 hostage negotiations give ample reasons for the delay. Moreover, the problems of the Reagan government in its later approaches to Iran belie the theory that Casey was wheeling and dealing with the ayatollah or his representatives in 1980. If Casey had had that kind of influence, the tangled and frustrating effort to work out an opening of some kind in 1985–86 would hardly have been necessary.

In this respect, as with the diversion to the Contras, it is easy for political opponents or sensation-mongers to blame Bill Casey, since he is dead and can no longer defend himself. In neither instance is there any credible evidence that Casey did the things alleged—and a great deal of reason for believing that he did not. I say this not only as someone who came to know Casey well, but also as the person who talked directly with him twice in the course of uncovering the diversion and was thus in a position to judge his reaction to unfolding events.

As for that investigation, let me turn, by way of concluding this subject, to the manner in which it was conducted. Again, concerning this inquiry, many assertions and speculations have been floated suggesting we were dilatory in conducting it, did not ask probing questions, stood around while Ollie North was shredding documents, and so on. A recitation of exactly what did and did not happen may thus be helpful.

To reiterate, at the outset, this was not a criminal inquiry, but rather an effort to reconcile conflicting statements about a complex, covert, compartmentalized effort that few people understood in full. Knowing the Iran initiative of 1986 was authorized and lawful, though covert, I had no reason to assume that I was embarked on a criminal investigation. Rather, my effort was to deal with honorable colleagues, in the

President's behalf, so as to pull together fragmented facts about a confusing situation.

The events that led to my inquiry began, as noted, with the publication of the *Al Shiraa* account of McFarlane's May visit to Tehran. At this time, I told John Poindexter, as we were talking after a cabinet meeting, that if the White House needed any help concerning the legal aspects of the affair, we at the Department of Justice would be glad to assist. I thereupon notified Chuck Cooper, who was head of the Office of Legal Counsel, to contact Comdr. Paul Thompson, Poindexter's assistant at the NSC, to review the legal background on the January finding.

On Monday, November 10, the National Security Council received a briefing from Poindexter in which he reviewed the history of the Iranian initiative. At this point, I learned that rather than being concluded in thirty-to-sixty days, the efforts had dragged on for nearly ten months. I also learned for the first time about the Israeli transactions of 1985 and that there had been dispute about them among Weinberger, Shultz, McFarlane, and Casey. A similar briefing was provided to congressional leaders on November 12.

The following week, on November 19, the President presented the whole matter to the public in a televised news conference. During this conference, he was asked whether a third country had been involved in the transactions, and he said no. I knew this was not accurate, and I called John Poindexter to express my concern. He replied, "Yes, we caught that, and we've just put out a correction."

John went on to say that the following day, November 20, there would be a meeting to review the testimony that Bill Casey would be giving to the Intelligence committees as well as to hear the informal briefing from Poindexter himself (as a White House official, under executive privilege, he would not have testified formally about such matters). He asked if I would attend this meeting, and I said that I would—delaying a trip to West Point where I was to make a speech that evening.

When I attended the White House meeting with Chuck Cooper, we found there was considerable confusion as to what actually had occurred. Bill Casey had a document prepared by the CIA, Ollie North had addenda and modifications to it, and someone on the NSC staff had put together a chronology of transactions. We talked over the matter for about an hour and a half, when I had to leave to catch my plane.

On my way to the airport, I received a call from my deputy, Arnold Burns, telling me he had just heard from the State Department (apparently from Legal Advisor Abe Sofaer) that there were problems with the projected testimony. Thinking he was referring to the differences and confusions I was already aware of, I told him I knew of the problem and that it was being corrected.

That evening, from West Point, I talked to Chuck Cooper by secure phone, and he told me there were yet more serious problems—George Shultz and Abe Sofaer's versions of events differed considerably from the one prepared for Casey; furthermore, the intelligence committees had people out at the National Security Agency getting copies of relevant communications traffic. I told him we should make sure the CIA general counsel obtained copies of that traffic as well, and that Casey should not testify to anything he was not completely satisfied was factual.

It is worth repeating that Casey had been out of the country at the time of the HAWK missile shipment of November 1985, a principal object of interest in these inquiries. No record or other evidence shows that he was aware of the peripheral, impromptu involvement of the CIA in that transaction when it happened. He therefore had to rely on information provided by others, which was why I stressed that he should testify only to matters of which he was absolutely certain.

As already noted, my view of the matter was that this was a highly compartmentalized situation which kept some people from knowing what other people were doing. The one thing I wanted to be totally sure of was that members of the administration not say anything that was incorrect, or that might appear to be covering up. To my knowledge at that point, nothing had been done that was wrong, but if the feeling got around that people were covering up or dissembling, that itself would be cause for alarm, as witness the Watergate situation.

One thing that Chuck Cooper told me, which seemed curious in context, was that Abe Sofaer had said he was prepared to resign if this thing were not resolved. While I did not understand the reasoning, based on the information I then had, this statement obviously added a further note of urgency to the proceedings.

When I returned to Washington the next morning, Bill Casey had already given his testimony on the Hill, and according to Chuck, had indeed deleted from his testimony anything he was not completely sure of. But the atmosphere of confusion was still prevalent, and I called Don Regan at the White House to set up a meeting with the President to get the matter sorted out.

Shortly after 11:00 that morning, I met in the Oval Office with President Reagan, Donald Regan, and John Poindexter. I told the President that, because of the sensitivity of the project, nobody seemed to know the whole of the story. It was therefore important that someone do an overview—a survey of all the facts and documents—to enable the people testifying before Congress to be absolutely accurate, and to enable us to give a straightforward account to the American people.

Reagan asked me if I would undertake such an inquiry, and I said I would. He wanted to get it completed over the weekend so that it would be available for the National Security Council meeting scheduled for the following Monday afternoon.

On that Friday afternoon, it also happened that FBI Director William Webster was in my office on another matter, and we discussed whether the bureau should help with the fact-finding. We both agreed that it should not—mindful that this was not a criminal matter, and that in the past questions had been raised when other presidents had used the FBI on noncriminal inquiries or activities.

In beginning our review, I asked Brad Reynolds and John Richardson to assemble a documentary record, while Chuck Cooper and I would interview as many of the principal players as we could. I called John Poindexter, told him I would be sending people over to look at the records, and asked him to assemble the information. He said they would have the documents available by the following morning. Then I started calling the people we wanted to talk to. The first one available was Bud McFarlane, who came on Friday afternoon. George Shultz had heard of my mission and called, offering to help. We made arrangements to see him the following morning at the State Department.

Chuck Cooper and I met with Shultz and Charlie Hill of his staff at 8 A.M. on Saturday. This conversation revolved around the HAWK missile shipment of November 1985 and Shultz's recollection of discussions at the time, very helpful because most of the confusion seemed to be about how and why the HAWK missile episode occurred.

A few hours later, that same topic dominated the discussion I had with Stan Sporkin, general counsel of the CIA. We reviewed the legal framework of the U.S. initiative of January 1986, the legality of withholding notification, and matters pertaining to presidential findings. I also learned more about what had gone on during 1985. While this was occurring, Reynolds and Richardson were at the White House, reviewing documents. About 1:30 P.M. Chuck Cooper and I met with Brad and John for our now-famous lunch at the Old Ebbitt Grill.

Returning to the Justice Department on Saturday afternoon, I placed a call to Cap Weinberger, but he was occupied with an illness in his family and I arranged to speak with him later. I also talked with Bill Casey and arranged to drop by his house on Old Dominion Drive on my way back home to McLean, Virginia, which I did shortly after 5 P.M. on Saturday.

In the course of this conversation, Bill related to me the information from Roy Furmark, previously referred to. Since I had not at this point told Bill about our discovery of the diversion, nor asked him about it, his revelation of the Furmark material could not have been prompted by anything I had said or any awareness that we already knew of the possibility of a diversion.

Some critics have wondered why I did not confront Bill directly on Saturday afternoon with questions about the diversion. My reasons were simple enough and, in my view, compelling. I had not yet had a chance to talk directly with North, and I did not want to discuss this with anyone until we had established the facts and learned whether the diversion plan contained in the memorandum had actually been implemented.

The next day at noon I met with our team, reviewed the status of our information, and looked over the documents that they had found. At 2 P.M., Ollie North came in and, with Brad Reynolds, Chuck Cooper, and John Richardson present, I questioned him on the implementation of the Iran initiative, the HAWK shipments, and related matters. He explained how he had become involved after the many problems that had developed in November 1985.

I then asked North about the diversion plan and the memo that had been discovered in his files. He looked embarrassed, obviously taken aback that we had found out about it, and then asserted that the idea for the diversion had been suggested by the Israelis. He told us that in talking to them about his efforts to help the Nicaraguan resistance, they had been sympathetic but had said they had no money for this purpose. According to North, the Israelis then suggested they could contribute money they received from the United States. North said he rejected this, inasmuch as it would be an indirect use of U.S. government funds and thus improper. His comments showed clearly that North appreciated the limitations imposed by the Boland amendment and other legal restrictions discussed earlier.

At this point, North said, the Israelis suggested overcharging the Iranians for the weapons being sold from the CIA, placing the excess money in an account that would be controlled by them, and then having those funds donated to the Contras. At that time North made no mention of Secord and "the enterprise," a factor that would come to light in the inquiries of the Tower Commission and later in the congressional hearings.

I asked North who else knew about the diversion, and he told us the only people in the U.S. government who could know of it, besides himself, were McFarlane and Poindexter. As noted, he did not say Bill Casey knew about it, nor did he indicate that the President had any knowledge of the diversion.

The following morning I met again with McFarlane to verify that he indeed had known about the diversion. He said he had, but that he had not told anyone else. It was during this conversation that I advised Bud not to hold anything back, not to try to "outthink" the situation but simply to tell all of the truth as he knew it.

Following this talk, I called Don Regan at the White House and said I wanted to have a meeting just with him and the President to report on what we had discovered. We met briefly in the Oval Office shortly after 11 A.M. But since the President had an 11:30 appointment with Chief Buthelezi of South Africa, I was unable to give him a full report, and the details had to wait until after the National Security Council meeting that afternoon.

After my brief conversation with Don Regan and the President, I met again with Chuck Cooper and Brad Reynolds. I asked Chuck, based on the facts we now had, to look into the question of whether there were any criminal implications of the diversion, and whether there was any basis for bringing the criminal division of the Justice Department into it.

When the NSC meeting was concluded at 4 P.M., I questioned John Poindexter about what he knew of the diversion, since I had not yet had a chance to talk to him. He confirmed that he did know of the diversion, but said he had told no one about it nor done anything to stop it. He was so angry with Congress, he went on, for what it had done to the Nicaraguan freedom fighters that he just decided to let it happen. Poindexter said he was telling me this because he felt I was the only person he could trust, and that he would be guided by my advice. He added that he realized he would probably have to resign.

Following this brief conversation, Don Regan and I met again with the President and I laid out the details of what we had discovered. We discussed the repercussions, including the probability that Poindexter would have to resign. The President replied that he wanted to think about it overnight and we agreed to meet again the next morning.

I then took the opportunity to see the Vice President, George Bush, to brief him on the situation. He said he had known nothing about the fund diversion and was as shocked as the President and Don Regan had been. I went back to Don Regan's office and we agreed to meet the following morning at 8 A.M. to discuss what we should recommend to the President, with whom we would meet at nine o'clock.

On Tuesday morning at 6:30 A.M., just as I was leaving for my office, I received a call from Bill Casey, who said he had learned about the diversion from Regan in a phone call the night before. I went by Bill's home on the way into Washington and discussed what we had learned. The conversation indicated that Bill had not known about the diversion of funds from the Iranian initiative. He later provided me with memoranda that CIA officials had prepared about the contact by and conversations with Roy Furmark to help us in further proceedings. At no time did Casey behave as a man who had something to hide or as one who was implicated in misdeeds. Also worth noting, no one ever suggested Casey knew of, or was involved in, the diversion scheme until after he died from a brain tumor in May of 1987.

In summing up the Iran-Contra situation, this manifestly was not a "constitutional crisis," nor did the actions of a few members of the government, aided by some outsiders, constitute a "threat to democratic government," as some hostile partisans—in Congress and in the media—have stated. Rather, it was a serious mistake by men who, in their zeal to advance legitimate national interests, took steps that were both unauthorized and unwise. The acts involved in diverting funds from the Iranian initiative to support the freedom fighters in Nicaragua were not done out of cupidity, self-gain, or other corrupt motives. Instead, angered at what they viewed as Congress "selling out" brave men fighting for democracy in Central America, these public officials with unblemished records took extreme steps which—despite the noble purpose behind them—damaged the administration, agitated the country, and ultimately resulted in great harm to the individuals themselves.

While I have described the impact on the Reagan presidency and the tremendous advantage that Iran-Contra gave to its opponents, we should not overlook the human tragedies involved. John Poindexter, then a vice admiral, was one of the most outstanding officers in the United States navy. Graduating at the head of his Naval Academy class, he had compiled a distinguished record of command and staff service over many years and had been promoted rapidly through the ranks. He undoubtedly would have been one of the top admirals in the navy, perhaps even chief of naval operations, but for the Iran-Contra episode.

Likewise, Oliver North was a decorated combat veteran, whose courage and heroism were matched only by his patriotic fervor. Perhaps no punishment could be worse for him than to have to leave the Marine Corps.

In addition to these principal figures in the Iran-Contra story, several other dedicated public servants have been caught up in the investigation and some have been forced to plead guilty to criminal offenses (most fortunately minor) rather than lose their life savings in defending themselves against accusations, many of which have been politically motivated.

The Iran-Contra affair and its aftermath taught a number of lessons, many of which were incorporated into governmental policy by President Reagan when he implemented the Tower Commission recommendations.

First, operations—including covert actions—should not be run out of the White House. While the more bureaucratic processes of the regular departments and agencies may seem cumbersome, they do provide greater accountability, proper authorization, and checks on poor judgment. By contrast, when "the White House" calls, few federal employees are willing to ask whether a request—no matter how preposterous—is really what the President wants or simply the brainchild of a low-level staffer.

Second, clandestine operations, particularly those entailing great risk, must be reviewed frequently by the President and the National Security Council to make sure the risks do not outweigh the potential gains, and to determine whether particular actions have become less feasible or less desirable.

Third, when great differences exist between Congress and the executive branch over goals and/or policies, hostility may cloud judgment on either side. Good faith is needed if the national interest is to be served. The impasse between congressional leaders and the President almost saw the installation of a second Marxist bastion in this hemisphere.

Finally, the events that followed the discovery of the diversion of funds to the Contras has revealed that the greatest threat to constitutional government and the liberties of the U.S. citizen comes not from people such as those involved in Iran-Contra, but from a relatively new congressionally-initiated institution: the independent counsel. The violation of the separation of powers doctrine, the abuse of power, the lack of accountability, and other equally serious problems inherent in the independent counsel concept, were all demonstrated in the Iran-Contra investigation. Suffice it to say here (the issue will be discussed in detail in the next chapter) that the Iran-Contra independent counsel process resulted in five years of extravagant spending by arrogant lawyers responsible to no one, harassment and intimidation that would not be tolerated in any real prosecutor's office, and the wrenching sight of patriotic citizens being subjected to injustice and financial devastation.

Ironically, after more than five years of congressional, legal, and judicial investigation, there has been not one definitive finding of illegality concerning the original Iran-Contra actions. Since then, the valiant efforts of the Nicaraguan freedom fighters have restored democracy to that country. And the same Iranian elements with whom President Reagan sought to establish communications are now dealing with the United States government on a regular basis.

22

THE PURSUIT
OF JUSTICE

WHEN I WAS CONFIRMED as attorney general in the second
Reagan administration in 1985, my predecessor, Bill Smith, turned to
me and said: "Ed, there will be days when you feel a lot like the
captain of the Olympic javelin team who won the toss and elected to
receive."

It wasn't quite that bad, but I soon discovered that taking charge of
the Department of Justice, with some 72,000 employees, a budget of
$3.6 billion, and an array of responsibilities that ranged from drug
enforcement to civil rights to judicial selection, was a colossal responsibility. The challenge was great, but I hope—and believe—that I met
it as the President, and the American people, wanted and expected.

From the outset of the administration, the topics that fell under the
jurisdiction of the Department of Justice were of key importance to
President Reagan and to the members of his administration, myself in
particular. Since matters of law enforcement, drugs, family policy,
civil rights, the courts, and so on, had been addressed by the President

304

from the very outset, I had been closely involved with them as counsellor to the president. As attorney general, I would be even more so.

In the realm of law enforcement, no function of government is more essential than to protect peaceful citizens from violent crime. By and large, of course, this is a function of state and local governments, not the federal authorities. There are many areas, however, in which the federal government can help; in certain cases, this is required by statute law, as well as by the law of common sense.

Among the most obvious of these are the functions of the Federal Bureau of Investigation, which not only has investigatory jurisdiction over federal crimes, but is vital at times in assisting state and local law enforcement. Federal agencies such as the Drug Enforcement Administration, U.S. Marshal Service, Immigration and Naturalization Service, Bureau of Prisons, and numerous other components of the Justice Department are also involved in combatting crime.

There is, moreover, a general obligation of the federal government to support the efforts of local law enforcement—not to thwart them, as has often been the case. As governor, as candidate, and as president, Ronald Reagan frequently talked about the problem of crime and how government at all levels was failing in its primary responsibility: to ensure public safety. Thus in the Reagan Justice Department we set about to strengthen law enforcement in many areas where it had been severely weakened.

In order to assure justice in the courts, for instance, the Reagan administration repeatedly tried to combat unreasonable restrictions on the use of truthful evidence in a criminal trial. Under the so-called "exclusionary rule," the courts were throwing out perfectly valid evidence (such as illegal drugs or stolen property discovered in the possession of a suspect) if some procedural error had been made by the police, no matter how minor the technicality or how great the good faith of the officer. Thus, as Justice Benjamin Cardozo once put it, "the criminal is to go free because the constable has blundered."[1] The real world meaning of such legalisms was summed up by a spokesman for the Illinois Attorney General's office in the 1970s:

"There are literally hundreds of persons guilty of narcotics and gun offenses who walk the streets, despite their obvious guilt, because the evidence essential to their conviction has been suppressed. . . . In one recent instance in my experience a person murdered a young teenage girl and hid her body in a rural farm area. The police got a warrant signed by a judge which gave them the right to search, but there was a technical deficiency in the warrant, and the court held that the very body itself, the nature of the crime itself, had to be suppressed."[2]

Lest I be misunderstood, both the President and I believed strongly in preserving the rights of all persons accused of crime, and we upheld the constitutional protections against arrogant and arbitrary actions by governmental authorities of any sort. But we believed that this could be effectively accomplished without an endless series of court-invented obstacles that defied common sense, obscured truth, and frustrated justice. We felt the government—particularly the judiciary—needed a major change in this area.

Our view of the matter, similar to that of former Chief Justice Warren Burger and other authorities, was that the proper way to ensure good procedure by the police was to discipline those who violated the law—not to bar the use of evidence that would help determine the truth. This view, unfortunately, was unpalatable to those who were hostile to law enforcement and more concerned about the rights of criminals than the rights of victims.

In like fashion, truthful and completely voluntary confessions of guilt were being excluded by the courts for procedural reasons (as, for instance, when a suspect admitted guilt to an undercover policeman without a lawyer present). The effect of these rulings was to make a legalistic game of criminal procedings, allowing many of the guilty to walk free. Such tendencies were also manifest in the lenient policies of probation, sentencing, and parole which had characterized much of the criminal justice system since the 1960s.

The net result of allowing criminals to continue preying on society was to increase our nation's crime rate in dramatic fashion. It is a little known fact that huge numbers of crimes are committed by a relatively small group of people who engage in criminal acts repeatedly. As attorney general, I frequently spoke of this—as in the following excerpts from remarks I made about corrections policy:

"Between 1960 and 1980 the number of serious crimes committed in the United States increased a frightening 322 percent. The number of arrests also increased, up 271 percent . . . [but] prison populations increased only 61 percent . . . [and] the capacity of state prisons increased a meager 27. . . .

"Last year alone [1985] nineteen states reported 18,617 early releases due to prison crowding. . . . Half of all convicted murderers released from state prison serve fewer than seven years. . . . Half of the rapists serve four years or less. Fifty percent of convicted arsonists do less than two years. Burglars less than a year and a half. . . .

"About 39 percent of convicted rapists, 35 percent of convicted robbers, and between 50 and 60 percent of those convicted for burglary or aggravated assault are not sentenced to prison at all. . . . Of all those sent to prison each year, about 84 percent have a prior conviction on their record; 67 percent have done prison time; 42 percent were on probation or parole at the time they committed the crime that landed them in prison. . . ."[3]

As those figures show, if recidivist criminals already caught and convicted had simply been sentenced to long prison terms and required to serve them, the amount of crime could have been substantially reduced. And if society could have apprehended and convicted still more, the ensuing reduction would have been that much greater.

These objectives, however, went counter to liberal theories of penology, which stressed the "rehabilitation" of criminals rather than the protection of society. Essential features of this liberal outlook were short, indeterminate, or nonexistent sentences for serious crimes; lenient terms for probation and parole; and a crusade to slow or halt the building of prisons, thus inducing overcrowding, which could be used as another pretext for turning loose convicted felons.

At the Reagan Justice Department, my predecessor and I carried on a continuing crusade against all these problems, arguing for tougher and more effective sentencing, stressing the protective rather than the "rehabilitationist" model of penology, and pushing for construction of additional prison space so that convicted criminals could be kept away from society.

Probably no issue in the field of law enforcement prompted greater concern in the 1980s than drug abuse, the associated toll in crime and death, and the ruined lives of many of the addicted. Accordingly, both in the White House and the Justice Department, we conducted an all-out offensive to combat narcotics trafficking and abuse.

The President and Mrs. Reagan personally sought to convey one all-important message: drug traffic was not only illegal, but also wrong and dangerous to the users. That was the theme of an extensive communications effort in which Mrs. Reagan played a central role—enlisting the aid of many civic leaders, private groups, and well-known athletes in a campaign to "Just Say No To Drugs."

It was fashionable in some circles to disparage these efforts, but in fact they were tremendously significant. In 1980 our nation had just emerged from two decades during which the use of marijuana and cocaine had been actively promoted or condoned by many celebrities, consumerists, media outlets, and advocacy groups—and even some public officials—who depicted drugs as harmless, fun, and trendy. The message transmitted to young people: There was nothing wrong with taking drugs.*

The end result was that, despite federal and state prohibitions, drug use had zoomed to astonishing proportions (one survey suggested that more than half the nation's high school seniors had used drugs at one time or another). No clearer indication was needed that observance of the law depended on a consensus of values—that restoration of an antidrug consensus was essential to the health and safety of the nation.

The administration, however, did not stop there. We mounted a multifaceted effort to reduce both the supply and the demand for illegal drugs. The President adopted a "zero tolerance" policy, which we emphatically pursued at Justice; this meant we refused to wink at the "recreational" use of marijuana or any other illegal drug. We

---

* This outlook is recalled by former Jimmy Carter speechwriter Patrick Anderson in his book, *High in America*. Anderson recounts a party in 1977 at which Carter drug advisor Dr. Peter Bourne snorted cocaine, and journalists on the scene declined to report the episode. "These were young reporters," Anderson writes, "who, although in theory objective, were in fact sympathetic [to the prodrug cause] . . . for they used marijuana and other drugs . . . In a sense the young media people and the young political people . . . were united as drug users and as victims of the double standard that surrounded drug use in America."

recognized, for example, that marijuana was harmful in itself, and that, as a "gateway" drug, it often led to other forms of drug abuse.

A widespread campaign to establish drug-free schools and drug-free workplaces complemented public information and education activities. At the same time the facilities and programs for treatment and rehabilitation of drug users was expanded through increased public and private resources.*

Among the measures we took to cut down on the supply were cooperative endeavors with the governments of drug-producing countries. We worked with Bolivia to eliminate clandestine cocaine production laboratories, thus reducing the market and the price for coca growers in that country, and we cooperated with Colombia to arrest and extradite drug kingpins who were managing this traffic. We also dramatically stepped up efforts at interdiction, in cooperative efforts involving DEA and customs and military forces, such as spotting and tracking small aircraft and boats carrying drugs to Florida and elsewhere. Vice President Bush directed the National Narcotic Board Interdiction System, which obtained, allocated, and coordinated the resources committed to this effort.

One of our most effective weapons against drug traffickers was to confiscate the assets of their criminal activity, such as expensive autos, yachts, businesses, and homes and convert the proceeds to the antidrug effort. To make this technique even more effective, we shared the proceeds with cooperating local law enforcement agencies to enhance their drug-fighting activities. We also improved the cooperation of federal law enforcement agencies with their state and local counterparts.†

Because of President Reagan's personal leadership, the United

---

* An important influence on our antidrug policy and action in America was Dr. Carlton Turner, a brilliant pharmacology professor from the University of Mississippi. He headed the White House Office of Drug Abuse Policy and served as the principal advisor on this subject to both President and Mrs. Reagan. Carlton was an unusual academic and scientist, as much at home working with police officers and narcotic agents on the street as in the classroom or laboratory.

† Some further specifics: As of 1985, we had thirteen Organized Crime and Drug Enforcement Task Forces comprising one thousand agents and two hundred assistant U.S. attorneys, plus their support staffs. In that year, our task forces seized $164.5 million in nondrug assets. Federal drug arrests increased about 20 percent in 1985, while arrests of major traffickers increased by 40 percent.

States had a comprehensive strategy and a coordinated antinarcotics effort, with vastly increased resources, among federal agencies. This was exemplified by the cabinet-level National Drug Policy Board, which I was privileged to chair, and which addressed both the supply and the demand sides of the drug problem.

Although the production, trafficking, and use of illegal drugs are still a serious problem in our nation and throughout the world, significant change occurred pursuant to Reagan's firm stand against drugs. Statistics show that the annual use (i.e., at least once during the year prior to the survey) of any illicit drug by high school seniors dropped from 54 percent in 1979 to 29 percent in 1991, a drop of over 45 percent. Likewise, annual use among college students during the period 1980-91 fell over 48 percent.

This dramatic turnaround, after nearly two decades of rising drug use among high school-age youngsters, reflects considerable change in public attitudes. The 1991 statistics showed 90 percent of high school seniors disapproved of even trying LSD, barbiturates, cocaine, or heroin, and nearly 70 percent disapproved of trying marijuana. This is a far cry from the attitudes shaped by the drug culture during the heyday of the 1960s.

Similar findings exist for all ages, according to the Office of National Drug Control Policy which reported survey results that showed between 1979 and 1991, drug use by Americans twelve years and older fell by 50 percent.

Perhaps the most frightening form of crime in the modern era is terrorism—touched on in chapter 15. While the episodes described there involved terrorism overseas, we have also had a terrorist threat within the United States. The Reagan government initiated a major effort to combat both international and domestic terrorism.

On the domestic front, terrorism/security problems shared many features with other kinds of crime. Increasingly, in the name of "civil liberties," a broad range of activities had been allowed to proceed unmolested, even though the clear intent was to foment terrorism, violence, or tangible injury to our national security. Civil libertarians insisted that we could move against such actions only after they had happened.

One effect of this peculiar mindset was to place incredible restrictions on the FBI—not unlike those imposed on the CIA in coping with national security problems overseas. Among the clearest examples was the case of the so-called Weather Underground, a violence-prone organization founded in the 1960s. This group had been involved in numerous riots, bombings, bank robberies, and other acts of terrorism.

In an effort to head off further violence, agents of the FBI intercepted telephone messages of a known Weather Underground contact in New York by entering the premises of the group. Not only was this branded as an outrageous violation of the terrorists' "civil liberties," but two agents of the FBI, Mark Felt and Edward Miller, were actually indicted and convicted by the Carter Justice Department for the offense.

In my view, and that of President Reagan, this was an unconscionable perversion of the justice process—sending the peace officers to jail, while allowing the terrorist criminals to walk free. I accordingly suggested to the President soon after he took office that he grant a presidential pardon to Felt and Miller, and he readily agreed.

The message transmitted by this presidential action was, I think, clear and unequivocal. America now had a chief executive, and an administration, that would stand with the people who took on the difficult and often dangerous task of defending society from violent criminals and revolutionaries, while at the same time protecting our basic liberties. It was a message I sought to reinforce during my years as attorney general, not only through measures to strengthen law enforcement but through direct contact, as frequently as possible, with police executives, sheriffs, and district attorneys around the nation.

On the international front, we likewise moved to strengthen our defenses against terrorist forces. Of major importance was the enactment of legislation in 1985 permitting U.S. authorities to track down and seek the arrest of terrorists overseas who had attacked American citizens. We also obtained extradition agreements with cooperating governments to deny terrorists safe haven, and arranged to have someone who was barred from one country also barred from the others.

Vital to promoting this international cooperation was my frequent

participation in meetings with my counterparts in foreign countries—
the cabinet ministers responsible for justice and law enforcement. For
the first time ever, the U.S. was granted associate status with the
TREVI Group, an organization of ministers from the European community nations. In leading our country's crusade against drugs and
terrorism I visited over twenty countries during my years at Justice.

As with street crime and drugs, the data showed the impact of our
efforts against terrorism. The number of terrorist incidents in the U.S.
dropped from 112 in 1977 to only seven in 1985 and and eight in 1986.
In 1985 alone, the FBI detected and prevented twenty-three separate
terrorist missions within the borders of the United States—and did so
without violating anybody's "civil liberties."[4]

Also of concern to the administration was the problem of obscenity
and pornography. Near the end of his first term, the President had met
with a group of citizens, religious leaders, and child welfare experts. As
they sat in the cabinet room for over an hour, these spokesmen explained
how a flood of obscene material was sweeping across the nation and
spoke of its effect on our young people. They demonstrated how the new
wave of obscenity was much worse than anything previously experienced, with its emphasis on the sexual degradation of and violence
against women, as well as the extensive sexual exploitation of children.

Having followed the legal situation concerning obscene materials
over the previous twenty years, from the time I had first become a
prosecutor in the late 1950s, I recognized that most of what then had
been prosecuted as "obscenity" was now readily available at most
airport bookstores. But even I was not prepared for the present depth of
depravity, nor was President Reagan. As a result of the meeting, the
President asked Attorney General Smith, who had also attended the
meeting, to appoint a Commission on Pornography to look into all
aspects of the problem and to recommend how law enforcement agencies and other governmental institutions should deal with it. Attorney
General Smith began immediately to assemble a broad-based group,
including experts in psychology, child welfare, First Amendment issues, education, medicine, and so on.

Shortly after I arrived at the Department of Justice, I picked up where Bill Smith had left off and formally appointed the commission; I met with them and gave them their charter: to provide the President, the executive branch, and Congress with a thorough look at the obscenity and child pornography situation. They were not to be swayed by politics or other extraneous influences, but to give an honest treatment of the subject.

At the end of a year's hard work, the commission brought in an extensive and well-documented report, demonstrating the prevalence of obscene materials and child pornography in our communities, documenting the harm and social danger being caused by it, and reporting that very little law enforcement action was being taken against it; this type of offense was not regarded as very important in comparison with street crime, drugs, and other types of offenses. The commission, however, showed not only the social danger of obscenity, but also the close ties between the obscenity industry and organized crime.

After reviewing this report with the president, the Justice Department proceeded to implement the recommendations. As a start, we established the Obscenity Enforcement Unit in the Criminal Division, led by Rob Showers, a talented attorney with extensive trial experience who had served on my staff.

In addition to our own enforcement activities, legislation was prepared to present to Congress in order to carry out the commission recommendations requiring legislative change. Model statutes were also developed for use by the states. As a result of these steps, there was a vast increase in investigations and prosecutions of obscenity and child pornography offenses by both federal and state prosecutors, as well as greater public awareness of the danger.

While matters of law enforcement were a top priority of the Reagan Justice Department, many other topics also fell within our purview. The President, for example, constantly emphasized the need to protect and preserve basic constitutional values, to restore the structure of American federalism, separation of powers, and limited government. This was integral to Reagan's view of government, and to the very notion of the rule of law in our society. As appropriate, we filed briefs in appellate courts and initiated other actions to support the legitimate powers of the states.

In addition, the Reagan Justice Department had a very active record in the field of civil rights. The President was adamant that we crack down on hate crime, discrimination, and organized bigotry in violation of the law—a top priority of the department. He believed, as did we, that justice should be administered impartially, without reference to someone's skin color, gender, religion, or ethnic origin.

That strong commitment, ironically, ran us afoul of the position of many 1980 "civil rights" proponents—a position that in the 1950s had been opposed as wrongful discrimination by leaders such as Martin Luther King, Jr. In this revised version of "civil rights," some contended that we *should* take cognizance of someone's skin color, or other minority attribute, in order to make it the basis of special treatment.

This was the essence of various "affirmative action," quota, minority-set-aside, and other schemes that had surfaced in the preceding decade. The most combustible example, perhaps, was busing school children for purposes of racial balance. But there was also a pervasive system of numerical quotas for hiring, promotion, admissions, and so on—all explicitly based on racial, ethnic, gender, or similar considerations.

Whatever the supposed reason behind these practices, the effects in terms of authentic civil rights were devastating. In a society that was allegedly color-blind and impartial in dealing with all its citizens, some people were singled out for different treatment precisely because of their color or ethnic origin, while others were necessarily turned away (though this was seldom mentioned) because of theirs.

This policy, in our view, went directly against two basic principles of a free society: that people are to be treated equally under the law, irrespective of who they are; and that advancement should be based on merit, rather than on racial, ethnic, or other distinctions. Disagreement about such matters provoked bitter controversy between the Reagan government and the "civil rights" establishment—a controversy that continues to this day. But the President's strong stand against discrimination struck a responsive chord among people of all races and backgrounds, and contributed to our nation's progress toward becoming a color-blind society.

Drugs, pornography, and quotas bring us to the so-called "social issues," a range of cultural and ideological disputes that deeply divided the nation in the 1970s and 1980s. In many conventional histories, President Reagan's interest in these matters allegedly waned after he was in office, even though they were important to constituencies that helped elect him. As the preceding discussion indicates, this analysis was profoundly mistaken. In questions pertaining to crime and drugs, busing, quotas, and pornography, the Reagan Justice Department was in the forefront in dealing with these issues.

In support of the claim that Reagan was indifferent to "social issues," some have observed that he concentrated heavily at the outset of his administration on his economic program and defense buildup. True, but this was necessary to get those aspects of the Reagan program through Congress promptly in order to revitalize the economy and restore our defense capability. This didn't mean, in any way, that the President was abandoning the other items on his agenda. It was simply a matter of timing and strategy.

It could, in fact, be argued that Reagan did even more about social issues, in a long-term institutional sense, than about the economy or our defenses. This point is seldom understood, however, because the social issue agenda, while important in itself, was an aspect of a much broader problem afflicting our system of government and society.

Most obviously, these issues reflected the liberal agenda that had permeated the U.S. during the 1960s and 1970s. Permissiveness on questions such as pornography, school prayer, crime, and drugs, and social engineering concerning family planning and abortion, quotas and busing, were distinguishing aspects of the modern liberal mindset.

These issues shared another trait as well: in every case, the controversies surrounding them had been created by *rulings of the federal courts*. Thus, to take the obvious examples, abortion, banning prayer from the schools, pornography, busing, and leniency toward crime all resulted from federal court decisions handed down with increasing frequency during the previous two decades.

The connection between these issues and the courts was not accidental. In almost every case, since the outcomes sought by liberal and leftist interest groups had been denied through the legislative process, they were pursued through litigation. Lawsuits in federal courts had become a method of conducting an end run around legislatures, and other elected officials, to attain results that couldn't be accomplished through the political system.*

In the Reagan administration, we thoroughly understood this problem. We also understood that the solution to the problem was restoring the constitutional rule of law, with the proper roles assigned to the respective branches of the federal government and with the system of checks and balances functioning in proper fashion.

The conclusion that the President drew was obvious enough: if the problems we confronted had come about because of judges, then something had to be done about the judges. This was of key importance, in his view, not simply because of the individual issues involved, but because restoring the proper role of the judiciary was critical to our system of self-government.

Accordingly, the selection of judicial personnel and reform of the judiciary became and remained important priorities of the administration. Given the lifetime tenure of federal judges, these could not be accomplished overnight. But Reagan battled for it during his entire presidency.

Over the course of his two administrations, the President appointed almost half of the federal judiciary—371 judges out of a total of 761. Of these, three appointees were Supreme Court Justices, 83 were appellate court judges, and 292 were federal district court judges. The

---

* This was most obviously true in the case of abortion, where efforts to liberalize state laws, with a few exceptions, had fallen short. In various busing and "affirmative action" cases, court rulings contradicted the meaning of the relevant civil rights laws, which barred discriminatory treatment based on race or ethnic origins. In the case of school prayer, crime, and other matters, the policies mandated by the courts were frequently opposed by vast majorities of the public—up to 80 percent and more in many cases.

remainder were judges on the court of international trade and other specialized courts.

In selecting judges, the administration established a rigorous process of interviews and background-checking. Both in the White House and at the Department of Justice I was intimately involved in the process and can attest that it was not only exhaustive, but that it established and adhered to the highest standards of professionalism and integrity.

In large measure, this continued and expanded upon the policy Reagan had followed in Sacramento. He was determined to choose judges who were qualified, not simply cronies of political supporters. Far more than is realized, federal judicial appointments had been based on patronage and political considerations, rather than on judicial fitness.

Traditionally, prospective federal district court judges have been recommended by the senators of the president's party from the state in which a district appellate court vacancy is located. If there is no senator in that state from the president's party, the members of his party in the House of Representatives make the recommendation. Obviously, this method lends itself to patronage considerations. Reagan adhered to this custom, but with important differences. For district court appointments we asked Republican senators, or members of Congress, to provide us with three names for each vacancy to choose from. If none of the proposed candidates was qualified, we asked for more names. In the case of Court of Appeals judges, the president accepted suggestions from senators or congressmen, but decided from among a wide range of candidates derived from many other sources as well.

The high quality of the judges selected through this process was affirmed by Professor Sheldon Goldman of the University of Massachusetts, who commented that, "assuming that the ABA ratings are a reasonably accurate assessment of the credentials of appointees, the second term appointments, on the whole, may turn out to be the most professionally qualified group of appointees over the last two decades."[5]

In addition to the nominee's professional qualifications, the president instructed us to consider his judicial philosophy. He wanted to name judges who would look at the Constitution and statute law and expound their evident meaning, rather than using loopholes or convoluted logic to reach some preconceived conclusion.

The President stressed this point when, in 1986, he announced two of his most important judicial appointments—Antonin Scalia as associate justice of the Supreme Court, and William Rehnquist as chief justice. To underscore the importance of naming judges who would interpret rather than make up the law, the President cited the example of the Founding Fathers:

"They understood that, in the words of James Madison, if 'the sense in which the Constitution was accepted and ratified by the nation is not to guide the expounding of it, there can be no security for the faithful exercise of its powers'. . . . For them, the question involved in judicial restraint was not—and it is not—will we have a liberal or conservative court? . . . The question was, and is, will we have government by the people? And this is why the principle of judicial restraint has had an honored place in our tradition."[6]

I had the privilege, both as counsellor to the president and attorney general, to play a principal role in the process by which such jurists were selected; while at Justice I would sometimes conduct the final interview of candidates before a recommendation was passed on to the President.

Critics of the President have alleged that his search for judges committed to a philosophy of judicial restraint was an effort to "politicize" the courts, since it posed "litmus test" questions to potential nominees. The truth was just the opposite. The President was seeking to depoliticize the courts, to ensure that they played a truly judicial role, rather than usurping the authority of the elected branches of our constitutional system.

The extent to which some judges had practiced judicial activism was evident not only in social issue rulings, but in a host of other topics. Federal courts had become involved in everything from running prisons and asylums to determining the proper hair length of students in the public schools. In one ruling, a federal judge found in the "penumbra" of the Bill of Rights a constitutional guarantee to attend a summer basketball camp; in another, a judge became involved in a fracas over selecting a high school homecoming queen; in yet another, a district court held forth on the evils of "mismatched carpeting and tile" in a public school.[7]

In this last case, which involved schools in Kansas City, the judge took it upon himself to order further spending to attain "the visual attractiveness sought by the court," along with other goals, plus a tax increase on the local citizens to pay the bills. In St. Louis, a federal court opined that a program of public school busing was "one of the most creative social experiments of our time" and ordered the school board to submit a bond issue to the voters to pay for its costs.[8]

In cases such as these, the federal courts had taken over the most essential functions of Anglo-American self-government—determining the level of public expenditures, and the measures that should be taken to pay for them. It was precisely to reserve such powers to the popularly elected branch of government that the English had fought many battles against oppressive kings, and that our American forefathers had fought a war of independence. Now the unelected judges of the federal courts were blithely arrogating such powers to themselves.

Such rulings were the by-product of the concept called "judicial activism" that had become dominant in too many of our law schools and had been practiced by too many of our jurists in the era of Jimmy Carter. Indeed, it was under Carter, not Reagan, that the judicial selection process was "politicized" and potential nominees asked "litmus test" questions about their stand on issues of the day. As one historian of the Carter selection process recalls, "both panel members and candidates reported that applicants had often been questioned about nine contemporary social issues. . . . The four areas which received the most attention were the Equal Rights Amendment, affirmative action, first amendment freedoms, and defendants' rights."*[9]

Reagan appointees were *not* asked such questions about political

---

* One Carter appointee, questioned by the Senate Judiciary Committee as to possible conflicts of interest between the Constitution on the one hand, and his private beliefs on the other, said that in the case of such a dilemma, "I would follow my conscience." He was confirmed.

beliefs, but they were interviewed on their understanding of the Constitution and their philosophy of judicial practice. The Reagan selection process thus took judges out of politics in two senses—first by minimizing if not eliminating entirely the problem of cronyism, and second by ensuring that the nominees were selected, not for their views on particular issues, but for their understanding of the judicial role and their fidelity to the Constitution.

The liberal penchant for posing "litmus test" questions was to become apparent in the 1987 confirmation fight over Judge Robert Bork, whom the President named to the Supreme Court to replace retiring Associate Justice Lewis Powell. With the Bork nomination, politics came crashing in on the judicial process in no uncertain terms.

Judge Bork is one of the foremost exponents of judicial restraint, and was thus well suited to fulfill the task that President Reagan thought jurists should perform. Moreover, Judge Bork was eminently qualified in terms of intellect, scholarship, and experience on the bench. That combination of factors, in the view of many, made him one of the best qualified nominees to the high court in history.

Faced with his distinguished qualifications, the liberal Democrats on the Senate Judiciary Committee subjected Bork to a whole series of "litmus test" questions, and indeed to a generic "litmus test" in terms of his philosophy. Because he did not accept their view that courts should engage in results-oriented political jurisprudence, they attacked him as "outside the mainstream" and thus unfit for service on the court. And they waged an unprecedented and intensive political campaign to discredit him with the American public.

The tone was set by Sen. Edward Kennedy, who claimed Bork's nomination would lead to an America where "women would be forced into back-alley abortions, blacks would sit at segregated lunch counters, rogue police would break down citizens' doors in midnight raids, school children would not be taught about evolution, writers and authors could be censored at the whim of government and the doors of the federal courts would be shut on the fingers of millions of citizens."[10] This was said before any hearings or examination of Bork's credentials had even taken place.

The effort of Kennedy and his allies to demonize Bork closely paralleled the attack that Jimmy Carter had mounted against Ronald Reagan in the campaign of 1980—once more demonstrating that, if you can't win on the issues, you attack the man. It also exhibited the high degree of collusion between the self-appointed "civil rights" lobby and the various elements of the liberal establishment. Provided with extensive funding from leftist sources, they trashed the constitutionally ordained confirmation process and turned it into a demeaning circus.

A full account of these proceedings has been provided in books by Judge Bork himself and other authors, so I won't repeat those details here. Essentially, however, liberal and leftist special interest groups, such as People for the America Way, the so-called Alliance for Justice, and others worked closely with Senate staffers and sympathetic members of the media to depict Bork as a judicial extremist. Author Suzanne Garment estimates the cost of the media campaign against him at up to $15 million.[11]

The anti-Bork campaign, like that later conducted against Clarence Thomas, showed how desperate and irresponsible the liberal interest groups had become. It was not only, as many noted, that these groups felt an important institution of government was slipping from their control, as had already occurred with the presidency; it was also that the courts had become their trump card against the people's elected representatives, and thus the most powerful factors in the permanent, unelected government.

Questions have been raised about administration tactics in responding to this, including insinuations that the White House was not sufficiently energetic in obtaining Bork's confirmation. Having watched these events closely, I know that President Reagan was absolutely committed to achieving the confirmation of his nominee and that he exhorted his staff to a maximum effort. Shortly after the Supreme Court vacancy first occurred, then-White House Chief of Staff Howard Baker and I met with members of the Senate Judiciary Committee and went over a list of a dozen people the President was considering for appointment.

From the reactions of some of the Democrat members, we knew that Bork faced a difficult battle. But we all believed it would be carried out with the dignity and decorum worthy of the Senate and with the respect that should be afforded a sitting judge. No one was prepared for the unprincipled conduct and outrageous attacks of Bork's opponents, including the slanderous television advertising and character assassination directed at the senators in their home areas. It was a bitter lesson that revealed the viciousness and moral bankruptcy of organizations that masqueraded behind a facade of high-sounding principles.

While the defeat of Judge Bork's nomination was a searing experience for him and for his family, and an obvious setback for the administration, it couldn't stop President Reagan from bringing about needed changes in the court. The Powell seat was ultimately taken by Judge Anthony Kennedy, whom then-Governor Reagan had recommended for appointment to the Ninth Circuit Court of Appeals in 1974. I had known Kennedy from our days together in California and respected him as an outstanding jurist of the highest qualifications and excellent judicial temperament.

In the Bush administration, Judge Kennedy was followed to the Court by David Souter and Clarence Thomas, both of whom had been under favorable consideration for appointment in the Reagan era. Along with previous Reagan appointees O'Connor and Scalia, these appointments brought into being a court that was truly committed to its constitutional responsibilities. Gauged by its long-term implications for our system of self-government, this may well prove to be the greatest legacy of the Reagan era.

Another major threat to constitutional government which the Reagan administration faced was the legislative opportunism that arose out of the Watergate controversy during the early 1970s. Congress had used this episode to expand its power in various ways vis-à-vis the executive branch, but no action was more far-reaching than the creation of a new statutory entity, the special prosecutor—later to be renamed the independent counsel. The purpose of this office was to provide for the independent, and presumably objective, investigation of allegations of criminal activity made against high-level executive branch officials. Promoted as a "good government" initiative in the 1978 Ethics in

Government Act, the concept may have been good in theory, but it has produced a bureaucratic Frankenstein.*

This new creature in the federal government structure, with its unprecedented statutory scheme and its breaching of the traditional separation of powers, had important ramifications that will continue into the future. The Reagan administration was the first to serve its entire tenure under the Ethics in Government Act, including the independent counsel provisions. While the new law was used to investigate certain officials in the Carter administration, only after 1981 did the nation learn how this statute could be utilized by a hostile and partisan congressional leadership to attempt to criminalize policy differences.

There are numerous constitutional, practical, and civil liberties problems with the independent counsel statutes—too numerous to discuss in detail here. An excellent book on the subject, *Ethics, Politics and the Independent Counsel*, by Terry Eastland, an experienced journalist and public official, was published by the National Legal Center for the Public Interest in November 1989. This impressive volume thoroughly documents the history, purpose, and problems of the independent counsel process. It describes how this "separate justice system" involves the creation of a unique and powerful official, outside the usual checks and balances of constitutional government, who is appointed by the judiciary, performs executive functions, and has a close and unusual relationship with the legislature.

One result of this arrangement has been to create a political weapon for a partisan Congress to use against a White House led by the political opposition. Eastland recounts how, after Reagan became president, congressional attitudes changed as legislative opponents of the administration saw how they could exploit this new power. Sena-

---

* Let me make it clear that these observations are not based on my own experiences with the independent counsels who were appointed in matters involving me. Indeed, in each of those two episodes, the independent counsel made a decision favorable to me, namely that no further proceedings were warranted. Furthermore, as previously mentioned, I have determined not to use this book to deal with the false allegations made when I was nominated as attorney general and thereafter. Perhaps that subject will be covered in a future work discussing more directly my own activities at Justice and elsewhere. The subject of this book, however, is President Reagan and his administration.

tors who had "bemoaned the adverse publicity surrounding the [Carter administration officials] investigations failed to complain about the negative publicity surrounding new victims of the law." Eastland ascribes this change to partisan politics: "A Democratic Congress had come to realize the extraordinary power over the Republican executive branch that the independent counsel statute could provide. The EPA case [a dispute between Congress and the president over executive privilege and the subsequent independent counsel investigation of administration officials concerning allegations of false statements and withholding of documents] in particular had taught congressional Democrats how the statute could enable them to trigger an independent counsel investigation over a policy dispute with the president. Suffice to say, Congress was of no mind to review the wisdom of a statute that could be used to criminalize American politics."

Theoretically intended as a safeguard against the abuse of power, the independent counsel turned out in practice to be a prime example of such abuse—threatening both the constitutional balance of our system and the liberties of affected individuals.

Among the functions that pertain to the elected head of the executive branch, none is more obvious than seeing to the "faithful execution of the laws." This means, self-evidently, seeking to ascertain whether the laws are being obeyed, determining if there is probable cause to believe they are not, and seeking indictments on that basis. It would be hard to name a function that is more quintessentially executive than this.

Under the independent counsel statute, however, this function is subject to great manipulation by members of Congress. Although the independent counsel is technically named by a three-judge panel upon the request of the attorney general, and is supposedly dismissable by the latter, the political and institutional realities are quite different. The limited statutory grounds for removing an independent counsel, the availability to the dismissed counsel of judicial review, and the political outcry that would ensue—let alone congressional hearings and inquiries—make such action by an attorney general virtually impossible.

The independent counsel, moreover, is not empowered to go after members of Congress—only members of the executive branch. This is the law despite the many political factors that make it most unlikely that an attorney general of one party would seek indictment of congressmen from another (as, for instance, in the case of lawmakers who were dealing with the Sandinistas in Nicaragua or the Bishop government in Grenada). Added to this is the fact that the counsel is subject to oversight by congressional committees, including reports as to a decision not to prosecute. The clear implication is that the independent counsel, or special prosecutor, is a weapon aimed solely and directly at officials of the executive branch in behalf of Congress.

This was exactly the way in which the independent counsel statutes were used during the Reagan years—most notoriously in the obsessive efforts of Lawrence Walsh, appointed in the Iran-Contra case. No less serious was the legal assault against Theodore Olson, who was subjected to a three-year inquiry that resulted in no indictment but that cost him legal fees of approximately $1 million.

The problem presented by the independent counsels is made worse because they have a much lower threshold to commence an investigation than does a normal prosecutor (appointment requiring only "reasonable grounds to believe that further investigation or prosecution is warranted"). Moreover, they focus on investigating *individuals* to see if they can find some crime that may have been committed, rather than beginning with a criminal *act* and establishing that a particular suspect was the guilty party.

Once set up in business, independent counsels are effectively answerable to no one. They are free to spend millions of dollars of taxpayers' money to see if they can find any grounds whatever for prosecuting a given individual, or group of individuals, on an open-ended basis. As Walsh has demonstrated in his (largely unsuccessful) search for Iran-Contra culprits, there is no logical terminus to the process, if the counsel is determined to keep it going.

The post of independent counsel thus hangs in organizational space—supposedly tied to other agencies of government, but in practical reality responsible to none. It is a further variation on the Washington theme of power without accountability, and thus a standing invitation to abuse.

The impact of this abuse can be very real to the individuals concerned. Terry Eastland accurately describes the plight of a public official who becomes the subject of an independent counsel investigation:

> You may discover that the independent counsel exists to investigate not some crime but you, personally, in the entirety of your public life. Ordinary citizens do not experience this kind of investigation. Your independent counsel, moreover, will have no other cases to worry about, which allows him untold time, and he has all the employees and resources he desires. Don't expect the Attorney General to reprimand your independent counsel if he treats you unfairly; the Attorney General has no political or institutional incentive to do that and would be publicly pilloried if he did take action.

* * *

In these many ways the separate justice system works inequities upon a class of individuals who otherwise would not endure them. What renders this constitutionally problematic is that there is no one to hold accountable for this inherent unfairness, or for any abuses of prosecutorial discretion by the independent counsel.*

---

* In 1987 the independent counsel statute came up for reauthorization. Because of its many defects, the Justice Department, after careful study, recommended to the President that the bill be vetoed. But the President, doubtless warned by political advisors that a veto would draw congressional and media criticism, signed the legislation on December 15, 1987. Still, hope remained among many White House staffers, and certainly at Justice, that the Supreme Court might ultimately save the day by declaring the law unconstitutional: the court was then considering the case of *Morrison v. Olson*, ironically an action involving three former officials of the Department of Justice.

In this case, which arose out of the controversy between the administration and Congress over the Environmental Protection Agency's exercise of executive privilege (discussed above), a former deputy attorney general and two assistant attorneys general challenged the authority of the independent counsel, asserting that the statute establishing that official was unconstitutional. Although the trial court rejected this contention, the Court of Appeals for the District of Columbia Circuit did hold the independent counsel law unconstitutional, stating that it violated several provisions of the Constitution, including the principle of separation of powers since it interfered with the president's authority under Article II (which sets forth the executive power of the federal government).

Ultimately, however, the Supreme Court failed to come to the same conclusion and, on June 29, 1988, reversed the decision of the Court of Appeals and, by a 7-1 vote, affirmed the constitutionality of the independent counsel act. To do so, it was necessary for the Court to depart from previous theories of constitutional doctrine concerning both the appointment of officials and separation of

As an experienced prosecutor myself, I have no quarrel with vigorous efforts thoroughly to investigate and prosecute violations of criminal law, no matter who the perpetrator might be—including high government officials. But I also know that a prosecutor who is answerable to no one, has unlimited time and resources at his command, and possesses an open-ended commission to try to find some wrongdoing by a given individual in a manner unconstrained by the Bill of Rights, is a serious threat to our basic liberties. Government by independent counsel is clearly akin to government by judiciary—an effort to rule outside the normal framework of our constitutional system, beyond the limits of accountability. It is a modern example of James Madison's warning that the "preservation of liberty requires that the three great departments of power should be separate and distinct." Failure to maintain that separation is, in Madison's words, "the very definition of tyranny."[12]

---

powers, and virtually to stand several prior cases on their heads. Justice Scalia delivered a vigorous dissent, in which he declared that the "decision on the basic issue of fragmentation of executive power is ungoverned by rule, and hence ungoverned by law." He set forth in detail the reasons why the majority opinion departed from "the judgment of the wise men who constructed our system, and of the peoples who approved it, and of two centuries of history that have shown it to be sound." Scalia's dissent was echoed by Terry Eastland's analysis of this decision:

In the final analysis, the Court's opinion in *Morrison v. Olson* is deeply unsatisfying. Not only is much of it unpersuasive on its own terms, and not only does it fail to ask important questions relevant to separation of powers, but in its most crucial parts, it provides no sense of being rooted in some clearly articulable principle of law.

Just as President Reagan undoubtedly had been concerned in 1987 about the outcry that would ensue if he should veto the independent counsel legislation, it is not unreasonable to speculate that at least some members of the Court felt similar constraints. Nevertheless, that decision and the statute it upheld remain the law of the land.

23

REFLECTIONS

CONSIDERED HISTORICALLY, the Reagan era was tremendously important in terms of what it accomplished for the United States and for the cause of freedom in the world. And it was equally important in the lessons it provided for the future.

Reagan demonstrated that principled and forceful leadership from the White House could make a difference in national policy—contrary to the 1970s' view of presidential impotence and paralysis. He showed that a political leader who believed in something—who had a vision for America—and who worked hard to accomplish his goals, could bring about significant changes, even though the odds seemed stacked against him.

Prior to Reagan's election, America had seen a succession of presidencies cut short by tragedy or turmoil. The assassination of John Kennedy, the Vietnam upheaval that forced the withdrawal of Lyndon Johnson, the Watergate-driven resignation of Richard Nixon, the brief tenure of Gerald Ford, and the erratic term of Jimmy Carter seemed to define the burdens and limits of the office. Prior to 1981, it was widely assumed that the job had gotten too big and complicated for any one person to handle.

In all respects, Reagan overturned such thinking. He was the first American president since Eisenhower to complete two full terms in office. He had strategies for dealing with our domestic and foreign challenges and, as we have seen, succeeded in carrying them forward, despite a vast array of obstacles. He exhibited a constancy of purpose through many vicissitudes. And he accomplished his mission.

The impact of Reagan's presidency upon the people of America was no less profound. As Jeane Kirkpatrick wrote in 1983:

> The elections of 1980 marked the end of a national identity crisis through which the United States had been passing for some ten or fifteen years. This was a period of great national self-doubt and self-denigration for Americans. Now there is a new national consensus in both our domestic and our foreign affairs, and that new consensus reflects a return of the nation's self-confidence—a returned confidence in the basic decency of Americans; a returned confidence in the legitimacy of American institutions; a returned confidence concerning the fundamental success of the American experience; and a returned confidence concerning the relevance of our nation's basic principles to the contemporary world.[1]

In economic matters, Reagan demonstrated his faith in the free market and proved that limiting the growth of federal taxing, spending, and regulation could spur the forces of recovery and stimulate market growth—a lesson that has been emulated around the world. He steadfastly backed a monetary policy that would slow the ruinous process of inflation. And by pressing ahead with deregulation of petroleum prices he ended the government-created "energy crisis" of the 1970s, while eliminating, with a few more strokes, the Council on Wage and Price Stability—the last vestige of those economic controls.

In foreign affairs, his accomplishments were equally remarkable. In the cases of Libya and Grenada he showed that the United States was no longer powerless to deal with foreign adversaries. Through the "Reagan Doctrine," he nurtured anticommunist resistance forces in Poland, Angola, Afghanistan, and Nicaragua. By rebuilding our defense capabilities, pioneering the Strategic Defense Initiative, and reviving our national will, he restored our position of leadership in the world—all of which helped greatly to bring down the communist empire.

What his critics like to call his "stubbornness" was essential in this. Despite his congeniality and flexibility, Reagan was remarkably steadfast when pursuing his key objectives. He was willing to accept 80 percent of what he was seeking today, but when tomorrow came he was back at the bargaining table using his skills to obtain the remaining 20 percent.

Many predicted, or hoped, that the Iran-Contra affair would break the Reagan presidency, but that never happened. While the episode resulted from and led to impediments against presidential action, Reagan's stature in office remained exceptionally high. When he ended his second term and handed over the reins of government to his vice president, he ranked as the most popular outgoing U.S. president since Eisenhower.

Symptomatic of Reagan's success was the exceptional degree of harmony within the Republican party while he was president. As he led the nation, he also united his party. Many of his predecessors had faced primary opposition within their own party when they sought reelection. Under Reagan, that thought simply did not arise. He was head of his party, domestic leader, and catalyst of global change. He had profoundly altered the people's view of the presidency.

That Reagan should have been the one to do this was especially ironic, given the many comments about his age, his background, and his incapabilities. Turning seventy just a few weeks after his inauguration in 1981, he was the oldest person ever to assume the Oval Office. Yet throughout his campaigns and his presidency, he showed that he had more than enough physical and intellectual resources for the job. Many, in fact, who were two or three decades younger had trouble keeping up with him.

Beyond his personal qualities, Reagan demonstrated what does and does not work in public policy. The President was a superb leader and campaigner—a point his adversaries came grudgingly to acknowledge, after many hard lessons. From laughing at him as an electoral pushover, they grew to respect—and to fear—his power as "the great communicator." Still, some never grasped that it was *what* he was communicating that gave his message its political impact.

In the view of most analysts, what mattered about Reagan was his skill at using television, his likeable personality, his common touch, and so on—all of which he undeniably possessed. But to stress these qualities as the principal reasons for his success is to reduce the issue to a matter of mere technique, which misses the point entirely.

The secret of Reagan's success was *not* that he was a skillful speaker and performer on television. If that were the case, hundreds of actors and public speakers might do equally well in politics, but other than he, none has so far been elected president. No, the key to Reagan's success was that he communicated timeless truths about America—home truths about freedom, limited government, hard work, and opportunity—and that these truths guided him while he was in office.

It was Reagan's appeal in terms of issues that his critics in the media (and even some of his own advisors) were unable, or unwilling, to comprehend. From the standpoint of Washington establishment wisdom, Reagan's issue positions were unrealistic, obsolete, or "ideological." It followed, then, that any success he enjoyed had to be in spite of his stands on issues, rather than because of them. This caused his critics to be perpetually surprised by his accomplishments. They could not comprehend Reagan's common sense approach and his identification with the fundamental values and interests of the American people which evoked such confidence and enthusiastic support.

The President often described Washington as "an island, surrounded on all sides by reality." Since he was not limited by the warped perspective of that "island," he could grasp the reality that existed among the people of his country.

But Reagan's political appeal would have been ephemeral if it had not "worked" in another sense as well—in dealing with the problems facing the nation. In the campaign against Carter in 1980, the answer to the question, "Are you better off today than you were four years ago?" was obviously no, and it worked in Reagan's favor. In 1984, the answer, of course, was reversed: the resounding yes accounted for Reagan's landslide reelection.

In restoring economic growth and dealing with our problems overseas, Reagan's policies "worked" for the American people, even as they offended the ruling sensibilities in the nation's capital. Limited government, personal freedom, and reduced burdens of taxation and regulation are the ingredients of economic success, just as the resolute defense of our security interests is the key to successful foreign policy.

These are the political and policy lessons that should guide the United States into its third century. Unfortunately, those with a different agenda—more governmental authority over people and institutions, greater centralized power in the federal government, and therefore higher taxes—have attempted to distort history and substitute their own mythology for what actually happened during the Reagan presidency. These people have tried to lessen the significance of their defeat by decrying the "decade of greed" (although private philanthropy and volunteer service rose to unprecedented heights) and the politics of "envy" and class warfare (although all segments of the economy benefited from the Reagan growth policies), and by criticizing the Reagan defense buildup as costly and unnecessary (although it caused the collapse of communism and enabled the U.S. and our allies to sweep to victory in the Persian Gulf War).

The purpose of these revisionist pundits* is to erase from public memory the achievements and the lessons of the Reagan years, and to fill the ensuing vacuum with the policies and practices of the 1970s—which caused the very problems that Reagan inherited. Throughout his campaigns and his two terms as president, Ronald Reagan led a crusade of ideas that brought change and progress to America. As Martin Anderson has written, "[I]deas need constant renewal, to be

---

*Martin Anderson, in his book *Revolution*, has described the role of the pundits in historical revisionism: "Most political scientists and historians and reporters are left-liberal Democrats—that is the way they vote, that is the way they think. In effect, what they have done is to carry on the political battle that their comrades—the professional political activists—had lost. The Left may have lost the presidency to Eisenhower in 1952 for eight years, but they won the history of that administration for the next twenty."

And that is precisely what is going on now with respect to the writing of the history of the Reagan presidency. Today most historians and political scientists, most editors of our major publishing houses, most newspaper and television reporters are living, breathing Democrats with deeply held political views.

passed from person to person as the generations change."[2] The apostles of negativism are seeking to disparage the Reagan record of the 1980s in order to deceive future generations.

While most of the lessons of the Reagan era stem from what was accomplished, others can be gleaned from its various trials and errors. In writing about the Reagan years, I have not hestitated to chronicle the mistakes made, the quests thwarted, and the opportunities missed. In many of these instances, the mere recounting of what happened has suggested how things might have been better done. But in several areas greater analysis is required.

The first problem concerns the federal budget process; its spending is out of control, producing annual deficits and a growing national debt. One lesson learned by President Reagan from the "Budget Debacle of 1982" (and learned again by his successor in the "Fiscal Fiasco of 1990") is that "budget summits" and tax increases do not solve these problems. They only lead to higher taxes, higher spending, and higher deficits—the worst of all worlds for the citizen-taxpayer.

But even more fundamental is the budgeting system itself. The Budget Act of 1974 was supposed to improve fiscal planning; the start of the fiscal year was even moved back three months (from July to October) to be sure the new budget was ready before the year began. Despite these measures, Congress has rarely met this deadline. What the budget act did do was to curtail drastically the powers of the executive branch and enhance those of Congress, thus altering the finely tuned checks and balances of our government.

One-sided congressional dominance over spending has been calamitous to the nation. In the eleven years prior to adoption of the budget act, federal spending averaged 19.4 percent of GNP, fairly close to the level of taxation, and federal deficits accordingly averaged slightly more than 1 percent of national output. But in the eleven years succeeding implementation of the act, spending has soared to an average 22.7 percent of GNP, while taxes have continued in their historic range. As a result, deficits have averaged 3.4 percent of GNP.

The abuses institutionalized in the budget act obviously need to be corrected. The "baseline" budget concept should be abandoned, and budgeting should be done in a common sense manner comprehensible to the average person.

Equally important, Congress should end the ludicrous practice of lumping all appropriation measures together in a single "bill" or continuing resolution (numbering hundreds of pages) which effectively denies the president the use of his constitutional veto power and forces him to choose between accepting numerous foolish and wasteful spending projects or shutting the government down entirely. (This technique has been used to force objectionable policy measures, such as the Boland amendments, on the executive.)

Changing these procedures would require no constitutional alteration; rather, it would basically restore the *status quo ante*, prior to adoption of the Budget Act of 1974. But these changes could only be brought about by mobilizing public opinion so as to counter the inevitable outcry of the many special interests that constantly seek to increase spending.

Two measures, however, that would dramatically improve the budget process do call for a constitutional amendment. The first is the line item veto. This would grant to the nation's chief executive the same kind of authority possessed by the governors of forty-three states— the authority that enables them to balance their budgets year after year. In the president's case, this veto power would allow him to delete or reduce specific items within the appropriations bills presented to him by Congress. Thus he could excise the "pork barrel" projects that now make up so great a part of the annual spending measures.

A second constitutional change would provide a balanced budget/ tax limitation amendment, requiring, on a yearly basis, that expenditures not exceed revenues, with total taxation and spending limited to a specified percentage of the gross national product. This would allow for reasonable (as opposed to extravagant) growth while curtailing deficit spending. A "safety valve" feature for emergencies would permit Congress to exceed the limits by a 60 percent vote of both Houses.

Another area of concern is the change that has taken place in our federal structure during recent decades. Congress has moved from the citizen-legislature, as intended in the Constitution, to a full-time

Washington bureaucracy that has increasingly encroached on the authority and prerogatives of the executive branch. This has had major implications for the presidency as well as for the quality of democratic representation. Our nation's founders intended that distinguished and successful citizens throughout the nation devote a portion of their lives to public service as members of Congress. Indeed, during the first quarter-century of the Republic, the average length of service for senators was less than six years and for representatives less than five.

Today, however, too many incumbents view the legislative branch as a career; for some, far from being a temporary departure from a successful private vocation, being on the public payroll is the best job they will ever find. In the House of Representatives, which was meant to be the body most responsive to the people and thus most susceptible to frequent turnover, members today have nearly permanent tenure— thanks to gerrymandering, the perquisites of office, and the numerous other political advantages of incumbency.

Furthermore, less congressional time and energy are being spent on actual legislation (as, for example, passing the budget bills on time) and more on attempts to micromanage and investigate executive agencies and departments. This, besides inevitably increasing the conflict between the two branches, has also reduced the civility and efficacy of political discourse and soured citizens on the government. At the time of this writing, public opinion surveys show disapproval of Congress running as high as 78 percent.

One remedy for this problem is the constitutional limitation of legislative terms, a practice now being adopted in several states. While I initially had my doubts about this proposal, and even now do not consider it a panacea for all the ills that afflict our system of representation, I see no other way to break the imperious political lifestyle adopted by Congress and to restore the concept of citizen-legislators.

A related improvement, which could be accomplished by legislative action (or by presidential veto if reauthorization is attempted), is to abolish the present independent counsel system. As described in chapter 22, few recent developments have been more inimical to the tenets of limited and balanced power, impartial justice, and the protection of individual liberty.

Eliminating this abuse would not conflict with holding executive branch officials to the highest standards of integrity and ethical behavior. The successful pattern of the past could be resumed: special counsel could be appointed by the attorney general under procedures designed to ensure objectivity and independence, and be made accountable ultimately to the voting public through the nation's elected chief executive.

Yet another concern deals with the administrative and operational inertia that frequently grips a massive bureaucracy like the federal government. Too often organizations continue well past their reason for existence, wasteful practices persist because nobody challenges them, and cost-benefit analysis is seldom used to evaluate the efficacy of public institutions. A president and his cabinet, no matter how dedicated to improving government, are inundated by the urgent business of daily operations. Just as outside organizations, such as the Heritage Foundation, the Hoover Institution, and the American Enterprise Institute, provide fresh policy insights, so too an independent examination is needed of the administrative, fiscal, and logistic operations of the federal government.

During Reagan's presidency, the Private Sector Survey on Cost Control, led by a dynamic business executive, J. Peter Grace, suggested remedies for waste and abuse in the federal government that would have saved $424 billion in three years, rising to $1.9 trillion per year by the year 2000. (President Reagan personally initiated this survey and patterned it after the Business Task Forces he established in California shortly after becoming governor.) While many of the proposals met with congressional, bureaucratic, and special interest resistance, the savings that did result were of tremendous benefit to the nation's taxpayers. .

A final concern has to do with the institution of the presidency itself. The exaggerated focus on members of the president's staff, the innumerable leaks from those holding top positions in an administration, and the preoccupation with internal power struggles have plagued all recent chief executives. At worst, they undermine valuable policy initiatives. At best, they dissipate public confidence in, and respect for, the nation's leaders.

George E. Reedy, former special assistant to President Lyndon B. Johnson, caustically described the inner workings of presidential staffs in the 1970 edition of his book, *The Twilight of the Presidency*:

> The inner life of the White House is essentially the life of a barnyard. . . . Below the president is a mass of intrigue, posturing, strutting, cringing, and pious "commitment" to irrelevant windbaggery . . . all too frequently [a] successful collection of the untalented, the unpassionate, and the insincere seeking to convince the public that it is brilliant, compassionate and dedicated. . . .

While Reedy's caricature certainly does not reflect the White House I knew, it might easily fit the perception of it by the public, or even by knowledgeable Washingtonians, given the media's constant hammering on the turmoil and treachery that beset the president's people.

Perhaps there is no way to correct this lopsided concentration on triva, given the proclivities of the press and politicians. But it would be interesting to see what would happen if a president limited White House contacts with the media to himself, the vice president, and designated members of his press office.

In closing this examination of the Reagan presidency, let me point out that his years in office concluded the second century of this nation's government under our written Constitution. Despite the problems, errors, and human frailties that have marked every administration from that of George Washington on, the Constitution has continued to provide the blueprint for governance, the citizenry's liberty and right of political participation have survived, and the people have prospered. When our country's fortunes have reached a low ebb, a leader has always arisen to revitilize our institutions and restore our confidence in ourselves as a people. In the 1980s, Ronald Reagan was such a leader.

The Reagan era presaged one of the most remarkable expansions of liberty and democracy in the history of man. Blessed with unquench-able optimism about the creative power of the human spirit, Ronald Reagan proved that freedom works, not only for the people of this land, but for those anywhere who have suffered from the excessive power of government. As the President himself put it: "We came to change the nation, and we changed the world!"

ENDNOTES

Chapter 1: Taking Command

1. Martin Anderson, *Revolution* (Stanford, California, Hoover Institution Press, 1990), p. 331

Chapter 2: Reagan as Leader

1. Anderson, *op. cit.,* p. 286

Chapter 4: Carter's Favorite Opponent

1. Lou Cannon and William Peterson, *The Pursuit of the Presidency 1980* (New York, Washington Post/Berkley Books, 1980), p. 143
2. Quoted by Charles O. Jones, *The American Elections of 1980* (Washington, American Enterprise Institute, 1981), pp. 61–62
3. Reagan's views on this subject are repeatedly disparaged, for instance, by Lou Cannon, in *Reagan* (New York, Perigee Books, 1984) and in *President Reagan: The Role of a Lifetime* (New York, Simon and Schuster, 1991)
4. See discussion in Anderson, *op. cit.*, pp. 127–139
5. *The American Elections of 1980*, p. 147
6. *Ibid.*, p. 155
7. *The Pursuit of the Presidency 1980*, p. 114

8. "October Surprise: The Making of a Myth," *Newsweek*, November 11, 1991; "The Conspiracy That Wasn't," *The New Republic*, November 18, 1991

Chapter 5: Preparing to Govern

1. Anderson, *op. cit.*, p. 167

Chapter 7: The Powers That Be

1. This episode is discussed with some variations in detail, by Hedrick Smith in *The Power Game* (New York, Random House, 1988), pp. 577–578, and Strobe Talbott, *Deadly Gambits* (New York, Knopf, 1984), pp. 224–225
2. Ronald Reagan, *An American Life* (New York, Simon and Schuster, 1991), p. 552
3. M. Stanton Evans, "Time To Clean House," Los Angeles Times Syndicate, April 29, 1982
4. Constantine C. Menges, *Inside the National Security Council* (New York, Simon and Schuster, 1988), p. 278
5. *Ibid.*, p. 108
6. *Ibid.*, p. 241

Chapter 8: Government By Leak

1. "Weinberger Blamed for Defeat on Build-Up," *Washington Post*, April 19, 1983; "Reagan Aide Called 'Disappointment,' " *Washington Post*, March 26, 1984
2. Suzanne Garment, *Scandal* (New York, Random House, 1991), pp. 73–74
3. "Eclipse of a Deputy," *Time*, July 12, 1982; "What's Behind the Attack on Ed Meese?" *Human Events*, July 17, 1982
4. *Honolulu Star Bulletin and Advertiser*, July 25, 1982
5. Remarks at meeting of the Philadelphia Society, September 22, 1990
6. Garment, *op. cit.*, p. 74
7. *Washington Post*, April 19, 1983
8. M. Stanton Evans, "The Smearing of Judge Clark," *Human Events*, April 20, 1983

9. *Ibid.*

10. "What Questions Did Mike Deaver Want Me Not To Raise?" *Washington Post*, May 24, 1988

11. *President Reagan: The Role of a Lifetime*, pp. 423–427

Chapter 9: Hit The Ground Running

1. *The Growth Experiment* (New York, Basic Books, 1990), p. 4

2. *An American Life*, p. 142

3. *Ibid.*, p. 231

4. Quoted in Anderson, *op. cit.*, p. 151

5. *Ibid.*, pp. 158–160

6. *Ibid.*, pp. 116–119

7. President Reagan's Inaugural Address, January 20, 1981, *Congressional Quarterly Almanac*, 1981, p. 11-E

8. *Congressional Quarterly Almanac*, p. 14-E

9. *A Program for Economic Recovery*, February 18, 1981, transmittal letter of the President

Chapter 10: Taxes and Treachery

1. Text reproduced in William Greider, *The Education of David Stockman and Other Americans* (New York, Signet Books, 1984), pp. 135–157

2. Stockman says: "The moment I heard about the contents of the Pickle bill I was determined to derail it." *The Triumph of Politics* (New York, Avon Books, 1987), p. 199

3. Laurence Barrett, *Gambling With History* (New York, Doubleday, 1983), pp. 349–350

4. Stockman, *op. cit.*, p. 338

5. Greider, *op. cit.*, p. 45

6. Quoted in Paul Craig Roberts, *The Supply Side Revolution* (Cambridge, Harvard University Press, 1984), pp. 202–203

7. *Ibid.*, p. 203

8. *Ibid.*, p. 204

9. Stockman, *op. cit.*, p. 455

10. Roberts, *op. cit.*, pp. 214–215

11. *Ibid.*, p. 218

12. *An American Life*, p. 314

13. *Ibid.*, pp. 314–315

Chapter 11: The Triumph of Reaganomics

1. *Consumers' Research*, April 1982

2. Quoted in Lindsey, *op. cit.*, pp. 46–47

3. Quoted in *Human Events*, October 3, 1981

4. Roberts, *op. cit.*, pp. 218, 301

5. *Policy Analysis*, Cato Institute, February 4, 1991, p. 5

6. *Ibid.*, p. 8

7. *The Wall Street Journal*, May 7, 1991

Chapter 12: The Man Who Won The Cold War

1. Quoted by Steve Hanke, *The Washington Times*, January 15, 1992

2. *An American Life*, p. 570

3. *Ibid.*, p. 555

4. *Ibid.*, p. 570

5. *Ibid.*, p. 682

6. *Ibid.*, p. 714

7. *Ibid.*, p. 559

8. *Ibid.*, pp. 551–552

9. *Ibid.*, p. 267

10. *For The Record* (New York, St. Martin's Press, 1989), pp. 330–331

11. *An American Life*, p. 559

12. Carl Bernstein, "The Holy Alliance," *Time*, February 24, 1992

13. *The Turn* (New York, Poseidon Press, 1991), p. 76

14. *Ibid.*, p. 89

15. *Ibid.*, p. 127

16. *Ibid.*, p. 162

17. *Ibid.*, p. 187

18. *Ibid.*, p. 319

19. *Ibid.*, p. 321

20. *Time*, January 1, 1990

Chapter 13: Rebuilding Our Defenses

1. Text of Reagan Address on Defense Policy, *Congressional Quarterly*, March 26, 1983

2. *Command of The Seas* (New York, Scribner's, 1988), p. 163

3. For their divergent accounts see Stockman, *op. cit.*, and Weinberger, *Fighting for Peace* (New York, Warner Books, 1990)

4. Reagan made such statements many times. See *An American Life*, p. 235, and Barrett, *op. cit.*, p. 175

5. For Weinberger's rationale and overview, see *Fighting for Peace*, Chapter II, "President Reagan's First Defense Budgets"

6. Lehman, *op. cit.*, p. 168

7. David Boaz, ed., *Assessing the Reagan Years* (Washington, Cato Institute, 1988), pp. 84, 86

8. For extensive discussion of this issue see Sam Cohen, *The Truth About the Neutron Bomb* (New York, Wm. Morrow, 1982)

9. *Congressional Quarterly*, March 26, 1983

10. For background on Soviet stratagems and changing European attitudes, see Talbott, *op. cit.*, pp. 39–41

11. Alexander Haig, *Caveat* (New York, Macmillan, 1984), p. 229

12. *Congressional Quarterly*, March 26, 1983

Chapter 14: Arms and The Man

1. *An American Life*, p. 257

2. *Ibid.*, p. 550

3. *Ibid.*, p. 547

4. "MX Missile Basing Mode Alternatives," Hearings Before a subcommittee of the Committee on Appropriations, U.S. Senate, June 16, 18, and 19, 1981, U.S. Government Printing Office

5. *An American Life*, pp. 258, 550

6. *Congressional Quarterly*, March 26, 1983

7. See also Weinberger, *op. cit.*, Chapter X, "The Strategic Defense Initiative"

8. *An American Life*, p. 679

Chapter 15: The Qaddafi Connection

1. CIA documents: "Memorandum from Robert Gates," February 14, 1982, plus additional CIA memoranda from April, May, and July 1985, released by Senate Committee on Intelligence

2. This information has already been made public. See Joseph Persico, *Casey* (New York, Viking, 1991), p. 499

3. Detailed discussion of this engagement and later action against Libya is provided by Lehman, *op. cit.*, Chapter 12, "Dealing with Qaddafi," and Weinberger, *op. cit.*, Chapter VI, "Libya"

4. Persico, *op. cit.*, p. 497

5. Barrett, *op. cit.*, and Cannon, in *President Reagan: The Role of a Lifetime*, dwell on this incident

6. Jillian Becker, "The Centrality of the PLO," in *Terrorism: How The West Can Win* (New York, Avon Books, 1986), pp. 100–101

7. M. Stanton Evans, "The Massive Communist Presence in Lebanon," *Human Events*, October 16, 1982

8. See Reagan's discussion, *An American Life*, pp. 417–435

9. Weinberger, *op. cit.*, p. 157

10. For North's account of the intercept see *Under Fire* (New York, Harper-Collins, 1991), pp. 199–215

Chapter 16: Conflict in the Caribbean

1. For background, see Timothy Ashby, *The Bear in the Back Yard* (Lexington, Mass., Lexington Books, 1987), pp. 80–101

2. *Congressional Quarterly*, March 26, 1983

3. The sequencing of these events has been pieced together by Cannon in *President Reagan: The Role of a Lifetime*, pp. 441–442

4. Again, Cannon gives almost a minute-by-minute chronology, *op. cit.*, p. 448

5. *Human Events*, November 12, 1983, and November 26, 1983

6. *Human Events*, November 12, 1983

7. *Ibid.*

8. *Grenada Documents: An Overview and Selection*, released by the Department of State and Department of Defense, September 1984

9. *Ibid.*

10. *The Central American Crisis Reader* (New York, Summit Books, 1987) p. 548

11. *An American Life*, p. 473–474

12. *Communist Interference in El Salvador*, U.S. State Department Document, February 23, 1981

13. "Response to Stories Published in *The Wall Street Journal* and *Washington Post* about Special Report No. 80," U.S. State Department, undated

14. *Background Paper: Nicaragua's Military Build-up and Support for Central American Subversion*, released by the Department of State and Department of Defense, July 18, 1984

15. *Congressional Record*, May 19, 1980

Chapter 17: "Dear Comandante"

1. Haig himself acknowledges such actions, but contends that they were insufficient, *op. cit.*, pp. 130–131

2. *An American Life*, p. 475

3. These and related policies are reviewed by Ashby, *op. cit.*, and by James R. Whelan and Franklin A. Jaeckle, *The Soviet Assault on America's Southern Flank* (Washington, D.C., Regnery Gateway, 1988)

4. For background, see Shirley Christian, *Nicaragua: Revolution in the Family* (New York, Vintage Books, 1986), pp. 225–226

5. Follow-up letters from Enders to Sandinista leader Daniel Ortega are excerpted in *The Central American Crisis Reader*, pp. 526–528

6. Whelan and Jaeckle, *op. cit.*, pp. 117–147

7. Christian, *op. cit.*, pp. 171–186, 224 *et seq.*

8. Far from being super-secret, this finding and program were quickly known to the press, but created no immediate outcry. See Bob Woodward, *Veil* (New York, Pocket Books, 1987), pp. 185–186, 210

9. "America's Secret War, Target: Nicaragua," *Newsweek*, November 1, 1982

10. So testified by Don Regan. Menges, *op. cit.*, p. 95

11. John Barry, *The Ambition and The Power* (New York, Penguin Books, 1990), p. 208

12. Woodward, *op. cit.*, p. 247

13. Ashby, *op. cit.*, pp. 87–88

14. Letter dated March 20, 1984

15. *Congressional Record*, April 24, 1984

16. Barry, *op. cit.*, pp. 500–503, 589

17. Quoted in *The Wall Street Journal*, April 17, 1984

18. Report of House Committee on Intelligence, May 13, 1983

Chapter 18: Discovering a Crisis

1. Theodore Draper, *A Very Thin Line* (New York, Hill and Wang, 1991), p. 505

2. Abol Hassan Bani-Sadr, *My Turn To Speak* (New York, Brassey's, 1991), pp. 27–28

3. CIA Memoranda; "Iran and Soviet Related Documents," released by the Senate Committee on Intelligence

4. *Ibid.*

5. Draper, *op. cit.*, p. 150

6. *The Washington Post*, January 18 and February 19, 1985

7. *The Washington Post*, January 19, 1992

8. Report of the President's Special Review Board (the Tower Commission) February 26, 1987, p. III-6

9. Draper, *op. cit.*, p. 194

Chapter 19: The Iranian Initiative

1. Regan, *op. cit.*, p. 18

2. *Report of the Congressional Committees Investigating the Iran-Contra Affair* (*Iran-Contra Report*), November 17, 1987, p. 160

3. Draper, *op. cit.*, pp. 323, 325

4. *Ibid.*, pp. 321–322

5. Gary Sick, *All Fall Down* (New York, Random House, 1985), p. 314

6. Bani-Sadr, *op. cit.*, pp. 29, 33

7. *Ibid.*, pp. 93–94

8. *An American Life*, p. 505

9. Draper, *op. cit.*, p. 167

10. *Iran-Contra Report*, p. 524

11. Draper, *op. cit.*, p. 182

12. *Iran-Contra Report*, p. 176

13. Tower Commission, p. B-38

14. See discussion of congressional leaks in *Iran-Contra Report* (minority views), pp. 575–579

15. *Iran-Contra Report*, p. 207

16. *Ibid.*, p. 477

Chapter 20: The Boland Amendments

1. Cannon, *President Reagan: The Role of a Lifetime*, p. 386

2. Quoted in *Human Events*, May 4, 1991

3. *Congressional Record* (CRS compilation), June 15, 1987

4. The chronology and permutations of the various amendments are set forth by Bretton Sciaroni in *Pepperdine Law Review*, Vol. 17, No. 2, 1990

5. *Congressional Record* (CRS compilation), June 15, 1987

6. Public Law 99-169, Intelligence Authorization Act for fiscal year 1986

7. *Iran-Contra Report*, p. 498

8. *Ibid.*

9. *Ibid.*, p. 487

10. *Ibid.*, p. 600

11. *Ibid.*, pp. 599–600

12. *Ibid.*, p. 495

13. *Ibid.*, pp. 607, 604

14. Quoted in *Human Events*, March 30, 1991

Chapter 22: The Pursuit of Justice

1. Quoted in Steven R. Schlesinger, *Exclusionary Injustice* (New York, Marcel Dekker, 1977), p. 98

2. *Ibid.*, p. 2

3. Edwin Meese III, *Major Statements of the Attorney General* (Washington, D.C., U.S. Government Printing Office, 1989), pp. 70–71

4. *Ibid.*, p. 144

5. Quoted in statement of Assistant Attorney General Stephen J. Markman, before the Senate Judiciary Committee, February 2, 1988

6. *Ibid.*

7. *Ibid.*

8. *Ibid.*; see also Meese, p. 60

9. Markman, *loc. cit.*

10. *The Washington Times*, July 2, 1987

11. "The War Against Robert H. Bork," *Commentary*, January 1988

12. Quoted in Meese, *op. cit.*, p. 27

Chapter 23: Reflections

1. Jeane J. Kirkpatrick, *The Reagan Phenomenon—and Other Speeches on Foreign Policy* (Washington, D.C.: AEI Press, 1983), p. 12

2. Anderson, *op. cit.*, p. 456

INDEX

Duberstein, Ken, 128, 144
Dukakis, Michael, 133

E

Eastland, Terry, 323–324, 326, 327
Economic advisors, 127–128
Economic policies, 119–132,
    148–162
  attempts to reduce deficit,
    158–159
  contribution to recovery, 156
  effect on annual real spending,
    160
  effect on disposable personal
    income, 156–157
  effect on stock market, 162
  federal spending reduction,
    133–147
  inflation decline, 155–156
  Martin Anderson formulation,
    124–125
  overview, 330
Economic Recovery Act, 132
Economy Act, 265–266
El Salvador, 224–226, 229–230
Election campaign, 3–12
  William Casey and, 8
Election campaign staff, 46–47
Enders, Thomas O., 231, 233
Entin, Steve, 128
Entitlement spending, 91
ERTA. See Economic Recovery Act
Ethics in Government Act, 322–323
Euromissiles, 182
Evans, Rowland, 141
Evans, Tom, 60

Executive Branch Management
    division, 58–59
Executive Personnel Advisory
    Committee, 63–64

F

Family Assistance Plan, 35–36
FAP. See Family Assistance Plan
Federal budget
  analysis of problems, 334–335
  cost of living adjustments, 90
  current services baseline, 90–91
  entitlement spending, 90
  nutrition programs, 92–93
  uncontrollables, 89–90
Federal government employees, 86–
    87, 93–94
Federal nutrition programs,
    92–93
Federal Reserve Board, 156
Federal Reserve System, 16–17
Federal revenues, 149–150
Federal spending reduction,
    133–147
  Debacle of 1982, 144–147
  presidential address, 141
Feldstein, Martin, 127
Felt, Mark, 311
Feulner, Edwin J., Jr., 60
Food programs, 92–93
Ford, Gerald, 43–44
Foreign policy, 96
  Contra aid, 233–235
  El Salvador, 229–230
  Grenada, 213–227
  Iran, 242–257